ENCOUNTERS WITH REALITY

1,001 Interpreter Scenarios

ENCOUNTERS WITH REALITY
1,001 Interpreter Scenarios

Brenda E. Cartwright, M.S., CSC, CI, and CT
Director, Sign Language/Interpreter Program
Lansing Community College
P.O. Box 40010
Lansing, Michigan 48901
517-483-1040 (phone)
517-483-5247 (fax)
BCartwright@lcc.edu

RID Press
Registry of Interpreters for the Deaf
333 Commerce St, Alexandria, VA 22314

Registry of Interpreters for the Deaf, Inc.

RID is a national membership organization representing the professionals who facilitate communication between people who are deaf or hard of hearing and people who can hear. Established in 1964 and incorporated in 1973, RID is a tax-exempt 501(c)(3) nonprofit organization.

It is the mission of RID to provide international, national, regional, state and local forums and an organizational structure for the continued growth and development of the profession of interpretation and transliteration of American Sign Language and English.

RID Press is a professional publishing arm of RID. The mission of RID Press is to extend the reach and reputation of RID through the publication of scholarly, practical, artistic and educational materials that advance the learning and knowledge of the profession of interpreting. The Press seeks to reflect the mission of RID by publishing a wide range of works that promote recognition and respect for the language and culture of deaf people and the practitioners in the field.

RID Press is a division of the Registry of Interpreters for the Deaf, 333 Commerce St, Alexandria, VA 22314, USA, (703) 838-0030, (703) 838-0459 TTY

www.rid.org

Library of Congress Control Number: 2009924863

ISBN 978-0-916883-50-8

Printed in the United States of America

Mixed Sources
Product group from well-managed forests and other controlled sources
www.fsc.org Cert no. BV-COC-070702
© 1996 Forest Stewardship Council
FSC

Contents

This text contains a variety of situations, as well as suggested responses. What are the relevant issues? How would you handle each situation? Discuss and compare your answers to the ones provided, as well as ones from colleagues.

Author's Preface

Being a professional interpreter can be a rewarding — but difficult and stressful — job. Often the interpreter may be the only person in the room able to communicate with the deaf client and is placed in the difficult position of controlling the flow of information. Interpreters are often faced with conflicting rights, needs and duties among their clients and others, requiring them to make important decisions quickly. In addition, interpreters cannot automatically assume that the client can be of help, since not all clients are familiar with appropriate procedures, behaviors or protocols. As working interpreters, we need guidelines to establish a framework for appropriate ethical behavior in a variety of situations — not only to protect interpreters, but also to protect the rights of deaf and hearing clients.

At a conference in 1964 (at Ball State Teacher's College), the Registry of Interpreters for the Deaf (RID) established an Interpreter's Code of Ethics. The code has been modified several times in the years since 1964, reflecting the profession's growth and development. (The current NAD-RID Code of Professional Conduct is presented in this book as Appendix A and will be referred to throughout this book as the CPC.) The purpose of the CPC is threefold: to serve as a guideline for ethical behavior of interpreters and transliterators, to protect the rights of hearing and deaf consumers, and to ensure the right to communicate of all parties. To achieve a high standard of professionalism, interpreters need to thoroughly master the CPC and practice it at all times.

As a professional working with the Deaf community, an interpreter may have a fine technical mastery of interpreting, a wonderful sense of humor, and all the best intentions in the world. However, if an interpreter behaves unethically, his or her career will be short. Few of us set out to be unscrupulous, but people can end up functioning in an unethical manner even with the best intentions, perhaps because they find themselves in a new or unexpected situation. No one working with the Deaf community can afford to be ignorant of the principles of appropriate, ethical behavior. As interpreters, all of our actions must be measured against the yardstick of the CPC.

What separates good interpreters from mediocre ones is their ability to apply critical thinking to each situation, behaving in a way that is respectful of their deaf clients and ensuring that their clients have all the information. Interpreters are held to high standards of truth, accuracy and discretion. At the same time, interpreters are thinking, breathing people who bring their own emotions and previous experiences along with them. The best interpreters are able to stay clear-headed and objective when faced with the unexpected.

In order to continue to improve their skills and achieve a high level of professionalism, interpreters need feedback, whether they be students about to launch a career in interpreting or seasoned veterans. Feedback is not always easy to get. In some geographical areas, for example, there are limited (or sometimes nonexistent) support systems available for obtaining feedback and the all-important processing that must follow. Finally, in order to internalize this process of continual improvement, interpreters have to practice it. A full knowledge of the CPC comes first, of course, and then interpreters need to practice applying the CPC in a multiplicity of situations.

This book provides a collection of scenarios with which to begin the feedback-processing cycle that can lead to excellence. The scenarios illustrate some of the unpredictable situations sign language interpreters may face during their careers. Unusual incidents, pleasant or otherwise, can potentially distract from the immediate task of facilitating communication, and this is when we need clear, quick, ethical thinking. While I cannot offer a magic potion for making interpreters superhuman, hopefully, these scenarios will shed some light on the nature of the profession and better prepare interpreters for the unexpected. Most importantly, they offer readers a chance to sharpen their thinking skills by analyzing the different situations and discussing them with others.

The purpose of these scenarios is to develop a basis from which interested parties can discuss ethical practices in both routine and controversial circumstances. The scenarios in this book cover issues of tact, judgment, stamina and the need for a sense of humor, as well as the mundane logistics of finding the assignment, physically arranging the participants for clear lines of sight, and the sometimes tricky business of getting paid for one's work.

Not all of the scenarios are of earth-shaking ethical or legal importance; some are related more to appropriate etiquette. Getting along in the professional world is important to us all. However, the major emphasis of the book is on the ethics of interpreting. It is my hope that the scenarios will make the CPC "come alive" by offering interesting situations and dilemmas for analysis and discussion.

The first section of each chapter includes responses from experienced interpreters and deaf consumers from all over the country. It should be noted that these responses represent only the opinions of those individuals; they are not necessarily mine nor any organization's views.

It should also be noted that not all of the scenarios show appropriate, ethical behavior; this is, of course, intentional. The point is to offer an opportunity for further discussion and reflection upon how you might react if you were in the same situation. The names, dates and places have all been altered, omitted, revised or disguised for obvious legal and ethical reasons, but bear in mind that all of the situations and encounters actually occurred, incredible as some may seem.

Whether you come to this book as an interpreter in training, an experienced interpreter wishing to sharpen your skills, a professional in a related field, or simply through personal interest, welcome to the world of interpreting. I hope these scenarios take you on a thoughtful, interesting and enlightening journey; that they offer useful practice in dealing with difficult or unexpected situations; and that they serve to stimulate further discussion of the ethical, professional and human issues we all face in our daily lives.

Acknowledgements

My appreciation to students and faculty at Lansing Community College, Ball State University, Madonna University, Mott Community College and the University of Milwaukee for field-testing these scenarios.

My appreciation also to Mary Klein, a talented deaf artist, for her illustrations. To the experienced interpreters and deaf consumers who contributed perspectives to the scenarios with responses:

Kathleen Alexander
Julie Armstrong
Ellen Altamore
David Bar-Tzur
Suellen Bahleda
Mary Barymore
Dawn Baumer
Marta Belsky
Janna Bennett
Sarah Benton
Claudia Bergquist
Lisa Betzer
Sandi Bommer
Glendia Boon
Helen Boucher
Pam Brodie
Richard Brumberg
Jeremy Brunson
Lisa Perry Burkhardt
Brent Burns
Keith Cagle
Judy Cain
Cindy Campbell
Tammy Cantrell
Judy Carlin
Edith Cartwright
Ari Asha Castalia
Ann Marie Christman
Janice Cobb
Josie Cole
Sheryl Cooper
Ed Corbett
Bobbi Cordano
Shannon Crider

Sue Deer-Hall
Janet Dobecki
Jenn Doerr
Catherine DuBois
Kathleen Edwards
Leslie Elion
Kelly Flores
Amy Free
Xenia Fretter
Brian Fruits
Suzette Garay
Lillian Garcia
Susan Gonzalez
Della Gorelick
Genie Gertz
Gino Gouby
Rob Granberry
Angela Grzemkowski
Richard Harris
Fred Hartman
Lisa Heglund
Mary High
Joan Hoffman
Steve Holland
Jess Holt
Jeff Jaech
Edna Johnston
Janet Jurus
Allisun Kale
Amy Kalmus
Beth Kennedy
Rebecca King
Mary Klein
Carmela Lucardie

Marian Lage
Daniel Langholtz
Donna Leahy
Joyce Linden
Albert Linderman
Connie Loper
Marian Lucas
Sara Lucas
Diana MacDougall
Heather Machonkin
Cassie Schellfeffer Manuel
Sharon Miranda
Marilyn Mitchell
Christa Moran
Jeff Mosher
Stevie Naeyaert
Brenda Nicodemus
Greg Owens
Ray Parks, Jr.
Leslie Pertz
Rico Peterson
Jeff Plaxco
Sandy Poplinski
Richard Postl

Justine Preston
Mary Reff
Ann Reifel
Rebecca Reihm
Gina Riccobono
Bambi Riehl
Karen Rivard
Amy Rowley
Bonnie Rudy
Melanie Samitz
Risa Shaw
Bonnie Sherwood
JoAnne Shopbell
Chris Skoczynski
Karen Staller
Jen Strauss
Steve Stubbs
Verne Taylor, Jr.
Linda Tripi
Maureen Wallace
Mary Wambach
Mel Whalen
Jess Watt
Janice Williamson

Publisher's Foreword

All of the scenarios in this book are taken from the real-life experiences of working interpreters; however, the names, places, genders, ages, locations and other details have in all cases been changed. Thus, all of the scenarios are fictional. If you think you recognize yourself or someone you know, rest assured that you are mistaken. (If you are still in doubt, you should know that the details of all the stories were changed by the author when she wrote them, and then again by the editor.) So, if some of these scenarios seem familiar, it is because certain types of situations are common in the interpreting world.

It should be noted that these scenarios often illustrate people behaving badly — clients, interpreters, hearing people and deaf people. The reason is that people who behave appropriately — and they are the majority — present few ethical dilemmas for interpreters. Therefore, these scenarios do not represent the "typical" behavior of interpreters, doctors, police officers, deaf people or anyone else. Quite the contrary, they represent the exceptions.

The first section of each chapter includes sample response(s) from experienced interpreters and deaf consumers. These are real answers from real people. Although their answers are thoughtful and insightful, you may not agree with them. They may not agree with each other, and they do not necessarily represent the position of RID. The purpose of this book is to stimulate thoughtful discussion and debate.

These scenarios illustrate the variety, and some of the challenges, to be found in the world of interpreting. We hope you enjoy them and learn something from them.

Challenges to Interpreter Ethics

- **Scenario 1**. I'm a staff interpreter at a community college and have just finished interpreting a sociology class final exam. A good friend of mine has the same final later today, and she begs me to tell her some of the questions I remember on the test.

AN INTERPRETER'S PERSPECTIVE: Even when it's a friend, you should maintain your professional standards by never revealing any information learned on an assignment.

A DEAF CONSUMER'S PERSPECTIVE: Tell your friend that, in your role as interpreter, information learned while interpreting is not to be shared with others.

- **Scenario 2**. It's been one of those days. My 8-year-old daughter decided to cut her own hair this morning, just in time for school pictures. Then I knocked over a pitcher of grape juice, so I not only had to scrub the floor, I had to change clothes. After all that, I am running late, and I ended up with a $150 speeding ticket. I gave the officer a piece of my mind, though. I finally get to my interpreting assignment in traffic court, and the officer called to the stand is the same one who just gave me a ticket.

AN INTERPRETER'S PERSPECTIVE: Disclose to the court that you're familiar with one of the people involved. The judge will most likely ask if that will affect your ability to remain impartial. That's something you have to honestly decide and let the judge know.

A DEAF CONSUMER'S PERSPECTIVE: You should go about your job just as you would if you did not know the police officer. In your line of work, you often encounter the same people over and over again (some you know and like, and others you may prefer to soon forget), but as interpreters the individuals present should have no bearing on your ability to do your job and do it well. If the officer recognizes you, then hopefully common etiquette would prevail, and he would keep quiet about your earlier interaction.

- **Scenario 3:** Recently I was interpreting a meeting where another interpreter was in attendance as a participant. At one point this person started telling tales of interpreting. These tales started out vague but quickly turned anecdotal and contained information that became quite specific. They not only included the content of what had been interpreted, but included where she worked as well. This was a terrible breach of confidentiality, and I was embarrassed for this person's obvious disregard for our CPC!

AN INTERPRETER'S PERSPECTIVE: When sharing interpreting related experiences with colleagues as described, it can indeed very quickly turn into an unethical situation if specifics are shared. Sometimes in an effort to be entertaining or help others understand a certain situation, an interpreter may feel the need to include the details. However, it is wrong, unprofessional, and unethical to do so. Concern for the profession and reputation of fellow interpreters should prompt you to address the situation with this person. How the situation is addressed is important. As a professional, you should choose an appropriate time to talk to your colleague. It could be that the interpreter was caught up in the moment and had not realized what she had done. There may have been no malicious intent whatsoever, and the interpreter's next reaction could determine your next move. If the interpreter appreciates the fact that you have taken the time to bring it to her attention and indeed had not realized how specific she had been, this could be the end of it — lesson learned. However, if the attitude of this colleague was one of arrogance or she trivialized the situation, then further action would be warranted. On a personal level, I would not recommend working with this particular interpreter in the future. In addition, if you work for the same agency or employer, you should also bring it to their attention, since the agency's reputation and integrity could be compromised as well. We all make mistakes, and none of us are perfect. However, like so many other situations in life, when we do make mistakes, even if they can be rectified, there are always consequences. Judges, doctors, lawyers, educators, and public servants, just to name a few, are all held accountable on a professional level for lapses in judgment. Similarly, interpreters are allowed into personal and occasionally intimate situations that they would not normally be privy to and, thus, bear a responsibility to those who have provided it. Disregard for the CPC sets the profession back. So for the sake of those who adhere to it, this person needs to be addressed and held accountable.

A DEAF CONSUMER'S PERSPECTIVE: Unfortunately, interpreters have been known to disclose specific information about an individual for whom they interpreted a conversation. This situation is not a rare one. Whether it is intentional or not, discussing personal information about another individual or a specific interpreting assignment is a breach of the CPC. Examples of information which breach the CPC may include but are not limited to:

- names
- addresses
- medical details
- financial situations
- family, employment or educational backgrounds
- emotional states
- any conversation content

At times, interpreters might reveal confidential information about a specific interpreting situation while in training sessions or even during casual conversations. In many cases, it may be accidental. Whatever the reason may be, this does not excuse the interpreter from being held accountable for breaking the CPC. Whether working for the general community, the educational system, or a video relay service (VRS) provider, the interpreter is always expected to act professionally and to keep all assignment-related information confidential. There is a time and a place for interpreters to share general experiences with other interpreters. The purpose of sharing experiences is for the enhancement of the interpreter's professional knowledge base and skill set. These enhancements can be made without revealing personal or confidential information. With regard to your specific situation, what you witnessed was very unprofessional, and it needs to be addressed. Consider the ramifications, for a moment, that such behavior could cause the interpreting profession if this kind of breach was commonplace among interpreters. It is in the best interest of all individuals involved for you to resolve the matter. I recommend that you approach the interpreter who discussed the conversation and, without criticism, explain why you felt that the discussion was inappropriate. Although this may be difficult, hopefully the interpreter will recognize the inappropriate behavior and avoid it in the future. Issues such as this one can be resolved as interpreters come together to respect all confidentialities in order to uphold the CPC.

- **Scenario 4:** I am the interpreter coordinator at an interpreter referral agency. My husband teaches in an interpreter training program (ITP) and is RID certified, and he does a lot of freelance interpreting in a community where he is very well respected. I hire him for assignments through our office since he is qualified, flexible, and dependable. However, we have been told that some interpreters in the community think I am being unethical because I am hiring my own husband. What do you think?

AN INTERPRETER'S PERSPECTIVE: I think interpreting can be a competitive profession and some people may wish they were getting the work instead of him. From what you write, he is a skilled and competent interpreter (I am assuming this is on the basis that he teaches in this profession), and you as a coordinator are lucky to have him as an employee. If you were not married, you would hire him for jobs; therefore, your marriage doesn't seem to be having an undue influence on you hiring him.

A DEAF CONSUMER'S PERSPECTIVE: I would have absolutely no objection to my interpreter being the coordinator's husband. As you already stated, your husband is qualified and is able to meet the interpreting needs of the community. I would expect that the assignments would be professionally and objectively handled. Given the consistent need for quality interpreting services in the Deaf community (and it is well known there is a shortage), it is my opinion that a qualified interpreter should have the opportunity to work.

- **Scenario 5:** Recently I was sent on an assignment by an interpreter referral agency to an elementary school. The agency knowingly sent an interpreter to team with me who is on probation and has been court ordered "not to be in contact with children under the age of 16." Upon arriving at the assignment, I informed the principal of my partner's restrictions. The principal dismissed the interpreter and contacted the referral agency regarding their decision to send this individual. The agency feels I should have contacted them instead of the principal. In my opinion, both the agency and the interpreter had a chance to inform the client. Did I do too much? Should I have done more?

AN INTERPRETER'S PERSPECTIVE: Although I don't know the full ramifications of your actions, such as how this affected your working relationship with the agency and the team interpreter with whom you might work in the future, it appears that you wanted to be sure that the interpreter on probation was removed from the school environment. You were successful in doing that, thereby keeping the kids safe, and perhaps meeting the letter of the law. I don't think whether you did too much or too little is an issue, but rather how you achieved the removal of the team interpreter. One approach I might have considered is to begin the discussion with the interpreter, verify with her that the probationary restrictions were still in place, and give your colleague the opportunity to remove herself at that moment. I always want to be careful about reporting my colleagues/agencies to consumers, thereby making me the "savior" in the situation. I agree that the interpreter and the agency missed an opportunity to inform the client earlier, and it was clearly inappropriate for an interpreter with probationary restrictions to be in that environment. I might have considered starting the discussion with the interpreter and the agency, verifying the restrictions, and reminding them that the assignment involved children. I know that sometimes we feel rushed at assignments, thinking that there is not enough time to make a few calls or sit down and discuss something. I'm often surprised how easy it can be to say to some clients, "Excuse me, may we have a few minutes to resolve a situation before this assignment begins? We'll try to take care of this as quickly as possible." If your team interpreter was under the probationary guidelines you stated, it was appropriate she was removed from the school environment. I'm guessing you felt pressure to make it happen as quickly as possible and felt that informing the principal was the shortest route to that result.

A DEAF CONSUMER'S PERSPECTIVE: What a situation! My first reaction to this was disbelief, and quite frankly, I was infuriated. How could an agency knowingly send this interpreter? Also, how could the interpreter even accept the assignment when she knew she could not work in that kind of setting? Then after I had time to mull it over, I started wondering if we had the whole story. After all, in small communities like ours, stories have a way of changing. You did the right thing based on the information you had. Unfortunately, we do have interpreters and agencies who disregard their own personal and professional ethics in order to fill a job when it may not be the right fit (and in this situation, it was absolutely the wrong fit). Your decision protected the children in the school, and you stood up for what was right. You had to make a decision on the spot, and the agency should be the one taking responsibility for sending the interpreter into this setting rather than placing the blame back on you. This interpreter is most likely in violation of the terms of probation.

- **Scenario 6:** My best friend is a teacher, and she often tells me that when she teaches history, she wants her students to "feel it." She says that when you feel something it makes it real and gives you a better understanding. Given that, I want you to imagine being at a workshop, listening to a colleague sharing information about an interpreting situation, and suddenly realizing they are talking about a member of your family! How would you feel? Imagine taking your deaf parents to see a "cancer doctor," and the interpreter, not only arrives late, but also leaves early and you are left to finish interpreting the appointment! How would you feel? Then the doctor says I would like to see the patient again next week. When you go to the receptionist to schedule the appointment, she says, "The interpreter has already scheduled the appointment to fit her schedule, two and a half weeks from now!" How would you feel? This interpreter's behavior is greedy and controlling, not to mention unethical. This is more than a job to me; this is my life! What interpreters do impacts my family and me. Literally, you have the power to destroy a life or facilitate knowledge and freedom. How would you feel?

AN INTERPRETER'S PERSPECTIVE: You ask how I would feel? I would be uncomfortable, irritated, or mad. However, I have to remind myself that we do not live in a perfect world. Your friend is right: teaching by sharing experiences is a wonderful tool. It accomplishes what your friend advocates — "feeling it so you have a better understanding." Many educators whom I respect use this method. As long as names and very specific identifying information are not shared, I am OK with describing interpreting experiences for teaching purposes, even if it's a member of my family. I also have had the experience of arriving late or leaving early. While irritating, I do understand that agencies sometimes face scheduling issues, and private practitioners can be blindsided such that their schedules go awry. However, if this were an ongoing issue, I would certainly be advocating that my parent or the doctor's office contact another agency or another private practitioner. I would also advocate that the person who hired the interpreters needs to explain to the interpreter (or agency) that making appointments to suit the interpreter's schedule is not acceptable. If they cannot comply, then find another interpreter. As for leaving an assignment early, was it a situation in which the doctor did not do a good job explaining the information? Or did your parents not have the prior knowledge needed to understand the information? I think that often we are too quick to blame the interpreter. However, we must certainly remember that people in general often leave the doctor's office not understanding everything. It certainly has happened to me. Ultimately, you have to decide if you want to talk to the interpreter directly about your concerns or file a complaint with the RID Ethical Practices System (EPS).

A DEAF CONSUMER'S PERSPECTIVE: First of all, you have every right to feel that your and your family's privacy had been violated. By giving too much detail in the example, this interpreter is breaking the tenet of confidentiality. Even if names have been changed, the Deaf community is very small, and people can figure out whom one is talking about. Granted, interpreters do learn from each other, but in workshop or teaching situations, they must be very careful to create examples that do not reveal the identity of clients from their local community. What interpreters should ask themselves is this: "What point do I want to make?" A good interpreter should be able to successfully get the point across without exposing the identity of any real people or situations. Secondly, regarding the interpreter arriving late, leaving early, leaving family to interpret or making appointments, it's black and white. A professional interpreter must show up on time, do their job, stay until the end of the assignment, and not try to control the situation. The interpreter's behavior is unethical, and the writer and her family have every right to "feel" violated, angry and devastated. At the very least, you should confront the offending interpreter. You should also tell the doctor's office that you do not wish to use this interpreter for any future appointments. Contact the referral agency and report these breaches of unprofessional behavior as well. Otherwise, consider filing a grievance.

- **Scenario 7:** A certified interpreter who is married to a deaf man did some interpreting for him before they were married. Now he is back in college for a second degree, and he has requested his wife to be one of his interpreters for all his classes. Is it appropriate for her to interpret his classes?

AN INTERPRETER'S PERSPECTIVE: In general, it is not appropriate for a hearing family member to interpret for a deaf family member. The reason for this is to protect the client's right to confidentiality, maintain the "neutrality" of the interpreter, and avoid any conflict of interest. However, there may be extenuating circumstances. Does this deaf person have unique linguistic needs that would be difficult for any other interpreter to meet? Are the other interpreters that are available markedly inferior in skill to the family member? Are there any issues related to his interpreting needs that would justify using a family member? If the answer to these questions is "no," then I believe it would be inappropriate to use a family member. However, if there are extenuating circumstances and the deaf person has requested a family member, then I think they have the right to make that choice. They are waiving their right to confidentiality in regard to that family member. The hearing family member should then maintain the same professional standards as she would for any other client. If she feels she cannot do that, then she should decline the job.

A DEAF CONSUMER'S PERSPECTIVE: This is a very sticky situation, and in most cases I'd say the interpreter should not interpret for her husband. She would have to be highly ethical in order to carry this off (e.g., no helping with homework, no reminding of what the instructor had said, no correcting notes.) There are interpreters that can do this, but it is not easy. My roommate interpreted for me for two years in trade school and was adamant that she would not help any more than she would if she wasn't interpreting. So she would help me with vocabulary, give her opinion on my presentations, proofread projects, etc., but that's it. The certified interpreter (wife) has to decide if she can do this, and the client (husband) has to be able to accept this without resentment.

- **Scenario 8:** A meeting was scheduled several weeks in advance by my supervisor for another deaf staff member and me to meet with the agency's attorney to answer questions about a client complaint. There was a last-minute change to the schedule, so my supervisor asked if I would mind taking an earlier time slot with the attorney. I agreed, but when I went to the meeting, my supervisor was there with the attorney, but no interpreter. I asked my supervisor where the interpreter was, and he said he'd interpret (he holds a CI). I thought perhaps the interpreter was running late and the attorney was short on time, so I agreed to go ahead with the meeting. Mind you, I wasn't comfortable with it because some of the complaints were about this supervisor. After my meeting, another deaf staff member met with the attorney. Later I asked, and it turns out that the supervisor interpreted for all of the staff members; no outside interpreter was ever brought in. When I told my supervisor that this appeared to be a conflict of interest, he became very agitated and said that if I had a problem with it, I should have requested an outside interpreter. We felt like that should have been a given and were very uncomfortable with it. What could we have done?

AN INTERPRETER'S PERSPECTIVE: As a former supervisor of deaf employees who is also a certified interpreter, I feel it is a conflict of interest for a supervisor to serve as an interpreter for deaf staff members. The issue of conflicts of interest is addressed in Tenets 3.3, 3.7, and 3.8 of the CPC. A supervisor's role is very different from that of an interpreter. A supervisor already has access to a lot of information about employees and doesn't need to make the situation more complicated by serving as an interpreter in even seemingly innocuous situations. This also calls into question the issue of confidentiality. By already possessing substantial information about deaf employees by virtue of being their supervisor, it compromises what little privacy the employees have by also serving as their interpreter. If the supervisor does not automatically draw this line, I would suggest that an interpreting policy be developed within the agency. The employees should discuss in what situations, if any, it would be appropriate for supervisors or other staff members to serve as interpreters for deaf employees. The policy manual also should include guidelines as to whose responsibility it is to request an outside interpreter — the supervisor, another staff member, or the deaf employee. I agree that this should have been a given, but apparently it wasn't to the supervisor. Therefore, a formal policy can be developed to make it not only a given, but a requirement.

A DEAF CONSUMER'S PERSPECTIVE: This is an unfortunate situation. It seems as if you were trusting that an impartial interpreter would show up late. Perhaps your coworkers were trusting that too. It would be interesting to know the reasons behind your supervisor deciding to become the interpreter. Perhaps it was to save money. Perhaps it was to make sure nothing was said about him. However, that would mean everyone is guessing. That is not helpful. So what can you and your coworkers do after the fact? You can ask your supervisor to schedule a second meeting with the attorney and hire an impartial interpreter. That should be your right, but asking the attorney about your rights might be the first step. Once you know your rights, you can approach your supervisor. You may all be concerned about losing your jobs. That puts you in a difficult position, but once you have knowledge and approach the problem in a positive, non-threatening manner, you may not need to worry. The other thing you can do, and it is your right, is file a complaint with RID. It is called a grievance and will need written information that states the legality of your complaint. Since your supervisor is RID certified with a CI, the grievance will be acted upon seriously and judiciously. This approach, filing a grievance, may feel more threatening to you, but it is your right.

- **Scenario 9:** Stevie Wonder is coming to town, and I absolutely love him! I am only a state QA level interpreter, but I want to contact the promoter and convince him to let me interpret. Is it OK to do that?

AN INTERPRETER'S PERSPECTIVE: There are a group of lawyers that have been deemed ambulance chasers. They wait around hospitals for individuals who have been injured in car accidents, etc., and may have legal claim to file a lawsuit. They have little respect among their colleagues and stain the legal profession. While you may be qualified to interpret the concert with your wealth of Stevie Wonder knowledge, it is not necessarily professional to solicit and then pressure someone into offering a job. Perhaps instead of trying to convince the promoter, a more professional approach would be simply to let them know you are available if they need someone and leave your contact information. Thus, if the promoter decides this will be a good idea, they can offer you a job. However, the interpreting profession looks bad if the promoter later finds out he was not legally required to hire an interpreter for the event or is dissatisfied with your services when he might have been better off with a nationally certified interpreter. Interpreting is a new profession, but a profession nonetheless. We, therefore, must depict this professionalism in every aspect of our work and remember that we are paving the way for every interpreter that comes after us.

A DEAF CONSUMER'S PERSPECTIVE: Yikes! You have to consider how this type of thing reflects on interpreters and the profession. Interpreters don't want to be known as greedy, and you must take care that your actions don't ever allow anyone to think that of them. Secondly, if you suspect you're not qualified, you're probably not. Are you risking your reputation? Go and enjoy the show, but as an audience member.

Other Scenarios

Identify the issue(s) involved and decide how you would respond. Discuss and compare your responses with your colleagues.

10. A dozen interpreters are hired to interpret a national conference that includes three deaf presenters. At the closing banquet, the interpreters are seated together at one large table in front. The deaf presenters choose to sit together at a smaller table off by themselves and visit. One of the deaf presenters comes up to you at the interpreter table and asks if you would mind joining them for dinner to interpret as needed. After dinner when the presentations begin, you get up to go back and join the other interpreters who will be taking turns interpreting the rest of the evening. The deaf presenters, however, ask you to please stay. You feel guilty enjoying yourself and not sharing the workload.

11. You're the sole interpreter for a celebrity roast. You're on the same dais with all the celebrities, and everyone is relaxed and jovial. The evening includes dinner and an open bar. There are waiters walking around filling everyone's champagne glasses. At one point a waiter comes by and asks if he can fill your glass. It's been a long day, and a glass of champagne sounds heavenly right now.

12. A deaf man is sent to a week-long conference in Hawaii, and his company agrees to pay all your expenses to accompany him. The deaf man spends his days on the beach and his nights in different bars. You both have a great time until today, when you get a call from the company's accounting office questioning some of the receipts you both submitted.

13. You're called to interpret for a series of meetings between the president of a local Deaf club and a developer who wants to buy the building currently occupied by the Deaf club. The developer plans to acquire and raze several buildings in the area to make room for some high-priced townhouses. During the course of the negotiations, the developer mentions that he has been unable to contact the owner of the building next door. You realize you could make a fortune if you contacted the owner of the building first, bought it, then turned around and resold it to the developer for four times as much money.

14. A deaf client contacts you to interpret for her, but you're already booked on that date. She asks you what you think of another interpreter that someone else recommended to her. You're familiar with the interpreter, but you honestly think these two people's personalities will clash. You would hate to say something negative, then have it get back to the interpreter.

15. You're at a Deaf club, and some of the ITP students you teach arrive. You watch as a deaf friend successfully picks up an ITP student. A few days later, the deaf man calls you and asks you if you could please tell him your student's phone number so he can call her.

16. You're a staff interpreter at a university where almost all of the classes are team-interpreted, even the 50-minute classes. One day you get a call at home to interpret a children's story hour at a local library. This is something right up your alley, but you're supposed to be interpreting a class at the university at that time. There's another interpreter in that class, so if you call in sick, you know the class will be covered.

Challenges Related to Qualification and Certification Issues

- **Scenario 17**. I'm a therapist at a substance abuse clinic who recently graduated from an ITP and just took our state QA test. I have been counseling a deaf client on a weekly basis and have always had a nationally certified interpreter with me in the sessions. My boss came in today and says, "Now that you've finished your program, the agency has decided to no longer provide an interpreter for those counseling sessions." They want me to communicate directly with the deaf client from now on.

AN INTERPRETER'S PERSPECTIVE: At first glance, you might think that your boss is being insensitive, but perhaps her request is reasonable. It may very well be that the deaf client would prefer to communicate directly with you rather than through an interpreter. The answer lies in both your skill and the preference of the deaf client. You should agree to discuss the possibility with the client — nothing more. Then share the pros and cons with your client. In the end, always adhere to the wishes of the client, not the supervisor. Whatever the outcome, use this opportunity to educate your supervisor about issues of consumer preference, skill levels, and other pertinent issues.

A DEAF CONSUMER'S PERSPECTIVE: I suggest you tell them that you're not yet certified and don't feel qualified (if you don't) to communicate directly with the client, especially in a situation as intense as counseling. Try explaining that when you're certified or have more experience, then you would be willing to handle this communication on your own. If you're not sure of your receptive skills (that is obviously very important), then having a certified interpreter present prevents any misunderstandings.

- **Scenario 18:** I haven't seen a particular interpreter at any workshops or conferences literally for years now. I know she doesn't care about getting RID continuing education units (CEUs) or losing her certification. She says, "Everyone knows my skills and will hire me anyway." Sure enough, she lost her certification, and she's still out there interpreting all the time and charging top dollar. No one ever asks to see her card. It's business as usual, which is so frustrating for those of us who put in all that time and money into following the RID Certification Maintenance Program (CMP) in a timely manner. Apparently, the rules don't apply to everyone, so why do we bother?

AN INTERPRETER'S PERSPECTIVE: It is too bad that all of us are not equally committed to keeping our knowledge, as well as our skills, up to date. We can only trust in the process and that someday their negligence will catch up with them. In the meantime, we should just worry about ourselves. I think we need to remind ourselves from time to time that our field is changing every week. There are new colleagues we meet, new high-tech signs to learn, and new ethical issues to address. We, particularly the more seasoned interpreters who are looked up to by those entering our field, can only maintain our status by continuing to know who's who and what's what in our field.

A DEAF CONSUMER'S PERSPECTIVE: It is truly unfortunate that there are interpreters out there working who don't believe and realize how important we believe it is for their career to keep up with current trends and issues. From my perspective, this reflects some of the "not-so-great" attitudes we've dealt with over the years, and it is certainly not acceptable by the Deaf community. On the other hand, those interpreters who continue to learn and enhance their skills are strongly favored by us. In the long run, I believe your attendance at workshops and conferences will only make you even more qualified and recognized by members of the Deaf and Hard of Hearing communities.

- **Scenario 19:** It just so happens that I've been collecting interpreter business cards for a long time now, and I'm convinced that anyone and everyone these days can call themselves an "interpreter" without any credentials to back up their claim. Truth be told, our consumers aren't always familiar with all our acronyms and the terminology we use for certification levels, so they can be easily misled. Here are some examples of titles I have in my collection from noncertified "interpreters": "ASL Interpreter," "State Certified Interpreter," "ITP Graduate," "Freelance Interpreter," "Interpreter for the Hearing Impaired," and my favorite — "Hearing Impaired Interpreter" — from a hearing person!

AN INTERPRETER'S PERSPECTIVE: "Consumer Beware!" That's really what they should print on their business cards, although I doubt we will ever see it. One of the reasons I'm a strong proponent of licensing is because of the need to establish standards to ensure that only qualified people are practicing in this profession. Many hearing consumers and even some deaf consumers don't know what it takes to become qualified. As more states get on the bandwagon with licensure, I believe this problem will start to disappear. In the meantime we need to continue to educate consumers so they can make an informed choice when it comes to interpreting services.

A DEAF CONSUMER'S PERSPECTIVE: First of all, I would ask the interpreter if he or she has certification from RID. If so, what kind of certification, and when?

If he or she has no certification, then I would ask where they got their training from and who their teachers were. If this person did not attend an ITP, then I would discuss the importance of getting formal training and certification, as well as the state laws requiring it. If this person was assigned to me from an agency, I would inform his or her supervisor about my concerns and suggest they not utilize this person in the future.

- **Scenario 20:** I am a teacher for the Deaf in a mainstreamed high school. Our program employs an interpreter aide who is trying to get her state certification. She has been requesting to move up and interpret higher level academic classes, as she feels it will improve her interpreting skills. At the same time, some of the students have come to me and indicated that they don't like to have her in the classroom because she doesn't sign fluently or fast enough and that sometimes she can't understand them when they sign to her. I find myself going along with the students' wishes as it is their education. The interpreter aide, though, is upset with my decision because she does not understand the students' needs come first.

AN INTERPRETER'S PERSPECTIVE: Both you and the interpreter aide are correct; the students come first. However, I can understand the interpreter aide's frustration; her interpreting skills will only marginally improve without significant time invested in hands-on opportunities. Can you team her with an experienced interpreter? If so, she can get actual interpreting experience and the students will not suffer if she encounters a problem while interpreting. What kind of mentorship opportunities can be set up for her? Are there courses she can take, and would the school district pay for them? These are all options you need to explore. If you show good faith efforts to help her improve her skills, then perhaps it will be less frustrating for her when you do have to tell her she can't interpret a particular class or assignment.

A DEAF CONSUMER'S PERSPECTIVE: The interpreter should not be in the educational setting at all. If she were a true professional, then I think she should realize it and get a mentor or help from deaf adults. Deaf children suffering because an interpreter is not skilled enough is unacceptable.

- **Scenario 21:** I just finished teaming with another uncertified, recent graduate of a local two-year ITP. Although I have worked with several graduates who were outstanding interpreters, that is not the norm. This guy could not keep up with the speaker at all and totally missed the whole content of what was being said at times. He failed to voice for the deaf client throughout the job, as well as the audience comments pertinent to the discussion. He wore unprofessional blue jeans and beach sandals. Finally, during break, he proudly told me he has informed many deaf friends that they may request him directly to save money rather than go through agencies. The agencies from whom I get my assignments work diligently to provide the most qualified interpreters for each job. I also know we all had to start from somewhere, but every single student who goes to medical school does not automatically come out a brain surgeon just because they stuck with it and graduated. If we are going to require college educational levels of our interpreters one day, don't programs need to refrain from graduating individuals who don't have the skills to interpret?

AN INTERPRETER'S PERSPECTIVE: This is a tough dilemma! Although it would be nearly impossible in this situation, we are not there to supervise and judge each other's abilities when teaming. I know that it happens, but to do something or say something about it would probably make this situation worse. I would do the best team work that is possible, but ask him about feeds and make sure that the participant's comments are voiced. If you think that he is not getting the comments because he does not understand the deaf people, tell him that you will voice for them. I am a note/message person. I would write notes to him and help with the processing and explanation of the topic by mapping and keeping notes. If he was not interested in doing the notes, then I would do the best I could and pray that the day goes fast! I would also ask him about working directly for consumers as opposed to going through the agency. I would hope that the deaf consumers could see for themselves how unprofessional this person appears and how "not ready" he is for interpreting. Many times, these types of situations take care of themselves. There is a bigger issue at hand here, and this interpreter addresses it. It is my opinion that programs need to be based upon skill. Just because someone completes his/her program does not mean he can interpret. I fully support an entrance assessment of language and skill. Progression through the program should be based upon skill. Another big issue is how we evaluate and assess. Well, that's for another day and another column!

A DEAF CONSUMER'S PERSPECTIVE: My reaction to this situation is that this interpreter certainly acted unprofessionally. It is very stressful when we as deaf clients do not get 100 percent access to communication. It makes me wonder because ITPs certainly teach their students about professionalism, dressing appropriately, and rendering the message faithfully. ITPs provide the best possible training for prospective interpreters. They teach these things to better prepare them upon graduation to be qualified and ready to interpret.

- **Scenario 22:** I'm very concerned that we are going to make our hearing consumers confused with yet more acronyms they have to figure out when determining who to hire to interpret. My business card already looks like alphabet soup: CSC, MCSC, CI and CT, NAD V. Is anyone else concerned or confused?

AN INTERPRETER'S PERSPECTIVE: I think it is very common in this day and age for professionals to have acronyms after their names on business cards and other promotional materials. For that reason, I would not be too concerned about the alphabet soup we currently have after our names. Of course, we need to be prepared to explain what these acronyms mean and refer consumers to non-partisan organizations or individuals to help them understand what is involved in hiring a qualified interpreter. I have noticed that some interpreters simply put certified after their name without going into great detail. Personally, I think if you want to say "certified," you should specify "nationally certified" or "state certified." With the advent of licensure in many states, I think it would be appropriate to simply say "licensed." Licensing is something most people understand. A license means you have met certain established requirements for your profession. If licensure in your state has levels, then you may want to note that, such as provisional, qualified, or master.

A DEAF CONSUMER'S PERSPECTIVE: Yes, I agree! I am a grassroots deaf consumer who has utilized interpreter services for many years. Fortunately, I have enough contact with interpreters that I have been able to figure out, over time, what all the initials mean (not necessarily stand for), but most hearing people who hire interpreters have no idea what they mean or what level of interpreter they are getting. Typically, if there are no complaints, they assume everyone was happy. I strongly support the idea of licensing interpreters because everyone understands this concept. We all know to hire licensed builders, licensed mechanics, licensed hairdressers, all of whom have met specific standards. Yes, some of them are better than others. At least with this terminology, we all have a better chance of everyone understanding and enforcing it. Let's keep it simple. Either you are licensed or not. If you don't have a license, you don't work.

- **Scenario 23:** I took the RID performance test four times before I passed. Apparently, I should be ashamed of this, but on the contrary, I'm thrilled I finally made it. I got very little support over the years from the Deaf and interpreting communities. Many people even told me that I should look for another career. This only made me more determined to prove them wrong. It wasn't easy. I took every class (many twice), attended every workshop for miles around, slowly but surely improved, and here I am. I know I will never be able to rest on my laurels, but these same people need to remind me often and publicly of how awful I once was. Please don't tell me time heals. What can I do now?

AN INTERPRETER'S PERSPECTIVE: Don't worry. We've all heard that myth many times, often in an attempt to comfort someone who is in pain. The reality is this: what time does, is pass. It's what we do while time is passing that makes the difference. I know people who have had huge tragedies in their lives and, because of the way they handled it, were doing fairly well relatively soon. I've also worked with people who have had misfortune in their lives who talk about it as if it were last week when in fact it occurred 15 years ago. They have kept it alive and recent for themselves. You are now a role model for all the up and coming interpreters, and you can teach them all the positive lessons you learned along the way. As for those colleagues you will continue to see at workshops and in the field, it's your attitude that makes the difference, not theirs. Congratulations on your accomplishment.

A DEAF CONSUMER'S PERSPECTIVE: If there is one thing I have learned, it is that who I am and how I act rubs off on the people around me. My background only impacts how I interact with others if I let it. Your struggle to become an interpreter is now part of your background. It does not define who you are as a whole. I have had many competent interpreters over the years. I did not care about their background (and I do know many of them). Again, it is who they are now that matters. So if I were you, I would stop focusing on how your struggle to become certified impacts others. You do not have to justify yourself to anyone. Unless there were some situations where you reacted poorly or were characterized by attitude, the past doesn't have to affect the future. You have the ability to be part of the solution. Be honest with yourself and others. Show them you are worthy of their respect, and remember the solution is within yourself. It will not be easy, but good luck.

- **Scenario 24:** I am an educational interpreter in the public school system. It was brought to my attention that I'm the only certified interpreter in our district. There are several interpreters who do not hold any certification (QA, RID, or NAD.) I looked up our Department of Education (DOE) policy regarding educational interpreters and basically it states:

1. "The required standard credential for all related service personnel providing educational interpreting for students who are deaf or hard of hearing shall be a current (state) level III or higher in both interpreting and transliterating and/or documentation of advanced interpreting skills and qualifications through current national certification from the Registry of Interpreters for the Deaf and/or documentation of advanced interpreting skills and qualifications through current national certification from the National Association of the Deaf (levels III, IV, V).

2. Maintenance of current credentials shall be the ongoing responsibility of any educational interpreter employed by the district for purposes of educational interpreting for students who are deaf or hard of hearing. Maintenance of records shall be the ongoing responsibility of the school district, and current credentials of educational interpreters must be filed with other personnel records.

3. Educational interpreters currently employed by the school district or those hired in subsequent school years must have a state rating of level I or II and have in place a professional plan of development leading to a state rating of level III or higher within a period not to exceed two school years. The two year professional plan of development may not be extended or renewed. These plans shall be filed with the school district employing the educational interpreter."

It appears as though the school system is not following regulations, and the interpreters are not attempting to get certification. What should my course of action be? Should I report this to the DOE? If I report it, I may experience repercussions. However, if I don't, I feel I am doing the students a disservice by not allowing them the qualified interpreting services that they deserve.

AN INTERPRETER'S PERSPECTIVE: As much as we would like to right the wrong as quickly as possible, going straight to the top may not be the best way to get this resolved. Follow the chain of command that you have in place in your district. I fear that there could be mass exodus of interpreters if you take it to the top and demand that the policy be followed to the letter, and that wouldn't be in anybody's best interest. Approach this as a win-win situation and get a professional plan put in place for interpreters. Have the district monitor the progress. Interpreters who are unskilled and know it (or even those who don't know it) will weed themselves out. Those who are willing to improve their skills and follow the district's plan will only benefit as their skills improve.

A DEAF CONSUMER'S PERSPECTIVE: As a deaf parent of a deaf child, I know firsthand that parents are the key. If parents complain to the school (e.g., during an Individual Educational Planning Committee meeting) that they are concerned about the certification level of the interpreter(s) working with their child, this issue must be addressed before signing off on the paperwork. If not, it becomes a legal issue. Many parents do not know their rights, the law, or the policies to which they and their child are entitled. They trust educational administrators to have the best interest of their child at heart. However, the administrators have too many children, and money is always a factor. Parents need to advocate for the best interpreters. Do you really want an uncertified interpreter modeling language for your child? You may have no idea what you're getting. Interpreter certification levels give you and the school some idea of how much information an interpreter is able to express and receive. Sadly, too often I see less skilled interpreters being placed in classrooms with the younger children because their interpreting/language skills match the level of the children. (In fact, this is where the most skilled interpreter is needed, during this critical acquisition period!) Educating parents is a key factor.

- **Scenario 25:** I am concerned about nonprofit agencies that historically have provided advocacy, information, and referrals who are now soliciting business from the deaf consumers they serve. Due to budget cuts, these agencies have had to resort to augmenting their funding by contracting out interpreting services. Unfortunately, we are seeing quality sacrificed at the expense of the deaf consumer. These centers may be taking advantage of the trust established with their consumers by directly asking for information regarding upcoming appointments they may have. Is anyone seeing this trend, and how are you handling it?

AN INTERPRETER'S PERSPECTIVE: This sounds like a problem for a variety of reasons. Deaf consumers have placed their trust in these agencies that are now practicing the alarming activity of double-dealing and trying to pad their own budgets by cutting off the top. They are probably biting the hands that feed them. Although this may not take place everywhere, downturns in the economy and federal funding affect directors in their pocketbook, and therefore, they start to think in terms of dollars instead of the individuals they serve. You may have realized by now that a short-term fix is never a permanent solution to a long-term problem. Often, it only makes the problem worse. By making cuts in the quality of interpreter services, these agencies are asking their clients to walk away confused or require further services that will tax the agencies' budgets further, rather than providing first-rate, high-quality interpreter services from the beginning of their relationships with their consumers. If you are personally hired on occasion by one of these agencies, perhaps it is best for your conscience that you part ways with their payroll and practices. If you are one of the interpreters who no longer works for this agency because of budget cuts, write off the loss for the time being and supplement your income by contracting with other agencies that don't resort to this practice. You can also be a good advocate for the Deaf community by becoming involved at the state and local level in NAD chapters, if you're not already, as well as stepping up your commitment to your local and state chapters of RID. In this manner, you can directly affect the quality of services at these agencies in the future, so budget constraints won't be a consideration for quality of interpreter services in your state and local agencies for the long-term.

A DEAF CONSUMER'S PERSPECTIVE: Where are the deaf customers' rights and options regarding whom they want as their interpreters? If an agency provides advocacy to deaf clients such as job coaching, independent living counseling, etc., that should include how to advocate for the interpreter of their choice as well. Part of this advocacy should be to provide resources to both the deaf and hearing consumers as to where and how to hire individual interpreters, interpreter referral agency contacts, and Web sites with FAQs. This resource list can include their own agency in addition to others. The decision should be totally up to the deaf person regarding whom to choose for her interpreter as long as the interpreter is qualified. If a deaf person is seeking advice or help from a nonprofit agency, they have the right to privacy; therefore, agencies should follow the CPC so that all client information remains confidential. The agency should not solicit business with their clients' upcoming appointments unless they are otherwise asked. Deaf people have the right to have qualified interpreters in all situations, and certainly some situations are more critical than others (e.g., medical, legal, counseling.) I know that some agencies provide unqualified and/or noncertified interpreters in order to make more profit and revenues for their agency. Some charge customers the same rate for certified and noncertified interpreters. As for me, I always ask for the names of interpreters that can be sent by the agencies so that I can accept or deny their services. They are not to send me unqualified interpreters whatsoever. That's because my position is important to my employer, and I want to get promotions. If I were to have an unqualified interpreter, I would be misrepresented and would be placed in an unequal position with my colleagues. This is the same for every deaf person! We all know that the nonprofit agencies that have historically provided advocacy are an essential part of our community, and we truly value the work that they do. We certainly don't want to see them fall under as some have because of lack of monies. If the agency is also providing interpreter referral services, they must use qualified interpreters so that the revenues can help the agency to stay afloat. Quality of interpreters and advocacy must not be sacrificed! Nonprofit, as well as other, agencies should provide options to their customers, rather than solely soliciting business for themselves.

- **Scenario 26**: I am a new and upcoming interpreter in the field, and recently I attended a presentation about job opportunities within a new company. I was impressed by their high standards and thought it sounded like a place I would want to work someday in the future. So you can imagine my shock and disappointment, when barely a month later, I found out that someone I knew had been offered a position that has no QA, no RID, no NAD certifications. I was ticked. What's the point of their song and dance about high standards if they say one thing and do another?

AN INTERPRETER'S PERSPECTIVE: A deaf friend who travels a great deal has told me he has seen interpreters working with a sign language book on their lap, spinning out incomprehensible drivel. This is "Warm Body Syndrome," where any interpreter (or person waving their hands) is seen as better than no interpreter. Part of the reason for this is the continued growing demand for interpreters, especially now that video relay service (VRS) providers are all the rage; many of the best interpreters are being drained out of the community pool as they find work in this setting. Community and educational settings are starved for interpreters and often hire those who have little or no experience. Some even hire people who have no professional training. We are not yet viewed as a full-fledged profession, but we need not give up hope. At the turn of the century, medical doctors didn't even need a high school diploma! We are coming up in the world, but we must continue to work to promote our status: as Deaf people, interpreters, ITPs, and agencies. Let's start with the largest social unit that is part of the problem: American culture. Who do Americans by and large look up to? Einstein? Picasso? Gandhi? No, sports stars, actors, and those wealthy from birth or other endeavors. Inability to generate income is looked down on, even if you are as brilliant as Einstein or as saintly as Gandhi. Our culture certainly does not value disabled people, including Deaf people. OK, it's hard to change society, so the next largest group is interpreting agencies. I hear of a lot of hypocrisy within this group. Preaching ethics, bemoaning quality, and then hiring the cheapest (least experienced, uncertified) interpreters or pulling qualified interpreters out of assignments for which they have already been confirmed and replacing them with staff to save money. When deaf people are accustomed to seeing under-qualified interpreters, many of them give up expecting anything different. Who could blame them? I would like to see agencies working with ITPs to improve the skills of recent interpreting graduates, perhaps pairing them with skilled staff or paid mentors from the community. ITPs need to research to figure out how to graduate or field students that are ready to interpret successfully in some settings. Mentoring with agencies might be one way, but there may be other things that can be done in terms of curriculum, pre-testing before entering the program, and exit tests required to get a degree. As individual interpreters, we could agree to mentor interpreters with whom we work, use discretion to make sure we are qualified to do a specific assignment, and be ethical in order to build esteem of the profession. Although it may run counter to American culture, we should de-emphasize pursuit of the almighty dollar, value continuing education (even if we don't get paid more after we have it), and spend time caring about the welfare of others, hearing and Deaf. "Be the change you want to see in the world." —— Mahatma Gandhi

A DEAF CONSUMER'S PERSPECTIVE: So often I hear about hospitals and court systems soliciting the services of unqualified and uncertified interpreters. While they are not above reproach, it seems a worse offense when an interpreter agency or call center, with full understanding of interpreter qualifications and certification standards, hires ill equipped individuals anyway. Unfortunately, the Federal Communications Commission (FCC) follows the Department of Justice's (DOJ) standards for interpreters, which is vague to say the least. My advice would be for everyone to go through an ITP, take their state QA exam, and set their goal for achieving RID certification. When accepting jobs, please do not accept jobs for which you are not ready, no matter how tempting the job or pay may be. If agencies, relay centers, etc. hire unqualified interpreters, then deaf and hearing consumers need to change providers. Eventually, they will be forced to look inward and either terminate unqualified employees or work with them to develop their skills. Interpreters and providers both should be following the CPC, but as we all know, you can teach someone about ethics but you can't force someone to be ethical.

- **Scenario 27.** I heard there are states that will jail people for interpreting without a license. I say, "It's about time!" People still do not understand how hard it is to become a successful interpreter and that only those who have certification or a license should work as interpreters. Do you agree?

AN INTERPRETER'S PERSPECTIVE: I agree that the general population does not understand how difficult it is to become a certified sign language interpreter, and I also agree that deaf children need certified interpreters. That said, I am making an assumption from your question, though it is not directly stated, that you believe it is in the school system where noncertified interpreters are working and, by implication, hindering the potential education of deaf children. Also, you state that an unspecified state has passed legislation requiring districts' use of certified interpreters or else they will be threatened with jail time which to me seems overly harsh. Another option is to introduce legislation that significantly penalizes the school district responsible for hiring the noncertified interpreters. This would eliminate the harsh threat of imprisonment and still accomplish the same goal. In doing this, however, you must recognize that changing an entrenched practice such as hiring noncertified interpreters may take two to three years to accomplish. Good luck with it.

A DEAF CONSUMER'S PERSPECTIVE: Just like I do not want a doctor operating on me who "almost" passed his boards, is "working towards" his license, or has been doing this for a long time without credentials, the same holds true for my interpreters. While most interpreters are not involved in life or death situations every day, they are interpreting enough life-altering events that they need to prove they are qualified for those assignments. Serious repercussions for "fakers" not only protect consumers but the interpreters as well. It is frustrating to watch time and time again as unqualified signers (I cannot even use the term "interpreter") steal jobs because they are cheaper and the person hiring them does not know any better. I hope that one day all states move toward this kind of standard because the bottom line is that it improves communication for deaf consumers.

- **Scenario 28.** My best friend and I both went through two-year associate's degree programs at the same time. Hers was in court reporting and mine was in interpreting. People seem to understand no one else can do her job because she uses a special machine. However, everyone seems to think they are interpreters. For example, at the school where I work there are six "interpreters," but only two of us have gone through a program or taken proficiency tests. Yet, all of us earn the same pay! My court reporter friend never has to deal with pseudo-court reporters; why do we have to tolerate pseudo-interpreters?

AN INTERPRETER'S PERSPECTIVE: It's most unfortunate that you are going through this situation. On one hand, I can understand the school system's logic in paying interpreters the same amount of pay (which is on the increase in most places); they are desperate to keep interpreters. Yet, I do understand the frustration that you are feeling at this point. My suggestion would be to schedule an appointment with the person who hired you and make her aware of this situation. Gather information, if you can, from other school districts or agencies in your area regarding their respective pay scales. Refer specifically to the range of pay according to skill, experience, education, and certification. You might even consider gathering information on the pay scale of teachers in your school district. I am sure you will find that a teacher who just graduated with a bachelor's degree in education is not on par with a teacher who possesses a master's degree in education.

A DEAF CONSUMER'S PERSPECTIVE: I would encourage you to educate the staff and administration regarding the role and qualifications of a professional educational interpreter. I don't think you should focus the issue on money. Instead, approach it as an opportunity to educate and advocate. Focus on the laws and rights of the deaf students. Lead by example and encourage your coworkers to take classes and go to workshops with you.

Other Scenarios

Identify the issue(s) involved and decide how you would respond. Discuss and compare your responses with your colleagues.

29. You have been a nationally certified interpreter for over 20 years. You used to do a lot of freelance interpreting, but over the last few years, you're more selective about what jobs you take. You have all the jobs you want and people know your work, so you decide to stop paying your RID dues. It truly won't affect the number of jobs that come in or your potential earnings.

30. You have just won free, front-row tickets to see the Indigo Girls — your favorite music group! Then you realize it's on the same weekend as a legal interpreting workshop you planned to attend. You do a lot of legal interpreting, and you know you need to attend to get up-to-date information on the field. It's been 10 years since your state had its last legal interpreting workshop.

31. You hear about a mentoring workshop coming up that sounds like it's right up your alley. Unfortunately, it's scheduled for the same weekend your family is having a huge reunion. This will be the only time you'll get to see some of your extended family members for years (maybe ever again.) You're also one of those RID members who procrastinated in getting their CEUs, and now the end of the CMP cycle is quickly approaching.

32. You're a nationally certified interpreter, and you have been freelance interpreting for almost 15 years. A workshop to train legal interpreters is coming to town. In your 15 years of interpreting, you have only interpreted in court once, for traffic court. You can't decide whether to go. You may not do much legal interpreting, but CEUs are CEUs. And you need plenty.

33. It's the last conference of the year for the CMP cycle, and you're still short two CEUs. The conference is on mental health interpreting. You're nationally certified with a master's degree in social work. Most likely, you could be presenting this conference instead of attending.

34. You have a much-anticipated day of pampering planned: a new hairstyle, a facial, a pedicure, and a massage. It turns out a great workshop on ASL grammar is scheduled for the exact same day as your beauty treatments. You know you should go to the workshop, but it took you a month to get this appointment.

35. You have one more semester left before you graduate from your ITP. The school where you're doing your internship asks you if you're interested in a full-time position. The money is great compared to what you're making now (nothing). However, it would mean that you would have to leave school.

36. You are an ITP student and are very busy at various practicum sites. Your friends complain that they never see you anymore. They say that, since you've starting interpreting, you are like a different person, never have time for them anymore, and "care more about deaf people than you do about your own friends."

37. You are an ITP student at a religious retreat for members of a Deaf congregation. Some interpreters are there as well and so you join them for lunch. One of the interpreters starts complaining to the group about the CMP program. She says she refuses to take the new RID certification test because she doesn't believe that, after three years, if you don't get all your CEUs, you should lose your certification.

38. You're a nationally certified interpreter attending a Weight Watchers meeting, not as an interpreter but to lose weight. Today you see that a new member has joined and is with an interpreter. You don't recognize either one. It's clear by the end of the meeting that the interpreter has some expressive skills, but her voicing skills are extremely weak. She makes the deaf woman look downright stupid.

39. You're offered an assignment in a courtroom. You're recently nationally certified (CI and CT) and would love to eventually do some legal interpreting, but you don't quite know how to go about it. Your mentor tells you to take the job, so you do. Once you're there, you realize this wasn't a good idea. The jargon is completely unfamiliar to you. They might as well be speaking another language.

40. You're a nationally certified interpreter and are asked to substitute for an interpreter who is ill. You're told the class is a college psychology course. You have taken some psychology courses, so you feel comfortable accepting the job. Once you're in the class though, you realize you're out of your league. You can't even spell half the words. Your partner, who has been there all semester, is feeding you practically everything. You feel you did such a lousy job that you don't even want to bill the university.

41. You're familiar with the deaf client and his language needs. However, the content of the meeting you're interpreting is way over your head, and you're just interpreting words, not concepts. The client is looking at you nodding his head, but you feel certain he's just being polite. There's nothing the speaker can say to make you understand, so stopping him would be pointless. The topic is just Greek to you.

42. You're a recent ITP graduate, and a deaf person calls you and asks you to interpret for her. She's aware of your skill level. She says she wants you to interpret for a doctor's visit. When you arrive at the doctor's office, you find out that this is not just a routine visit with her doctor. This is an appointment with a surgeon to discuss a very complicated experimental procedure he's suggesting for the deaf woman. This is way out of your league.

43. A church was advertising that they provide an interpreter for their Sunday services, so you and a deaf friend, who is also a CDI, decide to attend. However, you are disappointed to find, instead of a qualified interpreter, the pastor's wife is seated to his right in front of the congregation. She is slowly fingerspelling occasional words, and miming and gesturing everything else. After the service, the pastor's wife comes up to you and asks what you thought about the service and her interpreting.

44. You husband is a police officer, and one morning at 5 a.m., he calls you and says they need you to come in and interpret right away. They have set up a room with video equipment to tape the entire questioning process. You ask the deaf person some generic questions beforehand to establish a language base, and you realize the client has minimal language skills. You tell your husband you don't feel qualified to interpret for the man and suggest some other interpreters you know with more experience in this area. He begs you to at least interpret on tape as they read him his rights.

Challenges Related to Deciding Whether to Accept a Specific Job Assignment

- **Scenario 45**. A good friend of mine is also an interpreter, and she asked me if I would interpret for her deaf husband in therapy. This worries me because it's so personal, but at the same time, I'm honored to have been asked.

AN INTERPRETER'S PERSPECTIVE: Feeling a bit worried is different from knowing you shouldn't be on an assignment. Consider the possible fallout from doing such an assignment; for example, your friend may want to later discuss with you how the therapy sessions are going. Certainly, it's an unusual situation, but if you feel everyone is comfortable and your professional roles can be maintained during and after the assignment, I think you should do it.

A DEAF CONSUMER'S PERSPECTIVE: I would say definitely decline this assignment. It's too close to home. What if the friend asks what happened during the therapy? It would be very awkward to be in the middle of the husband and wife.

- **Scenario 46**. My deaf friend asks me to interpret her aunt's funeral. My own father is very ill and not expected to live six months. The thought of doing this funeral sets off a whole range of emotions. I try to explain this to my friend, but she persists and says she really needs me.

AN INTERPRETER'S PERSPECTIVE: You can't effectively interpret while blinded by your own grief. Although a friend in need is hard to deny, I would stand firm on my own personal and professional beliefs. To subject yourself to a funeral when you're awaiting the death of your own father wouldn't be wise, nor could you translate effectively under such emotional stress. The funeral is a significant event for your friend, and she deserves a quality interpreting job. You can be there for your friend in her time of need by helping to find another interpreter and offering to be with her before and after the funeral.

A DEAF CONSUMER'S PERSPECTIVE: You should diplomatically beg off and suggest some other qualified interpreters to do the job. The turmoil of trying to interpret while knowing your father doesn't have long to live would be too much for anyone. Interpreters are not superhuman. Your deaf friend deserves to have an interpreter who is fully focused on her aunt's funeral.

- **Scenario 47**. My deaf neighbor calls and asks me to interpret for her. As far as I'm concerned, she's been the "neighbor from hell." She took care of my dog one time while I was away, and he died! I don't "forgive and forget."

AN INTERPRETER'S PERSPECTIVE: It's important to recognize when your "emotional buttons" have been pushed and that you may not be able to interpret with neutrality. Listen to that inner voice. If it feels strong enough, gracefully decline the assignment.

A DEAF CONSUMER'S PERSPECTIVE: As an interpreter, you often have to learn to "forgive and forget." My suggestion would be to let go of the past and do the assignment.

- **Scenario 48**. I get a call from an interpreter referral agency to interpret a doctor's appointment. I recognize the name of the doctor, who has recently been in the news. They're calling him "Dr. Death."

AN INTERPRETER'S PERSPECTIVE: I couldn't maintain my professional demeanor in such a situation; I'd be too tempted to give my opinion. I would refer them to another interpreter.

A DEAF CONSUMER'S PERSPECTIVE: Knowing that you may not be able to maintain neutrality in this interpreting assignment, you should decline the job.

- **Scenario 49**. I met a young deaf couple who recently moved into the area. I see them from time to time socially and always enjoy their company. One day the husband contacts me to ask if I would interpret for him in court. He got a ticket for drunk driving and is making a joke of it. Two years ago, my brother was killed by a drunk driver who ran a red light. I turn down the job, but now find myself avoiding this couple because of the man's insensitivity to his drunk driving offense.

AN INTERPRETER'S PERSPECTIVE: You've already made the right ethical decision. You turned down the court assignment because you knew your personal feelings might affect your work. The CPC doesn't tell us what to feel. Having feelings is part of being human, and there's nothing wrong with that. It's only when you let your feelings interfere with your work that you enter the realm of ethics. If it's uncomfortable for you or the couple that you're avoiding, perhaps it's in everyone's best interest if you share your history with the couple.

A DEAF CONSUMER'S PERSPECTIVE: I would tell the deaf man I don't want to interpret a case in court that relates to drunk driving. I would explain briefly that a family member was killed by a drunk driver, and I don't consider it a laughing matter.

- **Scenario 50.** An interpreter colleague is getting married and asked me to interpret his wedding. I know the bride-to-be (also an interpreter) and that she has several gay friends. We learned only recently that the wedding will be held in a well-known gay church. My husband and I are deeply religious and do not approve of the gay lifestyle. Now I don't want to go. However, if I explain why I'm backing out of the job, I will risk alienating too many people with my personal views. What should I do?

AN INTERPRETER'S PERSPECTIVE: Do not interpret the wedding. The language in your letter reveals that you have a strong bias about gay people that could corrupt the neutrality of your interpretation. You write, for example, that you are "deeply religious" and "do not approve of the gay lifestyle." These statements suggest that being deeply religious and being gay are mutually exclusive constructs. Many gay people also consider themselves deeply religious, although they may hold religious beliefs other than your own. Further, your use of the words "gay lifestyle" reveals a commonly held stereotype, i.e., that all gay people live in a singular manner. Can we apply the notion of lifestyle to other groups — a "heterosexual lifestyle"? I believe you are using the words "gay lifestyle" as a euphemism for particular behaviors, specifically sexual relations, which you find offensive or perhaps sinful. Also, in your letter you state that you disapprove of gay people and this appears to extend to any church which welcomes them as congregants. Ethical dilemmas occur when we are faced with conflicting values. You value your religious beliefs. At the same time you value the harmonious relationships you have with your friends. You are uncertain how to reconcile both sets of values. Perhaps you can use this situation as an opportunity to further reflect upon your personal belief system. Take time to consider your values and all of the possible alternatives for acting on them. Then consider the potential consequences of each one. If you continue to feel that your values are being compromised by your presence in a church which embraces a particular minority group, then you should not attend, much less interpret, the wedding.

A DEAF CONSUMER'S PERSPECTIVE: You should be honest and withdraw. If I were a deaf friend of the couple attending the wedding, I would notice that you were not comfortable, and that might make me feel uncomfortable. I understand your feelings, and it is hard to face your friend and back out after you have already accepted the job. This is no different than having a Jewish interpreter of a Christian ceremony. Religious interpreting is a very personal thing. Besides your own personal feelings, there are two professional issues that you have to consider. You are dealing with a CPC issue. You have a duty to withdraw from any job in which you have a conflict — either personal or professional. This is a conflict of your beliefs, so you have a duty to withdraw. Who would know that you withdrew from the job? Only your friends (the couple) should know and they should already be aware of your convictions. You need to consider the feelings of your friend and your clients and not worry about yourself and what other people might think of you. This is probably the most important day in the lives of your friend and his fiancée. They deserve to have an interpreter who will feel comfortable and do the best job. That is obviously not you! You can tactfully say, "I would love to interpret for you, but that church conflicts with my beliefs, so I cannot do it. I'm sorry." Then give them your best wishes. This will give them the opportunity to find someone who will be comfortable for this wedding.

- **Scenario 51.** I recently team interpreted a large event for a predominately African-American audience. Afterwards people from the audience who didn't know either of us came up and complimented my African-American partner profusely and completely ignored me. The kudos are not the point. I wanted to take this job, but now I'm not so sure I should have. Do you have any insight?

AN INTERPRETER'S PERSPECTIVE: Well, one can look at this from two different perspectives. First, I will ask two questions. Perhaps this will help to understand both perspectives that I would like to offer. My first question: "Did you want to take this job because there were no other African-American interpreters available on that particular date?" If that is the case, then, yes, you should have taken the job. Programs that run long can be very emotionally and physically draining. This situation definitely calls for two interpreters, and if all means necessary were exhausted to find two African-American interpreters who were qualified to do the job, then it was completely appropriate for you to be there. My second question: "Did you want to take this job because you had studied or have immersed yourself in African-American culture and feel you have enough background to make the assignment 'work,' even though another African-American interpreter was available?" If this was the case, then you should not have been there. There are nuances that even the best interpreters outside of the African-American culture can't truly pick up on or even feel because the emotion runs so deep within African-American people. Very rarely do we come across someone outside of our race and culture who understands 100 percent. You just can't "get" everything, no matter how hard you try. This would be especially true when dealing with African-American events. There is an emotion that can be truly embodied only by those who have "been there."

A DEAF CONSUMER'S PERSPECTIVE: Very few minority students enter the field of American Sign Language (ASL) interpreting. Of RID's more than 15,000 members, nearly 90 percent are white women. Two to five percent of sign language interpreters around the country are African-American, Hispanic, or another minority according to colleges and a national registry. Is it any wonder then that an audience made up of African-Americans would react so enthusiastically to an interpreter who is African-American and is likely to be more familiar with their idioms and slang? Nuances can be lost when an interpreter does not share the same ethnic or cultural background as the client, not to mention the comfort factor that occurs from a common ethnic identity. You should ask yourself the following questions: Were you chosen for your skill? Did you render top quality interpreting services to the best of your ability? Were you sensitive to the situational dynamics (recognizing that you might not be able to convey colloquialisms as well as an African-American interpreter can)? Did you strive to respect your audience's sensibility, avoiding the temptation to "get down with them"? If your answers to these questions are yes, then you did the right thing in accepting the job, kudos or no kudos. The reaction of a mostly African-American audience is frankly understandable. That feeling of kinship and pride in one of their own has no bearing on how well you performed. Instead of feeling deflated because you were ignored or overlooked, applaud your team interpreter as well and consider this time an opportunity to develop a deeper understanding of this community. This is what it feels like to be an outsider, which minority groups and, in particular, Deaf people experience on a regular basis.

Other Scenarios

Identify the issue(s) involved and decide how you would respond. Discuss and compare your responses with your colleagues.

52. A deaf couple already attending Alcoholics Anonymous (AA) meetings approaches you to ask if you would interpret their weekly meetings. You're a recovering alcoholic and already attend these meetings, but the building where these two usually go with their sponsors is the same place your ex-husband attends. You and your ex had a messy divorce and have not spoken in years.

53. A deaf friend of yours asks you to interpret her wedding. You're stunned she would even ask you after all the negative things you've said to her about her fiancé. You don't even want to go to their wedding, much less interpret the darn thing, but she's still your friend.

54. A deaf man contacts you directly to interpret for him. He tells you he really likes your interpreting style and is very comfortable with you. You're flattered by his remarks, but, truth be told, voicing for him is your worst nightmare. You don't want to tell him that, but you've got to think of a way to get out of this.

55. A family close to your family has a deaf son who will be starting school soon. You have known this adorable child since he was a baby and have tutored him and his family in sign language for years. His parents ask you if you would consider being his interpreter in the mainstream program he will be attending because they know their son would make the adjustment easier with you around.

56. An interpreter referral agency calls you to interpret for a deaf client who lives in a housing project in a predominantly African-American area of the city. You have never considered yourself a racist, but you think the agency should have sent an African-American interpreter. However, you don't know if it's appropriate for you to say so.

57. Every year a church in your community has a big three-day revival out in the country. They have asked you to interpret all three days and are willing to pay you big bucks. They only plan to hire one person for the whole thing though, and you have heard these events can go on for hours, depending on how many people are being saved.

58. One of the deaf teachers in your ITP asks you to interpret a banquet she and her husband will be attending. You hem and haw, not because of your skill level (she's obviously very aware of your strengths and weaknesses as an "interpreter"), but because her husband always makes passes at you.

59. The college student you interpret for is just plain obnoxious and you can't stand him. You're counting down the days until the end of the semester. You're stunned when your supervisor tells you he came in raving about you and wants you for all his classes next semester.

60. The florist who did the flowers at your wedding is a good friend of yours. One day he calls you, thrilled that a deaf person has signed up to take his flower-arranging class. He enthusiastically asks you to interpret the class. You have no interest in interpreting a flower-arranging class, but you don't want to hurt his feelings. You know he's excited about working with you.

61. While driving, you witness a car accident, so you stop to see if you can help. In the first car, there's a deaf man and woman. They say they're fine, just a few bumps and scratches. You then go to the second car. The driver looks like he's dead, and the passenger is badly injured. Just then the police and an ambulance arrive and you direct them to the second car first. The police want to get your statement since you witnessed the accident. When the police attempt to talk to the deaf couple, they ask you to interpret for them. You have just given a statement indicating they were driving on the wrong side of the road.

62. You get a call from a hospital in the middle of the night asking you to come in and interpret. They tell you a deaf child has been severely burned in a house fire. His parents are also deaf but escaped unharmed. The child is in critical condition. Your worst nightmare is being caught in a fire, and you imagine everyone's emotions will be running high, including your own.

63. You have been asked to interpret for a club considering a deaf applicant. The club is exclusively for men, and so you're curious about getting inside a place that is usually off-limits to women. However, you can't help but wonder if your presence will adversely affect the deaf man's application.

64. You have been interpreting for the same deaf student attending medical school for several years. She tells you next semester she will be taking a class where they will be working with cadavers. You know right away that this is going to be a problem for you, so you tell her to try to find someone else. She begs you to reconsider because you're now very familiar with the terminology, and the two of you have set up many unique signs to meet her needs. She feels there's no way someone new could catch up at this point.

65. You're a state level QA III and have done quite a bit of interpreting in the medical field. An interpreter referral agency calls you and wants you to interpret an OB-GYN appointment. You start jotting down the information, and when the woman says the deaf client's name, you freeze. You hate interpreting for this woman. You privately call her "Hitler." She's so domineering and controlling, it's not worth any amount of money to do the job. Now, however, you have committed yourself and are afraid it's going to sound feeble to say you have a "personality conflict" with the client.

66. You're asked to interpret a divorce case for a deaf couple. Their kids go to school with yours, and so you have heard awful stories about the deaf parents coming to school and causing scenes. It has become a bitter custody battle, and you're not sure you even want to get involved considering all that you've already heard.

67. You're asked to interpret at a church whose views are very different from yours. You're curious, however, to see for yourself what this particular religion is like. You wonder if it's unethical to commit to a job only for a little while because you really have no interest in making this a long-term assignment.

68. You're called by the hospital at 3 a.m. because they have a deaf woman who needs an emergency C-section. You feel a little guilty when you say "no," but you need your beauty sleep. You have already got a full day of interpreting ahead of you tomorrow.

69. You're contacted by an interpreter referral agency to interpret at an attorney's office. You accept and start to write down all the pertinent information on your calendar. You stop though when you realize you recognize the name of the deaf client as someone who is suing a deaf friend of yours. You don't know the client personally, and you certainly don't ever have to tell anyone what you heard in the meeting. On the other hand, if it's about this pending lawsuit, you probably already know more about the situation than you should.

70. You're contacted to interpret for a deaf client just admitted to an after-hours crisis center. You ask the contact person for the client's name, which she refuses to tell you because she says that information is confidential. You explain you need to know the client's name to help determine if you're appropriate for the job. She still refuses to tell you.

71. You've just arrived home from a late-night party where you had too much to drink. You've only been asleep for about 30 minutes when the phone rings. It's the hospital. They have just admitted a critically ill deaf person, and they want you to come immediately to interpret. You feel hung-over, but the hospital pays a great late-night bonus.

72. Your best friend is a deaf woman having an affair. She knows she needs counseling and doesn't want to have anyone else interpret but you. She has taught in an ITP for years and knows every interpreter in town; most of them have been her former students. You agree it would be hard for her to have a former student as her interpreter, especially since the man with whom she's having an affair is a current student of hers. This assignment, however, would be hard for you.

73. Your daughter's birthday party is scheduled for 6 p.m. on Friday. On Friday, you get a call at noon to interpret in an emergency room at a hospital. You could use the money, but you also know that emergency room jobs can run much longer than expected.

74. You get a call from an interpreter referral agency to interpret a community education course about self-defense. It's weird that you get this call today because you were just thinking about signing up for a self-defense course anyway. Now you can interpret the course and learn all about it while being paid.

75. You're asked to interpret a board meeting for a large corporation. When you're given the name, you realize it's a company you used to work for many years ago, before you became an interpreter. You were fired (unfairly, you think), and you still harbor some bad feelings about it. On the other hand, they're offering a great hourly rate, and your old boss probably doesn't even work there anymore.

76. Your parents call and ask if you would go with them this Sunday to a nursing home to interpret for them and a deaf woman they met while visiting your grandmother. Your mom says the deaf woman's family never visits her and she's lonely. Personally, you've never gotten along with elderly people, not to mention you hate to give up a Sunday.

77. You have just left the doctor's office with a bandage on your left index finger. You slammed your finger in the car door and bruised the bone. The doctor says it won't hurt the finger to interpret, but it's extremely sore. You have an interpreting job scheduled tonight.

78. You have interpreted for a deaf woman in court on several occasions when she had been badly beaten by her abusive husband. A restraining order has been placed on him to keep him away from their home and children. One day while you're sitting in your car waiting for the light to change, you see the same deaf couple going into a restaurant together. The next day you get a call to interpret in court because the guy has beaten her up again. You're not the least bit sympathetic anymore.

79. You feel fortunate to have had the unique experience of interpreting for a deaf couple through their Lamaze classes and all the way up to the birth of their baby. Having spent so much time together over the last nine months, you feel very close to this special couple. Soon after the birth of the child, you hear the child became very sick and died. The parents ask you to interpret the funeral services, but they're embarrassed to admit that with all the hospital bills they can't afford to pay you.

80. You're at a picnic to which you've been looking forward for weeks with some Deaf friends. It's a beautiful day, and you're having a great time, when a young deaf boy falls and breaks his arm while he's playing. His parents ask you to go with them to the hospital to interpret. You really don't want to spend this beautiful Sunday cooped up in an emergency room, but these are your friends too.

81. You have interpreted for a deaf woman numerous times over the years, and the two of you have become good friends. She has always taken the time to introduce you to other deaf people in the community and looked out for you. Quite suddenly, the woman passes away, and her husband calls you and asks if you would please interpret her funeral. He says he knows that is what she would have wanted. You, however, have some serious doubts about your ability to keep it together during the service.

82. You have been asked to substitute interpret for a Sunday mass for a fellow interpreter who says she really needs a weekend away with her husband. Not only are you not Catholic, you're an atheist. Your friend has come through for you several times in the past, and you know how much this weekend means to her. You're sure you can get through one Sunday mass without disaster.

83. You're asked to interpret for a large conference. The Deaf audience will be large and quite varied. They tell you there will be only one interpreter hired for the main speakers, but you're thinking there should be at least two, especially for such a large audience.

84. You're called by an interpreter referral agency for an interpreting assignment. You write down all the pertinent information and then ask who your team interpreter will be. When you're told, you flinch because the two of you have completely different styles. For example, instead of feeding you a word or a sign if necessary, she will just take over. You hate to back out now and look like you're hard to get along with, but this assignment now no longer appeals to you.

Challenges Related to Deciding Whether to Accept a Specific Job Assignment Due to Qualification Concerns

---

- **Scenario 85**. I've finished my interpreter training as a straight-A student and then passed my state QA screening as a level III. I've been working full-time as an educational interpreter and I love it, but what I really want to do is get into legal interpreting. My sister is a lawyer and her firm just got a deaf client, so she calls to offer me a job interpreting for him. I don't have any practical experience, but I've seen every episode of "L.A. Law," "The Practice," and "Reasonable Doubt."

AN INTERPRETER'S PERSPECTIVE: I would call a friend or mentor who is an experienced legal interpreter, offer her the job, and ask if I could come along and observe. If she says OK, I'd call my sister the lawyer and obtain her permission to observe. I would then ask her to relay my request to the deaf consumer. If he says OK, then I'm there in the room, but not the on-duty interpreter. Arrange to have some debriefing time with the interpreter afterwards so you can ask questions such as, "Why did you do this?" and "Why didn't you do that?"

A DEAF CONSUMER'S PERSPECTIVE: Don't accept the legal interpreting job. Tell your sister to contact a referral agency or offer to help her find a qualified legal interpreter.

- **Scenario 86**. I get a call to substitute for a fellow interpreter at her church. Unfortunately, I haven't set foot inside a church since I was 12 years old.

AN INTERPRETER'S PERSPECTIVE: After interpreting in a church as a nonreligious person while a neophyte interpreter, I came to realize my limitations. Religious discourse differs from that of typical situations in which interpreters find themselves. To do at least an adequate job requires some knowledge of the text, the message, and the rituals the church practices. The adage "Someone is better than no one" doesn't always apply, especially when dealing with an important spiritual event.

A DEAF CONSUMER'S PERSPECTIVE: I can't imagine going to a church where the preacher hasn't set foot in a church for many years. By the same token, I wouldn't want an interpreter who hasn't been in church since childhood. I suggest they find an interpreter who has experience that is more recent.

- **Scenario 87**. I've been asked to interpret a theatrical performance. The last time I was on stage runs through my mind; it was a disaster. Granted, I was in high school and I was actually in the performance. I tell myself it'll be different this time because I won't actually be performing, just interpreting.

AN INTERPRETER'S PERSPECTIVE: Interpreting the performing arts requires special skills, knowledge, and experience. And it's definitely not for you if you're nervous being onstage. If this is something you want to get into, you'll need to prepare: obtain a copy of the script, attend a rehearsal or earlier performance, watch tapes of interpreted performances, read books on theatrical interpreting, and talk to interpreters experienced in that setting. You should also talk with the director about logistics — placement, sight lines, and lighting — to ensure you'll be able to hear the actors onstage.

A DEAF CONSUMER'S PERSPECTIVE: You should always preview a performance or rehearsal first. Personally, I prefer an interpreter who "performs" a little. It helps me relax and enjoy the whole performance. I would definitely not want an interpreter who was stiff and nervous.

Other Scenarios

Identify the issue(s) involved and decide how you would respond. Discuss and compare your responses with your colleagues.

88. A court calls you and says you have been specifically requested by a deaf man being held for attempted robbery. He has minimal language skills, and you're very familiar with his language level. However, you have never interpreted in court before. You know there's a lot more to it than meets the eye.

89. A ski resort in Colorado calls and asks you to interpret for a national convention of downhill skiers. You have never skied before and know nothing about skiing, but you would love to see Colorado. The ski resort is going to pay all your expenses.

90. A well-known deaf professor asks you to interpret a scientific presentation she's giving. While you're quite flattered that she asked you, math and science were always your weakest subjects in school, and you're afraid this is going to be over your head.

91. An elementary school in your small town is having a musical concert for their second- and third-grade students. The interpreter with whom they usually work for these events is sick, and so they call you to interpret the concert. You don't know a thing about music, and the concert is tonight!

92. As a recent ITP graduate, you have just completed your first freelance medical interpreting assignment. You really don't have much medical background or training; however, on your way out, the doctor's receptionist asks if you would be available to interpret a seminar the doctor is giving for his patients on Diosphoas-lengthening surgery.

93. In your 10 years as an interpreter, you've never done any performing arts interpreting, but you're interested in trying it. You're asked to interpret the musical "Hair" and think it would be perfect for your debut.

94. You have just graduated from an ITP and get a call to interpret at a school district where you're hoping to get a job. They're bringing in a deaf presenter to do an in-service on the needs of deaf children in mainstream programs. You know you're not ready to do that level of voicing but are afraid to admit that to the school for fear they will never consider you to work for them in the future.

95. You're a state QA level I interpreter with several years of interpreting experience under your belt. You get a call to interpret for a Deaf-blind client, but you have had no actual experience outside of some classes in your ITP. The pay is double what you normally charge because it's so physically demanding.

96. A congressman's secretary calls you to see if you'll interpret for a legislative committee meeting where the congressman is going to be discussing a bill that impacts the state school for the Deaf. The secretary indicates that she has been told that several people from the Deaf community have asked to testify. That sounds like a very stressful situation for you, and you're afraid you might blow something, which would then reflect poorly on the Deaf community.

97. You're enrolled in your ITP's internship class and establish a weekly placement at an elementary school. A school administrator approaches you one day at school and compliments your ITP as one of the finest in the state. He tells you the school still hasn't filled one full-time interpreter position, and he would like to offer it to you even before you graduate.

98. You're fresh out of an ITP and have taken and passed your state QA screening test and received a level II. According to your state guidelines, this level allows you to interpret in "limited" situations. You get calls all the time for jobs you know require skills beyond your screening level. You figure the interpreter referral agencies know your level and must know what they're doing.

99. Your all-time favorite deaf student has just graduated from high school and now is asking you to come and interpret for her in college. She has studied German all through high school and will be majoring in German in college. You two have actually learned the language together, and she says she feels the most comfortable with you. However, the university that she will be attending only utilizes nationally certified interpreters, which you are not.

100. Your uncle is the pastor of the church you have attended for years. The church has a nationally certified interpreter come in every week to interpret the service. You have just graduated from an ITP, and your uncle wants you to take over interpreting his sermons in order to save money.

101. You have been interpreting in a post-secondary educational setting for over a year. You're not nationally certified, but plan on it eventually. A mental health hospital contacts you directly to ask if you would be available to interpret weekly group sessions for deaf adolescents.

102. You have recently graduated from a well-respected ITP and are waiting for your state QA results, which should arrive in four to six weeks. Meanwhile, you get a call from a high school offering you a full-time job starting in the fall. Without a QA level, you feel uneasy taking the job. On the other hand, by the time the job starts, you'll probably be qualified.

103. You're a state QA level II who has just finished taking your QA screening exam again. You feel confident you have achieved an even higher rating. A deaf friend calls asks you to interpret for her in a traffic court in two weeks. There's a legal interpreting workshop this Saturday. You figure you could attend the workshop and get some pointers; then you'd be ready to interpret for your deaf friend in court.

104. You're an ITP student with a part-time job at a department store. Your boss finds out that you can sign, and the next time you come into work, she hands you a button she wants you to wear that says "ASL Interpreter." Your ITP professor has said you shouldn't call yourself an interpreter until you at least pass your state QA exam. What if she comes in the store and sees your button? On the other hand, your boss has a point too. Even with your beginning skills, you could probably help any deaf customers that come into the store.

Challenges in Ensuring Appropriate Attire

- **Scenarios 105.** Now that we're no longer limited to navy and black as our wardrobe color choices these days, I need advice. I'm seeing all kinds of contrasting colors on interpreters: shades of medium to dark gray, reds, greens, and browns, but I've also seen bright colors and pastels lately. I am not at all offended by this non-blue/black apparel trend, but would appreciate having your views.

AN INTERPRETER'S PERSPECTIVE: I started interpreting in the days of black and navy blue, and my favorite, smocks. Over time I came to realize, as apparently many other interpreters have, that different situations warrant particular clothing considerations. The number one issue is visual comfort and the avoidance of distractions or undue eye strain. In one-on-one interpreting situations of short duration with familiar consumers, particular colors or styles are less of an issue. I try to dress in clothing suitable to the situation, avoiding busy patterns or cumbersome styles, but the particular color is flexible. However, for assignments of long duration (i.e., several hours) with platform interpreting or with unfamiliar consumers, I still go with the plain contrasting colors (for my skin tone, black or other dark colors.) The reason is, for longer assignments, visual fatigue can become a factor. For platform interpreting, distance and background play a bigger role. For an unfamiliar consumer, it is unknown if the consumer may have some vision issues or vision loss requiring the darker color for background contrast. Again, we must assess the situation, but one thing is clear —— the smock is no longer in my wardrobe!

A DEAF CONSUMER'S PERSPECTIVE: Your question did not mention what kind of settings specifically. For formal, platform, or professional-like settings, the best practice in my opinion would be to dress from top to bottom with minimal contrasting colors. I am not in favor of black suits with white or soft (pastel) colors. With a black suit, I would wear maybe a dark gray shirt. In general, the color of your choice should softly blend all over making sure that your color choice shows contrast. (I guess we could call this the Regis Philbin Style.) Your shirt should be a similar color to your pants or skirt, not necessarily always black or dark blue. I must admit, I am not keen on bright colors and pastels on anyone. I think it either shows too much contrast or not enough. Colors should create a soothing and comfortable background for consumers to focus on. In a more casual and informal setting, I would suggest wearing similar types of clothing to those attending the meeting or function, to fit in but still be viewed as a professional in the setting. Follow the same rule, mentioned in the first paragraph: wear a similar color from top to bottom. Personally, I have added maroon and teal to my wardrobe.

- **Scenario 106**. I'm called to substitute for another interpreter at a nearby elementary school. When I ask the woman about the dress code at the school, she tells me to dress comfortably. She tells me most of the staff wear jeans and tennis shoes. I arrive casually dressed, only to find I'm scheduled to interpret Individual Educational Planning Committee (IEPC) meetings all day with parents, faculty, and administrators in attendance.

AN INTERPRETER'S PERSPECTIVE: Keep a spare set of clothes in your car at all times. If you're going "casual," bring something more professional along, and vice versa. It's a good practice.

A DEAF CONSUMER'S PERSPECTIVE: Experienced interpreters know that their car is also their "suitcase." Always, always have back-up clothes in the car for situations like this.

- **Scenario 107**. I'm team interpreting a televised gubernatorial debate. I realize too late that the way the lighting is set up, I can see right through my partner's dress and she isn't wearing a slip. It won't show on television because they're just showing us from the waist up, but everyone in the studio has a clear view.

AN INTERPRETER'S PERSPECTIVE: I would continue to do the interpreting job. I wouldn't want to embarrass her while we're doing this job. I might suggest to her after the job is over that in the future she may want to wear a slip with that particular dress and explain why.

A DEAF CONSUMER'S PERSPECTIVE: Too late is too late. At least we know the lower part won't be on TV. I'm sure the studio folks have seen such things before. You could write a note for her to read during the next switch, and she can figure out what to do before returning to the spotlight.

- **Scenario 108**. I have always been fascinated by body piercing, and after a few drinks on Friday night, I let some friends talk me into getting my tongue pierced. I wake up the next day and actually love it. I think it looks pretty cool. I have an interpreting job on Saturday, but I'm not supposed to take the stud out for any length of time yet. The deaf client is sure to notice the shiny, silver ball riding around on my tongue.

AN INTERPRETER'S PERSPECTIVE: The personal decisions you make can have an impact on you professionally. In particular, any change to your appearance will have consequences, and this is one example of that. You have to decide if the shiny, silver ball on your tongue will disturb the client or otherwise interfere with your ability to do your job. If so, either remove the object from your tongue or find a replacement interpreter. We're constantly "stepping into other people's lives," and we need to take that seriously. In some locales and situations, a tongue piercing may not be a problem; in most, it probably will be.

A DEAF CONSUMER'S PERSPECTIVE: Always plan ahead of time. If you wanted to have your tongue pierced, you should have planned to do it between interpreting assignments to allow adequate time for your tongue to heal.

- **Scenario 109**. I finally decide to do something about all those gray hairs that are spoiling my once-beautiful red hair. To my horror, my home dye job turns my hair bright orange — I look like Ronald McDonald! There's absolutely no way I can leave the house looking like this, much less show up at the business meeting I'm supposed to interpret in a few short hours.

AN INTERPRETER'S PERSPECTIVE: I'm good at scarves. I can think of no alternative but to find a substitute or cover my head with a scarf and try to have a good sense of humor about the situation.

A DEAF CONSUMER'S PERSPECTIVE: I would make the best of it. I would style my hair as usual and wear clothes to match. After the assignment I would run, run, run to the nearest salon!

- **Scenario 110.** I have noticed that my younger colleagues in semiformal interpreting situations often wear dresses minus the pantyhose. Is that ever appropriate for us as professionals? Is the new trend to go barelegged? Are pantyhose a thing of the past? I'm used to wearing pantyhose when I wear a skirt, but maybe I'm just being old fashioned.

AN INTERPRETER'S PERSPECTIVE: There are so many factors — whether the setting is indoors or out, etc. Since you mention that the settings are "semiformal," I am inclined to say that hose should be "de rigueur." If it was a luau or something less formal, bare legs would be perfectly appropriate. Geographic region may also influence dress. I believe people in Hawaii and Las Vegas tend to interpret semiformal in a more casual way than the rest of the country. Interpreters should look business-like, yet not call attention to themselves. So, if the other women in major roles in that setting are barelegged, again, that may be appropriate. Many shoes today are made specifically to be worn without stockings, some casual, some more dressy. However, I would expect interpreters in a semiformal setting to be dressed accordingly, in semiformal clothing which, in my mind, includes hose. Maybe it is a generation gap. As for myself, my feet get cold without hose unless I'm outside sitting in the sun!

A DEAF CONSUMER'S PERSPECTIVE: I believe one needs to take into account the setting and the time of the year that a semiformal interpreting situation takes place. Should that be at the beach or a resort area, it would be OK for an interpreter to go barelegged. If the weather is hot and the semiformal situation takes place outside, then going barelegged should not pose a problem in terms of dressing etiquette as long as the barelegged attire fits the occasion. In short, going barelegged depends on a number of factors, and you must clearly use your good judgment before leaving the house in the morning.

- **Scenario 111.** I think we can all agree that interpreters should remove body piercings, cover their tattoos, pull their hair back, limit jewelry, and not wear colored nail polish, but the generation gap is growing. For example, baggy pants are "in" for men and tight fitting clothing is "in" for women. How do you define professional appearance?

AN INTERPRETER'S PERSPECTIVE: Employers may already have dress code policies, so check with the referral agency to see if they have guidelines for maintaining their image. However, we all know that the type of dress needed for an assignment could vary from day to day or even within a given day. Ask yourself: does this match the environment and the participants of the assignment? It also might not be a bad idea to ask the interpreter coordinator who requests you. Few workplaces nowadays have specific dress codes. However, finding out as much as you can about the site in advance will assist you in choosing the most appropriate dress. It is true that preferences in personal styles may vary from interpreter to interpreter. Following the general business dress code is a safe bet. If you get a complaint from a deaf or hearing consumer, that should always be taken seriously.

A DEAF CONSUMER'S PERSPECTIVE: A true professional should not need to be reminded. You should surround yourself with like-minded professionals and you shouldn't have to worry about this. However, it should always come down to reflecting well on the client. We can tell you ourselves if we are unhappy with how you reflect upon us professionally as well.

- **Scenario 112.** I'm on call for a hospital and am working out at a local gym when I get paged. A pregnant Deaf woman is in the emergency room and needs to have a C-section immediately. I tell the hospital I'm on my way, but the minute I hang up I realize I have only brought sweats. To go home and change would only waste valuable time.

AN INTERPRETER'S PERSPECTIVE: Hospital personnel understand emergencies. Go do the job and apologize as necessary for your dress. Luckily, for a C-section you'll be in scrubs most of the time anyway. From now on, hang a change of clothes in your car for future emergencies.

A DEAF CONSUMER'S PERSPECTIVE: Actually, sweats are often perfect for a hospital situation. Most likely, no one will notice how you're dressed, much less have time for your apologies. I believe being comfortable is the key.

- **Scenario 113**. I'm a freelance interpreter, and I also work part-time at a computer store. I get a call at the store from my agency asking me to interpret a last-minute call for an in-house staff meeting. I'm just getting off work anyway, but I'm wearing jeans and a striped sweater. There's no way I can go home and change and still make it on time.

AN INTERPRETER'S PERSPECTIVE: Discuss this with the referral agency. Let them know what you're wearing and decide together if you should still do the interpreting. I would suggest keeping an extra set of clothes in your car from now on.

A DEAF CONSUMER'S PERSPECTIVE: The interpreter should always be prepared. Carry a smock or a change of clothes at all times.

Other Scenarios

Identify the issue(s) involved and decide how you would respond. Discuss and compare your responses with your colleagues.

114. At the high school where you interpret, it's spirit week. Monday is "Mismatch Day," and you decide to participate. You wear a checkered shirt and a pair of flower-print leggings. To top it off, you wear black nail polish. Your supervisor approaches you and reprimands you for your wardrobe choices today. She asks you to wear a smock over your clothes for the rest of the day and remove your nail polish immediately. Afterwards, you ask the deaf student if your outfit bothers her. She assures you she thinks you look cool, so you decide to disregard your supervisor's instructions. The next day your supervisor sends you copies of the school's appearance guidelines for interpreters. You counter her move by getting the deaf student to write a statement saying she doesn't care how you look when you interpret.

115. Off duty, you wear all the patterned clothing that you can't wear when you interpret. In case you have to take a last-minute job, you always carry a cover-up in your car. Today, you get such a call and you're wearing a brightly colored striped shirt, the kind that hurts your eyes if you stare at it too long. However, this is not a problem with your smock in the car to cover it up. You get to the assignment and open the trunk, only to find that your teenage son used your smock as a rag and now it reeks of gas.

116. You have been asked to interpret for the master of ceremonies at the Deaf Olympics. You know this is a sporting event, but you're not sure what to wear. When you arrive and are introduced to the master of ceremonies, he's wearing a tux. You're drastically underdressed and now you feel self-conscious.

117. You have just recently become engaged and are very proud of the rock on your finger. As an interpreter, you know a diamond of that size is very distracting when you interpret, but you just can't bear to take it off.

118. You show up to interpret at a youth center wearing a plaid skirt, solid fitted top, and heels. You inform the secretary at the front desk that you're there to interpret for a deaf youth at the center. The secretary tells you she can't admit you into the facility because of your inappropriate outfit. She says that this is a correctional facility for male youths, and the female staff members have a very specific dress code. You have no change of clothing in your car, nor were you told any of this in advance.

119. You're a staff interpreter for a large university that has an extensive agricultural program. You finish interpreting at the dairy farm and when you remove your coveralls and boots, you realize you now smell like a barnyard. You still have a full day of interpreting ahead of you.

120. You're asked to interpret a sports banquet for the girls' volleyball team. You misjudge the attire for the event, and you're underdressed. All of the girls and their families are in suits and dresses, and you feel conspicuous standing up in front where everyone can see you.

121. You're interpreting at a junior high school one day, and it's very hot outside. The school is not air-conditioned. In order to remain comfortable, you decide to wear shorts to work. Your supervisor comes up and reprimands you, but you tell her you don't understand. After all, the students are allowed to wear shorts.

122. Your new boyfriend is a tattoo artist. Your boyfriend finds them incredibly sexy and says he will do some for you for free, so how can you resist? You go ahead and get two, one that circles your ankle and a second one around your arm. It's summer and you realize nothing you own will cover the tattoos. Also, you can't very well wear socks with a dress. You get a call to interpret an 8-week college course. You hope the deaf student doesn't mind interpreters with tattoos.

123. While interpreting a high school graduation in a football stadium, a bird leaves a major dropping on your shoulder. You wipe it off with your sleeve, which only makes it worse. Now you have got smears on your suit in two places. The ceremony has just begun, and it feels like it's going to be a long afternoon.

124. You have recently given birth to your first child and are asked to interpret for your all-time favorite comedian. Reluctant to turn down such an opportunity, you arrange to bring your child backstage so you can breastfeed. Once the show begins, although the lights are shining brightly in your eyes, you can see a man in the front row making obscene gestures to you. He's grabbing his chest. You are, in fact, a large breasted woman, but this is offensive. You try valiantly to ignore this obnoxious little pervert, but he continues making gestures throughout the show. Afterwards backstage, your husband rushes up to you and says he tried to tell you that you were lactating, and you had two huge wet spots on the front of your shirt.

125. You have rehearsed for weeks for a theatrical performance you'll be interpreting tonight. You decide to take a quick nap to refresh yourself, and when you wake up you realize you have overslept and only have 20 minutes to get to the theater. You dress in record time, drive like a maniac, and walk on stage just as the curtain is going up. After the performance is over, you let out a sign of relief as you walk out to your car eager to go home and relax. As you approach your car, you can see your reflection in your car window. You groan as you realize you still have two pink curlers in your hair.

126. You walk up to relieve your team interpreter on stage only to realize too late that the draft you're feeling on your legs isn't from the air conditioning. Your skirt is tucked into your pantyhose from when you recently went to the restroom.

127. You're an interpreter in an elementary mainstream program where you tend to spend a lot of time sitting on the floor with the students or outside on the field for gym. You tend to wear very comfortable clothing. One day the classroom teacher you work with tells you she thinks you should start dressing more professionally.

128. You're called to substitute interpret at an elementary school. The first class of the day is gym class, and they're meeting outside on the muddy football field. You have to run up and down the field to interpret for the gym teacher. When you go back inside, your hose are ruined and the heels of your brand new shoes are caked in mud.

Challenges Related to Arriving on Time to Assignments

- **Scenario 129.** Being late is probably the number one most annoying thing an interpreter can do in my book, especially those interpreters who make a habit of it. In some situations I have felt it would have been better if the interpreter never showed up at all rather than embarrass us both by being so late. Honestly, don't you agree?

AN INTERPRETER'S PERSPECTIVE: Being on time is good; being late is bad. No disagreement there. That being said, if my current assignment at the hospital that was supposed to end at 2 p.m. drags on and on until 3 p.m., and my next assignment is a staff meeting, is it more ethical to stay until the hospital meeting ends, or should I leave at the appointed time regardless in order to be on time for the next one? Ethically, I am stuck because I can't tell you why I am late; all I can say is, "Sorry." No matter which decision I make, I can't meet everyone's need. Chronic lateness, however, is different, and unfortunately, interpreters who are chronically late are often rewarded for their behavior by the consumers (hearing and deaf) who fail to let agencies know there is a problem. I schedule interpreters for my company, and I've paid invoices from interpreters who charged me as if they'd shown up on time. Then I find out that they showed up an hour late or left an hour early. Unfortunately, if there is no follow-up, interpreters who demonstrate repeatedly that they don't respect the assignment might be hired again. Let the paying entity know how long the interpreter actually worked, and make sure she is paid correctly. If it's really better the interpreter not show up at all, let her know that being late more than a reasonable amount of time will mean the assignment will be cancelled and she won't be paid.

Scheduling interpreting assignments is at best a scientific wild guess because interpreters work with very unpredictable variables — people and time. It's hard to predict both with accuracy. Every interpreter is going to be late to an assignment occasionally, and that will continue to happen until people and time become predictable. Chronic lateness, however, shows that the interpreter holds little respect for the work and the people she serves. Behavior like that won't change without a consequence.

A DEAF CONSUMER'S PERSPECTIVE: Amen! Not only do I agree, in fact I think it is often the "better" interpreters in our area who are chronically late and guilty of this. It's almost like they know we have no other choice if we want the best interpreters available to us. Or maybe it's because they feel like after so many years of working in our community, they know us well enough that we'll just let it slide — and we do. Truth be told, my reason for not saying something to these few interpreters is I do not want to make them mad. Who knows, I may need them someday or end up having them in a situation where I have little choice, and then the situation is strained at best. I've been privy to interpreters talking about certain deaf consumers in the community whom they say they don't want to work because they are so demanding. I'm serious; we know sometimes you talk about us and sometimes we talk about you. If we were to talk amongst ourselves about an interpreter in the community who is known for showing up late (to be defined later), we all agree it's a bad thing, but none of us wants to be the bad guy and say anything. However, none of us like it. I work with a well-known interpreter trainer who tells her students, "If you are five minutes early, you're late!" She has another idea she shares with her students that I really like too. Instead of writing, for example, 4 p.m. as the start time in your day planner, get in the habit of writing 3:45 p.m. as the start time. Honestly, you'd be surprised because, when we talk about interpreters, it's not about your skills — it's your ethics and professionalism.

- **Scenario 130.** Which is better in your opinion: to be a few minutes late for an interpreting job when it is pouring rain or show up on time but soaking wet?

AN INTERPRETER'S PERSPECTIVE: If you arrive later (but dry), the consumers may be inconvenienced, annoyed, frustrated, anxious, etc. However, an appropriate business-like explanation and apology should soon set this matter aside and allow everyone to concentrate on the business at hand. I suspect the consequences will be more serious if you arrive drenched, but on time. Although you may be "on time" by the clock, you may not be ready to do the job. At least from my experience, it is difficult to concentrate on my interpreting task while dressed in uncomfortable, wet, clingy clothing and sodden shoes. These are not conditions conducive to producing your best work.

Secondly, imagine the effect on consumers as they try to concentrate on the business at hand and their communication goals, while trying to ignore the squishing sounds as you move around, the fine mist spraying off your fingertips, and the ever widening puddle on the floor beneath you (and these distractions will continue for the duration of the assignment!). After the assignment is the appropriate time to consider what reasonable alternatives might have prevented your dilemma. You might want to stop by a store on the way home and purchase the appropriate rain gear and an umbrella to keep in your car or interpreter's tote.

A DEAF CONSUMER'S PERSPECTIVE: Interpreters must make judicious safety-related decisions. If the interpreter is on a college campus, he or she can wait for a few minutes until the pouring rain has subsided, even though she should have an umbrella. As soon as you get to the classroom, you can privately tell the deaf student(s) succinctly the reason for being late. If it is to interpret for a doctor's appointment or a lawyer meeting, it would be best for the interpreter to call and let the parties know that you will be a little late due to heavy downpour. In other words, it is wise to be late for appointments as long as the parties involved (both hearing and deaf) know that you are on the way. Coming into an appointment soaking wet may not only reflect badly on the interpreter, but also the deaf consumer. Again, the interpreter's safety is the key to making sure that the communication process will work, no matter how late the interpreter arrives to the appointment.

Other Scenarios

Identify the issue(s) involved and decide how you would respond. Discuss and compare your responses with your colleagues.

131. One day you're at the gym working out before an assignment, and you have your eye on the clock. About 20 minutes before you need to leave, you run into an old boyfriend at the gym who's still as "hot" as ever. He comes over with a big smile, and your heart starts beating wildly. You completely lose track of time, and before you know it, you're definitely late. You jump in your car and dash off to the assignment arriving late, looking like a mess, and smelling like a gym locker.

132. You have been booked for a two-hour assignment and at the end of two hours, the speaker shows no sign of slowing down. You have got another job scheduled in 30 minutes, and you need to leave right now. You tell the deaf client you have to go and she becomes angry. She says it's almost over. You hate leaving things badly between the two of you, but nothing is going to resolve this now. And you've just got to leave.

133. You've been interpreting all day for a deaf student in a veterinary program at the university. As you're driving to your next assignment off campus, you realize you smell like a kennel. You have just enough time to run home and change, but you're out of gas and out of money, which means you'd have to stop by the bank and the gas station too.

134. You have an interpreting assignment that starts at 11 a.m. You get a last-minute phone call to do another assignment at 10 a.m. You explain that you already have an assignment at 11 o'clock, but the doctor's office swears it will only take five minutes. It's for a re-exam. You agree and when you arrive, sure enough, there's no wait and you're both ushered right in to see the doctor. However, it turns out the client's wound is swollen and infected and so the doctor needs to reopen the wound. Meanwhile, the clock is ticking away towards your next assignment for which you still need to allow for drive time and to find parking.

135. On the first day of class at the university where you interpret, you figure you have the wrong classroom when no deaf students show up. So you walk all the way back to your office and find out it's the classroom next door. You walk all the way back, but by now, the class has started. You try to enter the classroom through the door closest to where the professor is standing, and he stops his lecture and tells you that all late arrivals must enter through the back door. You clearly see the deaf students seated in the front row but don't want to antagonize the professor further. However, if you go in through the back door, you'll just have to walk all the way up to the front of the classroom.

Challenges in Dealing with Hearing People Unfamiliar with Interpreting and Deaf Individuals' Needs

- **Scenario 136.** I work in an educational setting. Fortunately, there are two other interpreters here so we do get an opportunity to team when there are school-wide events. In the past there has been little pre-planning for events until 20 minutes (or less) before the start time. Repeatedly, I have tried to solicit pre-planning time from the administration, but until that occurs, I just do the best I can. Is there a way you can suggest that I can appropriately approach this situation without looking like the pressuring villain instead of the rational interpreter that I am?

AN INTERPRETER'S PERSPECTIVE: It seems there are two problems that you are facing: the non-interpreting personnel do not understand the dynamic of interpreting (and your need to have as much information before the fact); and that there are several and maybe numerous personnel whom must be dealt with to raise and resolve the issues. Trying to do this on a case-by-case basis will not only take a lot of time, but will too often take place when you, other interpreters, speakers, meeting facilitators, students, etc. are all under stress. What might work is if you and your fellow interpreters could compose a factual yet tactful memo explaining the reasons that you need certain information (e.g., lighting, seating).

This memo could be given to your supervisor, the principal, teachers, and anyone who might possibly be involved in the scheduling or coordination of a meeting or event. One way to title and word this memo could be "Cheat Sheet for Great Communication" and/or "Good interpreting happens when the interpreter(s) knows as much as possible in advance." This allows the closest approximation to "simultaneous" communication between two languages. Outlines, agendas, speaker notes, and bios (especially when there are many names; it's very hard to guess the spelling of names that are unfamiliar), as well as topics to be covered, should be provided ideally at least two days in advance of the event. This not only assures that the interpreter(s) can provide smooth and efficient information, but that the deaf or hard of hearing students or attendees can receive information that allows them to understand, respond, laugh, reflect on the subject, etc. within a time frame that is close to those who can hear. Some additional information could be typical things that may not be known to those who do not use or really understand the art and science of interpreting. I am a great believer in the concept of telling anyone anything if you do it in the right way, so your concerns about being a "villain" can be addressed through your mode of providing this information. A final thought: depending on the age of the students, it could be very helpful to have discussions with them about what you ideally would like to encounter in the interpreting set-up and background information. This will educate and empower the students to hopefully speak up on your behalf and their own in the future.

A DEAF CONSUMER'S PERSPECTIVE: From your letter it is difficult to tell who you are soliciting for pre-planning material. When there is a school-wide event, find out who is in charge of coordinating that event and then track that person down in person! When you have contacted the coordinator, don't expect "her" to hand you the material, but rather get the names and telephone numbers of the person(s) from the department(s) that will be performing or the outside contact person that will be in charge of music for the words. Offer to make copies yourself, and then do the same for all the various speakers, explaining how having the words to songs and an outline to speeches helps you provide a clearer, more precise interpretation of their work. Hopefully, if the same departments provide the programs in the future, your job of soliciting material ahead of time will become second nature to them, and they will think to make copies and outlines for you without asking (oh, in a perfect world). You also say that you have two other interpreters who can share the responsibility of tracking down the material prior to events. Also, remember to start several weeks in advance, tell them when you need the materials, and then follow up with the speakers and music leaders. Finally, remember that thank-you notes still go a long way in maintaining goodwill!

- **Scenario 137**. I'm interpreting an AIDS awareness workshop. First, there's a video of couples performing various sexual acts. Then the presenter uncovers a table displaying a variety of sexual devices and contraceptives. The presenter asks for volunteers from the audience to help him demonstrate some of the items. Everyone giggles but no one volunteers, so he's forced to demonstrate everything himself. He has several household items that in a pinch can double as prophylactics, and he begins to demonstrate how to use them safely. The next thing I know, the presenter is wrapping my hips with plastic wrap.

AN INTERPRETER'S PERSPECTIVE: In a pleasant but professional manner, I would explain that in order to do my job as an interpreter, I need to focus on my interpreting, and that participating in any way is too distracting. I would suggest that he involve those who are supposed to be participating. I would keep my comments succinct, end the discussion quickly, and get back to my job.

A DEAF CONSUMER'S PERSPECTIVE: You should tell the presenter to use one of the participants instead of you. You're working, and the presenter didn't ask you about this before the presentation. Your feelings should be respected.

- **Scenario 138**. I am an interpreter in a group parenting class where most of the parents are there because they've been court-ordered for child abuse. The deaf client is taking the class voluntarily to improve her parenting skills. Every time she participates in class, the other parents laugh because of the sounds she makes when she vocalizes. I know the client will no longer participate if she finds out that the other parents are making fun of her.

AN INTERPRETER'S PERSPECTIVE: I would continue to interpret what is going on. I would tell the others that it's difficult to hear the instructor when people are laughing and ask them to please stop.

A DEAF CONSUMER'S PERSPECTIVE: Just interpret everything that is going on. The interpreter could approach the instructor with the idea of covering parenting tips with a disabled child, which would naturally include some education on etiquette and respect toward everyone, regardless of "differences." I would insist, however, that the interpreter remain in the role.

Other Scenarios

Identify the issue(s) involved and decide how you would respond. Discuss and compare your responses with your colleagues.

139. While interpreting for a college class, the professor starts rambling, and you and everyone else in the class are having trouble following her. Finally, the deaf student raises his hand, but the professor doesn't see it. The student asks his question anyway, which you voice. The professor turns to you and bawls you out. She accuses you of trying to undermine her authority.

140. While interpreting in a post-secondary educational classroom, the professor keeps referring to you as an aide, or even worse, a helper. Both you and the deaf student have corrected him several times, but it's obvious how he views your role in the classroom.

141. You're interpreting a long list of questions that a receptionist in the emergency room is asking the deaf patient. The client repeatedly states that he's feeling dizzy. Finally, the receptionist turns and snaps at you saying, "Look, I'm almost done here. Just sit down if you're dizzy!"

142. You're interpreting a physical, and the nurse keeps talking to you instead of directly to the patient. She says, "He weighs 240 pounds," to which the deaf man

jokingly replies, "I don't weigh that much!" The nurse looks at you and says, "No, you don't weigh that much; I said he does!"

143. You're interpreting at an all-day group therapy session. Everyone in the group is going around the circle introducing themselves. When it's the deaf client's turn to introduce himself, instead of telling everyone his name and where he's from, he says, "My mother f— –ked me," and that's it. Later that morning when the group has a short break, you're in the break room alone sipping a cup of coffee, and one of the other patients comes in and sits down next to you. She says, "I heard what you said about your mama and I'm real sorry."

144. You're interpreting for a deaf woman who has undergone major surgery and is just coming out of sedation. An intern walks in to check her chart, and the woman suddenly starts signing a lot of swear words. You voice her remarks, and the intern calls for security. When they arrive, the intern tells them to remove you from the hospital.

145. One day while you're interpreting for a deaf client in a doctor's office, the doctor starts reprimanding the client about her excess weight. The deaf client becomes angry with the doctor and tells him "to mind his own f— –king business." Afterwards, as you're gathering your coat and your bag and the client has walked out of the room ahead of you, the doctor stops you in the hall. He tells you he's appalled at your behavior and will be reporting you for talking to him like that, especially in front of the poor deaf patient.

146. You're interpreting at a doctor's office for a deaf woman complaining of rectal itching. The doctor has the patient lying on her side with her knees pulled up tight to her chest. You're situated in a chair by her face while the doctor is examining her. You can't hear the doctor so you keep asking him to repeat himself. He finally requests you come stand next to him so you can hear him better.

147. You're interpreting for a deaf woman who has been in labor for many hours, and it's finally determined that she will have a C-section. The doctor and the client tell you to take a quick break and grab something to eat in the cafeteria. The client insists she can lipread until you come back. While you're getting something to eat, you're paged and asked to report to OB-GYN stat! Worried that something terrible has happened, you rush upstairs. You run into the deaf woman's doctor storming down the hall and he says, "I thought she said she could read lips. She hasn't understood one damn thing I've said to her while you were gone!" The whole time he's yelling at you, he's still wearing his surgical mask.

148. While you're interpreting a church sermon, the pastor looks over at you every time he says the phrase, "If you don't resist the temptation of sin, you would surely be damned to hell, and you'll never enter the gates of heaven." The pastor, thinking he's pretty slick, starts signing the sign he thinks he figured out is the sign for "heaven." Unfortunately, he's got the wrong sign, and now he's standing at the pulpit signing "hell" every time he says "heaven."

149. You're contracted to interpret at a festival on one of the side stages. A storyteller begins to wander from her storytelling and starts discussing the type of men she prefers. You interpret as she compares her boyfriend's physique to yours. She goads the audience into encouraging you to turn around to show everyone your behind.

150. You're interpreting a show that features several comedians. In between comedians, you stay on stage, as the transitions are generally quick. However, during one particularly long wait for the next comedian to come out, you see a little boy in the front row pointing at you. He says loud enough for everyone to hear, "Mommy, she's not funny at all!"

151. On the first day of a college class, you introduce yourself to the professor, explain your role, and then get a chair and place it facing the deaf student near the professor. The professor asks you to move a little further away. The deaf student says she doesn't mind, but soon after the professor begins lecturing, you find that the man speaks in a very soft voice and you can barely hear him. You start scooting your chair closer to hear better. The next thing you know the professor is coldly asking you to please move farther away — you're distracting him.

152. It's the kindergarten teacher's first day working with an interpreter. When you voice for the little deaf boy, "I have to go to the bathroom. Can you help me with my buttons?" the kindergarten teacher freaks out. She says to you, "Look, I'm not into that kind of thing. This arrangement is not going to work out!"

153. Your friend's deaf, teenage daughter asks you to interpret for her to get a manicure. She has a hard time communicating while her nails are wet with polish, and in her frustration, she signs something and smears the polish. The client demands that the manicurist re-do her nails, but she's obviously fed up with such a difficult client and refuses.

154. You're contacted by a theater group to interpret one of their productions. You're excited at the prospect and ask the director all kinds of questions, which he answers reluctantly. You're puzzled by his response but enthusiastically jump in anyway. After several rehearsals with the same reluctance shown by the director, you ask a production assistant if the guy is that way with everyone. She tells you, "No, he really didn't want an interpreter involved, but management says we have to comply with the Americans With Disabilities Act (ADA)."

Challenges Related to Violations of Clients' Rights

- **Scenario 155**. I am standing in the cold rain interpreting while the football coach talks to his players about whether or not to have practice today. None of the boys want to practice, but the coach tells them their opponents for this week's game are probably practicing right now. One of the players shouts, "No, they don't practice; they're pu– –ies!" The coach immediately looks at me and says, "Don't sign that!"

AN INTERPRETER'S PERSPECTIVE: We have all faced this situation many times in our careers. There are so many dynamics taking place at once that it's challenging to manage. The coach obviously needs education about the role of an interpreter, but this isn't the time or place. One way to handle this situation is to give quick eye contact to the coach and indicate with a nod that you have heard him, then continue to interpret everything, including the fact that he told you not to interpret the message. Encourage the Deaf student to self-advocate in this instance. If he's reluctant, however, try to meet with the coach later to clarify your role.

A DEAF CONSUMER'S PERSPECTIVE: The interpreter must interpret the statement, along with the coach's statement, "Don't sign that." You aren't there to censor anything but to facilitate all communication, regardless of vulgarity. Additionally, you're there for the deaf student, not for the coach. The coach's statement not to interpret the remark would deny the deaf student full participation in the practice. If the coach gets upset, explain that the CPC obligates you to interpret everything and not to take a censorship role.

- **Scenario 156**. I interpret in a college course where I'm convinced the professor hates all people, especially interpreters. Today he's showing some slides in class and so he turns off the lights. When the deaf student asks for some kind of compromise for a light source, the professor steadfastly refuses the student's request.

AN INTERPRETER'S PERSPECTIVE: This is a tough one. RID frowns upon the appearance of paternalism, and taking up the cause for this consumer would definitely be that. However, you could offer to interpret the student's complaint to the disabled students' office.

A DEAF CONSUMER'S PERSPECTIVE: Follow the lead of the deaf student. If the student wants to make a formal complaint, go with the student to facilitate that communication.

- **Scenario 157**. I'm asked to interpret for a hearing wife and her deaf husband, who are having a baby. I have attended all the childbirth classes and am almost as excited as the expectant couple. On the day of the delivery, I'm in the delivery room with the mother-to-be, her husband, the doctor, and several nurses. The room is rather crowded, and in the middle of the delivery, the doctor orders me to leave the room. He says I'm in his way and that the mother-to-be can interpret the rest of the delivery for her deaf husband.

AN INTERPRETER'S PERSPECTIVE: This is not the time to start an argument with the doctor. On the other hand, the father should have as much access as any hearing father. To emphasize the point that I'm there for both the doctor and the couple, I would both sign and voice the statement, "The doctor just told me that I'm in the way and wants me to leave. What do you (the father and mother) suggest I do?" If the parents decide it's best that I leave, I would leave. If they want me to stay and they explain this to the doctor on their own, I would interpret this, perhaps adding the phrase, "Joe (the father) is saying," to emphasize that it's the consumer who is demanding equal access. If they want me to stay but don't advocate for themselves, I would ask the father if he would like for me to explain (quickly, of course) why an interpreter is necessary and even some of the legal aspects of providing interpreting services in a situation like this. If the father agrees, I would do so politely in both spoken English and ASL.

A DEAF CONSUMER'S PERSPECTIVE: Under no circumstances should the interpreter leave! Perhaps the interpreter and husband will need to shift their positions to create more room while maintaining visible communication.

- **Scenario 158**. I was interpreting at the home of a deaf person for a meeting with his counselor. This meeting was interrupted by a phone call for the counselor who took the call. During this time, I interpreted the side of a conversation that I could hear. After the call, the counselor apologized to the deaf person for the interruption and then turned to me, smiled, lowered his voice and said, "For future reference, my calls are no one's business but my own!" What could I have done?

AN INTERPRETER'S PERSPECTIVE: You did the right thing by interpreting what you heard of the counselor's phone call, and I hope you interpreted the snide remark after the phone call, too! If it were truly no one's business but his own, the counselor should have gone out of ear shot to talk. This incident reinforces the need for the interpreter to have a pre- and post-session with the counselor. If the counselor had known in advance your ground rules stating that you will interpret anything you hear, he may have taken the personal phone call in a place where you couldn't hear. If you had explained the "rules" before the call and the counselor still chastised you, you could have reminded the counselor of that specific ground rule in the post-session.

A DEAF CONSUMER'S PERSPECTIVE: After the session, I would encourage you to go to the counselor and explain the role of an interpreter. I would say that you have the responsibility to interpret everything that is said in the room for both the deaf client and the counselor. The road goes both ways. I would also add if he wants to take a private phone call, he has the option of leaving the room.

- **Scenario 159.** I have been a nationally certified interpreter for many years, and I have a long-standing contract with a large medical facility in town. Recently I was interpreting there with a client when a deaf person who is new to town walks in bringing her own "interpreter" (a friend). Ultimately, deaf consumers can utilize whomever they want to interpret and may have a variety of valid reasons for doing so, but now the new coordinator doesn't want to offer my services to new deaf patients if they're willing to bring their own to save on costs. I have worked very hard to get this medical center to always utilize nationally certified interpreters (even if it is not me). What do I say, if anything, to the deaf woman, the friend, or the medical coordinator?

AN INTERPRETER'S PERSPECTIVE: This is an issue between you and the medical facility with which you contract; it would be appropriate to address that issue with the medical coordinator only. There are several issues you can bring to the attention of the medical coordinator: liability, complying with federal and state law, and quality control. If you address it from these perspectives, the medical coordinator may be more willing to listen. You can point out that the medical facility is liable if the deaf person receives treatment but doesn't understand instructions or procedures (because the interpretation was ineffective) and then subsequently is injured as a direct result of lack of understanding. Generally, you can get information about federal and state laws governing provision of interpreters from your state division on Deafness and Hard of Hearing office that you can then provide the medical coordinator. Having this documentation will strengthen your argument. You can also point out that the liability issue really goes back to quality control; if the medical facility does not hire qualified interpreters, then they have no control over the quality of the interpretation and put themselves into a precarious situation.

Approaching either the deaf person or the friend would be difficult for a couple of reasons: approaching the deaf person could be perceived as being paternalistic and oppressive. Approaching the friend could appear as though you are being territorial and are disgruntled that the medical facility did not use your services. Either situation would require a great deal of finesse. However, given that the deaf person is new in town, she may not realize that the medical facility has a contract, or she may be used to bringing her own interpreter. If any of the above is true and you feel that you have a good friendship with her, you could mention that the medical facility contracts with qualified interpreters and give her the contact information for the medical coordinator.

A DEAF CONSUMER'S PERSPECTIVE: Since the deaf woman is new to town, I can see where she might unknowingly rely on a friend she knows in town to interpret for her. I would suggest asking the medical coordinator if there is a way for them to inform new patients on one of their questionnaires or brochures that interpreters are provided upon request. Meanwhile, introduce yourself to the deaf woman as the facility on-call (nationally certified) interpreter and welcome her to the area.

- **Scenario 160.** I was interpreting for a deaf inmate who had been given a ticket because he disobeyed a direct order. An officer had given a note that read: "urine drop now." The prisoner says he didn't understand what those words meant, and based on what I've seen of his language, I believe him. Should I have spoken up? He got seven days in the hole because of this.

AN INTERPRETER'S PERSPECTIVE: Yes, you should have spoken up. You are there to facilitate communication both ways. You're considered the expert in communication, as well as the differences and challenges for individuals whose native language is not English. Therefore, I think you should explain to the hearing officer that the prisoner is not fluent in English and that you are using ASL to communicate. Would they have found a Japanese prisoner guilty if he didn't understand a written command? No. People think because you're born in America that English is your first language.

A DEAF CONSUMER'S PERSPECTIVE: If this happened while I was interpreting, I would have asked for clarification of the meaning of the note. The inmate didn't understand what the note meant, so I would have conveyed that to the officer. Communication needs to be clear between all parties involved, and that is the job of the interpreter to help facilitate that exchange.

- **Scenario 161.** For years I have interpreted at a large ophthalmology clinic in town. This morning one of the secretaries I've come to know takes me aside and shows me a memo written by the doctors outlining their "new procedures" for when a deaf patient calls to make an appointment. It said: "When a deaf patient calls for an appointment and requests an interpreter, first suggest they bring a friend or family member. If that doesn't work, then tell them the staff is willing to write notes back and forth. Finally, and only if the options above don't work, should you agree to provide an interpreter." Holy smokes, what should I do with this information?

AN INTERPRETER'S PERSPECTIVE: Holy smokes is right. If I have learned anything in my life, it is that I can't change other people's minds, I can only change myself. My philosophy is that if this is the way an organization feels about my profession, then I don't need their money or their business. However, what do you do about the deaf clients that are involved also? I am thinking if this secretary has approached you, she is not on-board with the doctor's plan. I would print a copy of the standard practice paper on medical interpreting from RID and give it to the secretary. You may also contact your state agency on Deaf and Hard of Hearing or a local advocacy agency to send out some additional information as well. After that, it's out of your hands. Sadly, everyone is trying to cut costs these days, and we may look like a pretty easy cost saving measure. Also, just because doctors go to school for so long, doesn't always mean that they know anything!

A DEAF CONSUMER'S PERSPECTIVE: Unfortunately, this situation occurs often. Most often it is not written in a "formal" policy, as in the case here. Sadly, there are situations where the office simply has a "not accepting new patients" policy whenever receiving a TTY or relay call. All of these are violations of the Americans with Disabilities Act (ADA). This can be a sticky situation for you as the interpreter. If you choose to really take a loud stand, it could really reflect negatively on you and consequently on your clients. Remember, as interpreters we are also cultural brokers and advocates. In this situation, it is clear that you do need to take on that role of advocate. I would do so, however, quietly and as diplomatically as possible. I would explain to the secretary about the Americans with Disability Act and further point out how and why this policy violates that law. At that point she might choose to explain that to her supervisor or coworkers. If she chooses not to, I would on my own contact a local or state deaf advocacy organization and have them follow up with this office. These groups will often explain the law, give them resources that they need to make that policy change, and/or pursue matters legally to institute that change. In most cases when faced with a possible lawsuit, protest, or sanctions, the offending organization will decide to comply.

- **Scenario 162.** While interpreting for a deaf client, he says he's reluctant to schedule a follow-up visit because he can't afford to pay for both the office visit and an interpreter. When he sees me looking at him with a puzzled look on my face, he pulls a copy of my invoice. The doctor's office has forwarded it on to him to pay in addition to their bill. I reluctantly mention to him that the Americans with Disabilities Act (ADA) requires doctors to pay for interpreters. He says he knows that and has talked to his physician about it several times. He says his doctor keeps insisting the two of them don't need an interpreter because they get along just fine writing notes back and forth. I'm not sure how much I should say here?

AN INTERPRETER'S PERSPECTIVE: I'm assuming, since your invoice was given to the deaf client by the doctor's office, you were hired directly by the doctor's office. If it were through an agency, I would ask them to handle it.

According to the RID Standard Practice Paper "Interpreting in Medical Settings," health care providers are responsible for hiring interpreters under the ADA and they cannot legally charge the patient for those interpreter services. Given the law, my assumption when accepting the assignment would have been that my invoice would be paid by the doctor's office. When it came to my attention that my invoice was given to the Deaf person to pay in full, I would do the following: after getting the client's permission to speak with the doctor's office, I would tell them that I had submitted the bill with the understanding that it would be paid by the doctor's office which requested my services. It has come to my attention that the invoice had in fact been given to the client with a demand to pay in full, and that it is illegal to bill the client for interpreting services. I would tell both the client and the doctor's office that I couldn't work there again until the payment issue was resolved.

A DEAF CONSUMER'S PERSPECTIVE: This situation is difficult for an interpreter to have to face, but personally, I think there must be a boundary line between the interpreter and the client. I do believe that interpreters should be involved in the Deaf community, but the client needs to be responsible and request an interpreter in advance through the doctor's office. If the client did this and they still denied him his right to an interpreter, then this client would need to go through some sort of legal process to resolve it. If the client hired you knowing there would be an obstacle for you to get paid, then that is not fair to the interpreter because they put you in the middle of a situation for which you are not responsible. However, if the doctor's office booked you, then the doctor is responsible for paying you. This doctor needs to be educated about his patient's rights to an interpreter.

Other Scenarios

Identify the issue(s) involved and decide how you would respond. Discuss and compare your responses with your colleagues.

163. The elementary school where you interpret enrolls a new hearing student who has deaf parents. You inform your supervisor you would be willing to interpret their child's parent/teacher meetings, etc. However, your supervisor says if they don't ask for anything, he's not going to volunteer anything so don't open your mouth because the budget is already tight.

164. You have just won an all-expenses-paid trip to Hollywood for you and a guest, and you decide to take your deaf roommate. You both love game shows and so you make arrangements to see one while you're there. The show randomly picks contestants from the audience. Lady luck is still smiling on you because your roommate gets picked. You both scream appropriately and go running down to the front to meet Bob Barker. You go along to interpret, but suddenly they break for a commercial. You're both told they will need to pick someone else because they can't have a deaf contestant.

165. You're interpreting for a deaf client in jail, who is accused of armed robbery, and he's being given a psychiatric review. The deaf client answers "yes" to every single question the psychiatrist asks, and finally the psychiatrist asks him, "Can you read my lips?" The deaf client, of course, again answers "yes." The psychiatrist turns to you, dismisses you, and says he will take it from there.

166. In a rural hospital without fancy birthing rooms, you're called in to interpret for an expectant mother. There's nothing separating the deaf woman and the hospital staff but a curtain. The doctor is on the other side of the curtain discussing complications with a nurse, and you're interpreting everything. The doctor sees you through the crack of the curtain and realizes that you're interpreting his remarks. He goes nuts and tells you to stop interpreting until he tells you he's ready to talk to the patient.

167. You show up at an elementary school to substitute interpret for the regular interpreter who is out ill. After you interpret the first 30 minutes of class, the teacher says that you can leave. You're stunned and ask her what you have done wrong. The teacher replies, "Oh my goodness, you didn't do anything wrong. It's just that the regular interpreter only stays in the classroom for a few minutes every day, and then she goes down to the lounge and reads or does her homework for the rest of the day. I assumed you would want to do the same thing!"

168. A deaf man hires you to interpret a meeting he has set up with the personnel director at his job. When you both walk into the director's office, he tells the deaf employee that he was not aware he was bringing his own interpreter. Seated in the room is someone whom you know is still a signer, not an interpreter. The director insists that since the company has hired this woman, the deaf man must send you away.

169. You're in the hospital, but not as an interpreter; you're a patient. Across the hall is a deaf person who has minimal language competency. You go over to visit him from time to time, and it's very difficult most of the time to follow what he's saying. After you get out of the hospital, you go back to visit the man and see a sign above his bed that reads, "DEAF BUT READS LIPS WELL."

170. A deaf person has asked you to volunteer to interpret an addiction treatment meeting for him. After the initial introductions, a member of the group asks if you're also a recovering addict. The deaf client explains your role to the group, but the other members agree that they're not comfortable with an outsider at their meeting. They ask you both to leave.

171. You're substitute interpreting an English class, and they're having a spelling test. The regular interpreter and the student have established signs for all the words they have been practicing, but you have no idea what they are. You approach the teacher about how to fairly resolve the situation, and the teacher's only response is, "Oh, well."

172. You're hired to interpret for a 16-year-old deaf client taking his driver's license written test. You have been asked to sign the test in ASL because of his lack of English skills. One of the employees at the motor vehicle office comes over, accuses you of cheating, and takes the client's test away. She rips up the test and refuses to give the boy another one unless you agree not to "help" anymore.

173. A doctor is complaining to a deaf patient about the cost of having an interpreter at every office visit. The deaf client asks the doctor to look at it from another perspective: that all 300 of his patients are paying 50 cents more per office visit so that he can have equal access to the doctor. You think that's a great way to look at it. However, the doctor continues his harangue until the deaf patient finally agrees to only request an interpreter for emergencies. They will go back to paper-and-pencil communication.

174. You walk into a hospital room to interpret for a deaf client, and he and his wife tell you they think they made the doctor mad. You ask them why, and they say the doctor was just in and wouldn't wait for an interpreter, and so they asked him to write notes. They said they could see he wasn't happy about it, and to make matters worse, they couldn't read his writing. When they told him this, he threw down the pen and left.

175. At the church where you interpret, an upcoming retreat is announced. Immediately after the service, the person in charge of the retreat comes up to you and asks you if you know if any of the deaf parishioners are interested in attending. He tells you he hopes not because he didn't budget for any interpreters at the retreat.

176. You're asked to interpret for a deaf couple planning a Jewish wedding. While you're interpreting, the deaf couple is told by the Rabbi that they must speak their vows in Hebrew or else they won't be allowed to get married. The couple leaves dejected and tell you that this is the third Rabbi they have tried. They all say the same thing.

177. During a college class, the professor brings in a film and there's no way to leave on just some of the lights; it's either all the lights or pitch black. You pull out a flashlight from your purse (your ITP teacher told you to always be prepared), but the professor demands that you turn it off.

178. While interpreting a college class, the second week into the semester the professor stops his lecture and asks the deaf student to move to the back of the classroom. He feels the interpreting is distracting the rest of the students.

179. You're interpreting a college art class where the instructor doesn't give the class a break. You approach the instructor after class to explain that you need at least one break in a two-hour block. The instructor reluctantly agrees to a four-minute break. At the first break, however, as you're starting to leave the room, she starts giving the class instructions. You come back in the room to interpret the instructions, and she looks over at you and says, "Go ahead and take your break. The deaf student will only miss four minutes. We'll catch her up later."

180. You're sitting with a deaf client in municipal court waiting for your turn to be called up. You interpret what is going on in the courtroom for the deaf client while you wait. Finally, the bailiff calls the deaf client's case and informs the judge that the client is deaf. The judge angrily responds, "I know he's deaf because this interpreter has been disrupting my courtroom all morning waving her hands." He then turns to you and says, "Your responsibility is to interpret only what is germane to this deaf person's case, and if you can't abide by that, I will make sure we don't pay for your services today."

181. As a CDI, I was interpreting an Individualized Education Plan (IEP) meeting for a deaf father who requested a deaf interpreter. His son's teacher could sign but not well enough for him to understand 100 percent. During the IEP, any time she signed she insisted the father watch her and not us (the interpreters). Does she have the right to insist on this?

Challenges in Accurately Interpreting a Message

- **Scenario 182**. I'm voicing for a deaf person telling about her recent trip to Australia. Someone in the audience asks her what types of cars they have in Australia. She responds by saying, "They were mostly European cars like VWs, Mercedes, and (she spells) V-u-l-v-a-s."

AN INTERPRETER'S PERSPECTIVE: Unless I knew her to be a joker-type person, I would assume she meant "Volvos" and would voice it with the correction. I might also fingerspell v-o-l-v-o to her at that moment, if it were a small group or people known to her. Depending on our relationship, I might mention it in passing after the assignment.

A DEAF CONSUMER'S PERSPECTIVE: I would want the interpreter to voice "Volvos."

- **Scenario 183**. I'm interpreting for a science class, and the lesson today is on reproductive anatomy. The teacher asks the students how many ovaries a female has, and a student raises his hand and answers "two." The teacher then asks how many testes a male has, and the same student raises his hand and answers "four." The teacher laughs and says, "Having that many would make you nuts." I don't get the joke.

AN INTERPRETER'S PERSPECTIVE: If I don't understand something, I can't interpret it. I would pause and ask for clarification before moving on. It's my responsibility to make sure I convey all information accurately. Asking for clarification or for something to be repeated is the only way to make sure.

A DEAF CONSUMER'S PERSPECTIVE: At that point, it may be inappropriate to ask for clarification from the teacher. I would interpret the information literally, perhaps fingerspelling the words. Then follow the student's lead if more information is requested.

- **Scenario 184**. I'm an interpreter for a high school deaf student who goes to a resource room for reading. While he's reading aloud he points to an unfamiliar word and indicates he doesn't know what it means, so I voice, "What is this word?" The teacher then begins to sound out the word phonetically and looks to me to interpret the pronunciation. I realize she's clueless, so I try saying, "What does this word mean?" This time, she over-enunciates the pronunciation of the word for my benefit, still not catching on to the real question.

AN INTERPRETER'S PERSPECTIVE: I would either interpret the pronunciation to the deaf student and let him participate in the discussion, or I would tell her that I, the interpreter, was unclear with my question. I would then restate the question by pointing to the word and asking, "What does the word (x) mean in the dictionary?"

A DEAF CONSUMER'S PERSPECTIVE: If the interpreter strictly abides by the CPC, she will interpret exactly what is happening and let the student clarify his question. The interpreter can make a subtle facial expression to the student indicating that the teacher missed his question.

- **Scenario 185**. I'm interpreting for a college course on World Studies. Today there's a guest speaker with a lot of facial hair, which makes it almost impossible to recognize any facial expressions. Plus, I can barely understand his thick accent. I've asked him to repeat himself several times, but I'm still lost. I glance around the room, and those students who are still awake appear to be as lost as I am.

AN INTERPRETER'S PERSPECTIVE: If the professor is lost, he knows you'll be too. You should interpret the fact that it's difficult to understand the speaker. The fact that you've tried several times unsuccessfully to ask for clarification should also be conveyed through your interpretation.

A DEAF CONSUMER'S PERSPECTIVE: The interpreter should inform the deaf student of the situation. As a deaf student, I would ask the interpreter to keep interpreting to the best of her ability. After class, I would inform the professor that the interpreter and notetaker were unable to obtain the information completely and ask for suggestions. Perhaps the guest speaker is willing to provide a copy of his lecture notes.

- **Scenario 186.** I'm interpreting an upcoming concert that includes some songs in a foreign language. I have found translations and I think we should interpret the lyrics for these songs. My team interpreter is adamant that we should not interpret them. He says if the hearing members of the audience don't know what is being sung, why should the deaf audience? He adds that not interpreting these songs gives us a chance to rest. I need some guidance here.

AN INTERPRETER'S PERSPECTIVE: There are several views that could be expressed on this point, but first let me say that if you think the assignment is exhausting or long and that you are going to need a "rest," that is the purpose of having a second interpreter. It is not so that you both can rest at the same time. One option is to ask deaf people whom you know if they plan to be in attendance what they would prefer. Another option is to ask the person/organization doing the hiring what they would prefer you to do. Interpreting the songs into ASL will definitely add another dimension to the concert, and while it may not be expected, it is certainly another aspect of the job.

A DEAF CONSUMER'S PERSPECTIVE: Yes, I would want the interpreters to interpret the words/meaning of the foreign songs. While it is true that not everyone in the hearing audience will be able to understand the words either, they at least will still be able to hear the sound and emotions of the music. So, in my opinion, I think a deaf audience would love to have the opportunity to continue to "listen" and enjoy the songs as well, with signed translations from the interpreters.

- **Scenario 187.** While interpreting for a patient, the patient is told she has stage four melanoma. The doctor tells her, "You need to get your affairs in order." However, I notice he never says the word "die." Do I?

AN INTERPRETER'S PERSPECTIVE: I feel like this is a judgment call on your part as interpreter. Why did the doctor decide to say it in this way? In hearing culture, we hardly ever say what we mean. We ask companions if they are hungry instead of asking them if they want to go out for dinner, or what they are doing later instead of asking them to go to the 9 o'clock movie. In this case, the doctor may have said this out of respect for the consumer, and his hearing culture is telling him that it is not appropriate to flat out say, "You are going to die soon." This may be an opportunity for cross-cultural mediation. You as the hearing interpreter understand exactly what the doctor means and could interpret the sentence using expansion techniques so that the deaf consumer understands as well. However, if it seems like the doctor is purposefully being vague, then it is your duty as interpreter to be vague as well. Fingerspell the phrase and use quotations to emphasize that the doctor is using figurative language. It is then the consumer's responsibility to clarify what exactly the doctor means by this phrase. Perhaps the consumer is bilingual and understands the doctor's meaning. It is the doctor's responsibility to explain the prognosis, and if he needs to clarify by being more direct, then he needs to have the opportunity to do so.

A DEAF CONSUMER'S PERSPECTIVE: Depending on the language of the client you could interpret the meaning from English to ASL with a list of examples: (1) inform the family, (2) see a lawyer, and (3) make plans. You do not have to use the word "die" either. You could interpret exactly what the doctor said, and let the client ask for clarification. If she still doesn't seem to understand, then you could interpret that she doesn't understand as her response.

- **Scenario 188.** At the church where I interpret regularly, the weekly scripture reading is done by members of the congregation. Invariably, a few

of the readers are nervous when they read in public. They don't speak into
the microphone, and they read so fast, they're practically unintelligible.

AN INTERPRETER'S PERSPECTIVE: If you've been interpreting in this
setting regularly, this isn't something new and unexpected. There isn't much you
can do to improve the congregation's public speaking abilities, but you can probably
get a copy of each week's scriptures to read before the service. Keep the copy in
front of you during the service to refer to as needed.

A DEAF CONSUMER'S PERSPECTIVE: If you don't understand, most likely
no one else in the congregation understands either, so you should sign, "The speaker
is not clear." I would also suggest that you talk to the minister about this problem.
Perhaps he could talk to the readers each week before they read.

Other Scenarios

**Identify the issue(s) involved and decide how you would respond. Discuss
and compare your responses with your colleagues**.

189. You're the interpreter for a dry and long-winded professor. Fortunately, he
puts his lectures on an overhead word-for-word and then reads them to the class.
This makes it easy for you, but you feel somewhat guilty spending 15 weeks doing
nothing but impersonating Vanna White.

190. You're interpreting in a high school class where the teacher is lecturing and
writing on the board. All of a sudden, the chalk makes that awful screeching sound
it sometimes makes and everyone in the class, including you, jumps. The Deaf
student is insistent you explain what just happened, but meanwhile the teacher has
resumed lecturing.

191. The guest speaker for a Rotary Club meeting for which you're interpreting has
a very strong accent, and you're having a difficult time understanding what is being
said. As you look around the room, you see that most of the other people in the
audience are straining to understand too.

192. You're asked to interpret a luncheon given by the PAWS with Purpose
organization. During the luncheon, the deaf client is surprised when the committee
honors her with a plaque for her work with hearing-ear dogs. She's asked to say a
few words as she accepts her award. You mentally switch gears to voice for her, but
she's crying with joy and her signing is unclear. You're struggling, but stopping her
won't help because she's totally caught up in her emotions.

193. You're interpreting for a deaf man who is hard of hearing. The client speaks for himself but looks at you when the doctor asks a question. When the man says "injection," it sounds like "ejaculation" instead.

194. You're just starting your career as an interpreter when a deaf woman at the church where you interpret asks you to interpret a meeting between her and her pastor. You agree, but once you're in the meeting, the deaf woman gets so caught up in her story she starts signing faster and faster. You start to lose her and keep asking her to slow down, but it soon becomes a lost cause.

195. At the doctor's office, the doctor tells his deaf patient that she's expecting triplets, and the patient is thrilled. She's so excited she stops signing and only uses her speech to communicate. However, it's unintelligible to you, and when you keep asking her to remember to sign, she says she can't — she's just too excited and nervous. She seems to have a million questions for the doctor, but you can barely make out what she's trying to say. In fact, the doctor is helping you put it together. You hate to dampen the moment, but her not signing affects your ability to do your job.

196. You agree to interpret for a comedian. You two have rehearsed together several times, and you're really looking forward to the show. When the comedian walks out on the stage though, she gets stage fright and her timing is way off. Her jokes fall flat and no one in the audience is laughing. The deaf audience though is howling because you have a little lag time and the information is still all there. You wonder if you should be botching it up somehow so the deaf audience doesn't laugh.

197. You and a colleague are interpreting a psychology lecture given by a deaf woman with an M.D. After the formal presentation, the deaf woman asks if there are any questions from members of the audience. In response to one question from the audience, you hesitate because you know the deaf psychiatrist's response is not clear. You're not sure if the doctor misunderstood the question or is purposefully being vague.

198. You have been interpreting for months for a deaf man studying to become a clown. On the night of his graduation, there's quite a crowd present. At the end of the evening after the graduates have made their way across stage to pick up their diplomas, an unfamiliar song is played. It's one of those long, drawn out songs where all the words tend to blur together. You're unable to distinguish "life" from "love" from "light."

199. You're interpreting a theater production where you have a particular character you're shadowing throughout the show. At one point, your character is sitting and reading a newspaper. You're right behind your character, and the urge to ad lib by looking over the character's shoulder and interpreting some of the articles is overwhelming.

200. You're interpreting for a comedian at a comedy club where there are several deaf people in the audience. The comedian is singling out people in the audience and making jokes at their expense. At one point, one of the deaf people laughs, and it's a very loud, distinctive laugh. The comedian does a whole series of jokes now about what her laugh sounds like — a coyote, a crying baby, a cat in heat, etc. You can see that the deaf woman doesn't realize the comedian is talking about her because she keeps looking around and laughing loudly.

201. You're on stage ready to interpret a concert, and when the music begins, you hear a voice but no intelligible words. You panic and look down at the speaker thinking it must be broken, then over at the singer. You see the lead singer is singing with the microphone too close to her mouth. You're completely thrown for a loop but compose yourself and interpret the rest of the songs as best you can.

202. You interpret for a very shy deaf boy who is a freshman in high school. The boy's history teacher is notorious for putting down his students. He tells his students things like, "If you read the chapter, you wouldn't give me such stupid answers." One day the deaf student raises his hand to answer a question. He's nervous and signs the wrong answer. You know the teacher is going to put him down if you voice the date wrong, when you're sure he just transposed the numbers.

203. You're hired to interpret a probation hearing at a prison. The hearing officer gives you a curt, unfriendly greeting and says he is ready to begin. The deaf prisoner is brought in, eager to talk. The officer shuts him up and says he'll have his turn later. As the hearing begins, you have to ask the officer several times to slow down, and he's obviously annoyed. After he finishes telling the prisoner all the evidence against him, he asks the prisoner for a response. The prisoner says he didn't understand anything the hearing officer said because the interpreter had to sign so fast to keep up with him.

204. You're substitute interpreting for a fellow interpreter at a church revival. You started in the interpreting field in a church setting, so although revivals are unfamiliar to you, religious terminology and concepts are not. You gladly agreed to help your friend. As the service becomes more animated, literally thousands of people in the huge hall are crying, swaying, singing, and feeling the Holy Spirit. Everybody except two people, however — you and the deaf consumer.

Challenges in Interpreting Profanity or Content that is Inappropriate, Sexual or Rude

- **Scenario 205.** In biology class, the teacher is doing a science demonstration that involves blowing into a straw and pushing air and water into sand. A student from the back of the room makes a comment about the teacher's "blow job." I can see all the student's eyes turn to me to see my reaction and how I will sign it.

AN INTERPRETER'S PERSPECTIVE: All students are fascinated with the "dirty" signs. My job is to make communication equal. The deaf students have just as much right to hear the derogatory remarks as the hearing students do.

A DEAF CONSUMER'S PERSPECTIVE: Of course, the interpreter shouldn't intentionally give the kids a thrill. Instead, I would suggest fingerspelling the words. If they're using words like "blow job," this is probably an older group of kids. The deaf student probably knows the term without you having to sign it or make any obscene gestures.

- **Scenario 206.** I was interpreting for a deaf man at a doctor's appointment. He had requested a male interpreter but was told there were none available. In the name of expediency, the client agreed to have a female interpreter. The doctor is examining the man's genitals, and the client is becoming obviously increasingly embarrassed. The doctor, thinking he's being funny, says "What's the matter, hasn't a woman seen your penis before?"

AN INTERPRETER'S PERSPECTIVE: Interpret the question and let the client respond. You should also provide some appropriate verbal interpretation of the client's obvious embarrassment. You could also offer to wait outside until the examination is completed. In that case, you should ask the doctor to hold off communicating until you return.

A DEAF CONSUMER'S PERSPECTIVE: I would suggest simply interpreting the sentence as is and let the Deaf client tell the doctor off.

- **Scenario 207.** I was interpreting for a deaf client at a job interview, and he's being interviewed by a very attractive woman. When the interviewer stands and walks over to a file cabinet, the deaf client makes a sexually suggestive remark about her to me.

AN INTERPRETER'S PERSPECTIVE: I wouldn't voice it this time, but I would tell the Deaf client that, as an interpreter, I have to interpret everything that is said or signed. Then interpret all future remarks.

A DEAF CONSUMER'S PERSPECTIVE: Interpret every single word he said! He did this to himself, and hopefully this is a mistake he won't repeat in the future!

- **Scenario 208**. I interpret in a high school history class in which the teacher basically ignores the deaf student and rarely calls on him. One day when the deaf student is the only student with his hand up, the teacher has no choice but to call on him. When the student gives the wrong answer, the teacher looks at the rest of the class and says, "We might as well forget David is here; he never knows the right answer anyway."

AN INTERPRETER'S PERSPECTIVE: Ouch! Interpret everything. The deaf person has a right to know when someone is being rude or degrading, no matter how much it might hurt at the time.

A DEAF CONSUMER'S PERSPECTIVE: Interpret the teacher's remark and look for reactions from the deaf student. Hopefully, the deaf student will challenge that statement directly with the teacher. If not, I would report it to an advocate or supervisor who could make a decision about how to handle it.

- **Scenario 209**. I am interpreting for a deaf man accused of masturbating in public. The prosecutor says "masturbate" at least 100 times. The sign I'm using is very graphic, so even non-signers in the audience know what I'm signing. Now they are snickering every time the word is signed.

AN INTERPRETER'S PERSPECTIVE: I would interpret the laughter from the room, fingerspell masturbate, and ask the deaf man if he has another sign I can use that is less graphic. If he doesn't care about me using the graphic sign, I would continue to use it. The snickering won't bother me, and the judge is in control of the courtroom.

A DEAF CONSUMER'S PERSPECTIVE: Ignore all the snickering and let the judge put a stop to it. If the client is capable of following fingerspelling, you could spell out "masturbate" or you could sign "play self" instead of doing the graphic sign. It's best to check with the client in advance for sign preference.

- **Scenario 210**. I'm interpreting for a deaf man at a dentist appointment. The dentist tells the client he has two very small cavities and that they should probably be fixed now. The dentist says Novocain won't be necessary because the cavities are so small. The client, however, admits to a low

threshold for pain and says he prefers a local anesthetic. The dentist refuses
and derisively tells the client to "Buck it up and be a man!"

AN INTERPRETER'S PERSPECTIVE: Continue to interpret faithfully what
the dentist and patient say. Why should deaf people be denied access to the full,
miserable experience of going to the dentist?

A DEAF CONSUMER'S PERSPECTIVE: If the dentist won't provide the
requested anesthetic, I (as the deaf consumer) would leave. Since the cavities are so
small, it's not an emergency, and I can decide to reschedule another appointment, or
another dentist!

- **Scenario 211**. A deaf patient is in the dentist's chair enjoying the effects
  of nitrous oxide (laughing gas) and feeling a little loose. The deaf woman
  starts expressing her feelings about the very cute dentist who "has awfully
  strong hands" and "cute, curly chest hair." We're walking out of the
  dentist's office together when the client turns to me and sheepishly asks if I
  think she should find another dentist.

AN INTERPRETER'S PERSPECTIVE: A good stock response to questions like
this is, "Gee, I don't know." I might even say something I never say in any other
context: "I'm just the interpreter." There's no need to go over what your role is,
citing the CPC. Most deaf adults understand that doling out opinions is not what an
interpreter is supposed to do. Perhaps in this instance, the patient is simply reacting
to the interpreter as another adult who witnessed her embarrassing behavior and not
as an interpreter. (This doesn't change the interpreter's obligation to adhere to the
CPC, however.) If this is a recurring problem with this client, it may be necessary
to clarify the ethics involved, as always in a friendly and non-condescending way.
After that, never bring up the subject of the dentist or the appointment again.

A DEAF CONSUMER'S PERSPECTIVE: Hopefully, the interpreter has enough
sense not to voice what the deaf woman is expressing. The interpreter should let
the client know that she didn't interpret her comments due to the effects of the
"laughing gas." It's up to the deaf woman to decide whether to change dentists.

- **Scenario 212**. I interpret in a technology class where I am the only female
  in the room. The students often make crude remarks about women, and the
  class always looks over at me and cracks up while I interpret them. I can
  see my deaf client is embarrassed for me, but he laughs along with the rest
  of them.

AN INTERPRETER'S PERSPECTIVE: In any classroom the teacher bears
responsibility for controlling student behavior, whether it's kindergarten or graduate

school. I would approach this problem as a discipline issue. If you talk about this issue by placing focus on yourself, on how you feel, or how this behavior is hurting you, statements like that leave room for others to suggest you are too sensitive or that, "Boys will be boys." Instead, talk about the class behavior in terms of outcome: it is disruptive, impedes the student's access to instructional material, and impedes the interpreting process. Use words that carry legal impact. Always talk to the teacher first. The field of education is fraught with politics, and it is better to begin the problem-solving process in the classroom.

If that fails, the next step is to ask to talk to your immediate supervisor (not the teacher's). Your supervisor should handle the matter from there. Be clear in what you expect. I would ask my supervisor to have the classroom discipline issue dealt with. If that doesn't resolve the issue, I would then ask my supervisor to move me to another class, since I cannot perform effectively in a hostile work environment.

A DEAF CONSUMER'S PERSPECTIVE: In a perfect world, the deaf client will speak up in the interpreter's defense and scold the class for making crude remarks about women in general, and you, the interpreter, in particular. But, in today's real world, the way to handle this is for the female interpreter to lodge a formal protest with the teacher about the boorish behavior of the class (including the deaf client who laughed along with the rest of them). If the teacher is not able to do so, then you yourself should file a harassment complaint. Why? We do have harassment laws, and if we do not invoke those laws to protect people, harassment of any form or substance will continue to no end. It is high time to make our laws work so that we can all live in a more perfect world.

- **Scenario 213.** A student with Tourette's syndrome is registered with the Disability Services Office at our university. The student is taking a class with a deaf instructor. The instructor utilizes two sign language interpreters and a CART writer. The student will frequently make inappropriate/ obscene outbursts. The interpreter signs all the outbursts. The student has filed a complaint with our office that such makes him uncomfortable. He says that the outbursts have nothing to do with the subject discussed. I'm wondering where this falls in your ethical guidelines?

AN INTERPRETER'S PERSPECTIVE: As an interpreter, am I now supposed to figure out what is relevant and what is not? I interpret cell phones ringing because it interrupts the flow of the class. However, I would never as an interpreter go out of my way to draw negative attention to someone. I think that the instructor should be aware when an outburst happens so she knows what is happening and can conduct her class accordingly with that knowledge. These outbursts could be interpreted in a subtle way as to not draw even more attention from the other students in the class.

It would be wise for the interpreters and instructor to decide if and how she wants to be informed each time an outburst happens.

A DEAF CONSUMER'S PERSPECTIVE: I utilize both CART and interpreter services where I work. The CART writer's first responsibility is to write the spoken word which is pertinent to the lecture and questions from students. In addition, I would expect her to write any environmental sounds or briefly describe any unusual happenings in our immediate surroundings. Everyone else in the room is aware of the outbursts from the person with Tourette's, so I think the CART writer and the interpreter should ask the deaf professor if/how they want to be informed of these outbursts.

A CART WRITER'S PERSPECTIVE: As a CART provider, if I hear it, I write it, unless otherwise directed by the CART consumer(s). Lots of things that happen in a classroom don't have anything to do with the subject being discussed, but a CART provider should not pick and choose what to write or not write. Environmental sounds or other non-word noises or happenings are also communicated via parenthesis, such as: (applause), (cell phone rings), (sneeze). In this particular situation, balancing the need for communication accessibility, while maintaining respect for and sensitivity to the individual with Tourette's, might best be accomplished by researching terminology used by Tourette's groups to describe vocalizations. For example, "(vocal tic)" would seem to be an appropriate parenthetical to use for the utterances. Assuming some discussion with the deaf instructor before class has occurred with regard to understandable words, appropriate or otherwise, they should be written as well. However, a possible variation may be to put them within the parenthetical, e.g. (vocal tic: Darn you all). If a transcript is provided after the class, a discussion should occur in regard to leaving vocal tic utterances in the transcript.

- **Scenario 214.** During high school football games (where I interpret for a deaf player) the coach often calls the other team very insensitive and derogatroy names. I finally got fed up and decided to file a complaint with the school administration. Now I'm being labeled a troublemaker, and everyone is treating me like an outcast. This is my hometown!

AN INTERPRETER'S PERSPECTIVE: You made the decision to file a complaint and you had to know there would be both negative and positive results of such an action. On the negative side, it's interesting that the entire community is aware of your "nonpublic" complaint. On the positive side, maybe this will help improve the school system where you want to send your kids.

A DEAF CONSUMER'S PERSPECTIVE: All decisions come with consequences, some of them unintended. It is well within your right to file a

complaint if you feel one is warranted. It may be that there is a policy for district
employees governing speech and conduct when in the presence of students.
Regardless, many would agree with you that the type of language used by the
coach was situationally unacceptable. Others may see it as the coach being a
good motivator in an emotionally charged situation. Strong language, swearing,
and vulgarity are a part of sports in today's world. It is generally not "officially"
acceptable in high school sports, but it is readily accepted in college athletics.
Coaches, athletes, and fans are exposed to it on television *ad nauseum*.

You have the free will to make choices as an interpreter, an educational professional,
and as an individual. As an interpreter, you could decide to no longer interpret for
the student during football games. As an educational professional, you could decide
to take the coach aside and state your concerns. As an individual, you could decide
to file a complaint, which you did. Realize, though, another interpreter in the same
situation may not have been offended at all. Your decision was well within your
rights, but in my opinion, it is not an interpreting issue as much as a personal one.

Other Scenarios

**Identify the issue(s) involved and decide how you would respond. Discuss
and compare your responses with your colleagues.**

215. At a seminar you have just finished interpreting, the keynote speaker comes
up to you and asks if you would mind interpreting for him, as he would like to say
something to the deaf woman who attended the seminar. You agree, but instead of
the professional conversation you anticipate, he starts hitting on her and ends up
passing her the key to his hotel room.

216. You interpret for a deaf high school student who has gone through some rough
times but is trying to straighten out his life now. He knows he's been considered a
troublemaker in the past, but you can see he's trying to put that behind him. During
one class, the deaf student raises his hand to answer a question. He gives the wrong
answer, and the teacher says, "See what all those drugs did to your brain?"

217. At a company meeting, the deaf employee for whom you're interpreting keeps
interrupting the meeting with inappropriate and hostile remarks. You can clearly see
everyone in the room rolling their eyes and whispering about her. The supervisor is
unfailingly polite, however, and listens to all her remarks. The deaf woman doesn't
sense her coworker's negative reactions behind her.

218. In a college biology class, the professor is handing out the students' quizzes,
and when he gets to the deaf student's paper, he says, "Obviously no rocket scientist

here." You interpret the professor's remarks, and the student says, "Screw you," and leaves the class. The professor turns to you and says, "Why did you tell him? I was only kidding."

219. While interpreting at a college for a doctoral student, the professor passes out a class assignment. After the deaf student reads it, he signs, "I'm not going to do this assignment. This is a silly waste of time." You're not sure if this is a side comment to you or if he expects you to voice this to the professor.

220. You interpret for a deaf football player. Tonight there was an out-of-town game, and you rode the bus with the team. The team stops at McDonald's to get something to eat and you interpret the boy's order. He thinks he's being funny when he adds swear words to his order (e.g., "f– –king large fries"), and he looks to see what you'll do.

221. You're hired to interpret for a deaf woman at a job interview. While the two of you are sitting in the waiting room, you see two of the secretaries watching both of you and snickering. They mock the vocalizations the deaf client makes when she signs. You're torn between going up and putting the secretaries in their place or hurting the deaf woman's feelings when you tell her what the secretaries are saying. You don't want to upset her right before her interview.

222. You're interpreting a job interview, and the interviewer briefly turns his back to the deaf client to check something in his files. While his back is turned, he continues to ask the deaf applicant questions. The deaf applicant, thinking he's sharing a joke with you, answers the question, but his facial expression and body language are sarcastic. He's making fun of the interviewer.

223. You're interpreting a study group for a deaf college student who notices a girl sitting near him squeezed into her chair. He signs to you (which you don't voice), "Look at that girl. She's so fat she can't fit in that chair." Between pointing at the girl, making the very visual sign for fat, and the fact that he's looking right at her, the girl figures out what he's saying, and you see her turn away very hurt.

224. You're interpreting at a high school basketball game for a deaf student on the varsity team. After he fouls out of the game and is taking a seat on the bench, a man in the crowd yells, "Good riddance, Deafie!" The deaf boy sees everyone looking at him uncomfortably and looks at you to find out what he missed.

225. You're interpreting for a closing on a house when the discussion is interrupted by a phone call. The realtor takes the call and begins speaking in Spanish to the person on the other end of the line. You're trilingual and understand everything he's saying but don't interpret his conversation to the deaf client. Your face begins to turn red involuntarily as you overhear the realtor making graphic sexual comments to the person on the other end. The deaf client wants to know what's wrong and why your face is so red.

226. You're interpreting for a deaf man meeting with the township's zoning committee. The committee has denied his request for re-zoning, and the deaf man is very upset about it. He starts swearing at the commissioners and threatening them. You can't help but think this will only make the situation worse, especially in such a small, conservative town where they don't forgive or forget easily.

227. You're interpreting for two deaf women at a business seminar. The man running the seminar is obviously talking down to the deaf women and treating them like children. One of the deaf women signs, "I have had enough of this bulls----t. Let's get out of here." You're not sure if she's talking to him for you to voice or to the other deaf woman.

228. You're interpreting in a culinary class, and the chef makes a derogatory remark about the intelligence of deaf people. The class laughs and he turns to you and says, "Don't interpret that."

229. While interpreting for a deaf college student, the student continually makes side comments to you, which you acknowledge, and then you continue interpreting. The professor notices the student signing and you not voicing any of it, so he asks you what she's saying.

230. You are interpreting for a college class on comparative religion. A Catholic priest is talking to the students about his vow of celibacy and his commitment to living a pure life. Your deaf client raises his hand and signs a question. He wants to ask the priest if he has ever had sex. You don't think the question is appropriate.

231. You're interpreting a wedding. When they get to the part where the minister asks, "If anyone objects to this marriage, let him speak now or forever hold his peace," a deaf man in the audience stands up and starts signing that the groom is a jerk and doesn't deserve to marry this woman. The rest of the audience is looking to you to interpret this.

232. You recently interpreted a Planned Parenthood presentation at a deaf group home. A week later you're called back to discuss a complaint lodged by one of the deaf men from the home. He says that during the presentation you signed sexually suggestive remarks specifically to him.

233. You're interpreting for a high school human growth and development class where the topic for today is anatomy and hormones. Suddenly, during the lecture

you see the deaf student's eyes become as large as saucers and her face becomes beet-red. She has just realized what the teacher is talking about, and she covers her eyes and keeps signing, "That is not polite. That is not polite." She refuses to watch you.

234. You're a nationally certified interpreter who is mentoring an ITP student. The ITP student is interpreting in a junior high school class under your watchful eye. You see the student try to sign the "new" sign for Japan, and instead it looks very sexual. The hormonally overcharged male deaf student loves it and starts laughing. The student suddenly realizes what she signed and giggles. The classroom teacher looks over at you and demands to know what is so funny!

235. You're interpreting in an automotive class where you're the only female in the room. One day the instructor makes a crude remark about women, and the class looks over at you and cracks up. You can see your deaf client is embarrassed for you, but he's laughing as well.

236. You're asked to interpret for a male client enrolled in a sexuality class at an addictions treatment program for men. You suggest a male interpreter might be more appropriate for the situation, but you're told the last one "couldn't handle it." You assume they mean his skill wasn't up to par. When you arrive and start interpreting, you realize it's the content. It's very graphic and very raw. The men in the group deliberately say things just to see how you'll sign them. The deaf client just sits there.

237. Your deaf client is a large woman who grew up on a farm and doesn't have much in the way of social skills. She doesn't wear a bra (and she definitely should) and dresses right of the '40s. It's embarrassing to interpret for her because you never know what she's going to say next. Nine times out of ten, it's rude, inappropriate, or both.

238. While interpreting a vocational trade class, the instructor uses a racial slur in telling the class that over the many years he's been a contractor he's seen all kinds of electrical jobs. The class of white males just chuckles. The instructor carries on, but you can't get past his racist remark.

239. While interpreting for a deaf couple at a car dealership, the salesman leaves the cubicle for a moment to confer with his boss. You can distinctly hear him tell his boss, "I've got a couple of deaf-mutes in my office. I'm going to have to earn my commission tonight!"

240. While interpreting in court, the prosecutor continually uses the phrase "deaf and dumb" whenever he refers to the deaf client. Surprisingly, no one seems to mind except you, including the deaf client.

241. You're interpreting for a deaf couple attending a classic car show. While you're walking around interpreting, you notice that people are pointing and staring at all of you. You're surprised since most people nowadays don't make a big deal when they see someone signing. By now your deaf clients have picked up on the stares, and now the husband is irritated. He starts pointing back at people and swearing. Of course, he expects you to voice his anger.

242. After major surgery, the deaf patient is still somewhat under sedation when the doctor comes in to check on her. The patient's responses are quite sexual, and the doctor becomes visibly embarrassed. The next day you're back to interpret for the doctor's rounds, and he never makes eye contact with the deaf patient. Before you leave, the patient requests you to stay for a moment and asks you what she should do because she remembers bits and pieces of what she said. She repeats it and asks you for verification.

243. You're interpreting for a deaf woman in the middle of getting a Pap smear when her doctor starts explaining something unusual he's seeing to the patient. He's having trouble expressing himself clearly, so he tells you to come around and take a look. The deaf woman realizes what is about to happen and signs, "No, no!" The doctor then smugly replies, "Oh, so you don't want the interpreter to know you're not really a blonde."

244. You're at a wedding reception that you have been hired to interpret. Right now, you're just standing around talking to the newly married deaf bride. You overhear her hearing groom and his best man reviewing the details of last night's bachelor party. You and the bride are no more than two feet away, and she's going on about how happy she is.

245. An elementary deaf student you interpret for is meeting her speech therapist, and the first thing the student asks is, "What is wrong with her (the speech therapist's) teeth?" Since the child is pointing to her own teeth as she asks and the woman doesn't sign, you could temper the question somewhat. However, for a speech teacher, the woman does have really bad teeth.

246. While interpreting for a deaf student in an elementary classroom, the student asks a question and the teacher's response is unusually harsh. However, you go ahead and interpret her response. The child starts crying, and the teacher starts belittling her even more.

247. You interpret for a deaf boy in Cub Scouts, and his father usually doesn't attend the meetings, whereas the other fathers come often. One day the other boys start teasing the deaf boy, saying they don't believe he really has a father because they have never seen him. They call him a "mama's boy." The deaf boy tries to be brave, but you can see the tears forming in his eyes.

248. You interpret for a deaf high school student who is very good looking and knows it. He's cocky and arrogant, but all the girls are crazy about him. One day a girl who sits next to him in class compliments him on his new glasses. The deaf boy looks at her with disdain and says, "Thanks. Too bad I can still see you."

249. You interpret for a deaf junior high school boy, and he's lovestruck by a girl in one of his classes. He has been trying for weeks to get up the nerve to talk to her. One day you overhear the girl and her friends making fun of his speech. He sees them looking at him and asks you what they're saying.

250. You're interpreting for a deaf boy attending a summer basketball camp. Today the campers are learning how to rebound and shoot lay-ups. The deaf camper is tall, skinny, and extremely uncoordinated. His shoes are actually his older brother's and are too big. His feet thud on the floor as he tries to run up and down the floor. The coach continually makes fun of the deaf kid, which you interpret, but most of the time, he's not watching you. All the kids are laughing at him now.

251. You're interpreting for a young deaf girl one day when her speech teacher offers her a cookie as a reward. The little girl declines, so the teacher jokingly asks her if she's on a diet. The little girl replies, "No, but you're so fat you should be!"

252. You're interpreting for two deaf boys in a seventh-grade health class. The teacher is explaining the changes that girls' bodies go through during puberty. By the time he starts explaining how the breasts increase in size, you realize neither boy is making eye contact with you anymore. They're staring intently at your chest.

Challenges in Maintaining Impartiality

- **Scenario 253**. A new doctor in town got my business card from a colleague, and I got a call from his office to interpret for a deaf patient. During the course of the appointment, the deaf woman reveals that she's pregnant and wants an abortion. The doctor angrily says, "I won't even discuss that option with you." I can't help remembering how my best friend needed to have an abortion when she was seventeen.

AN INTERPRETER'S PERSPECTIVE: Being an interpreter means remaining impartial and simply interpreting the content and intent of the message. This can be difficult at times. You should interpret the doctor's statements accurately and with facial expression conveying his emotion. However, I would use two hands when signing any "I" statements (using one hand to sign "I" and the other hand to point to the doctor) to make it clear that it's the doctor who won't discuss that option, not me. Additionally, I would use gentle, caring eye contact and facial expressions while the doctor is not speaking to convey my own sympathy for her situation.

A DEAF CONSUMER'S PERSPECTIVE: As an interpreter, you're there to relay messages between the deaf consumer and the doctor, nothing else. After leaving the doctor's office, you could comfort the deaf consumer and suggest seeing another doctor.

- **Scenario 254**. While interpreting for a deaf client at a doctor's office, the doctor is describing a new alternative treatment for heart disease. My own father had the same treatment this doctor is suggesting, and he died from a massive heart attack during one of the treatments.

AN INTERPRETER'S PERSPECTIVE: Since we're in the middle of a doctor's appointment, I would feel it's my obligation to continue interpreting despite my discomfort. I would use my focusing techniques to remind myself that we're not talking about my father, each case is different, and the results for my father have nothing to do with the results for this patient. If there's a need for follow-up interpreting, I will graciously decline.

A DEAF CONSUMER'S PERSPECTIVE: I wouldn't say anything during the appointment. Afterwards, depending on my relationship with the client, I might explain what happened to my father and encourage the deaf person to seek a second opinion. I believe it's OK to intervene when it's a matter of life and death.

- **Scenario 255.** I am a staff interpreter at a state college, and a student for whom I interpret is filing a suit against two of her three instructors. The claim is completely unfounded, and I have been asked by the instructors to document the happenings in class. There are concerns of this progressing to mediation/investigation, and the expectation is that I share my documentation should I be called as a witness. Is this something I can do ethically?

AN INTERPRETER'S PERSPECTIVE: Fortunately, it sounds as if you are being asked to begin documenting what happens in the class, which gives you the opportunity to carefully explain why that won't work! I would begin by asserting that, first of all, it is impossible to do the job of interpreting and also be documenting what is going on, partly because of the physical limitations — a person can't write and sign at the same time. You might also emphasize that an interpreter does not retain everything even from a 50-minute class, so writing notes afterwards would be ineffective. My second step would be to remind the instructors of an interpreter's attempt to remain neutral. I would rely on information the Disability Services Office should have already provided the instructors regarding the interpreter's role and ethical considerations pertinent to classroom interpreting. Remind the instructors of that information and use it to rebut their request. I would inform them that, if I had been asked to document what happened in the classroom by the student, I could not do that either. I would encourage the instructors to bring in a third party — a department chair, a dean — to do any observations or documentation. Finally, I would make sure that my supervisor was fully informed about the situation so she could offer support as the situation unfolds.

A DEAF CONSUMER'S PERSPECTIVE: I sympathize with you being put in the middle between the instructors and the student. However, by your statement that "the claim is completely unfounded," you really have taken a side. The deaf student has just as much right as any other student to file a suit and have it succeed or fail based on its own merit and not on your opinions or documentation. You are in the class to provide equal access to communication. You are not the student's keeper, "narc," or big brother/sister. Of course, you are human and have opinions, but you keep them to yourself. The instructors are naturally looking for an ally in you, but that's not your job. These are adults, and there is a complaint process that should be the same for everyone. You should enlist the support of your supervisor to remind everyone of the scope of your responsibilities, if you aren't successful doing it yourself. Otherwise, you are in a no-win situation. The instructors feel betrayed because you won't take their side. The student no longer trusts you, and possibly, future students who hear about your involvement with this won't trust you. Keep your opinions to yourself, and focus on getting through the rest of the semester with your head low and your hands doing the best job possible.

Other Scenarios

Identify the issue(s) involved and decide how you would respond. Discuss and compare your responses with your colleagues.

256. A deaf man was involved in a car accident, and you're now interpreting his statement to the cops. The deaf man is being arrogant in his responses, and the police officer is annoyed. The officer tells the deaf man he killed three people, and the deaf client says, "So what?" His complete disregard for human life gives you the creeps.

257. A high school class for which you interpret is discussing various cultures and religions. The teacher starts discussing Mormons, a religion that happens to be the one in which you were raised. He's really mutilating the fundamental beliefs of your religion. The bottom line is some of the things he's attributing to your religion are just not true.

258. While interpreting in a college classroom, the professor makes a rude remark about mixed marriages. The deaf student raises her hand and tells the professor her husband is African-American. The professor is not the least bit remorseful about his remark and, in your opinion, he only gets worse. The deaf student starts feeling harassed and asks you to interpret one day after class as she approaches other students in the class. She's asking them to sign a petition to take to the dean of the school.

259. You have been an avid runner for years and compete in many local races. You have been training hard and, in a few short weeks, you'll be competing in your first marathon. You're offered an assignment interpreting a sports clinic and jump at the opportunity. The main speaker briefly discusses the positive aspects of running but then spends the rest of the hour going on about how detrimental running is to the human body. He's a swimmer and believes swimming to be the perfect sport. You find yourself irritated at his obvious bias.

260. You were raised by Jewish parents, and you strictly follow the teachings and practices of the Jewish faith. While interpreting in a high school history class, the teacher is lecturing about World War II, and he tells the students the Holocaust was a complete fabrication and that it never occurred.

261. You're interpreting an Interpreter Educational Planning Committee (IEPC) meeting for a deaf high school student who is sitting in the meeting with his mother and a school administrator. The deaf student is crying and pleading with his mother because he has just been told he will be getting a cochlear implant. His mother is furious that he doesn't want it and tells him that her insurance won't cover it, they're paying a lot of money to help him, and he should be grateful. The student threatens to run away from home, and the school administrator tells him, "It's for your own good." No one is asking your opinion at this moment, nor is it appropriate for you to volunteer it, but this is hard work.

262. You're interpreting at a doctor's office for a deaf client. The client recently tore his rotator cuff in a football game. His doctor has recommended an orthopedic surgeon. You recognize the surgeon's name from your own personal experience with him in the past. In your opinion, he messed up a similar surgery on you and you would never go back to him.

263. You're interpreting at a doctor's office for a young unmarried girl who is pregnant and desperately seeking an abortion. You know the girl and her family because you all attend the same church. You're very involved in your church's pro-life movement.

264. You're interpreting for a deaf client meeting with a counselor from Planned Parenthood. The client specifically asks the counselor if she can get pregnant while she's having her period, and you're surprised when you hear the counselor assure her she can't!

265. You're interpreting for several deaf clients from a group home brought into the doctor's office for their annual checkup. One particularly meek and mild deaf woman, who usually never says a thing, surprises everyone when she very clearly requests condoms.

266. You were brought up in a very religious, family-oriented home. The deaf woman you're interpreting for is poor, unmarried, and pregnant with her fourth child. All the kids have different fathers. You can't help thinking how unfair life is. This woman turns babies out left and right, doesn't want them, and can't take care of them, while you and your husband have been trying for years to have children.

267. During a meeting between a deaf high school student and her guidance counselor, the counselor is expressing her concern over the student's sudden drastic drop in grades. The girl breaks down in sobs and tells the counselor that she has been sleeping with one of her teachers, the same teacher whose class you're supposed to interpret in 30 minutes.

268. You're driving to an assignment, and the car in front of you cuts you off. You honk and give him a dirty look. He sees you and just shrugs. You arrive at the site and sit in your car a moment to cool down, when that same man pulls into the slot next to you, gets out, and signs, "Aren't you my interpreter today?"

269. A deaf client with a weight problem has admitted herself to a well-known weight loss clinic. The clinic prides itself on its high success rate and permanent weight loss. You're hired to interpret for the deaf woman's entire stay. At a group session you're interpreting, the group leader is screaming at the women and humiliating them for their poor eating habits.

270. A deaf woman calls you to interpret a bridal shower that evening. She apologizes for the short notice, but she says the interpreter she originally hired had to go out of town for a family emergency. You take the assignment, and during the shower, someone knocks on the door. It's a male stripper. You're a founding member of M.O.P.E., Mothers Against Pornographic Entertainment.

271. You're hired by a correctional facility to interpret for a group of convicted child molesters. As you're interpreting their weekly counseling sessions, you're amazed at some of the deaf inmates' lack of remorse. One day one of the inmates tells the therapist that his accuser, an 8-year-old girl, was at fault and that she came on to him.

272. While interpreting a seminar, the speaker makes derogatory comments about overweight people. He goes so far as to say that overweight people are just lazy and their eating habits are out of control. You're overweight, and out of the corner of your eye, you see the speaker looking your way.

273. You're admittedly overweight, and one day you have to struggle to remain in your role as you interpret a meeting between a deaf woman and her nutritionist. The 5' 1", 100-pound deaf woman is obsessed with losing five more pounds so she can wear a thong on the beach in Jamaica. You see the nutritionist critically looking you up and down like she thinks it's you worried about getting into a thong bathing suit.

274. You're interpreting for a doctor making a presentation about cochlear implants. He's going on and on about the merits of cochlear implants. He then tells the audience of mostly parents of deaf children what a waste of money interpreters are and that they're only a crutch. He finishes by saying he wished interpreters would have the decency to find a more productive profession. All eyes are on you, and the deaf client now shrinks into his seat.

275. While substitute interpreting at a small rural all-white church, the minister starts preaching about how African-American people are the descendents of Cain and are damned to hell. You look around, and the congregation is enthusiastically agreeing with his remarks.

276. You're substitute interpreting a church service for an interpreter friend of yours who is ill. Today's sermon is about the abomination of homosexuality. Your brother, who is gay, was recently attacked, and it was determined that it was a hate crime. It makes your skin crawl to hear people butting into two consenting adults' private lives.

277. You're a nationally certified interpreter who also has an M.S.W. degree. You're interpreting at a lawyer's office for a deaf client who is going through a divorce. He tells his attorney his wife's name, and you realize she's a client of yours. They evidently have different last names, and you didn't realize they were married.

Challenges Related to Distractions While Interpreting

- **Scenario 278:** When I voice for deaf clients, I tend to utilize a lot of lag time before I actually begin to speak. In the audience, though, there is always someone who knows just enough sign language to be dangerous and continually blurts out words thinking she is helping me. But of course, it makes it worse. Now I'm distracted, and the audience is wondering what the heck is going on. What can I do in these situations?

AN INTERPRETER'S PERSPECTIVE: In these situations you need to let the audience member know that her blurting out words is interfering with your ability to do your interpreting job. How you would approach this depends on several factors: Can you get the attention of your team interpreter? Can you signal whoever is in charge? If you can enlist someone to privately approach this person and let them know that your work is being compromised, you can avoid making any more of a scene than has already occurred. If no one is readily available and it is possible to stop the speaker, do so and explain that you are having a logistical problem and need to speak to someone in charge. Otherwise, you just carry on as best as you can ignoring this person, and let your work show that you are the professional and know what you're doing.

A DEAF CONSUMER'S PERSPECTIVE: Assuming that there are at least two interpreters working, the team interpreter can quietly go talk to the well-intentioned "helper" in the audience. In order to minimize disruption, the initial contact could be brief and polite, simply asking this person to refrain from calling out verbal prompts. In addition, you and your partner could offer to meet with this person during the next break to explain the importance of processing time for professional and highly skilled interpreters such as yourself. Reassure the individual that you and your partner are there to support each other if and when you need a feed. Calmly explain why it is disruptive to have someone calling out from the audience (it creates a distraction, discomfort, and embarrassment) which you are sure is not their intent. Finally, thank this person for her desire to help because truly I'm sure it was genuine in her mind.

- **Scenario 279.** I am an educational interpreter and have begun to notice a disturbing trend involving the use of Sidekick text messengers at work. As with the advent of cell phones, I am seeing interpreter ethics take a nosedive in this area. I understand the importance of the Sidekick, especially for deaf users. If students choose to use this device at inappropriate times (such as during class), that is for the teacher and administration to address (just as they would for cell phone usage). However, what I'm seeing is the use of text messaging between students and interpreters or between interpreters. I'm sure some of the messages are valid (work-related), but I also know that they are chitchatting when team interpreting is supposed to be happening. One student told me that she actually had to get the interpreter's attention to continue interpreting while the interpreter was busy with her Sidekick. On the other hand, an interpreter told me she experienced a deaf teacher who stopped teaching her class to answer her Sidekick. I do not own a Sidekick so I could really use another perspective.

AN INTERPRETER'S PERSPECTIVE: Although I do not own a Sidekick, Blackberry, T-Mobile, or text/picture phone, their inappropriate use has really been a cause of concern for me as well. I agree with you that classroom teachers and administration should be addressing the use of these devices during class time whether the student is deaf or hearing. I have been on the receiving end of a team interpreter who has been inattentive while serving as my support. There are several tenets under the CPC which apply to this situation: "Interpreters conduct themselves in a manner appropriate to the specific interpreting situation. Interpreters demonstrate respect for consumers. Interpreters demonstrate respect for colleagues, interns, and students of the profession." So, rather than causing the situation to escalate by filing a grievance, I would recommend a frank discussion, whether they be interpreter colleagues, teachers, or consumers. If the situation does not change, perhaps it is time to move to the next step, but by all means bring it up at your local affiliate chapter meetings. Unless it is an emergency situation, what you are describing is just rude, and a reminder is needed of what constitutes professionalism and boundaries.

A DEAF CONSUMER'S PERSPECTIVE: This is a great question because this speaks to access and equality. It is my opinion that pager etiquette depends on the setting. The deaf teachers in our school use their Sidekicks to communicate because it is no different than a hearing teacher who stops teaching to answer the phone. Teachers pick up the phone for a variety of reasons (e.g., to ask about an IEP meeting, confirm the date of a field trip). When there is a P.A. announcement and an interpreter is not in the room, the office sends the message to all the deaf teachers on their pagers. The interpreters in my building also use them to communicate with each other. For example, when a deaf teacher sends out the following page, "An interpreter is needed in the nurse's office." There will often be a flurry of responses such as, "Can someone else get this? I'm in the office," or "I've got it." Also, emergencies may arise that necessitate outside communication. For example, if your sister-in-law is rushed to the hospital with chest pains, you may need to explain that to those present so they have some understanding of your situation. In this new communication age, personally and professionally we need to check our pagers.

Our deaf students, as future users of this technology, need to see us appropriately using our text messengers as well. This needs to be clear with the students, staff, and administration with whom you work.

Other Scenarios

Identify the issue(s) involved and decide how you would respond. Discuss and compare your responses with your colleagues.

280. You have been contacted to do some interpreting for a deaf worker training at a pizza parlor. While you're interpreting the manager's directions on how to build the perfect pizza, you see a roach in the black olives.

281. You're interpreting for a deaf client at a formal banquet. You're seated opposite the client and interpreting during dinner. You ate before you came, but your stomach is gurgling loud enough for people to hear. You're not hungry; your stomach just has a mind of its own sometimes. The people seated around you begin to make a fuss about getting you something to eat. The deaf client is trying to have a conversation with a potential customer and is annoyed by the distraction.

282. You're interpreting at a deaf senior citizens' center where the presentation today is on the importance of hygiene. You notice an elderly woman in the front row who has every hair in place, full make-up, and is wearing a neatly ironed dress. When you look down at her shoes, however, you see she has on two different colored shoes. It strikes you as funny and you begin to giggle. It's obviously very inappropriate, but you just can't stop.

283. While platform interpreting, you see other interpreters in the audience signing back and forth, criticizing some of your sign choices. You try to block them out, but they're distracting.

284. You're voicing for a well-known deaf person in town for a presentation. The room is packed and noisy, and at one point you get lost and stop the speaker for clarification. Behind you, loud enough for you to hear, some interpreters in the audience are making derogatory comments about you for missing something "so simple."

285. In the culinary class for which you're interpreting, the chef insists that you wear a white jacket and hat for sanitary reasons. The jacket he gives you is too big, and the hat slides all over your head.

286. While interpreting a college lecture, the professor continually comes over to where you're sitting with the deaf student and picks lint off your shirt (both real and imaginary).

287. While interpreting an AIDS march, you're suddenly surrounded by hecklers making derogatory remarks. One woman starts screaming at you to repent. It's extremely difficult to concentrate on the speaker with her screaming at you.

288. You're interpreting an all day meeting, and a woman next to you pulls out her nail clippers. The clicking from the clippers is driving you nuts. You tell yourself to hold on and it will all be over in 20 minutes. You then see the woman pull out an emery board and some smelly nail polish.

289. You're interpreting for a deaf woman being prepared for surgery. While you're both riding the elevator on the way down to the operating room, a staff person in the elevator asks you where you learned to sign. You try to be polite and briefly answer her, but this person doesn't stop. She wants to talk on and on and follows you both to surgery.

290. You have just started interpreting at a small conference when your pager goes off. You quickly glance at it and see it's a number your family uses when there's an emergency. You have no partner in this situation, and you figure it will be at least an hour before there's a break.

291. A deaf client calls and asks you to interpret an interview with a prospective employee. The restaurant she has chosen is a place you usually avoid because of previous bad experiences. They have been rude to you and your deaf friends. Thinking that maybe things have changed since you were there last, you don't say anything and take the assignment. As you sit down at the table, you can hear the staff complaining and arguing about who is going to take care of your table.

292. You're interpreting a mass in church, and a man in the audience passes out. People rush over to see what is wrong, but the priest is ignoring the commotion and just continues with the service.

293. You're team interpreting with a very handsome male interpreter. You switch back and forth every 20 minutes. As he's feeding you a sign, suddenly you notice something white in his crotch area. You realize he has split his pants, and his underwear is visible. No one notices while he's standing; only you can see it when you look to him for a feed. It throws you off, and you can tell from his expression that he's perplexed as to why you're ignoring his feeds.

Challenges in Starting to Interpret or Continuing to Interpret in the Middle of an Assignment

- **Scenario 294**. I am interpreting a school field trip to the zoo, and truth be told, I'm not really fond of animals. In fact, the smell is starting to make me sick. There are lots of bugs flying around, and during a presentation that I'm interpreting, one flies in my mouth. I'm ready to scream. I've had it!

AN INTERPRETER'S PERSPECTIVE: The straw that breaks the camel's back is often the one thing that makes an experience laughable. Chalk it up to experience and think about what a great story you'll have at the next interpreters' morbidity and mortality conference. Do what you must to finish the job. Remove the fly from your mouth, take a deep breath, and realize all bad days come to an end and this one will be over soon too.

A DEAF CONSUMER'S PERSPECTIVE: Assuming you either didn't know what you were getting yourself into or this was a requirement you couldn't get out of, I would say just grin and bear it. In the future, avoid trips to the zoo. It isn't fair to penalize the client because you can't concentrate on the assignment.

- **Scenario 295**. I'm interpreting a home economics class, and the group is making taffy. I stick my fingers in the bowl for a taste, and now it's all over my hands. My fingers keep sticking together and I can't fingerspell, much less interpret.

AN INTERPRETER'S PERSPECTIVE: Sometimes we become so involved in a comfortable, regular setting that we forget our primary duty. In order to remedy this sticky situation, explain to the students and teacher in a diplomatic way, "Mea culpa, I need to wash my hands to continue my job." Then run to the nearest sink, wash your hands, and get on with the job as soon as possible.

A DEAF CONSUMER'S PERSPECTIVE: You shouldn't distract or hold up the class. Quickly wash or wipe your hands, and get back in role as soon as possible.

- **Scenario 296**. I'm interpreting a dendrology class, and the professor decides to take the class outside and identify some nearby trees. However, the weather takes a sudden turn for the worse, and now it's cold and windy. All the students are huddled in their coats shivering. I don't have any gloves, my fingers are cold and stiff, and it's becoming painful to interpret.

AN INTERPRETER'S PERSPECTIVE I would tell the student that my hands are freezing, and I can't continue to interpret. If the student doesn't say something to the teacher, then I would tell the student that I'm going to talk with the teacher about it. I would then inform the teacher I can't interpret in this cold without gloves. Perhaps someone else has some gloves I might use? Or perhaps the class needs to move back indoors.

A DEAF CONSUMER'S PERSPECTIVE: Inform the professor your hands are no longer functioning; therefore, you're unable to do your job as an interpreter. Then let the professor make the final decision. I'm sure the whole class will thank you!

- **Scenario 297**. I have agreed to substitute for a church's regular interpreter, and she arranges for me to meet with the minister an hour before the service to review his sermon. However, the minister shows up late, and it turns out he's only subbing for the regular minister. He doesn't have his sermon written out, and he speaks so quickly that I'm exhausted after only 20 minutes. The service is scheduled to last another hour and a half.

AN INTERPRETER'S PERSPECTIVE: This is one of those times when all the information isn't going to be interpreted if I hope to stay alive for the next two hours. I would slow myself down and just go for concepts, almost summarizing what he's saying. No one's going to be tested later on the information, nor is anyone's health being compromised, so I think it's OK to summarize. After the service, I might talk with the minister and do my spiel, or I might just let the regular interpreter know so she can talk with the regular minister about future subbing situations.

A DEAF CONSUMER'S PERSPECTIVE: Warn the Deaf congregation you weren't adequately prepared for the minister's presentation but that you'll do your best. Perhaps you could stop the minister from time to time if you're exhausted and need pacing.

Other Scenarios

Identify the issue(s) involved and decide how you would respond. Discuss and compare your responses with your colleagues.

298. You're interpreting at a beautiful wedding reception. In between toasts, you're enjoying the wonderful food provided. However, you don't realize the "punch" you've been drinking contains alcohol. When you stand up to interpret the next toast, you're feeling a little woozy.

299. There's going to be a puppet show at the elementary school where you interpret. You're told there are several characters/puppets in the show and it will last almost two hours. That's a long time without a break, but you are the only interpreter at the school.

300. You have been interpreting a business meeting for the last two hours. The meeting is running longer than expected because emotions are running high. To ask for a break would break the flow of the emotions, but you're completely exhausted!

301. You're one of several interpreters hired for a regional interpreter conference. The building's furnace is out of order and the room is downright freezing. The participants have their coats on and your fingers are turning blue. You're ready to quit.

302. Admittedly, you ate too much at your favorite restaurant for lunch. Half an hour into the interpreting assignment, your stomach starts to cramp, and you know it won't be long before you need to run for the bathroom. Unfortunately, there are no breaks scheduled during this two-hour block, and you're all alone.

303. Today you're supposed to interpret an orthodox Jewish wedding, and it's 90 degrees out with 90 percent humidity. The synagogue's air conditioning has broken down, and with your long-sleeved dress, you're absolutely melting. You feel yourself becoming faint as the sweat unattractively pours out every pore.

304. While interpreting a two-hour presentation, you're informed at the break that your son has had an accident at school, and they need you at the hospital to sign release forms. You're alone at this assignment, and it would be next to impossible for the agency to send someone over to finish up the last hour.

305. You have recently bought a new sweater and you wear it for the first time at an interpreting assignment. Suddenly you start to itch something fierce, and you realize the sweater you're wearing probably has wool in it. You're allergic to wool.

306. You're a recent graduate of an ITP and have agreed to interpret at a conference at your church, where you also interpret every Sunday. Your team interpreter is on stage and you realize two things. First, he's much better than you, and the difference is going to be quite dramatic when you get up there; and second, you didn't realize that the conference would attract over 1,000 people, including a large deaf audience. You're now glued to your seat. Your partner has given you several subtle signals he's ready to switch, but you're too scared to move.

307. You're in a courtroom interpreting when it suddenly seems to have become very hot, and you're starting to sweat profusely. Your clothes are soon soaking wet, and you look like a participant in a wet T-shirt contest. You're very embarrassed, and no one else seems to be sweating.

308. You're interpreting in a low-income deaf client's home and are invited to partake of a snack. The family tells you it's venison, which is not your favorite meat, but you have some anyway to be polite. As you're chewing and interpreting, the deaf family starts explaining to the hearing client that they found this deer dead on the road. You know Miss Manners would say either swallow it or use your napkin discretely, but you're having an extremely hard time interpreting right now with that lovely thought in your head.

309. You're hired to interpret a bingo game at a local Deaf-blind club. You're the only interpreter, and after each number is called, you see a sea of Deaf-blind adults in front of you all reaching out and waiting for you to put the information in their hands. It's an overwhelming feeling, and it's starting to get to you.

310. You're interpreting a counseling session for a deaf man and a therapist. The man has been living on the street and stinks of body odor and urine. The odor is so pungent that twice during the session the therapist had to leave the room. You're about to throw up too.

311. You have accepted a week-long assignment at a job training center. You arrive and are introduced to the deaf client, who is being trained to count nuts and bolts. She has a tray of nuts on one side of her and a tray of bolts on the other side. You realize you're going to spend all day, every day, interpreting, "No, the square ones go in that tray."

312. You're interpreting for a doctor's appointment where the procedure for doing a throat culture causes the deaf client to vomit. Just looking at vomit makes you want to vomit. You look down and see some vomit got on you. You start to gag.

313. While interpreting for a live TV talk show, the host and the guest are discussing first aid techniques to assist people who choke on food or other objects. When you sign "stuck" you accidentally jab your windpipe too hard. You're suddenly gasping for air while live on television. You try desperately to maintain your composure, but tears are running down your face as your face turns red.

314. You have just graduated from an ITP and taken your first freelance job, which is to interpret an upcoming play. You'll have plenty of time to rehearse, so you feel good. The night of the play, the curtain rises and you look out into the audience and see your first ASL instructor, the director of your ITP, and your mentor sitting in the audience, and you freeze. The play begins and you literally can't move.

315. You're interpreting a live concert for one of your all-time favorite performers. You're having a great time when, after one of the songs, the lead singer walks over to you and tells the audience how much he appreciates having an interpreter for his songs. He asks if you would mind coming up on stage and interpreting the next song standing next to him. You freeze like a deer caught in the headlights.

Challenges to an Interpreter's Emotional State While Interpreting

- **Scenario 316**. I am interpreting in a high school science class as they are dissecting cats. I can't help but think about my own little "Fluffy" at home as I watch the students start pulling out various organs. I feel myself starting to get upset.

AN INTERPRETER'S PERSPECTIVE: If you can stomach it, hang in there. Maintain eye contact and avoid looking at the dissection if you can. Don't get caught off guard next time. Check over the class syllabus for future lesson plans that may be difficult for you to handle.

A DEAF CONSUMER'S PERSPECTIVE: Interpreters aren't machines; they're human beings with feelings. I completely understand where the interpreter is coming from. Take a quick break for a drink of water, and when you've calmed down, finish the job. Afterwards, race home and hug your cat!

- **Scenario 317**. I'm interpreting a school field trip to the local zoo. In the reptile house, the docent is showing the kids a snake. I can't help myself; I hate snakes. Although I know the snake is harmless, my face and body register obvious fear, and I cringe physically away from the docent.

AN INTERPRETER'S PERSPECTIVE: It's OK to show that you're a real person sometimes, and if snakes creep you out, then snakes creep you out. The kids might even appreciate seeing you show your "human" side and will probably think it's funny, which is OK too. If you can switch with another interpreter who is not bothered by snakes, do so at once. If that's not possible, you're going to have to tough it out. Get as close as you can but as far away as you need to be. (An interpreter passed out on the floor is no good to anyone). Remember this is a valuable learning experience for these children. Once they're done with the snakes, ask for a short break and try to shake off that creepy feeling. Remind yourself that this is just one of those wild experiences that interpreters have. I always like to remember that there's probably no other job in the world that would put me in so many different and unusual situations, good and bad, and how much richer my life is as a result.

A DEAF CONSUMER'S PERSPECTIVE: If there's a team interpreter, I would immediately ask to switch. If I'm solo, then I would just move as far away from the snake as I possibly could. I would also do my best not to look at the snake.

Other Scenarios

Identify the issue(s) involved and decide how you would respond. Discuss and compare your responses with your colleagues.

318. While interpreting a videotape at school, you find yourself moved to tears. The story is very powerful and moving, but more than that, it's that time of month and so you're very emotional anyway. Everyone is looking at you standing there with tears running down your face.

319. You are interpreting in a college classroom where the professor and the students are discussing the right to die. The professor starts using his own father as an example and goes into detail about his father's death from emphysema. He discusses the quality of life aspect and says he supports Dr. Kevorkian's efforts. Your own father has recently been diagnosed with cancer, and listening to the professor's graphic description gets you thinking about your own father. You start to get scared and upset at the thought of what his future holds.

320. During a break in class at the university where you're a staff interpreter, the deaf student tells you about one of her roommates who is having an affair with a married professor. Your heart stops when she says she doesn't remember his last name, only his first name and department in which he works, because you realize it's your husband. The deaf student doesn't even know your husband works for the university.

321. You're interpreting a well-attended lecture by an expert on child abuse. The large auditorium is completely packed when you suddenly have a memory of being sexually abused as a child. Your knees turn to jelly, and you feel yourself starting to fall apart.

322. You're interpreting for a deaf woman at a doctor's appointment where she finds out she's pregnant. The client cops an attitude and flippantly says, "No big deal, I've had four other abortions." Not only are you a card-carrying member of the Right to Life organization, you and your husband have been trying to conceive for eight years now with no success. Her comment hits you like a knife to the heart, and you become sick to your stomach.

323. You're interpreting for a deaf couple meeting with their attorney, and the attorney is yelling at the couple because they owe him a lot of money. He's telling them he won't help them anymore because he hasn't seen a dime of his money, and so on. The whole time he's yelling, he's addressing you, not the couple. He's in your ear and breathing down your neck while he's screaming at them.

324. While interpreting in a college classroom, the professor tells a very funny story. When the professor continues his lecture, you still have tears running down your face, and you can't stop laughing. You can see the other students looking at you concerned because of your tears.

325. You're on your way to an interpreting assignment when your car breaks down. You open the hood and check a few things, but you're no mechanic. A young guy pulls up and offers to call a tow truck for you, but you say, "No way, my budget can't handle a $100 tow." So he offers to nudge your car to see if you can start it while it's rolling by popping the clutch. Sure enough, it starts, but then just as you get back on the road, a cop turns on his flashing lights and pulls you over. He gives you a ticket for driving without a seatbelt. By the time you get to your interpreting assignment, your hands are black and your mood pretty well matches them.

326. You're called in to interpret at a large veterinary clinic. The deaf client's cat was deliberately run over by a neighbor and is in very bad shape. You're usually fairly stoic, but in this case, when you see the cat, you start to cry at the thought of someone's deliberate cruelty to an innocent animal.

327. At an Individualized Educational Planning Committee (IEPC) meeting that you're interpreting, the deaf parents are battling with the administration of the mainstream program their children currently attend. They vehemently want to pull their children out of the school and send them to the residential school where they themselves once attended. The administrator tells them he will fight them all the way because of the astronomical cost to the local school district to send their kids to the state school. He looks at you and says, "It only costs us $15,000 a year for this little lady sitting here." At that moment, you're ready to quit and tell him where he can stick his measly $15 grand a year.

328. A deaf friend tells you she would consider it a wonderful wedding gift if you would interpret her wedding. Unfortunately, you two were once lovers and it ended by her decision, not yours. Over the years, time has healed those wounds somewhat, but not nearly enough to ask this of you. Like a fool, however, you say yes. Moments before the wedding is set to begin, you realize you have made a bad, bad decision.

329. While interpreting for a dying deaf man and his priest, the deaf man says he has a confession to make. He says, "I shot President Kennedy; it was a conspiracy." You laugh out loud at the man's last attempt at humor. The priest turns to you and snaps at you for laughing at a dying man.

330. You accept an ongoing assignment at a local community college. You arrive and find that the deaf student is a guy you met a few months ago at a wedding. At the reception, you both became intoxicated, and you ended up going home with him that night. You don't even remember his name. It's very uncomfortable for both of you right now.

331. You can't help yourself; every time you look at the deaf client, you picture your old boyfriend. It ended badly, and you can honestly say you hate him. Unfortunately, your deaf client could be his twin.

332. While interpreting a presentation, the speaker starts making condescending remarks about women. Some of the men and women in the audience start leaving, and the presenter just laughs and then turns and gestures to you and says, "At least we have one woman here today who knows her place and just does what she's told."

333. You're interpreting for a deaf client accused of sexually abusing his child. The child is brought into the courtroom, and your jaw drops because this could be your child's twin. You finish the day but tell the judge you want to find a replacement. He orders you to continue interpreting the trial so as not to break up the continuity of the proceedings and possibly allow for any question of a mistrial.

Challenges Related to Dealing with Attraction While on the Job

- **Scenario 334**. An extremely attractive deaf man from out-of-town is giving a presentation in my area. I interpret for him, and afterwards he asks me to join him back at his hotel room. My first thought is, "Why not? I'll probably never see him again."

AN INTERPRETER'S PERSPECTIVE: Chances are, you will see him again. Remember that he's a client, not just a man on the street. Lust is a powerful emotion, but ethics should supersede your desire for a night of romance.

A DEAF CONSUMER'S PERSPECTIVE: The Deaf community is a small world, and so you may unknowingly be establishing a reputation among deaf men. Also, if your interpreting agency finds out, you could be in trouble. Give it a pass.

- **Scenario 335.** I was interpreting at an all-day assignment for a deaf business man manning his company's booth. Whenever we were alone at the booth, he would continually make suggestive remarks. At first, I tried to just ignore it. I told him to "knock it off," but that didn't stop him. Instead, he would say, "I don't mean sexual harassment. I'm just an open person." What should I have done or what can I do now?

AN INTERPRETER'S PERSPECTIVE: Unfortunately, I too have made the same mistake over and over again. Instead of stopping the person who is being inappropriate right away, I tend to hope it will just go away if I ignore it. However, like you, it never does; it gets worse. This man knew he was crossing a line and tried to cover it up by calling himself an "open person." A spade is a spade. He is sexually harassing you. Instead of beating yourself up for letting it continue and feeling like somehow you let it happen because you were being polite (several times in fact), it's time to start taking action. Typically, when women address the problem seriously, the person will try to deflect it by saying that you misunderstood or are overreacting. (This I know from experience.) In your heart of hearts, you know you didn't misunderstand, and you know what he is trying to do, as disappointing and difficult as it may be to believe when you're taken off guard. If you don't stand up for yourself either directly with him or with his supervisor (or all of the above), you've allowed this man to move on to the next, unsuspecting female. In my situation I didn't listen to my gut, and I wish I had — if not for me, for the next female interpreter who came after me. If this guy hears it enough, he'll learn. However, if he still doesn't get it, he should have to suffer the consequences. Trust yourself. It's wrong and it needs to stop.

A DEAF CONSUMER'S PERSPECTIVE: Sexual harassment is sexual harassment, and there are numerous local, state, and federal laws governing this. Anytime unwelcome sexual advances, jokes, talk, or touching occurs, it is immediately defined as sexual harassment. Your main job is to facilitate communication, and this requires the use of mental, emotional, and physical faculties. When this is compromised, your ability to fully use your faculties is greatly diminished. Tell him, "I'm here to interpret, and I can respect that you are an 'open person'; however, I am a person too. Those comments are unwarranted and make me feel extremely uncomfortable, and they are unwelcome. If you choose to continue doing this, I will report this to the federal agency (if you were hired through them) or to the hiring party and explain what has occurred and request a replacement be sent." Also, explain to him you will be leaving as soon as the call is made.

Other Scenarios

Identify the issue(s) involved and decide how you would respond. Discuss and compare your responses with your colleagues.

336. For the past several months, you have interpreted weekly counseling sessions for a young deaf couple and their therapist. Although they have their share of problems, they seem very committed to each other. Inside you can't help but root for them as every week they overcome another hurdle. After one session the counselor asks to speak to you for a moment, and out of the clear blue, he asks you for a date. This guy is so far out in left field that you have no idea where he's coming from. You swear you have never given him the time of day before this, much less any indication you're anything but professionally interested in this situation.

337. You are hired to interpret at a banquet. There's a speech before the dinner. No remarks are planned during dinner, so the deaf client invites you to join her for the meal. You're thrilled because you're starving. You eat and still interpret conversations around the table. The man sitting next to you turns and asks you if you would like to go out for drinks afterward.

338. You have a college class you're interpreting this afternoon, and your boyfriend asks if he can come along and watch you.

339. You're an attractive, young, female interpreter who has recently gotten a job interpreting at a high school. One of the deaf students is a muscular, attractive, young man involved in several sports. One afternoon while you're waiting outside for your ride after school, he approaches you and makes a romantic overture. You tell him that his behavior is not appropriate. Fortunately, your ride pulls up and you leave. The student doesn't take the hint, and he won't take no for an answer. He keeps bothering you.

340. You are asked to interpret for a deaf client going in to see her gynecologist. You have interpreted for this physician in the past and have never seen anything but the most professional decorum. However, today for some reason, he's making questionable innuendoes. At one point during the exam, you look over and see him wink at the client. You think it must have been your imagination. However, then the client asks you to leave because she's uncomfortable with you there. She says she can handle the rest of the visit herself.

341. You have just received your CI and CT and are interpreting a court case. One of the attorneys involved in the case has been coming on to you more every day. You try discouraging him subtly, but subtle doesn't seem to work with this guy. It has become uncomfortable for you in the courtroom because now he stares at you the whole time you're interpreting.

342. You're interpreting a swimming class. One day after class, the instructor tells you he would prefer it if you would wear a swimsuit to class. You're puzzled because you never have to get in the water. You ask him why and he says, "I want to get a better look at your behind."

343. Your high school deaf student asks you to interpret for her at a prom she will be attending for gay and lesbian students. You're honored she feels comfortable enough to even ask you. You're having a great time until one of the chaperones starts to hit on you. You're uncomfortable now and ready to call it a night, but the prom is not supposed to end for a couple more hours.

344. You're interpreting a job interview and can't help but notice that the deaf client is staring lustfully at your chest. You feel your face turning red, but you continue interpreting. After the assignment, the first words out of the deaf client's mouth are, "Will you go out with me?"

Challenges to a Person's Health or Physical Well-Being

- **Scenario 345**. I was interpreting in an auto mechanics class, and the teacher was explaining to them about torches and the appropriate mixtures. My husband owns an auto shop so I'm somewhat familiar with the subject. I was watching the deaf student put his mixture into his torch. I was pretty sure he didn't follow the instructions and that, if he lit the torch, he could blow up the place. Without waiting for the instructor to come over and check his work, the student started to light his torch. I couldn't help myself; I interceded, and he wasn't too pleased.

AN INTERPRETER'S PERSPECTIVE: Common sense tells you to value the lives of others over any professional code. In a situation like this, yes, I would probably say or do something.

A DEAF CONSUMER'S PERSPECTIVE: If you value your life, then you should definitely tell the student to check with the instructor before lighting the mixture.

- **Scenario 346**. I'm interpreting for a deaf client in the process of being bawled out by the case manager of the group home where he lives. The client becomes upset and keeps asking, "(Your name sign) mad at me?" The case manager tried telling the client he's the one who is mad, not the interpreter. The client, however, is unconvinced and now he's getting mad at me. He is in my face and threatening me with physical harm if I don't "shut up."

AN INTERPRETER'S PERSPECTIVE: This situation could most likely have been prevented. When difficult information is being shared, I will frequently point to and reference the sender of the information. I also use a sign name or other identifier ("boss" or "manager," for example) to make clear the information is not originating from me. If these tactics fail, I would require a break at this point, as well as separation between myself and the deaf consumer. Depending on the procedures in the group home, I may talk with the case manager about how to proceed. Under no circumstances would I continue to place myself at risk of physical harm.

A DEAF CONSUMER'S PERSPECTIVE: The interpreter should say, "You're misunderstanding me! I (my name sign) am not mad at you. She (pointing to the case manager) is mad at you." Then I would let them continue their discussion.

- **Scenario 347**. I'm in a restaurant enjoying some authentic Mexican food when I notice a young deaf couple at a table in the corner. They're so engrossed with one another that I don't go over and say hello. They're obviously enjoying themselves. Suddenly I hear someone in the kitchen shout, "Fire!" Incredibly, the deaf couple doesn't notice the mass exodus, and my husband is shoving me out the door.

AN INTERPRETER'S PERSPECTIVE: The fact that I know the couple is deaf and unaware of the potential danger would require that I get their attention. Hopefully, there's some object handy that I can throw toward them while being whisked out the door. If not, and if my life isn't at risk, I would break free of my husband's grip, run over to the couple's table, get their attention by tapping their shoulders or banging on the table, and quickly sign, "FIRE!"

A DEAF CONSUMER'S PERSPECTIVE: All romance aside, I'm sure the couple would greatly appreciate it if you let them know about the danger.

- **Scenario 348**. I have recently become sensitive to many perfumes and colognes. Consequently, interpreting has become quite a challenge. It seems like everyone drenches herself with cologne, and I end up with terrible headaches. My services are in demand, but I feel awkward insisting the clients not wear any fragrances before I accept the assignment.

AN INTERPRETER'S PERSPECTIVE: I would handle this situation just like I deal with situations where I anticipate smoking. When you receive the request, be very straightforward about your limitations. Tell them, "I would really love to do this job, but I can't work in situations where there are strong perfume scents. Do you happen to know if any of the people involved wear perfume? Can you please find out? I'm afraid I can't commit to this job until I know if I will be able to work without getting a migraine headache. Great, thanks a million!"

A DEAF CONSUMER'S PERSPECTIVE: As a freelance interpreter, you won't be able to control every work situation to minimize personal discomfort. For regularly scheduled assignments, you can try to work out an agreement with the clients. You may want to check into medical treatments to reduce the severity of your symptoms or look into a career change.

Other Scenarios

Identify the issue(s) involved and decide how you would respond. Discuss and compare your responses with your colleagues.

349. On the day of an interpreting assignment, you find yourself suffering from a severe case of the flu. You know the chances of finding another interpreter at this late hour are minimal. You open your medicine cabinet, but the only flu medicine you have are those pills that make you sleepy.

350. While interpreting at a deaf client's home for a home visit with a caseworker, you notice the deaf woman's child playing on the kitchen floor with a box of matches. The other two adults don't see what is happening, as you're the only one who can see the child from where you're sitting.

351. You're interpreting for a week-long trip to the Grand Canyon. Part of the trip requires a very steep descent into the canyon. The 17-year-old deaf client starts having difficulty breathing, and when you suggest he let the group leader know, he bristles at your interference and insists you leave him alone.

352. You're out of town interpreting a conference. Afterwards when you and the deaf client are walking out to your cars, you both see an elderly man having some car trouble. The deaf client asks you if you would mind interpreting again while he sees if he can be of any assistance. The deaf client is giving instructions to the elderly man for jumping his car battery that you know for a fact are inaccurate and potentially dangerous.

353. At the end of the week, your thumb is extremely sore, but you forget about it over the weekend. First thing Monday morning in math class, the pain shoots through your hand the first time you make the sign for "long division." There's still a week more of long division scheduled this week.

354. The deaf client is being trained to work in a kitchen, and you're interpreting as the instructor asks the man to peel potatoes. The client isn't happy about this task and an argument breaks out. The instructor is insistent, and so the deaf client grabs a large knife and starts waving it around.

355. You are called into the emergency room to interpret for a deaf woman who has fallen down a flight of stairs and broken her hip. At the hospital, you jump out of your car and take no more than three steps before you slip on the ice in the parking lot and hurt your arm. As you walk in, you're not sure if you're an interpreter or a patient.

356. You are interpreting an arraignment in district court one day when the judge passes down his sentence and informs the deaf client that he will be going to jail. The deaf client nods his head, then gets up from his seat and turns to be escorted out of the room. As you turn away to gather up your things, you see a flash of orange. It is the deaf client, and he's climbing over tables trying to attack you.

357. A deaf parishioner comes up to you after you finish interpreting at church one day and asks you to interpret for him at his weekly Alcoholics Anonymous (AA) meetings. You tell him you would be happy to go with him and rearrange your schedule to fit in his meetings. The first night you're surprised at the amount of smoke in the room, and by the end of the evening, you're physically ill from second-hand smoke.

358. You have accepted an assignment that is once a week for several weeks. The meetings are to be held in the deaf client's home so the social worker can discuss family issues with the whole family. However, on the first day, you find yourself experiencing an allergic reaction to the family's two Chihuahuas.

359. You're hired to interpret for a deaf client training for a job at a local restaurant. At one point during the day, the client is accused by the manager of stealing paychecks from other employees. The deaf client starts screaming in front of a large number of people currently in the restaurant. The manager quickly says to forget it and the client walks away. Later when another employee tries to show the client how to do something, the deaf client throws another tantrum, but instead of backing down, the employee takes a swing at the deaf client. He misses and hits you instead.

360. You're called into a hospital emergency room late one night for a deaf client with a blood alcohol level of .20. He was very aggressive when he arrived, so the hospital staff had to restrain him. Now the man has calmed down, and so the staff unstraps his wrists so you two can communicate. Suddenly the man grabs your arm and starts cursing at you.

361. You have interpreted three checkups for a deaf couple's baby at a health clinic. Each time the baby is seen by a different doctor, but all three doctors say that the baby is not gaining weight like he should. The parents always tell the doctors that their son is just a fussy eater. The last doctor wrote on the baby's chart, "This is a 'failure to thrive' baby," and orders a visiting nurse to make a home visit to assist the parents. Appointments were made for the home visit, but the parents always canceled them at the last minute. You see the parents and the baby at the Deaf club one weekend, and the baby is bluish and too weak to cry. You see the parents telling another couple how they resent the demands a baby makes on them.

362. You're interpreting for a deaf student on the university's gymnastics team as she meets with a doctor. The doctor advises her to not participate in any sports due to a heart condition. He refuses to sign off on her physical. It is weeks later and the physical isn't mentioned again. The girl is still participating in gymnastics. At today's gymnastics meet, she's short of breath, and her coach asks her if she would like to stop. She assures him she's fine and wants to continue.

363. You're interpreting for a fund-raising event to support AIDS research. One of the presenters tells the audience the only way to stop the virus is to get rid of the African-Americans and homosexuals, who are deliberately spreading it to the white heterosexual world. Suddenly things are being thrown from the audience at the presenter, and you're dangerously close to being hit too.

364. In the remedial math class that you interpret, the teacher is consistently late. Today the students get out of control and a fight starts. Knives are drawn, and you physically have to separate the two fighting students.

Challenges to Maintaining Confidentiality

- **Scenario 365**. My mom has always been interested in what's going on in my life. I was home last weekend for a visit, and she asked me about my work. She doesn't want specific information about my clients; she just wants to know what types of situations I have interpreted. She doesn't have anything to do with the field of interpreting and doesn't even know any deaf people. Can I tell her?

AN INTERPRETER'S PERSPECTIVE: The reason the confidentiality tenet exists and is placed first and foremost in our CPC is that it is crucial to the development of trust between deaf persons and their interpreters. The deaf client needs to know that anything that is interpreted, any information exchanged, is owned by the parties involved — the deaf and hearing consumers — and not by the interpreter. It is essential that we earn that trust daily by adhering to this basic tenet.

In this situation I would explain that I do a variety of work in all kinds of places and give some examples, such as funerals, surgeries, trials, artistic performances, concerts, and other places. I would also explain my work is confidential and that I wouldn't want to place her in an awkward situation if one of my interpreting friends or deaf friends talks to her about my work. Keeping information confidential protects her, my clients, and me. I would point out that the work I do is very specialized, and it's easy to figure out who did what if I share specifics about any job.

A DEAF CONSUMER'S PERSPECTIVE: I would go ahead and share the most basic information with my mother and my own "take" on the situations. Generic information can be shared without violating the CPC.

- **Scenario 366**. I had a job interpreting for a therapy session, and I wrote, "Therapy — Stv. Miller" in my date book. My date book is never out of my purse and no one ever sees it. However, of course Murphy's law, one day I lost my date book. The next session my client, Steve Miller shoves my lost book in my face and furiously signs, "My boss found this at the bank and saw my name. Now he knows I have therapy. Thanks a lot!"

AN INTERPRETER'S PERSPECTIVE: By revealing information in your date book pertaining to setting and client, you have indeed breached the confidentiality tenet of the CPC. Although you said, "My date book is never out of my purse and no one ever sees it," obviously it *did* get out and someone *did* see it. Therefore, it's an excellent lesson for you. You need to revamp the notation system in your date book so that the information won't be decipherable. All you can do in this instance is apologize sincerely and explain that this incident has caused you to review your business practices so that this will never happen again.

A DEAF CONSUMER'S PERSPECTIVE: This is precisely why no names should ever be used in a date book. You never know when you'll lose it. Always use a code for regular interpreting jobs. For regular interpreting jobs, you should certainly be able to remember who the client is. It's a clear violation of the CPC to identify your clients in any way, including in a date book. You should apologize profusely to the client and offer to remove yourself from the job. It's the honorable thing to do under the circumstances. Hopefully, the client knows that, legally, his boss can't take any action as a result of his having therapy.

- **Scenario 367**. I am an interpreting student and I have two set practicum sites. One is a middle school and the other is at Alcoholics Anonymous (AA). When the middle school interpreter is signing off in my journal, she scans my signature page and says, "Oh, who else are you working with?"

AN INTERPRETER'S PERSPECTIVE: The tenet of confidentiality prevents us from revealing any information about any of our assignments, including the fact that the service is even being delivered. I would give a vague response such as, "I'm working at a lot of interesting assignments." I think many times interpreters ask each other this question innocently, without meaning to intrude on confidential information. We all need to be reminded of our promise to adhere to the CPC; therefore, I might underscore my answer with a comment such as, "Thank you for giving me an opportunity to practice following the CPC." This subtly reminds the practicing interpreter of the breach she invited without preaching to her, which wouldn't be appropriate from a student.

A DEAF CONSUMER'S PERSPECTIVE: I think it's relatively safe to state you're working in a recovery program and gaining a lot of experience in that field. Most interpreters I know do comment on the types of jobs they have worked on without divulging names of clients or sites. The interpreting world is small — the Deaf world far smaller. It's almost common knowledge who has worked where and with whom. If the middle school interpreter persists, simply say you're uncomfortable giving any more information, as you're new in the field and would like to honor the CPC.

- **Scenario 368**. One night I looked in my cupboards and realized I needed to run to the store. As I was walking down the frozen food aisle, I bumped into one of my neighbors. She asks how I am and I tell her I'm fine. She then remarks that she's seen my car a lot at the doctor's office (an interpreting site of mine). She says she knows that her deaf cousin has been sick a lot and wonders how she's feeling these days.

AN INTERPRETER'S PERSPECTIVE: The CPC is very clear about situations like this: we must not reveal any information about any assignment, including the fact the service was even performed. The best response in a case like this is to have a sentence ready that deflects the person's question without sounding rude or insensitive to her genuine concern for her cousin. I might say, "Oh, I'm sure she'd be happy to hear from you. Why don't you call her?" I might even offer to pass on her concern to her cousin if I happen to run into her. Do not reveal whether or not you interpreted for her cousin or any information regarding her health that you learned while interpreting.

A DEAF CONSUMER'S PERSPECTIVE: If it's common knowledge, you could comment on the deaf cousin's health and then direct the conversation back to the cousin, instead of your being at the doctor's office frequently. Encourage her to talk with her cousin. You could even offer your interpreting skills so the neighbor can communicate with her deaf cousin.

- **Scenario 369**. I've been interpreting for a deaf couple attending marriage counseling. The husband tells his wife that he has had several affairs but claims he doesn't want to leave her. He names the women with whom he has had affairs, and several of them are women I know. Later that week I see a deaf woman that the husband named. The woman comes up to me and says her "boyfriend" told her I was interpreting his counseling sessions. She says he's leaving his wife for her and asks if he has told his wife yet.

AN INTERPRETER'S PERSPECTIVE: I would say something like, "I'm sure you understand why your question is inappropriate. Please don't ask me about any interpreting assignments again."

A DEAF CONSUMER'S PERSPECTIVE: I would say, "I'm sorry, but I can't divulge any job-related information." If she persists, walk away.

- **Scenario 370**. I get a last-minute call to interpret a staff meeting at a local television station. During the meeting I learn that K.D. Lang is in town for a surprise performance and staying at a nearby hotel. She's my best friend's favorite singer. She would owe me for life if I called her and told her the juicy tidbit.

AN INTERPRETER'S PERSPECTIVE: Sometimes we become privy to information while interpreting that challenges every ethical bone in our bodies. Always remember why you have access to that information and what your role is. You have been hired as a professional interpreter, and with that job title, professional recognition, and pay, comes the moral responsibility of adhering to the CPC. The confidentiality tenet is a code we must live by, regardless of how innocuous divulging a tidbit may seem. Even the smallest lapses have a way of snowballing and coming back to you or others in ways you never anticipated. Be safe, not sorry.

A DEAF CONSUMER'S PERSPECTIVE: This would be a definite violation of the interpreter's CPC. If you talk about the little things, how do your clients know you don't talk about all your assignments? This is not your information to share.

- **Scenario 371**. I'm on my way to an interpreting assignment when my car breaks down. I immediately get on my car phone and call the interpreter referral agency about getting a replacement. The only person available is someone I privately call "Big Mouth." The assignment is a therapy session, and I know the client is very vulnerable. "Big Mouth" gets on the phone and asks me for background information so she can prepare for the session.

AN INTERPRETER'S PERSPECTIVE: If I truly felt that the deaf client's right to confidentiality was at risk, I wouldn't disclose any information to "Big Mouth," and I would ask the agency to call the therapist's office and reschedule the appointment. The integrity of the therapy session is too important to risk allowing it to happen with an unethical provider.

A DEAF CONSUMER'S PERSPECTIVE: Don't say a single word regarding the details of this assignment. You know her reputation, so there's no excuse for you to fall into her trap. Reschedule the appointment.

- **Scenario 372**. I have been interpreting for a young deaf woman in counseling. It's Valentine's Day and she gives me a pin she has made herself. I pin it on my shirt, and later that day another deaf person comments, "Oh, I see Julie made you a pin. She gave me one too. Where did you see her?"

AN INTERPRETER'S PERSPECTIVE: This question doesn't require a precise answer. You can simply say, "Yes, isn't it beautiful!" If she continues to probe, give a vague answer such as "I saw her the other day" or "I bumped into her on the street." The person asking the question does not need to know that it was given to you at an interpreting assignment.

A DEAF CONSUMER'S PERSPECTIVE: You don't need to get into specifics. You can simply inform her that, yes, it was indeed a gift.

- **Scenario 373**. I'm an interpreting student at an internship site with a working interpreter. During some down time, the two of us are chatting, and she tells me about the time when a deaf client became ill and vomited on her shoe during a job interview. Later a deaf pal of mine tells me a hilarious story he just heard about a deaf friend of his who threw up during a job interview.

AN INTERPRETER'S PERSPECTIVE: This is a tough situation because it's through stories like these that new interpreters get "snapshots" of what interpreting is really like. Assuming no names or locations were divulged, I'd just laugh at my friend's story. However, you might want to approach the working interpreter under the guise of resolving your own confusion about the ethics of revealing this type of information. Hopefully, she will think twice next time. If I noticed a pattern of information sharing that was inappropriate, I would consider filing a grievance.

A DEAF CONSUMER'S PERSPECTIVE: You should remain neutral and act as if this is new information. Don't make the situation worse by saying you heard it before from another interpreter.

- **Scenario 374**. I'm at a weekly dinner outing with a group of deaf and hearing friends. Everyone starts talking about one member of the group who for the last month has always come up with excuses not to show up. Someone cattily says, "She must think she's too good for us now that she's working for that law firm." I happen to know that this person was recently fired from her job because I've interpreted a couple of job interviews for her. I also know the reason she's stopped coming to dinner is because she can't afford to eat out and is embarrassed about it.

AN INTERPRETER'S PERSPECTIVE: You say nothing. It's not your business to disclose this information, friends or not. It's very much your obligation to keep quiet.

A DEAF CONSUMER'S PERSPECTIVE: Say nothing. Adhere strictly to the code of confidentiality.

- **Scenario 375**. A nationally known deaf actress is giving the commencement speech at the college where I work as a staff interpreter. I have been a fan of hers for years, and I'm thrilled to be selected to interpret for her. The commencement goes well, and as a bonus, I get to spend the day at various receptions with all the college bigwigs. What a day! When I get home I'm on cloud nine. I'm dying to pick up the phone and call someone, anyone, to talk about my day.

AN INTERPRETER'S PERSPECTIVE: Certain information is public knowledge. Commencement speakers are usually publicized, and there's a good chance that the event was covered by the media, or at least videotaped for the school. I would feel comfortable sharing the fact that I was the interpreter for the ceremony where so-and-so was giving the commencement speech. I think you could mention what her speech was about. Anything that happened in public I believe is public information. However, there's a clear line to be drawn. I would be careful not to share any information that didn't occur in public. For example, I wouldn't mention anything about which bigwigs she chatted with or what they said because these would be considered private conversations.

A DEAF CONSUMER'S PERSPECTIVE: I'm thrilled that there are jobs that interpreters enjoy so much. However, the CPC clearly states that confidentiality must be observed. I don't see a problem in sharing with a friend that you just had a great day and now are on cloud nine. That's probably as much as you can say without breaching confidentiality.

- **Scenario 376**. It's Friday morning and I have just interpreted a telephone conversation for a deaf person. During the call the person on the other end talked about her new boyfriend and their plans to spend the weekend together at his cabin, which she describes in detail. Later that week I run into an old friend whom I have not seen in over a year. She announces she's engaged and fills me in on all the details. She describes a recent romantic getaway the two of them enjoyed, and it sounds like the same cabin the other woman was describing.

AN INTERPRETER'S PERSPECTIVE: You have no business divulging any of this information. You can't be sure it's the same cabin anyway, and it's not your role to create problems and raise issues. I would continue to interpret as usual and not get involved. If your friend tells you later about what a two-timing creep her fiancé was, I would feign surprise.

A DEAF CONSUMER'S PERSPECTIVE: You can't be sure there's a conflict here. Simply keep quiet and enjoy your friend's happiness in being in love.

- **Scenario 377**. I have just spent an intense day interpreting at a nearby prison, and now my best friend and I are kicking back watching a video. I'm not really paying attention, though; my mind is still processing the events of the day. As I sit there, deep in thought, my friend looks over and asks me what's wrong. I know she would never tell anyone.

AN INTERPRETER'S PERSPECTIVE: I would tell her I'm feeling a little preoccupied with some of my work, apologize, and either try to get into the evening's entertainment or tell my friend that I guess I'm not up for company right now and call it a night. I might consider talking with an interpreter confidante if I feel that I need to process my experiences with another person.

A DEAF CONSUMER'S PERSPECTIVE: Just say you've had a long, hard day today. Don't compromise on confidentiality. This is something I have a hard time dealing with; I have a hard time trusting interpreters. I've heard too many horror stories about interpreters who blab.

- **Scenario 378**. I'm the interpreter for a deaf football player at the local university. During a game, the deaf player gets knocked unconscious by a 300-pound player on the opposing team. The team doctor runs out and calls me over. He wants to find out any health-related information of which I might be aware.

AN INTERPRETER'S PERSPECTIVE: If I'm aware of any health-related information, I would tell the doctor. Then I would tell him whom to contact to get specific and accurate information.

A DEAF CONSUMER'S PERSPECTIVE: I would find out if his family is present. If not, I would share whatever information I had on the player and let the doctor know that it might not be accurate. If I knew my interpreter well, I would want her to assist the doctor with information on my health. If the interpreter didn't know me very well, I wouldn't like it if she volunteered any information.

- **Scenario 379:** A deaf client just confided in me that she has herpes. Ethically, I know not to tell anyone, but I feel I need to talk with someone because I'm in shock. Is it wrong to confide in a close mutual friend?

AN INTERPRETER'S PERSPECTIVE: Sometimes, in spite of our best efforts to maintain clear boundaries, clients share information with us that we would prefer not to know. Whatever the reasons are for your reaction of shock, it is clear that you need to explore your feelings in an ethical, appropriate way. Confiding in a close mutual friend will only complicate matters and place you in jeopardy with the deaf client and the mutual friend. First, allow yourself to experience the shock and examine why you feel this way, then make an appointment with a qualified counselor or mental health professional who can provide a safe, confidential environment where you can vent your emotions without violating ethical practices. From my perspective, confiding in a close mutual friend is definitely *not* the way to go. If your reaction leads you to not making yourself available for professional tasks with this client, you will have drawn one more person into the dynamics who does not need to be involved. If the deaf client wants the close mutual friend to know, that's entirely her decision.

A DEAF CONSUMER'S PERSPECTIVE: There are two issues I see here which
may require you to do some self-analysis: what kind of relationship you have
with this deaf client and your feelings of shock. You indicate that the deaf client
confided in you, which tells me that the client considers you to be more than just
an interpreter. Ideally, the relationship between the interpreter and client would
be the same as between a doctor or lawyer and their clients — more businesslike.
Realistically, however, this is often difficult. For example, interpreting for a student
seven hours a day, five days a week, nine months out of a year, how can you not
become personal? You need to determine how far your professional and personal
boundaries extend with this client (and others) and how to maintain them. Possibly
the client and you share some of the same circle of friends, which may end up
getting back to the client. If you really do need to discuss this, it may be better to
talk about it with the client directly. This way, not only would you be able to keep
it between the two of you, you could also discuss your roles and redefine your
boundaries for the future. Finally, the news of the disease seems to have hit you
hard, so perhaps you have become too close, or perhaps you are conservative or
even just naïve about this topic. Be honest with yourself; know your comfort levels
and accept assignments that fit those levels to better prepare yourself in the future.

- **Scenario 380.** I have a somewhat complicated situation on which I would
  like to get your opinion. Since we are not interpreting all the time, the
  other interpreters and I on staff are asked to do things around the office that
  generally do not interfere with our role as interpreter. One client is going
  through a nasty divorce/custody case, and part of the visitation agreement
  is that the baby exchange takes place at our office so there are witnesses
  who can document everything. The husband often calls his lawyer from the
  office with tons of lies about what is going on, and since we're interpreting
  the calls, we know it but can't do anything about it. The wife's attorney
  now wants to subpoena us to testify about what we interpreted. Interpreter/
  client confidentiality is not legally binding like lawyer/client, right? So if
  we get called in, do we explain the CPC and hope that satisfies the attorney
  and court?

AN INTERPRETER'S PERSPECTIVE: Since the conversations between
attorney and client are privileged, that privilege also covers your interpreting
work. However, the wife's attorney can tell you to testify. If the attorney asks
any questions about the content of the conversation between the husband and his
attorney, you can assert the attorney/client privilege on behalf of the client. The
attorney can ask questions about any conversations you might have had with the
husband when the attorney was not present, such as during your preparation. These
conversations are not privileged, and you would need to answer those questions
truthfully. The attorney can also ask questions about your qualifications. The only
way you could share information from the husband's meetings with his attorney

would be if the husband waived that privilege and allowed you to speak to the wife's attorney. One concern would be if there were other people present when you were interpreting phone calls. Having a third person present destroys that privilege. In that case, you would have to testify regarding the interpreting work you did between the husband and his attorney. Another concern that comes up in this situation is your feelings about the husband. You seem to have made some decisions about the husband's truthfulness, and this raises a concern about your ability to carry out your interpreting without allowing this attitude to affect your work. It may be best to have another interpreter work with the husband. Sad as it is to say, people may choose to lie, whether they are deaf or hearing. There are ways, without the interference of an interpreter, to discern that someone is lying.

A DEAF CONSUMER'S PERSPECTIVE: The visitation agreement probably did not indicate that the interpreters are not to be used as witnesses, either when they are interpreting or not. This makes it very hard on the interpreters. However, the exchange agreement was set forth as a means to provide a "neutral environment" in the eyes of the law. Both parties involved probably neglected to account for the interpreter's role in the situation. The same would apply if the husband was using a relay operator instead of you, the interpreter. Whether the husband is manipulating the interpreters to his benefit or sincerely believes the interpreters cannot divulge information from the interpreted phone calls is something I find curious and I wonder about. My answer here would be that interpreter/client confidentiality is as binding per our express understanding when we as deaf consumers utilize interpreters in everyday practices. In addition, if the child in question is not in any immediate or foreseeable danger, the interpreters should not have any reason to testify. If you cannot work with the husband in question due to internal conflicts or complications, don't do it.

- **Scenario 381.** I interpreted for a client in a hospital recently and looked at her medical chart. Now either the client is lying about her condition (which is much more serious than she is letting on), her doctor hasn't been clear with her, or worse yet, the previous interpreter wasn't clear. To be safe, should I admit I looked at her chart?

AN INTERPRETER'S PERSPECTIVE: If you hadn't raised the prospect of the previous interpreter or the physician possibly not being clear, this would have been a "slam dunk." The client's privacy comes first. Even though it is best to be honest, the client's privacy extends beyond her medical chart. She gets to choose whether or not to discuss her condition with you. This is assuming, of course, that she knows the full extent of her condition. It is possible that her doctor is being paternalistic or the previous interpreter was somehow not clear. However, it is far more likely she is stonewalling you or in denial. P.S.: MYOB (mind your own business).

A DEAF CONSUMER'S PERSPECTIVE: If an interpreter looked at my chart, I would fire this person on the spot! It is so wrong for an interpreter to look at a client's chart. If this was me, I would never want this interpreter again in any situation. How could you even begin to think that it was right? What made you think you could look at it without the deaf client's permission? You'd better have a pretty good explanation because I would file a grievance and request to have your certification revoked!

Other Scenarios

Identify the issue(s) involved and decide how you would respond. Discuss and compare your responses with your colleagues.

382. A college deaf student asks if you would mind interpreting a quick conversation with a classmate before class starts, and you readily agree. The conversation, however, turns out to be about getting a copy of last year's quizzes for one of their classes.

383. A deaf woman at the church where you interpret has asked you to interpret for her during her baby delivery. Everyone in the congregation is aware you'll be interpreting for her, as the deaf woman has shared that information with all her friends. It's getting pretty close to the due date, and so when one Sunday the deaf woman doesn't come to church, everyone naturally assumes she had her baby and comes up to you for confirmation. In reality, there have been some complications which you have interpreted, but you're not sure how much you should share.

384. A vocational rehabilitation counselor contacts you to interpret for a deaf client going for a week of job training. He says that he would like you to report to him after the training to discuss how things progressed.

385. An interpreter tells you she needs to talk to you about an assignment confidentially. No names, dates, or places are given, but you soon figure out who the deaf person is by the description. She's concerned that it's unethical for her to even discuss this with you, but she says she's distraught. You assure her you'll never tell a soul (except your sister, who is also an interpreter and whom you trust not to say a word).

386. Every week for months, you have interpreted a long-standing counseling appointment on Thursdays. This Thursday you can't make it, and the deaf client knows you'll be finding a substitute. You arrange for another nationally certified interpreter to cover for you, and she wants to know the nature of the counseling sessions before she commits in case there's a conflict of interest. You're a little nervous about telling her too many details but think her reasoning makes sense. Soon her questions and interest have gone beyond deciding whether she's comfortable with the job. Now she's just plain being nosy.

387. On a break from an interpreting assignment in a hospital, you run down to the cafeteria for lunch. You run into several deaf people who say they come there all the time because the food is great and reasonably priced. They ask whom you're there to interpret for today.

388. One day a deaf friend of yours, whom you know to be very promiscuous, informs you she has tested positive for AIDS. She asks you to interpret a doctor's appointment for her because she doesn't want any chance of this leaking out. When the doctor asks her to list her previous sex partners, the list is quite extensive and contains names of other deaf friends of yours, both male and female.

389. Over the past few months, you have been interpreting for a deaf client attending Alcoholics Anonymous (AA) meetings. One night you and some friends go out to a restaurant, and you see the client sitting at the bar, barely coherent. You still have enough time to slip out of the restaurant before the deaf man spots you. You think this might save both of you some embarrassment, but what in the world are you going to tell your friends?

390. The high school deaf student for whom you interpret likes to think he's part of the "in" crowd. He often tells you about drugs being passed around at the parties he attends. He does in fact hang out with a rough crowd, so maybe his stories are true. One day the school principal approaches you and tells you the deaf student and a group of his friends have been picked up by the cops for selling drugs. The principal asks if you know anything about the student using drugs.

391. The mother of a deaf student in high school for whom you interpret is your childhood friend. You're not close anymore, but one day she asks you to lunch. She tells you she's worried about her daughter and her new boyfriend. They stay out beyond curfew, and she's worried they're sleeping together. She wants to know what you have seen at school.

392. Two high school deaf students for whom you interpret sit next to each other in every class and are very good friends. The teacher asks one of the girls to go out in the hall so he can talk to her alone. You go with them to interpret, and when you come back, you're by yourself. The other deaf student asks you what happened in the hall.

393. While at the Deaf club enjoying yourself, a group of deaf people at another table calls you over to ask about the condition of one of their deaf friends who is in the hospital. She has told one of them you were her interpreter.

394. While interpreting a deaf student's statement to the police in the principal's office, you suddenly realize that the teacher the student is accusing of molesting her is also your daughter's teacher.

395. While interpreting a parent/teacher conference, the deaf student's deaf mom turns to you and tells you she knows her daughter trusts you. That is why she wants you to tell her if you know whether her daughter's having sex so she can take steps to make sure she's protected. She assures you she won't confront her daughter; she just wants to get her on birth control rather than risk a teenage pregnancy.

396. While interpreting for a young deaf woman at a doctor's office, she's given the results of her AIDS test. She tests positive and becomes very upset. She tells the doctor she hates men and says, "Now they're all going to pay." A few weeks later, you see the same woman out partying at a night club. One of the guys you're with zeros in on her, says, "Tonight is my lucky night," and heads over to meet her. He says, "Wish me luck!"

397. You have just interpreted for a sick, deaf client in the hospital who has elected to spend his remaining days at home. He doesn't want anyone to know that he's dying. A mutual friend calls you wanting to plan a surprise party for him when he gets home.

398. While interpreting in a mental health setting, you suddenly make a connection between your deaf client and a friend of yours who works for him. Your friend is ready to quit her job because she says this guy has terrible mood swings. The psychiatrist is prescribing some medication for the deaf man that he says will make a big difference within a few weeks. You hope your friend can hang on.

399. While waiting in the doctor's office with the deaf client, you find out through casual conversation that she grew up in the same neighborhood as your husband. Her brothers were good friends with your husband, but she never knew your husband. She tells you all about what her brothers are doing now, and when you get home, you're dying to tell your husband. You wonder if that would be breaking confidentiality.

400. You accompany a deaf actor to a Hollywood gathering. As the evening progresses, the actor meets an interesting woman who knows a little sign language. The two become friendly, and so he asks you to leave them alone for the rest of the evening. On your way out, a reporter lurking in the bushes asks you to comment about the "happily" married deaf actor and the young starlet he's with now.

401. You have been interpreting for a deaf girl in a vocational training program for several months. Every day she complains about her home life. It sounds like normal teenage angst to you. One day she doesn't show up for school, and after a week the principal tells you she has run away from home. He asks you if you have any idea why she might have left home.

402. You have been interpreting for months for a deaf couple getting counseling from a marriage counselor. You have a lot of respect for this counselor because of how much he accomplished with this couple. One day a deaf friend tells you she and her husband are having problems and asks you to recommend a counselor.

403. You have had a rough day. The deaf student for whom you interpret in a college math class failed his first test. He told his instructor that he failed the test because you don't interpret the information clearly in class. The professor plans to call your supervisor to set up a meeting. You're really bummed when you meet your best friend for dinner. She wants to know what is up with you and promises to just listen and not tell a soul.

404. You have just finished interpreting a company's upper management meeting regarding the company's future. It has been rumored in the community that the company is selling out, and this will affect thousands of people in the community, one of whom is your favorite aunt. You know she would be eternally grateful if you told her what you learned in that meeting. All the employees have been anxiously waiting to find out if they still have jobs.

405. You have just finished interpreting a two-week, summer school, sleep-over program held at a university. As you and the deaf teenager are waiting for her dad to pick her up, she begs you not to tell her dad about a minor infraction of the rules that occurred with her friends. Chances are the director of the program has already called her parents, but the student says she wants to tell her dad herself on the way home.

406. You have just finished interpreting an assignment where both the defense and prosecuting attorneys are very high-profile. Your husband is currently in law school, and that night he asks you for details on how these two lawyers handled the case. The deaf client is a friend of both of yours.

407. You have just finished interpreting in a courtroom, and a deaf woman approaches you in the hall and says it was her husband for whom you just interpreted in court. She knew he was supposed to be in court today, but she didn't want him to know she was there because he would be mad. She begs you to tell her what was decided because she doesn't trust him to tell her the truth.

408. You have just interpreted for a young deaf couple who just found out, not only are they pregnant, they're having twins. Everyone, including you, left the office on an emotional high. You have a few errands to run, and you run into the wife's deaf mother at the store. She says she knows you always interpret for her daughter, so she asks you how the doctor's appointment went today.

409. You're an ITP student getting practicum hours at a mainstream junior high school. One weekend you and some of your classmates go to a Deaf club, and you see one of the deaf students from your practicum there with her deaf parents. She introduces you to her parents and then runs off to play. Right.away her mother starts grilling you about her daughter's progress in school.

410. You're asked to take over interpreting a counseling assignment at a county mental health facility. The previous interpreter is stepping down because she admits she doesn't feel qualified to continue. You accept and she gives you a little background information to better prepare you. After several sessions, the deaf client tells his psychiatrist he's infected with the HIV virus. A few weeks later the initial interpreter contacts you and asks how things are working out. You can tell she's fishing for information.

411. You're at a classy social event on a Saturday night at a hotel. A friend is introducing you around and steers you over to another couple. Before you recognize the woman, she recognizes you and says, "Oh, we already know each other. She interprets for me every week in Weight Watchers."

412. You're brought in from the outside to a closed meeting of a state government agency for the Deaf where budget cuts are being discussed. A good friend of yours works for the agency, and her job is one of those to possibly be eliminated. During the meeting, they discuss the strengths and weaknesses of each position, and it turns out your friend's job is safe. Your friend and you have dinner plans that evening, but she's good and doesn't ask you to divulge any information. You know, though, she's extremely worried about job security. You hate to see her going through all this anxiety when you know that her job is safe.

413. You're hired to interpret an OB-GYN appointment. The deaf client is 15 years old and sexually active with her 16-year-old boyfriend. She tells the doctor she thinks she may be pregnant. The tests come back positive and immediately she starts talking about getting an abortion. Afterwards she asks you to please not tell anyone about her condition.

414. You're interpreting a stockholders meeting where they're discussing things like salaries, upcoming developments, and profit projections. You finish early, so you call your husband and ask him to meet you around the corner for an early dinner. The company for which you just interpreted is your husband's company's main competition. His company is having some financial problems right now, and you know what you heard this morning in the meeting might make a big difference to your family's future.

415. You're interpreting at a doctor's office when a deaf teenager finds out that she's pregnant. On Sunday you see her mother at church, and she asks you what medicine the doctor gave her daughter for her "flu" because she didn't see any prescription.

416. You're interpreting for a deaf couple at their doctor's office. The husband is explaining to the doctor how much they want children and that they have been trying to start a family for months. This is the wife's second marriage, and she obviously hasn't told her new husband everything about her past. You interpreted for her several years ago when she had her tubes tied. She doesn't make eye contact with you at all.

417. You're interpreting for a deaf person in the process of getting a $100,000 life insurance policy. The deaf person currently looks healthy but has had some health problems in the past that you have interpreted. He has been HIV positive for the last five years. His HIV status, though, never comes up during the interviews.

418. You're interpreting for a deaf woman in a doctor's office when she finds out she needs some major surgery. She tells the doctor that she doesn't want her husband to know about it until she has some time to think about it. At home that night, you get a relay call from the deaf woman's husband who demands you tell him why his wife is so upset.

419. You're one of the interpreters in a high-profile murder case. It's all over the news, and every day when you walk out of the courtroom, reporters bombard you with questions. On your answering machine at home, you get a call from "The Jerry Springer Show" offering you a princely sum to appear on his show to talk about the case.

420. Your brother is a stockbroker and is constantly trying to get you to invest in the market; however, you're definitely on the conservative side. One day you're interpreting for a deaf woman and her stockbroker over the phone. The deaf woman has tripled her money in a very short time on a new stock. That night your brother is over for dinner, and he starts in on you again about buying some solid, blue chip stocks. Instead, you surprise him by saying you want to invest all your savings in the stock you learned about today. He's stunned and questions you on why and how you decided on that particular stock.

421. Your husband's boss has a deaf teenage daughter. The girl attends weekly counseling sessions which you interpret. Your husband comes home one night and says his boss is pressuring him to find out from you what is happening at his daughter's sessions.

422. A small group of ITP students are working together at a practicum site. Afterwards you all go to lunch. During lunch one of your fellow students begins to talk about another practicum site she attends every week. Another student, who needs practicum hours, begins asking the first student questions about the site to see if she can come too. Names, dates, and places are discussed.

423. Some deaf friends of yours will soon be celebrating their 10th anniversary. The husband asks you to accompany him to a travel agency to interpret, as he plans to take his wife on a surprise cruise to the Bahamas. Afterwards he writes you a personal check for your services. Later that week his wife comes to your home and demands to know what your relationship is with her husband. She has found out that he wrote you a sizeable check from their personal checking account, and she wants to know exactly for what.

424. You get a call from an interpreter referral agency to interpret this coming Thursday for a Deaf client. You check your calendar and you see you're already scheduled to interpret for that same client at the same time but somewhere else. The deaf client has hired you directly, so you're fairly confident your site is where the deaf client will actually be.

425. You have just finished an interpreting assignment that you think you may have really botched. You don't know what you should do next. You call another interpreter to ask her advice, mentioning no specific names, dates, or places, just the dilemma and possible solutions. The interpreter tells you she won't discuss anything with you because she considers it unethical to discuss interpreting jobs.

426. You have just interpreted an Individualized Educational Planning Committee (IEPC) meeting for a deaf student and her deaf parents. It turned out to be quite a heated debate over what services the deaf student should receive and the quality of interpreters in the school system. Afterwards another staff interpreter at your school comes up and asks you what went on in the IEPC meeting because she saw the deaf student's parents storm out of the building earlier.

427. You interpret every week for a deaf person attending Alcoholics Anonymous (AA) meetings. Your next-door neighbor also attends, but so far it hasn't been a problem. Today, however, he comes over to your house under the pretense of borrowing something. It soon becomes obvious his real goal is to grill you about your cute deaf client.

428. You recently interpreted for a wealthy, elderly deaf man in his lawyer's office when he made out his will. He has decided to leave his estate to his cats unless his only living relative, his deaf niece, is married by the time he dies. He states he has no intention of informing her about this. This same niece is a friend of yours.

429. You walk in the house, and your husband is upset. You were interpreting in an emergency room, and the assignment ran way over what you expected. Now dinner is cold, and your husband says he doesn't understand why your interpreting jobs always seem to run overtime. As you try to explain, you feel like the bounds of confidentiality are beginning to slip a little too much.

430. You're one of the few nationally certified interpreters in your area. One day you're interpreting for a deaf client who has brought along a hearing friend. On break, the friend asks whether you interpret for another deaf friend of his who is currently in prison. You do, so you don't want to lie, but you don't want to break confidentiality either.

431. You've been interpreting regularly at a hospital for a very sick deaf child. Today the child died, and you come home obviously upset. Your husband is very concerned. It seems almost inhuman not to be able to say even one thing about what happened and how you feel.

432. You happen to be very good friends with a 16-year-old deaf boy's parents. He's in an inpatient treatment program for a drinking problem. The clinic utilizes you for all their interpreting needs. You feel like you can be objective in this situation, but every day his parents call you at home asking you how their son is doing.

433. From time to time you interpret at a children's hospital with mostly terminally ill kids. You have just finished interpreting a radiation therapy session for a little deaf girl who is dying of cancer. As you're leaving the girl's hospital room, an elderly man approaches you and says he's from the Make-A-Wish Foundation. He asks you if the little girl would be a good candidate for their organization.

434. You're interpreting for a deaf person applying for a job. From previous interpreting assignments with this client, you know he takes lithium for his manic depression. The client knows he will be given a drug screening and tells you he has stopped taking his medication in order to pass the drug test. During the interview, the client, who is normally very articulate and competent, becomes agitated and incomplete. Suddenly in the middle of a response to a question, he abruptly gets up and says he's going to the bathroom. As he leaves the room, the potential employers turns to you and asks you what's wrong.

435. You're the interpreter for a deaf woman who was witness to a robbery and testified in court. Following the court appearance, you're on your way out to your car when a news reporter recognizes you and requests an interview to educate the public about Deaf people. When you hesitate, he assures you that anything said in a courtroom is public domain anyway.

436. You're interpreting for a young deaf couple recently married but now in need of some marriage counseling with their pastor. You're not their regular church interpreter, but that's fine because they wanted someone from outside their faith. Their regular interpreter's nose is out of joint, though, and she calls you at home under the pretext of looking for advice on something else. You can tell, however, she's just dying to ask you about the counseling sessions.

437. A well-known deaf person in your community has recently passed away, and the cause of death is not announced. The family requests a small private funeral at which you interpret. The rumor mill has it the deaf man was a closet homosexual and that he died of AIDS. People keep asking you if you're going to interpret the funeral so you can tell them what he really died of.

438. After much prodding from a deaf friend, you agree to go out on a blind date. The blind date however turns out to be none other than the hearing husband of a deaf client for whom you interpreted in marriage counseling last week. You immediately grab your deaf friend and pull her into the ladies room. She asks, "What in the world is the matter with you?"

439. After interpreting for a deaf woman receiving cancer treatment, you walk back out into the waiting room. Her family comes up to you and starts asking all kinds of questions about how she's feeling and what the doctor has said about her prognosis, etc.

440. Early one morning you interpret for a deaf client who is told she's pregnant. Later that same day, you get a call to interpret in an emergency room. It turns out to be the same deaf woman, who's been brought in unconscious from a drug overdose. You know that mentioning to the doctors that she's pregnant may be an important factor in treating this woman.

441. A deaf woman at the church where you interpret comes up to you and tells you this is her last Sunday. She has found another church she prefers to attend. You continue to interpret every week at the church, and one Sunday the pastor comes up

to you and asks specifically if you know what happened to the deaf woman. He says he hasn't seen her in a few weeks.

442. You're interpreting for a deaf client who is undergoing physical rehabilitation at a hospital. You and your family attend the same church as the client. Because you're one of the few people at church who can communicate directly with this deaf person, everyone assumes you're also privy to every detail of his life. Well-meaning, fellow parishioners grill you at church every Sunday about how well the client is responding to treatment and when she will be back.

443. You have been interpreting for a very popular deaf girl attending weekly counseling sessions in school. She has recently gotten pregnant and is seeking information about how to get an abortion. One day her parents come to school specifically to see the girl's counselor, but she's out sick that day. The principal calls you in to talk to them instead.

444. You're interpreting at a visitation center for a 9-year-old deaf boy who is having a supervised visit with his hearing father, who doesn't know sign language. He's only allowed supervised visits two times a month because of allegations of child abuse. During today's visit, the boy's father is telling his son that the pressure of having a deaf child is what caused his marriage to fall apart. While you're interpreting this, you see the look of devastation on the boy's face, but he stoically says nothing. After his father leaves, the boy's mother arrives, and the boy starts crying uncontrollably. She demands you tell her what her ex-husband said to upset her son!

445. You're interpreting for a young deaf girl who finds out from her doctor that she has a sexually transmitted disease. Her mother is in the waiting room, but because she's over 18, the doctor says he won't tell her mom. He gives her several prescriptions and then you're done. In the waiting room, the girl's mom demands to know what the doctor said is wrong with her. The daughter refuses to tell her, and so the mother pounces on you for information.

446. You're scheduled to interpret for a 14-year-old deaf girl for a routine physical with her physician. The girl tells her mom she's old enough to see the doctor alone and to wait in the waiting room. While in with the doctor, she asks him for information about birth control. He gives her a few pamphlets and says he can't prescribe anything without parental consent. The girl tells him her mom would kill her if she knew she was even asking. Afterwards as you're all leaving the doctor's office, one of the pamphlets falls to the floor. The girl's mother picks it up and assumes it's yours. She looks at it more closely and angrily says she doesn't appreciate you exposing her daughter to such "pornographic material."

Challenges in Being Privy to More Information (About a Situation) Than Is Being Interpreted

- **Scenario 447.** I am interpreting a medical appointment, and while the deaf patient is getting undressed, I step into the hall. I overhear the nurse and doctor laughing, and the nurse says it looks like Sea World because the patient looks like Shamu the whale. I don't say anything, but when we all go back into the room together, I see them look at each other and smirk. The deaf patient, however, also sees this exchange and asks them what's so funny.

AN INTERPRETER'S PERSPECTIVE: In this situation, you're off the hook. Just translate the Deaf patient's question. Now they have the ethical dilemma. Do your job and learn from their insensitivity.

A DEAF CONSUMER'S PERSPECTIVE: I think it's important for the deaf client to have a trusting relationship with the doctor. If the doctor isn't capable of such a relationship, the client has a right to know. Place the responsibility back on the doctor and say, "The patient would like to know what is so funny."

- **Scenario 448.** I recently interpreted for a deaf woman filing an insurance claim. She claims she fell at the grocery store and can't use her left leg for six months. The following Monday, I go to my first yoga class and in walks the same deaf woman.

AN INTERPRETER'S PERSPECTIVE: I say use your discretion here. You might decide to decline any future assignments for this woman because you wouldn't be able to remain impartial. You know too much "outside" information.

A DEAF CONSUMER'S PERSPECTIVE: Avoid making judgments about the woman. Perhaps yoga is a part of her therapeutic treatment. If you know the woman well and feel that your interpreting might be affected by your suspicions, you might ask her about it casually another time.

- **Scenario 449.** I'm interpreting for a deaf man at a counseling appointment. He expresses concern that he isn't a "real man" because he and his wife have tried for years for her to become pregnant with no success. Unfortunately, I have interpreted for his wife at a doctor's appointment in the past and know she's taking birth control pills. Obviously, something doesn't add up here.

AN INTERPRETER'S PERSPECTIVE: It's not your role to empathize with the husband or condemn the wife for her deceit. This man is in counseling; let the counselor do his job and you do yours. Stay in role.

A DEAF CONSUMER'S PERSPECTIVE: You must not reveal information from other interpreted situations. It's the counselor's job to help the client, not yours.

- **Scenario 450.** Recently I was interpreting at a large hospital for a deaf man being told he needed surgery. When the doctor explained the procedure, he was very reassuring. That's why I was shocked when on my way out of the room I overheard him tell his interns that his success rate for this type of surgery is only 78 percent. No mention of that significant fact was ever made in front of the client. What are my options here?

AN INTERPRETER'S PERSPECTIVE: This appears to be a teaching hospital based on what you've said. Often discussions between physicians and interns are not intended for patients and their families. If it wasn't presented in front of the patient, then it wasn't meant for him to hear. The physician may intend to share this information at a different time, or this information may come from the surgeon during the pre-op appointment. Second guessing the motivation of a physician and his team can put interpreters into a risky place. Medicine is not perfect and the prognosis may be incorrect. If a patient approaches the procedure based on information given to him, their recovery rate may improve based on their positive attitude.

A DEAF CONSUMER'S PERSPECTIVE: This is a challenging situation. If these comments were made in the room the patient was in, even if made by the doctor under his breath, the interpreter must interpret this information to the client. If it happened in the hallway or behind a closed door, then there are two choices that are acceptable: (1) Do nothing. You need to ask yourself this question: If the patient was hearing, would he have missed this information as well? Perhaps there is a reason that the doctor did not tell the patient this percentage. If the patient really wanted to know the success rate, he could have asked himself, but maybe he didn't want to know. A recent article in the "New York Times" discussed the impact of a message of "false hopelessness" given by doctors to their patients. Studies found that doctors, in an effort to avoid lawsuits, are giving patients bad news and this sense of hopelessness. Patients who do not have hope often will set low expectations for themselves and do not do well. Whereas, patients who have been given hope by their doctors and believe the outcome will be best often do much better. Perhaps that is what the doctor is trying to do in this situation. (2) Because the interpreter was within earshot of the doctor, she could say, "Oh, I'm sorry; I didn't interpret that information to the patient. Would you like to explain that and I will come back into the room with you?" Hopefully, the doctor will, but if not, you should leave it alone. The information may come out in another pre-operative meeting, or the client may look it up on his own.

Other Scenarios

Identify the issue(s) involved and decide how you would respond. Discuss and compare your responses with your colleagues.

451. A deaf couple from out of state is house hunting, and you have been asked to interpret for them as they drive around town with a realtor. The couple seems to have fallen in love with one house, and the realtor really starts pushing the couple to "grab it because it won't last long." Having lived in the area most of your life, you know this house has been on the market for almost a year, and in your opinion, it's still way overpriced.

452. A deaf couple is buying a house and you're hired to interpret for their mortgage application. It's obvious from their expressions that they're shocked when they're told about all the extra expenses involved in getting a mortgage. When the loan officer leaves the room for a minute to make some photocopies, they turn and ask your opinion about this company's rates. Actually, you do know about another bank that currently has lower rates with fewer expenses.

453. During a meeting between a deaf woman accused of child abuse and her lawyer, the attorney excuses himself for a moment and leaves the room to attend to an urgent matter. During the meeting the client has consistently denied any wrongdoing, claiming she's a poor, misunderstood woman who loves her children and would do anything for them. While the lawyer is out of the room, the deaf woman starts complaining bitterly about the children and what a "pain in the ass" the kids are. When the attorney walks back in the room, the deaf woman reverts to her meek and submissive demeanor.

454. You're scheduled to interpret for a deaf client meeting with a loan officer. The client is told that the officer scheduled to meet with her is ill but to wait and someone else will be meeting with her shortly. In walks the replacement loan officer, and it's none other than a man you once dated. To say that the relationship ended badly would be an understatement, but he doesn't bat an eye when he sees you. However, he's being a total idiot toward the deaf client, and you can't help but think there's some connection.

455. Last month you interpreted for a deaf college student for a meeting at school where she signed up to study abroad next year. Today, you're interpreting for the same student at a job fair on campus. She tells you she needs to save some money for the fall when she goes abroad. She's interviewing with a potential employer who wants his employees to commit to more than just the summer. He says he doesn't want to waste his time and money on training people who leave at the end of the summer, and he asks her if that will be a problem. Without missing a beat, she tells him that will be fine.

456. The deaf high school student for whom you interpret doesn't pay attention in class. His teachers constantly have to remind him to pay attention, and he's failing his classes. At his Individualized Educational Planning Committee (IEPC) meeting, his parents insist their son doesn't need an interpreter.

457. While interpreting for a deaf man at his doctor's office, he's told he needs to have a series of tests done as soon as possible. When the receptionist calls the lab, she tells the client that they have an opening if he can get there in 20 minutes. The next opening is not for another two weeks. The lab is across town and the receptionist gives him directions. You interpret the directions, but since you live on that side of town, you know that if he follows those directions, he'll never get there in time.

458. While interpreting in a college math class, the instructor keeps inverting the "more than" and "less than" symbols in his problems. You can't help but notice that all the students in the class look confused, including the deaf student.

459. You have been interpreting at a high school for years, and you're fairly attuned to what is going on at the school. One day you're interpreting for a deaf student who has two college interviews on campus. During the first interview, the student tells the interviewer he's the senior class treasurer. In the second interview, he tells the interviewer he's the senior class president. You know neither to be true.

460. You have interpreted numerous times for a Deaf-blind client who gradually lost his sight over the years. He makes wooden toys and furniture by touch, and a couple of times a year he takes his things to sell at arts and crafts shows. He has asked you to interpret people's questions at a show, and you see someone try to give him a five dollar bill instead of a twenty.

461. You know a lot about cars, and so you're asked by a deaf friend to accompany her while she test drives some used cars at a dealer. The salesperson shows the client one car's engine and raves about what great shape it's in. You can see that the engine has been cleaned but that most of the parts are worn, and overall the engine is in bad shape. Obviously, the sales person is hoping your deaf friend knows nothing about engines.

462. You're interpreting a health intake for a deaf prisoner, and the man is only able to communicate through incredibly slow and laborious fingerspelling. He answers all the nurse's questions correctly, but he repeatedly mixes up his "d's" and "f's," which you know is a common mistake hearing students make when they're just learning to fingerspell. That sets off a warning bell in your head, and so you fingerspell, "Your mama wears combat boots," instead of the nurse's next question. The prisoner doesn't bat an eye and answers the nurse's question appropriately. You ask him about his mama again for the next couple of questions, and the prisoner instead responds to the nurse's verbal questions appropriately.

463. You're interpreting an intake evaluation at an abortion clinic. The deaf client is asked how many terminations she has had in the past. The nurse explains there are possible ramifications if a woman has had more than two terminations. You have interpreted at two previous abortions, so you know this is at least the woman's third termination. The deaf woman tells the nurse that this is her first termination.

464. You're interpreting for a psychiatrist and a deaf client meeting for the first time. The psychiatrist asks the client to tell him his family history and why he's seeking counseling. At the end of the session, the psychiatrist tells the client that he's very pleased with their progress and that he feels he got a lot of valuable information. However, having known this deaf client almost all your life, you know that not one word of the "valuable information" is even remotely close to the truth.

465. You're sent to interpret for a deaf couple who are meeting with a fertility specialist. When you meet the couple, you recognize the husband as someone you interpreted for years ago when he had a vasectomy. The doctor informs the couple that the tests show that the reason they can't conceive a child is because the husband is sterile. The wife begins to cry, and the husband acts surprised.

466. While sitting in the doctor's waiting room for almost an hour, the deaf client spends the whole time telling you about his symptoms. When you finally get in to see the doctor, the man barely says anything and won't answer the doctor's questions.

467. You arrive at a hospital to interpret for a deaf couple you have known for years. The husband has suffered a severe stroke and is completely paralyzed. When the doctor asks the wife what measures she wants taken to save her husband's life, you're surprised to hear her say, "Do whatever it takes. I don't want him to die." You know the very topic has been discussed by the couple in your presence, and quite the contrary was decided.

468. You're asked to interpret in a medical setting for a deaf man for whom you interpreted when he was in high school. The doctor is going to prescribe some

medication for his depression. When the doctor asks him if he has ever taken any medication for this condition, he says "no." You know, however, that this is untrue because you used to interpret for him years ago when he tried to commit suicide.

469. You're interpreting for a deaf client who is having a cyst removed from her cervix and the doctor is using electrocautery. The client says she can smell something burning, and the doctor laughs and says the burning smell is "her." The client's face freezes in horror. She doesn't say anything else. She's terrified, but the doctor doesn't know because he can't see her face.

470. You're interpreting for a deaf patient at a doctor's office. The patient has listed a whole set of symptoms and complaints, and after several tests, the doctor prescribes heart medication. The doctor asks the deaf man if he's taking any other medication and the patient answers "no." However, you have also interpreted for this client every week in a mental health setting and know he's taking psychotropic medication.

471. During a psych evaluation, the client was asked who his social worker was. The client said he didn't know. I am a CDI, and since I have interpreted for this client many times, I know the name of the social worker. However, I didn't say anything. Right after the psych evaluation, the client met with his attorney, and the attorney asked him the exact same question. He spelled her name perfectly. I suspect he just didn't want to answer before.

Challenges Related to Stepping Out of the Interpreter Role

- **Scenario 472.** Recently I was interpreting in court for a deaf client who was meeting for the first time with his court appointed attorney. He is required to attend counseling, but I feel he truly does not have the wherewithal to know where to begin to find a counselor for himself. His attorney is unfamiliar with community resources as well, so they both turned to me for help. My primary job is to facilitate communication, but obviously I know people and places they could call. In your opinion, how far can interpreters go to bridge the gap?

AN INTERPRETER'S PERSPECTIVE: Yes, the interpreter's primary job is to facilitate communication. However, we are also cultural-mediators, and because of our experience, background, education, etc., we may have information that will help facilitate the communication between two (or more) parties. I believe that sharing community resources *is* facilitating communication — a part of our job, especially if the parties involved have been referred to you for your assistance. If you feel uncomfortable giving information at that time, you can refer them to a place/person (community services for the Deaf) who could give them the same information. I've done this in the past and it was always welcomed by both parties.

A DEAF CONSUMER'S PERSPECTIVE: Interpreters often have information about various referral and service agencies that deaf people themselves may not know about. If the interpreter knows the community and the available resources, she can certainly state and provide that information in a manner which does not detract from the first priority of facilitating communication. In this situation, both the deaf person and the attorney looked to the interpreter for help, so I think it is very appropriate for the interpreter to provide that information, unless doing so would create a conflict of interest. Specific information could be provided right then or could be deferred to the end of the meeting when the interpreting has been completed. It would not be appropriate, however, for an interpreter to stop interpreting, interrupt a dialog that the deaf person and the attorney were having about the need for counseling to interject that you, the interpreter, have information on where those services can be obtained. In general, though, I do believe that it is well within the interpreter's purview to provide community referral information when asked.

- **Scenario 473.** I am an ITP practicum student doing some observation at a middle school. I arrive before the interpreter with whom I work, and the deaf student comes in and shows me several large bruises. I ask her what happened and she starts crying. She signs, "My father — no, I mean I fell down the stairs. It was my fault!"

AN INTERPRETER'S PERSPECTIVE: Tell the child you're concerned about her and will ask her mentor to talk with her when she arrives. You should try not to show the alarm you feel, and reassure the child that you won't talk about this to other students or anyone other than her mentor. The school most likely has policies for handling this type of situation, which need to be followed strictly. If you don't know what your responsibilities are, you should ask the mentor.

A DEAF CONSUMER'S PERSPECTIVE: I would ask the teacher if there has been evidence of abuse in the child's home life. Even if the teacher told me not to get involved, I would probably go to the school counselor and report it. I don't think it's wrong to intervene when a child's safety is at stake.

- **Scenario 474.** I don't think interpreters always remember who the boss is. I recently had an interpreter who presumed too much. She tried to set up my future doctor appointment based on her schedule. (It is *my* appointment. It should be *my* schedule). She obviously assumed my future plans included her as the interpreter. Apparently, enough of her clients allow her to do this kind of inappropriate behavior. How do we stop interpreters from treating us like children?

AN INTERPRETER'S PERSPECTIVE: It sounds like your interpreter prematurely dropped out of her interpreter role and became an interpreter coordinator. Whether that was because she was a self-employed interpreter and didn't want to lose a revenue opportunity or felt she was the only interpreter who could interpret for you, whatever the reason, it doesn't matter. I am sorry you had to experience that. I do not condone this interpreter's behavior. In my opinion, the interpreter should have stayed in her role throughout the interaction while you were scheduling your next appointment. This would have empowered you to make your own decisions as to when to schedule your next appointment. If you used an agency for this appointment, I would make sure that they were made aware of the situation and you have a profile filled out with your preferences of interpreters. Please do not judge all interpreters from this one experience. I would ask you, the deaf consumer, to help those of us who know how to stay within our roles by stepping forward and confronting those few interpreters who forget. You can empower yourself (and other deaf consumers) by taking control in these situations and letting the hearing consumer know what you want if (or when) the interpreter is out of line and that you want to be consulted as to which date works best for you.

A DEAF CONSUMER'S PERSPECTIVE: We all have to understand the balance of a finite number of human resources available to us; interpreters do not fall out of the sky like lawyers and doctors. The reality is that there are always going to be unfilled interpreting assignments. This is due to the ongoing problem of a lack of qualified interpreters. Interpreters are more able to provide services to more consumers when consumers and interpreters both are willing to work out scheduling together. This makes much more efficient use of the interpreter's availability. Your interpreter may have assumed a positive consumer-interpreter rapport exists between you two just because you utilize her services. However, this is no different from the doctor you are seeing who assumes you will return to see her for future appointments. It sounds like your appointment may be a recurring one. If so, there are benefits to using the same interpreter for your recurring appointments, as the interpreter has the cumulative contextual knowledge to interpret effectively for you. This may be why she took charge and offered her availability of specific times for the next appointment. Neither deaf consumers nor interpreters are the "boss." You may be coloring your interpreter negatively because she made a different assumption than you. There is no way I can speculate without being there myself as to why she exhibited this behavior toward you, but I do recommend that you have a heart-to-heart talk with her about it. Go ahead and assert your feelings and expectation of her as a professional. You, the consumer, have a lot of clout in interpreter selections for future appointments requiring interpreter services.

- **Scenario 475.** I recently was hired to interpret for a lecture being given to health care professionals. The lecture included some tips on how to work with the interpreter (e.g., talk directly to the deaf patient, don't ask the interpreter questions about the deaf patient, everything said will be interpreted, everything signed will be voiced). We (my team interpreter and I) were on stage and when one of us was "off," she sat in the front row of the auditorium. The deaf speaker was very knowledgeable, and there were many questions from the audience. One question was specifically about the interpreting profession, and so the presenter asked my partner to come up on stage and answer the question in detail. The next question from the audience was also about the interpreting profession, and so my partner took over interpreting while I answered the question. I told the audience that I wasn't used to answering questions while working, but because the speaker had given me permission, I would. However, I needed the question repeated so I could process it. After the assignment I could tell my partner was miffed by my response. I have felt badly and wonder if I made the other interpreter look bad and myself look arrogant with my comment?

AN INTERPRETER'S PERSPECTIVE: I am not sure why your partner was miffed. When you first saw that she seemed upset, that was the best time to find out what was wrong; however, it is never too late to resolve bad feelings. Tell her that she seemed upset about something after you made your comments on stage. You weren't sure if you should say something at the time, but now you would like to find out if it was something you said. Another possibility is that your partner was upset she didn't get to answer both questions. This seems petty; she was the first one to be asked to comment, and she should have been flattered. You said, "The presenter asked my partner to come up on stage and answer the question." This tells me she was not interpreting at the time she was asked to comment, so she shouldn't feel personally criticized by what you said. Perhaps she was angry because you said something with which she disagreed. If so, you may want to speak to her about which statement upset her. When you know what it was, you can explain why you feel the way you do and ask for feedback. It could be she realized after you spoke that she did something wrong and displaced her anger onto you, although she had only herself to blame. She should not be angry with you for having your own opinion about something, but it might be good to know where you differ in case you have to team with her again. The two of you need to either come to some acceptable compromise or agree to disagree and not team together. This incident underscores how important it is for all of us to have a discussion before team interpreting about: how and when to take turns, how long the turns will be, whether the partner wants an active feed, how each partner likes to be fed, and so on. One suggestion I have put into practice is to have a pad of paper so my teammate and I can write notes back and forth when either of us is not the principal interpreter. Your partner should also learn to "share rather than glare." That is, tell her teammate what she needs, and what is bothering her, as well as make the effort to work things out. Although we strive to be experts in other people's communication, we often are so used to staying out of the picture that we don't know what to do when we need to communicate our needs, even when this would be beneficial.

A DEAF CONSUMER'S PERSPECTIVE: Since the deaf client is the one who gave your partner (and you) permission to step out of the roles, she (and you) did the right thing by answering the questions from the audience. It sounds to me, in your "teachable moment" with the audience about the role of an interpreter, you came off sounding like you were also subtly (or not so subtly perhaps) reprimanding your partner for jumping right in. It isn't your place to do that. The client took his chances with her answer, as well as knew that you were left alone without a team while she did it. By saying she answered "in detail" must mean apparently she took quite a bit of time responding. For you to then get on the microphone and point out something interpreters shouldn't do while working is poor form. If you're looking for me to say you did the right thing and your partner shouldn't be miffed, I can't. I'd be miffed too for judging me, in front of an audience no less.

- **Scenario 476.** I interpret for a college student who has recently lost a lot of weight. She often complains about being unable to sleep or eat, and she always looks like she is about to start crying. She is over 18. Do I say or do anything?

AN INTERPRETER'S PERSPECTIVE: As someone who worked at a university for many years, I can say that the answer to this is probably not one you will like. If it is a public university and the student is 18 years of age or older, all you can really do is offer resources. Even then, I would only recommend this if you felt you had a relationship with her beyond interpreter-consumer. Every school with which I have dealt has some sort of free counseling service for students. Therefore, if you felt comfortable, perhaps you could pass along a brochure. If it is a private university, there is a little more flexibility, and in that case I would talk with the professor. The professor should have a better idea of what can be done, and it may be more appropriate for her to be the one to initiate that conversation with the student with you serving in your role as interpreter. Unless the student becomes a true danger to herself or others, there is little else that can be done due to confidentiality concerns regarding the client.

A DEAF CONSUMER'S PERSPECTIVE: There seems to be a lot going on in this student's life. If she threatens to hurt herself or commit suicide, that is something that would need to be reported to the proper authorities. The confidentiality of the client is superseded by the health and welfare of the client. The same holds true for reporting child abuse situations. As a human being first and an interpreter second, I believe that you can give her some options regarding how to help herself. If she does not follow any of your advice, that is her prerogative.

Other Scenarios

Identify the issue(s) involved and decide how you would respond. Discuss and compare your responses with your colleagues.

477. You're interpreting for a deaf woman getting her stitches removed following breast reduction surgery. The doctor turns to you and says, "Come here and look at my work of art!"

478. You're interpreting for a deaf client at her workplace where she's the only deaf employee. She seems to have minimal interaction with her coworkers. After the meeting they announce a buffet will be served in the cafeteria. The deaf woman says she doesn't want to eat alone and asks you to please come eat with her.

479. You're interpreting for a deaf woman having a baby with only the assistance of a midwife. The baby's arrival comes rather quickly, and the midwife starts asking you to help her. Things are not going well. The midwife insists the Lord will provide. Meanwhile, you're becoming very nervous about your involvement in this in the first place.

480. A deaf woman asks you to interpret for her and her husband for birthing classes. The local hospital provides these classes, so you know the hospital should be required to provide an interpreter. Your friend is offering to pay you herself because she doesn't know to request an interpreter through the hospital.

481. You have been interpreting regularly for a deaf woman who is terminally ill going in for various treatments. One day after a doctor's appointment, she asks you if you would please go with her and help her shop for her casket.

482. You are interpreting for a deaf woman applying for some financial aid at a community college. The woman and the financial aid officer are filling out the forms together. Using the figures that the deaf woman provided the financial aid officer, it's soon very clear that after 15 years of working for the same company the Deaf woman's earnings are incredibly meager. The financial aid officer turns to you and says, "Don't you think Mary needs a good attorney? She's clearly being taken advantage of at her workplace."

483. A deaf client has just finished her first OB-GYN appointment and can't wait to get out of there. On your way out, you stop to go to the bathroom. On your way out to your car, the nurse comes running out to the parking lot hoping to catch the deaf client. Apparently, they need another form filled out, and she asks if you would mind coming back in and filling it out.

484. A deaf couple is meeting with a counselor to discuss various options for job retraining. The husband has recently been diagnosed with Usher's Syndrome and needs to start making plans for the future. The deaf man hasn't told his employer about his condition yet and is afraid he will be fired when they find out. The counselor is urging the deaf man to hurry and tell his employer so he can get release time from work to go back to school. The wife turns to you and asks you in all earnestness what you think they should do.

485. A deaf student has been caught cheating on an exam and is meeting with the principal. The principal tells the student he won't suspend him this time, but that he's sending home a note to his parents for them to sign. A few days later on the way to the principal's office the deaf student proudly shows you the signed note. You know his mom's signature, and you can tell this is a forgery.

486. A deaf woman is meeting with her supervisor, who is reprimanding her for being loud in the office. The supervisor says her coworkers are complaining about it. The deaf woman vehemently argues that this is an unfair complaint because she's deaf and can't monitor her volume. The supervisor turns to you and asks you if what she's saying is true. They both look at you for an answer.

487. A real estate agent calls you to interpret for a deaf couple interested in buying a very expensive house. She says she has checked their financial report, and they're more than qualified to afford the home. She says she thinks if she comes with an interpreter, the couple will be impressed and more likely to purchase the home. You agree to interpret, regardless of her motives, but the deaf couple decides not to buy the house. That night, the agent calls you and wants to discuss why you think the sale fell through.

488. The deaf high school girl for whom you interpret has some serious self-esteem issues. She almost never eats anything at lunch, and she's obsessed about being fat. When she sees someone else eat anything fattening, she starts talking about fat grams. It's ridiculous because she's already rail thin. Over the last three months, you begin to notice she is steadily losing weight. After lunch you walk into the bathroom and hear someone throwing up. Out of concern, you wait around to see if you can be of assistance. Out walks the deaf student. When you ask her if she's OK, she says lunch just didn't agree with her and she's fine now. You can't help thinking she might be anorexic or bulimic.

489. The elementary deaf student for whom you interpret has a history of chronic illness. One day in class, he falls and hits his head. His teacher doesn't mention it to anyone, including the school nurse. Later you see the same student holding his head, and he looks ill. The teacher doesn't seem to notice, so you bring it to her attention. She brushes it off as nothing.

490. While interpreting a counseling session between a social worker and a pregnant, unmarried, unemployed deaf woman, you're surprised to hear the social worker really pushing the deaf client to get an abortion. You know the situation looks bleak, but the social worker only seems to be giving the client one option.

491. While interpreting in a high school for a shy deaf teenage boy, he surprisingly starts asking you about how he should go about asking a classmate out on a date. You're supposed to be interpreting, but you would hate to lose this moment when he's finally opening up to someone and tell him to wait until later to talk about it.

492. You get parental permission to take a deaf student to an NTD performance. When you go to the student's home on Sunday to pick her up, you're overwhelmed by the awful stench when you walk in the house. The house is filthy, the student's hair is matted, and she's wearing the same clothes you saw her wearing on Friday.

493. You interpret the directions for the American College Test (ACT) being administered to all the high school students, and then you sit and wait until the test time is up. While waiting, you see one of the deaf students cheating off the student across from him.

494. You're interpreting a meeting between a group of deaf people and the executive director of an interpreter referral agency who is not fluent in sign language. The deaf people are complaining about several of the interpreters the agency utilizes. They tell her the interpreters have great skills but lousy attitudes. The deaf people contend they would rather have a less skilled interpreter with the right attitude than a skilled interpreter with a lousy attitude. The executive director says he doesn't understand what they mean by the "right attitude" and asks them to explain. One deaf woman points to you and says, "Like her!" She then asks you to explain what she means.

495. You're interpreting at a bank for a deaf couple inquiring about a mortgage. The bank manager leaves the room to make copies of their tax forms, and the deaf couple immediately turn to you and ask your opinion on the terms of the mortgage.

496. You're interpreting for a deaf client training for a job in a bicycle repair shop. The job involves basic repairs and odd jobs around the shop. The employer is very rude and abusive to the client and denies him any breaks. The client complains about the employer to his Vocational Rehabilitation (VR) counselor, who turns and asks you if the deaf client's allegations are true.

497. You're interpreting for a deaf client who is being given explicit instructions for taking medications that he's told he must follow exactly. Afterwards when the two of you are walking out of the doctor's office, you see the client wadding up the paper with the instructions and tossing it into the trash.

498. You're interpreting for a deaf friend who wants to buy an expensive stereo system. The salesperson explains all the different features available and then starts to pressure the deaf customer into buying the stereo from him today. It's obvious to you that the salesperson works on commission, but you can see that your friend now feels obligated to buy the stereo.

499. You're interpreting for a deaf man who lives in a group home, and he's explaining to the police how his roommate attacked him. The man's story is very difficult to follow, and the police officer keeps saying he's confused. The officer finally stops you and says, "This makes no sense. I'm not filing this report," and he leaves. The deaf man is afraid to go back to the home for fear his roommate will kill him and asks to go home with you.

500. You're interpreting for a deaf person negotiating for a new car at a dealership. The salesman steps away for a few minutes to get approval from his manager. The deaf client turns to you and asks you if you think she's getting a good deal. You always use a professional car buying company because you hate the whole negotiating process. The deaf woman is paying the sticker price from what you can see.

501. You're interpreting for a deaf woman in labor when she encounters complications and is put under anesthesia. The baby dies during the delivery, and you're the first person the deaf woman sees when she comes to. The first thing she asks is, "Where is my baby?"

502. Your deaf neighbor comes running over to your house asking if you would go with her to the vet to interpret because her cat is vomiting up blood. She tells you where her vet is, and you realize it's the same one that mistreated your dog, who later died. You found out later that he's under investigation for malpractice. You now go to a great vet who's even closer to where you both live.

503. You're interpreting a meeting between a deaf student and her professor. During the meeting the professor offers to tutor her at his home to help improve her grades, which you think is unusual. A fellow staff interpreter meets you coming out of the professor's office and asks what you think of "Professor Romeo."

504. You're interpreting for a deaf woman attending a conference at a very nice hotel. On break you go into the bathroom, and you hear some scraping and sniffing in the next stall. Your client comes out of the stall, and she's sniffing and has white powder on her nose.

505. An elderly deaf lady who lives on your block has been taken in by a phony real estate scheme and left virtually penniless. She is a proud woman and won't tell anyone, even her children. The only reason you know is because you interpreted for her when she went to an attorney to try to fight back. The attorney, however, told her there was nothing she could do. You see the woman growing more frail and thin every day, but you're not sure if it's appropriate for you to intervene.

506. You're interpreting for a deaf patient in an emergency room. He knows he's dying and his family is on the way from out of town. He's afraid they won't make it before he dies. He asks you to please listen as he tells you things he wants each of them to know in case they don't make it in time.

507. While interpreting a job interview, the interviewer asks the deaf applicant about her marital status. The single mom looks at you and says, "That's an illegal question. What should I do?"

508. You have just interpreted for a deaf boy in court alleging that his mother sexually molested him. On the way out of the courthouse, his mother comes up to you and begs to tell you her side of the story. You decline and say you need to get to another assignment. She starts sobbing and sits down on the steps as people start staring at both of you. You have always been a sucker for a woman crying and start to console her.

509. At the high school where you interpret, some of the deaf students are behind grade level, and your position allows for some one-on-one tutoring, which you really enjoy. Another interpreter in the school system confronts you and says you're ruining it for everyone else by not functioning solely as an interpreter.

510. You're interpreting a meeting, and the presenter asks you if you wouldn't mind plugging in the TV/VCR because you're seated close to an outlet. However, during the time it would take you to get up, go over to the VCR, unravel the cord from the stand, walk it over to the outlet, and then go back and sit down, you know you'll miss some information.

511. You're interpreting for a deaf team leader in a meeting who says he needs to leave the room for a moment to go back to his office to check on something. A significant amount of time later, everyone is still waiting for him to return. Finally, someone suggests you go and get him.

512. While on your way to an interpreting assignment, you are stopped by a train. Sitting in your car, you notice a man going from car to car with a sign hanging around his neck. It says, "I am deaf and homeless." He knocks on your window and shows you a tin cup. You recognize the man from the local Deaf club, and you know perfectly well that he's far from broke and definitely not homeless.

513. You're a staff interpreter interpreting a college theater class where the professor is showing the students how to dye fabric. That evening you go to the bathroom, and your urine is bright purple. You rush to the university's emergency facility and see several other students from class there as well. It turns out the dye used in class will penetrate your pores and get into your system. The students are planning to complain to the professor's boss that they weren't warned about this. They want to force the college to pay their medical bills. They ask you to join them for this meeting.

514. While interpreting a church meeting where they're budget allocating, one member of the congregation raises her hand and suggests the church buy each of the poor deaf members hearing aids so they won't need interpreters anymore. You wait for a response from the deaf parishioners, but there is none.

515. While interpreting a discussion group, the moderator makes an effort to include you in the discussion. You politely decline, but he doesn't give up easily. He insists you have relevant experience and that your comments would be helpful to the group.

516. You're team-interpreting a budget meeting for upper administration at the university where you work. A faculty member is complaining to the president about high faculty wages and excessive spending on things like new buildings. The president responds by telling the faculty member the university has hidden human expenses such as interpreter costs. He says, "For example, do you realize we're required to provide accessibility at all our meetings at $100 an hour for these interpreters?" You and your team interpreter exchange glances and wonder where that fabrication came from.

517. A deaf man whose deaf lover has recently been hospitalized asks you to interpret a phone call to his partner's doctor. He tells the doctor that he believes the hospital staff is not treating his partner kindly and suspects it's because he's deaf. The doctor disagrees. He believes it's because the staff is still uncomfortable with AIDS patients. The deaf man placing the call is in shock and doesn't say anything. Finally, the doctor suggests that the man call him back later. The deaf man is crying and tells you, all this time, he and his lover never understood the term "acquired immune deficiency syndrome" to mean AIDS. They both thought he had cancer.

518. An HIV-positive deaf patient for whom you're interpreting has just left the room for a moment to give a urine specimen. The doctor is reading over the patient's chart and turns to you and asks, "Do you think the deaf patient understands any of this?"

519. In the middle of the night, you get a call to interpret in an emergency room. A deaf patient has had a stroke, and the staff keeps telling his deaf wife that he's not going to make it. Finally, the doctor comes in with the test results and announces that her husband is going to be just fine. The deaf woman is thrilled at first, but then she's angry at all the mental anguish the staff has put her through. She tells the doctor she will be reporting this to the hospital's administration. He tells her it's not necessary as she probably just misunderstood the staff. She looks to you for confirmation of her take on the situation.

520. You're called into a hospital emergency room to interpret for a 10-year-old deaf boy who has deaf parents and was involved in a bicycle accident. The boy has suffered severe trauma to his head, and to check the boy's responses, the doctor is asking him questions such as, "Who is the vice president?" or "What is the capitol of the United States?" The boy just shrugs his shoulders to each question. The doctor becomes very concerned and suspects the worst. However, you can't help but wonder if the boy were asked questions such as, "Who is the president of the Deaf club?" or "Where is the Deaf club?" he might respond better.

521. You're interpreting at a doctor's office for a deaf patient for whom you interpret regularly in various medical situations. The doctor asks her to make a list of her medications, which she does, but she says she takes a lot and can't remember them all. She turns to you to go over her list.

522. You're interpreting for a deaf couple about to become parents. The wife's delivery is a difficult one, and suddenly you see the doctor put his foot up on the delivery table. He then quite forcefully pulls the baby out of the mother while he yells for you to get him a nurse.

523. You're interpreting for a deaf woman and her husband at her doctor's appointment. The woman finds out she's pregnant with not one, but multiple babies. The doctor informs the couple that they need to discuss the possibility of "selective reduction." The woman breaks down and says to you, "As a woman, what would you do?"

524. You're interpreting for a young deaf girl in a hospital who has minimal language competency. The child is signing predominantly with her left hand, and you see the nurse getting ready to put an IV into her left hand.

525. You're interpreting for a deaf woman making a presentation to a large audience. As she signs, a button comes loose on her blouse, and now there's this gaping view of her lacy red bra, which everyone can clearly see. No one else says anything. She's on a roll and obviously doesn't feel the draft.

526. A young deaf student's parents are visiting their child's classroom. The teacher tells them that their daughter has few social skills and her communication still involves many home signs. She suggests that the parents take some sign language classes to better communicate with their daughter. Since you're familiar with several sign language programs in the community, the teacher suggests that the parents talk to you about which program would best suit their needs. The parents, however, turn to you and ask, "When will our daughter quit playing deaf?"

527. During lunch duty you've noticed that the 6-year-old elementary student for whom you interpret doesn't know how to use his eating utensils properly. During the child's Individualized Educational Planning Committee (IEPC) meeting, the teacher doesn't bring it up. You feel it's important, but you're interpreting the meeting for the child's deaf parents and are not asked to participate.

528. You interpret for a deaf second-grader that comes to school with a large bruise on his cheek. When the teacher asks him what happened, he says he fell out of a tree. However, during the course of the day, you notice that this usually bright, happy child is having trouble paying attention and gets the shakes. During recess the little boy comes up to you and starts crying and says his dad came home drunk last night and hit him and his mother. His dad has threatened him if he tells anyone, so now he's afraid to go home.

529. A college student for whom you interpret asks you to interpret a meeting in her professor's office after class. You know she often meets with her professor after class, but she usually speaks for herself in one-on-one situations. She tells her professor she's suing him for sexual harassment, that you are her witness, and that's why you're at this meeting.

530. You hold IC/TC certification and are interpreting in court. While you're interpreting, the defense is asserting to the judge you're not a "fully qualified interpreter."

531. While interpreting for a deaf client, you can't help but notice that she seems to be upset about something. During a break she confides that her husband, who is currently in the state penitentiary, is soon going to be released. He has threatened her and her children numerous times, and she's afraid of what he might do to them when he gets out. She asks for your opinion on what she should do.

532. While interpreting in municipal court, the judge asks you to tell him your credentials and then asks the deaf person if he's satisfied with you as his interpreter. The client says, "No, I want a CSC interpreter, not a CI and CT." The judge asks you to explain the difference to him.

533. A deaf person who had been hit by a train was in a coma. He and his deaf brother lived together. As the weeks turned into months, the brother was evicted from their apartment for failing to pay the rent, so he started sleeping at the hospital. The hospital hired me (a CDI) to interpret a meeting with this brother to explain that he couldn't continue to stay at the hospital. The client said he understood, but that he had nowhere else to go. After the assignment, I made some calls to find him emergency housing. I know it wasn't part of my job, but I knew I could help him. Was I wrong?

534. I was interpreting in a courtroom when the judge asked the client if there were other CDIs available in another part of our state. The client responded that he didn't know. However, since I have been a CDI for many years, I am very familiar with other CDIs in our state. I want to know if it would be OK to stop and share the information with the court.

Challenges in Maintaining Appropriate Boundaries with Clients

- **Scenario 535.** I do a lot of freelance interpreting and have a solid client base. I've heard through the grapevine (both from deaf clients and interpreters) that my colleagues are talking behind my back. They say I'm "unethical" because I send my deaf clients birthday cards, flowers, or my kid's hand-me-downs to their kids. Personally, I think they're just jealous I have so much work. Those things aren't unethical, are they?

AN INTERPRETER'S PERSPECTIVE: There's no question that relationships can develop between interpreters and their clients. Because the Deaf community is small, members may assume multiple roles and the line between "friend" and "interpreter" can become blurred. However, as a professional interpreter, it is your responsibility to maintain certain standards of conduct. One important standard is to establish and honor appropriate boundaries between yourself and your clients.

What are "appropriate boundaries"? Professionals set boundaries by being supportive but separate from clients. Boundaries are established so that professional judgment and client objectivity are not compromised in any way. Interpreters are in a position of trust and power and, thus, have opportunities to manipulate or influence relationships with clients. Actions that seem "nice," such as gift giving, may be questioned later as being done for personal benefit or may lead to feelings of obligation by clients. The exchange of gifts and favors is appropriate among friends. However, you need to consider the implications of entering a client's personal support network. Giving or receiving a card or small impersonal gift is acceptable on significant occasions but should not be encouraged as general practice. You can be "nice" in a professional way by establishing and maintaining appropriate boundaries.

A DEAF CONSUMER'S PERSPECTIVE: The Deaf world is a small one, and it seems that most people who become interpreters begin to socialize in the Deaf community while they are learning the language. In this situation, friendships can develop before the hearing person is placed in a professional relationship, and friends can become clients. Because of the nature of the job, interpreters walk a fine line in keeping personal and professional relationships separate. You mention that you have a solid client base. I assume that you know these clients well and consider them to be friends as well as clients. I think it is thoughtful of you to remember your deaf clients when they are sick or have birthdays. However, I would caution you to be careful that you do not compromise your relationship with them.

As a deaf consumer, I would appreciate a birthday card or a get-well card because they are inexpensive expressions. However, spending more money on gifts or flowers would make me uncomfortable, and I might feel that I needed to reciprocate. I would be offended by the offer of used clothing, unless we were really good friends. Also, sending cards to all your clients no matter whether you are close friends, casual acquaintances, or simply have a working relationship with them sounds like you are looking for business. It's similar to insurance companies or other businesses that send cards or calendars to a list of all their clients. An interpreter should never present a card or gift during a job. This would be a conflict of interest, confusing the professional and personal relationship. Finally, I think that you should seriously consider why you are sending cards and gifts and to which clients you are sending them. Other interpreters in the community may feel that you are taking unfair advantage of your position by "buying" clients, rather than getting jobs because of your skills.

- **Scenario 536.:** What do you suggest for those times when we interpret in situations with the same deaf client all day for several days in a row, and we probably appear joined at the hip? I know spending every minute together is perceived by the hearing professional as making me unable to be neutral. Often trying to distance myself from the deaf client makes things confusing and hurtful when in fact we are sharing this experience together. What would you do?

AN INTERPRETER'S PERSPECTIVE: In these situations I try to resist being the sole conversation partner for the deaf client, which can be perceived as a biased majority of two. For the deaf client, the ease of conversing with another person who uses ASL can isolate the two of you in a sea of hearing people. When not actively working (e.g., social times, meals), I look for opportunities to clue the deaf clients in on some of the topics happening around us. Often just mentioning the discussions going on at the table or while waiting in line, for example, will allow the deaf client to participate and become part of the conversation. By interpreting these side conversations, I give the client the opportunity to join them. I also take my cue from the deaf person on how much she wants to participate. If these are peers, colleagues, or coworkers, I try to limit my own participation in spoken conversations during off-times. I will answer questions addressed to me personally, but deflect much of the conversations back to the deaf person for their response. After all, this is their business, not mine. So there are times I do chat with a deaf client, but to appear as a professional doing a job, I look for ways to avoid being the only conversation partner. I find opportunities to take breathers (restroom breaks or a short walk outside to get fresh air) and clear my mind, so as not to seem joined at the hip.

A DEAF CONSUMER'S PERSPECTIVE: As a deaf person who has experienced situations like this where I am the only deaf person at a multi-day conference, I do depend on the interpreter to interpret, as well as to keep me company. I am aware that the interpreter does need breaks and I respect her wishes. However, I expect the interpreter to stay with me as much as possible to interpret what is happening and be there if I choose to socialize with the other conference attendees. I know that this can be an awkward situation for some interpreters, and if I sense that they are not comfortable with being overly friendly with me, I will respect that and give them more space. In general, it is my belief that the deaf client is the one who should choose how much time they want to spend with the interpreter, and the interpreter should respect that since they are being paid to be there for the deaf person.

- **Scenario 537.** I am a training consultant for an employees assistance program. One of the topics I teach is sexual harassment. I recently taught a seminar on this topic in a local agency which employs and provides services for the deaf. One of the points I discuss in my training is the issue about touching (hugging, etc.) clients or consumers. In a previous career, I was a drug and alcohol therapist and have also been the clinical director of a private psychiatric hospital. In my workshop, I talk about those of us in the "helping professions" who have been used to being "touchy feely," hugging and touching clients. I also talk about our litigious society and how we need to be very careful of touching clients and try to limit or eliminate the practice. It is sad that we have come to this state, but again, lawsuits — even frivolous ones — have ruined companies, agencies, and individuals. The interpreters in attendance took exception to my comments, saying that Deaf culture would not allow interpreters to cease and desist from touching and hugging their consumers. The deaf employees echoed the sentiments of the interpreters. I again said it was a sad state of affairs, but I think this is the way all professionals are heading. I would welcome your comments in this regard and could use them in further training with our company's clients who both employ and service the Deaf community.

AN INTERPRETER'S PERSPECTIVE: Yes, it is a sad commentary on today's world when we have to consider that any move we make could have serious or even legal consequences. That being said, I have found ways to combat misunderstandings. First of all, I never make the first move to hug a deaf consumer. If the consumer wants to hug me, that's her choice. I hug in open places so that lots of people can see what I'm doing. If anyone asks why or gives me an uncomfortable look, either I explain the cultural aspect of leave-taking and hugging and how it's a sign of respect (if the deaf person's too young to say something), or I ask the deaf person if she wants to explain or would prefer I explain it. In a permanent assignment, like in a school system or a psychiatric ward, you might want to have staff training about Deaf culture in tandem with your presentation. That way, you have made the staff aware of both sides of the issue, and they will be more cognizant when they have a real life encounter. The other way I try to deal with touching and hugging is within the interpretation. A number of years ago, I worked in a school which had a sheriff's county's officer employed onsite. A deaf student wanted to talk with the officer and tapped him on the shoulder. In hearing culture, when dealing with someone of authority, you don't tap them on the shoulder, especially if they carry a loaded weapon! However, in Deaf culture, tapping someone on the shoulder is a way to get attention and a sign of respect (i.e., if I respect you and your opinion, I'll want to talk with you). When the deaf student went to tap the officer on the shoulder, I voiced it as, "Excuse me, officer." It could also have been voiced as, "Sir?" This helped relieve any misunderstanding between the hearing and deaf individual.

A DEAF CONSUMER'S PERSPECTIVE: It is difficult for me to accept this "sad state of affairs" as you put it. Yes, it is true that your advice is contrary to historical Deaf cultural norms. However, it sounds to me like the interpreters in attendance who were advocating for touching and hugging their clients were in fact demonstrating their own need to be "warm and fuzzy" helping professionals who "take care" of deaf adults. It was not surprising to me, just unfortunate that the deaf adults in attendance supported them. As a young, professional deaf adult, I don't want this kind of relationship with interpreters. In fact, I would prefer interpreters keep our professional relationship just that, professional. If I see you off duty and we choose to acknowledge each other, that's different. By and large, I appreciate interpreters being friendly, but I see a distinct difference between that and an interpreter being familiar with me, especially while she's on the job.

- **Scenario 538.** I interpret for a deaf high school student who believes he has good speech skills. However, I find his speech difficult to understand. Today, I saw him in the cafeteria trying to talk to one of the cafeteria workers, and she clearly doesn't understand him. After lunch he starts telling me about the "stupid cafeteria worker." Is it my place to say something?

AN INTERPRETER'S PERSPECTIVE: Ahh, high school…where the goal of students is to be "cool." After the encounter with the cafeteria woman, this student probably had a moment of feeling seriously un-cool, and to save himself the embarrassment, he made her the "stupid" party of their interaction. You say he thinks he has good speech skills. He may have this opinion because people like his family and doctors have told him so, or maybe he thinks his speech skills are good because it would be far too deflating to his self-image to believe the opposite. We find ourselves weighing which might be more damaging to his developing image: to give him a hint that maybe the woman in the cafeteria isn't stupid and actually can't understand his speech? Or to let him continue to go through his class, the lunch line, and life with more encounters that leave him blaming other people? Since this isn't as superficial as telling someone that his Abercrombie & Fitch shirt from last year is "sooooo out" and he can change it tomorrow, deciding to say something to this student requires you to take into consideration his ability to empower himself about the issue. If you tell him that people struggle to understand him, can he do anything about it? If he's worked hard on his speech skills for several years and does not want or cannot work on his speech anymore, then the comment leaves him feeling deflated and hopeless to change the un-cool. Additionally, think about your relationship thus far with this student in terms of how much he trusts your professional opinion. If he accepts your opinion and wants to do something about his speech skills, make sure to offer support and resources. Have a private conversation to know if he wants your feedback about his speech in the future. Another issue embedded in this situation is your responsibility as a school employee to encourage and enforce respect for all adults working there. Let him know that it's not appropriate for him to use you as a repository for his badmouthing other employees.

A DEAF CONSUMER'S PERSPECTIVE: In the educational setting, sometimes roles and responsibilities can become unclear. There are times when interpreters probably feel more maternal or that they need to educate the clients/students. In this situation I do not think that you should share your observations with the high school student. Telling this information to the student would be counseling, advising, or sharing your opinion, which clearly breaches the interpreter's commitment to remaining impartial. It is quite possible that this student has experienced this reaction in the past from others and is simply expressing his frustration with the communication difficulties. If you were to share with him your opinion (which happens to be subjective), you could cause, among other things, emotional distress, embarrassment, and damage to your relationship with him. In this situation it is the role of the student's speech and language practitioner to evaluate and remediate any speech difficulties or communication issues.

- **Scenario 539.** A prominent deaf consumer for whom I interpret fairly regularly smacks when he sucks on hard candy (which unfortunately is often). I have been in high level meetings with him, and the room is completely quiet except for the person talking and the sound of him smacking his candy. I'd feel weird telling this distinguished man, who is 20 years older than me, about this!

AN INTERPRETER'S PERSPECTIVE: Perhaps you've had the experience of walking around with a bit of spinach on your teeth all day and not realizing it. Finally, at the end of the day, you look in the mirror and realize that you've had a bit of spinach on your teeth since lunch, and no one bothered to tell you. Perhaps your colleagues and friends didn't want to say anything for fear they would "hurt your feelings."

It's possible that you are the only one who is bothered or disturbed by the noises made by his candy smacking habit. It's also possible that everyone else doesn't want to say anything because they don't want to "hurt his feelings." Age difference or not, if it's causing others around him to snicker or lower their opinion of his competence, it would be just and right to inform him that when he eats hard candy he makes a distracting noise by "smacking." As interpreters, we can make the call as to whether to tell consumers to "turn off their voice" on occasion. This particular consideration might be another call of courtesy, not only to the deaf consumer, but his hearing colleagues at high-level meetings as well. Tell him kindly, but discreetly (not during the actual offense, but perhaps before the next meeting begins) that when he eats candy he makes noise. Hopefully, he'll take it as well as if you'd mentioned unsightly spinach in his teeth!

A DEAF CONSUMER'S PERSPECTIVE: While I know I would want to know if I make noise, I also know sometimes hearing people are overly conscious about making noises when the room is quiet. I have had interpreters tell me to stop moving in my chair or that I make noises with my mouth while signing. While I appreciate knowing this, I also think "how" the interpreter tells me is equally important. Ultimately, it is my choice to decide what I want to do. Sometimes I will decide what I wish to do based on the attitude affecting this environment. For example, if I am tired of bowing down to hearing people, maybe I will continue to make the noise. If this is a workplace where deaf awareness is good, then the hearing people who work there will be more sensitive to the behaviors of deaf people. In turn, maybe I will feel like I could "be myself" and continue to make the noises. There are several reasons why your deaf consumer might be continuing to make the noises. However, you should not feel that this bad behavior reflects on you as an interpreter.

Other Scenarios

Identify the issue(s) involved and decide how you would respond. Discuss and compare your responses with your colleagues.

540. A deaf student at the college where you interpret invites you to his fraternity party Saturday night, not to interpret but as his guest. You have never been to a Greek party but have heard they can be fun. The school's interpreter handbook doesn't have a specific policy for fraternizing with the students; on the other hand, all the other staff interpreters are married, and it's probably never been an issue.

541. After an interpreting assignment, the very attractive deaf client asks you out to dinner. You're attracted, single, and new to town so you gladly accept. After dinner he asks you back to his place, and although you had a great time, you turn him down. He takes your number and promises to call, but weeks go by and he never calls. Later you find out he's married to one of your new deaf clients.

542. You're interpreting for a deaf woman every week who had an abortion years ago and is now in counseling trying to come to terms with it. You run into the woman and her husband at the mall and go up to say, "Hi." She turns away and acts like she doesn't know you, dragging her husband along with her. The next week at counseling she angrily tells you that her husband doesn't know about the abortion or the counseling and to stay away from her outside of work.

543. On Monday morning when you enter the classroom at the high school where you work, the deaf student is there as usual waiting to tell you every detail of her weekend. You're the only person in her life who can sign, and she relies on you a great deal for her socialization.

544. You are giving a deaf-blind client and her service dog (a big, lovable, black dog) a ride home after a day of interpreting. The client warns you that her dog doesn't like to sit in the back seat, and so you all manage to crunch into the front seat of your little Honda. In spite of your precautions, the dog gets sick all over your car. You can hardly ask the client to clean it up, but this is more than you bargained for.

545. You're interpreting for a deaf woman at a three-day training program. She has a bad cold and keeps sneezing and coughing, and she never covers her mouth. She's also very physical, and she keeps touching you. Even when you aren't interpreting, she hangs on to your arm just in case you do say something. You're not sure you can finish this job.

Challenges in Handling Clients' Inappropriate Requests or Behavior

- **Scenario 546**. I go with a deaf friend to the beauty salon to interpret between her and the stylist. My friend ends up looking like GI Jane, and she's mad at me instead of the stylist. I hear from the grapevine she's telling people it's my fault and that I'm a lousy interpreter.

AN INTERPRETER'S PERSPECTIVE: If I have a good reputation in this community, I would probably let the comments go because people trust me and know my interpreting skills. If I'm new and trying to establish my reputation, I would contact the deaf friend and talk out the situation, explaining that I was interpreting and not styling her hair. I would offer to go back to the stylist and interpret while she complained and perhaps received a re-style.

A DEAF CONSUMER'S PERSPECTIVE: Ignore the gossip. You can't undo rumors, and if you talk about what happened, it breaks the confidentiality. You should confront your deaf friend and clear this up.

- **Scenario 547**. I'm interpreting a very boring presentation, and the deaf client has indicated she would prefer to chat instead. If I stop interpreting, it will be obvious that something's amiss, but the client is the one paying me. I figure it's her dime and her call. I stop interpreting.

AN INTERPRETER'S PERSPECTIVE: Been there! It's always nice to have a good rapport with a client; however, this situation sounds like it may be getting too chummy. I would feel rude carrying on an obvious conversation during a presentation, regardless of my role or who is paying me. I would indicate to the consumer that I wouldn't feel comfortable just chatting and would rather go on interpreting.

A DEAF CONSUMER'S PERSPECTIVE: Regardless of who is paying, the interpreter should continue to interpret. After the assignment both should discuss the situation, and the interpreter should explain her reasons for continuing. Only if the client leaves the room should the interpreter stop interpreting.

- **Scenario 548**. The deaf high school student for whom I interpret will do just about anything to get attention in class. He throws spit-balls, belches, farts, picks his nose, you name it. After a while I realize I just don't like the kid, and so I ask my supervisor to switch me with another staff interpreter. My supervisor is surprised at my request and says the deaf student and his parents have recently specifically requested that I be his interpreter again next year. I'm surprised and somewhat flattered, so I decide to give the student another chance. The next day in class, the first thing he does is start rooting around inside his nose. This time, when he flicks it in the air, it lands on me!

AN INTERPRETER'S PERSPECTIVE: I would go back to the supervisor and say that I made a mistake and I can't continue to interpret for this particular student. It's a good idea for students to have some variety in their interpreters anyway, so they don't get too dependent on any one person.

A DEAF CONSUMER'S PERSPECTIVE: I would confront the student. I would say, "If you behave inappropriately one more time, I will talk to the supervisor and ask to be replaced with another interpreter." I don't believe that interpreters should have to take this kind of behavior from their deaf clients.

- **Scenario 549.** In the postsecondary setting where I interpret, one particular deaf student frankly doesn't have much in the way of social skills. She is just plain mean to everyone, and it's uncomfortable and embarrassing to be around her. She's either rude or inappropriate or both. Her hearing classmates, upon meeting their first, real live deaf person, try to be friendly but more often than not walk away completely turned off. Please don't tell me to simply not take assignments where she is the client; as a staff interpreter, we don't always have that choice. She knows she's a "challenge." I suspect she gets off on it!

AN INTERPRETER'S PERSPECTIVE: Maybe your experience relates to cultural differences. Some things hearing people might label rude, Deaf people might attribute to the fact that they are "Deaf-blunt." As interpreters we do not regulate anyone's behavior, and it can be difficult with students, both deaf and hearing. Offering Deaf awareness activities on campus might be one way to develop understanding between hearing and deaf students and give them a different arena in which to socialize. Also, all students (deaf and hearing) need to learn the ropes of interacting in a university setting, and I think we as interpreters need to take a hands-off approach on this one.

A DEAF CONSUMER'S PERSPECTIVE: It is hard to determine whether the student in this situation is in fact having a "true" social skill problem or if there is some misunderstanding about what is "culturally acceptable." Sometimes as a deaf person, it is hard to "park your culture at the door" and behave in ways that are considered acceptable to our hearing peers. For example, it has been my experience that it is not socially acceptable to interrupt people without letting them finish, but it's not clear to me from watching the interpreter when I can and can't interrupt.

Appropriate registers are not always there for me to be cued correctly, and for years I thought "jumping in" and cutting people off was the way to get your point across or make yourself heard. Of course later I learned to trust the interpreter or professor that I would have a chance to participate. Without knowing more specifics, I assume the "rudeness" or "inappropriateness" is due to a lack of understanding the subtleness in the hearing culture. For example, hearing people equate being blunt with being rude, whereas deaf people consider it being honest or direct. Without more specific information, I would not be so quick to say it's the student's problem, but would look at the situation a while to determine what exactly is causing this perception.

- **Scenario 550.** In an educational setting, a student had asked me to accompany her to interpret a conversation with one of her teachers. On the way to the teacher's classroom, I asked, "What did you need to see Miss X for?" The deaf student responded, "It's none of your business; you are the interpreter and you will do what I tell you to do!" Needless to say, I was shocked at this answer. I always try to prepare myself and avoid misunderstandings. For example, before going into a doctor's office, I ask the client why they're there to prepare myself as well as to get a feel for the client's signing style, etc. I am not being nosy; I feel this response was very curt and rude. Is this how we are viewed?

AN INTERPRETER'S PERSPECTIVE: I think there are numbers of issues at play. First, there is your question and reasoning behind it. I applaud your rationale; you were trying to be prepared for the event and gauge the deaf person's sign style/ preference. That's great! However, I wouldn't have asked why the student wanted to see the teacher. It may be misconstrued as fishing for information. If this was a first-time assignment, I think the most I might ask would be, "What does the teacher teach?" That way, the subject being taught would prime my brain for certain terms and/or grammatical aspects of ASL and English. For example, if you're measuring a young student's signing preference, you could ask about another less threatening topic. One question I use is "What is your favorite game?" Lots of times, young kids will answer by talking about their favorite video game. They're more relaxed, and it helps me find a good starting point for matching their preferences. The second issue is the deaf student's response. Remember that she is young, and part of being a student is learning how to be a savvy, yet polite, consumer. If this educational setting is your full-time position, you should talk with the student as soon as you can after the interpreting event. Be honest, but not authoritative. Remember, diplomacy can be your best friend. You might want to tell her that it always helps the interpreter to have something to start with, both content and communication preferences, so that you can be ready to interpret. This way, the student might volunteer necessary information next time without an interpreter having to ask.

A DEAF CONSUMER'S PERSPECTIVE: That sounds familiar to me. I have seen and heard this reaction from students. I believe the student is learning how to utilize an interpreter. Some students will use too much power without common sense. Often deaf students are told that interpreters don't have the right to be nosy about their personal lives, but at the same time they do not understand how the CPC really works for them too. This student probably didn't even think ahead about the fact that the interpreter is going to find out what the topic will be in a few moments anyway; they just don't know why you ask those kinds of questions. After the initial meeting (not right away, but later on), you should have a nice, comfortable talk with the student about why you ask these kinds of questions. Explaining this would be beneficial. Some students need help learning how to utilize interpreters and what to expect later in the Deaf community. Eventually the student can decide whether the interpreter's questions are appropriate prior to situations. This student is still learning.

- **Scenario 551.** I was interpreting in court for a young deaf man charged with both possession of marijuana and driving while intoxicated. The judge finds him guilty. As he's taken into custody, he asks me to tell his brother, who is parked out front waiting for him, what happened. Am I really supposed to go looking around the parking lot for some guy sitting in his car?

AN INTERPRETER'S PERSPECTIVE: Do not go find the brother to tell him the verdict. Where is he again? Parked out front somewhere? Well, he's just going to have to find out from the bailiff (when he finally comes in because he wonders what's taking so long) to whom you dutifully interpret your client's remarks.

A DEAF CONSUMER'S PERSPECTIVE: I would suggest you tell his brother (if you can find a man sitting in a parked car) that he needs to go to the courthouse.

Other Scenarios

Identify the issue(s) involved and decide how you would respond. Discuss and compare your responses with your colleagues.

552. While interpreting for a deaf student during a college history test, the student surprises you by asking for some answers to the test. When you try to laugh it off, he tells you he's serious; he needs help. He hasn't studied.

553. You're a freelance interpreter interpreting in a Vocational Rehabilitation (VR) office. As the deaf client is looking down filling out his paperwork, the VR counselor looks at you and says, "Do you think John can do this type of work?"

554. You're asked to interpret a sex education seminar for some teenagers living in a residential treatment program. The boys, including the deaf teenager, are loud and obnoxious when the presenter demonstrates the correct method for putting on a condom. You feel like you don't deserve this kind of disrespect. The presenter may have to take it, but you don't. When one of the boys flips a condom at you, you snap and tell him to "behave."

555. You're interpreting a company meeting where the deaf employee falls asleep. He's seated in the front row, and you keep interpreting, so only a few people notice he's asleep. He then starts making grunts and groans in his sleep. Now every single person in the room knows he's sleeping, but not a soul has the nerve to wake him.

556. A female college student for whom you interpret is very open about her preference for women. One day her parents come to campus to visit, and the student introduces you to them. The student's mother tells you, "We're so happy to finally meet our daughter's boyfriend."

557. One Sunday the speaker at the church where you interpret is using German phrases to illustrate his point. Not knowing any German, you inform the deaf parishioners that he's speaking German and then wait until he speaks English again to start interpreting. A deaf man in the audience, however, becomes angry, stands up, and announces to the congregation that the interpreter is incompetent! He says, "German language or not, it was spoken, and interpreters must interpret spoken language!"

558. The mother of a deaf-blind client asks you to interpret a doctor's appointment for her son. The mother wants to be present for the appointment but admits her son wants to go alone. She says if he asks who is in the room, not to tell him she's there. She says she is willing to pay top dollar for your services and that she's only acting in the best interests of her son.

559. While interpreting for a deaf patient in a doctor's office, the patient is complaining that he has been coming in for months with the same symptoms, and he's still not feeling any better. Finally, the doctor admits he just can't figure out what is wrong with the deaf man. The doctor then turns to you and asks you to step out of the examining room as there is something he would like to discuss with you.

560. You're interpreting in court for a deaf client for whom you have interpreted for years. This is the client's first time in court, and he's nervous. He tries to have side conversations with you for reassurance. You tell him you'll need to voice everything he says just like you'll sign everything anyone else says, and he says he understands and stops talking. He then does it again a few minutes later, and so you voice his remarks. You can see he's surprised and hurt; he just meant that comment for you. Now the judge is yelling at him.

561. You're scheduled to interpret an Individualized Educational Planning Committee (IEPC) meeting for the deaf parents of an elementary student. The parents have brought two hearing family members, who can also sign, with them for support. While the meeting is going on, the family continually has little side conversations going on, signing back and forth. You start to voice these conversations as well, and the two hearing family members insist you stop because they're "private" conversations.

562. While interpreting for a deaf client attending a staff meeting at the manufacturing company where he works, the deaf man became very angry with his boss. He gets up, and as he's walking out of the door, he signs "A‑‑‑hole!" His boss then turns to you and asks why the man was so angry.

563. At lunch at a downtown cafe with some friends, you're approached by a deaf client's therapist, who is at a nearby table. The therapist asks you why the deaf client didn't show up for an appointment. You have no idea, and can't he see you're off duty now?

564. While interpreting a company training class, the instructor apologizes to the deaf employee because the next video is not closed-captioned. The deaf employee responds, "Then I'm going to go have a cigarette, and my interpreter can fill me in when I get back."

565. You have been interpreting in an assisted living/group home every morning for the last two weeks when the manager of the home approaches you and says he'll be calling your agency requesting another interpreter. When you ask if there's a problem with your work, he says that your interpreting is fine, but the last interpreter they had helped the clients with their household chores and you don't.

566. You interpret for a deaf student enrolled in a pre-law class. The lecture class is held in an auditorium and always packed. The deaf student doesn't always show up. If she does, she always arrives late, so finding a seat up front becomes a problem. One day the student arrives late, and there are no seats left up front. She demands the professor make someone move. He tells her seating is first come, first served, and that if she is truly concerned about seating, she should get there on time like everyone else. She demands you give up your chair next to the professor and stand up to interpret the two-hour class.

567. You're scheduled to interpret for three deaf adults attending a job training program, but only two have shown up by the time the training begins. Thirty minutes later, the third deaf participant arrives, and the job trainer asks you to go ahead and get the third participant "up to speed" while the other two are working.

568. From time to time you interpret for a deaf woman known for being an incurable gossip. She's one of those people that, even if you just nod your head to something she says to be polite, she will tell people you're the one who said it. You're interpreting for her today and really working hard to keep things on a professional level, but the deaf woman still tries to sidetrack you.

569. Halfway through a two-hour workshop, a 10-minute break is announced. During the break you rush for the food because your blood sugar level has dropped, and you're feeling light-headed. The deaf client comes up to you in line and asks you to interpret what everyone is talking about. You have not even been to the bathroom yet, and that too is high on your list of priorities for the break. When you explain this to the deaf client, she says, "You just want free food. You're too fat anyway."

570. While waiting to see a doctor in the emergency room, your deaf client asks you if you're gay. Rather than lie, you say, "Yes, but I'm not open about it, and I hope you can respect that." Weeks later, you hear from interpreters and deaf people alike that this guy is telling people you "came on to him." This is as far from the truth as possible, and you would like to find and confront him.

571. You're interpreting a photo shoot for a deaf model. The photographer requests that the client disrobe, and she quickly complies. You're surprised, and she laughs and signs to you, "Compared to you, I look great."

572. One summer day in a college classroom, you're interpreting the professor's lecture, and you notice that the deaf student, who is wearing shorts, keeps crossing and uncrossing his legs. You figure he's just trying to get comfortable. Suddenly out of the corner of your eye, it becomes obvious that the student is not wearing underwear. When you look up at the deaf student's face and see his smirk, you know he's doing it on purpose.

573. You're interpreting for a deaf couple attending family counseling sessions with their teenage hearing son. Every session, without fail, the teenager points out to his parents and the therapist the sign choices you make that he thinks are wrong. When asked about it by the therapist, you explain that there are many ways to sign something, just as there are many ways to say something in English. After several more weeks of this, you're ready to spank the boy yourself for trying to make you look bad, but everyone else is just indulging him.

574. In a high school cooking class, the students are baking cookies all day for a student fundraiser. The deaf student is left in charge of watching the oven. She's to make sure the cookies go in and out in a timely manner. The student doesn't pay attention, leaves the cookies in too long, and now they're all slightly burned. When the classroom teacher comes back to check the cookies, she says none of them will be able to be sold. She snaps at you for not helping the deaf student watch the cookies.

575. While interpreting a college course, a well-intentioned professor constantly stops his lecture and asks if you're keeping up. You always smile and say "yes," but then he starts talking in slow motion, thinking he's doing you a favor.

576. You're interpreting for a deaf client getting some tests done on her bladder. After about an hour of testing, one of the nurses is in the room putting away equipment. The deaf patient verbally thanks her for her assistance. The nurse freezes for a moment and then turns around and says to you, "Make her do it again. I want to hear her say it again!"

577. You're interpreting for a deaf student in a mainstream elementary classroom on the first day of school. You and the other students watch in amazement as the teacher follows the deaf student around the room, clapping her hands behind the student's back to find out whether she's really deaf.

578. An elderly deaf man is hit by a car while crossing a street. He's rushed to the hospital, and you're called in to interpret. His wife meets with the surgeon and is told that her husband needs surgery immediately or he will die. The doctor tells the wife they need her to sign consent forms, and she refuses because she feels his quality of life will never be the same. The doctor looks at you and angrily says, "You're my witness. She's as good as murdering her husband."

579. You have agreed to interpret at a church which is not of your faith, but you enjoy a great deal. The pastor of the church tells you that you'll need to become a member of their church in order to continue interpreting there.

580. You're asked by the family of the bride to interpret a wedding for a deaf couple you have never met before. You accept and arrive at the church, only to find yourself being introduced to everyone as the bride's good friend. The girl's parents ask you if you would mind seating the guests and making sure the guest book is signed.

581. You have agreed to shadow interpret a play. The play is a comedy with lots of prat falls and slap-stick humor. During a dress rehearsal, the crew decides to play a practical joke on you, and you end up at one point alone on the stage in the spotlight. After the dress rehearsal, the director asks you if you would mind if they incorporate you into the play because your reactions are so priceless.

582. You're hired by the parents of a deaf client with Usher's Syndrome. The client is new to the city and will be starting college on Monday. The parents request that you acclimate their son to his new environment and show him around the town. You sit down with the client and suggest a variety of places the two of you can go, but the client is very clear about what he wants to do. He asks you to take him to some of the bars in town, and he specifically wants to meet some topless dancers.

583. A high school teacher whose class you interpret every day is very disorganized. She's always asking you to help pass out papers, hook up the VCR, take attendance, find her lost grade-book, etc. You want to be helpful, but you're not sure where the line is between you doing your job and her doing hers.

584. While interpreting a video in a college class, the deaf student falls soundly asleep. When the professor turns the lights back on, the deaf student wakes up and asks you what the movie was about.

585. While interpreting for a deaf client at her workplace for weekly meetings between her and her supervisor, you can't help but notice that all the deaf client seems to do every week is whine and complain. Her supervisor is extremely patient and understanding, but she explains to the deaf woman that none of the deaf woman's coworkers want to work with her anymore because she always tattles on them. This doesn't sink in, and every week it's the same complaints. You find yourself dreading going to this assignment now. You think about trying to get a replacement, but the holidays are coming up and the steady money is nice.

586. You're interpreting in a two-week, pre-employment course. After a few sessions, a pattern develops. The deaf client comes to class, signs in, stays for about 15 minutes, then disappears until the end of the day. She reappears just in time to sign out and catch a ride home with her mom. The instructor finally corners her one day before she leaves. The student tells the instructor that her mom has grounded her from seeing her boyfriend and so she leaves to see him. The instructor tells her he will need to discuss this situation with her mother. She turns to you and says it's all your fault. If you weren't standing around all day, no one would have noticed she was gone.

Challenges in Working with a Team Interpreter

- **Scenario 587**. One day I was team interpreting, and the deaf client turned to me while my partner was interpreting and started chatting with me about mutual friends and colleagues.

AN INTERPRETER'S PERSPECTIVE: Give a polite but brief response to the client and resume attending to the lecture. If the client continues to chat, remind her that you need to pay attention to the lecture so you're prepared to interpret it. Certainly, there are occasions when chatting is appropriate, but you shouldn't let it get out of hand.

A DEAF CONSUMER'S PERSPECTIVE: I'm guilty of this. I will sometimes chat with the "off" interpreter, especially if what is going on is boring. I realize this is frustrating for the "on" interpreter; however, I would expect her to keep interpreting so I can keep an eye on her and know what is going on. Also, I wouldn't like it if the "off" interpreter told me to be quiet and pay attention; after all, I'm an adult. One possible solution is for the "off" interpreter to say, "I'm sorry, I'd like to chat, but I have to pay attention in order to feed my partner. Let's chat at the break."

- **Scenario 588**. My team interpreter constantly flicks her hair away from her face while she's interpreting. During the first break, the deaf client asks her to do something about her hair because her movements are distracting. My partner insists that she doesn't like the way she looks with her hair pulled back and promises to try not to touch her hair anymore. It doesn't work. She continues to flick her hair every few signs. Frustrated, the deaf person asks me to finish up solo.

AN INTERPRETER'S PERSPECTIVE: During a break, speak with the team interpreter privately regarding her hair and the deaf client's comments. I think putting closure to the issue with the client is also a good practice. Tell her that you believe the issue has been resolved and will continue to team with your partner. Maintaining consistent working standards, in this case not agreeing to interpret the last three hours by yourself, sets a precedent that all working interpreters and consumers should follow.

A DEAF CONSUMER'S PERSPECTIVE: You could help encourage and remind her to discontinue those movements.

- **Scenario 589**. I am team interpreting, and for some reason, my partner starts to feed me every single sign from her seat. At first, I try to watch what she's signing, but it's just too much. I can't watch her and listen at the same time. People start to notice the two of us. It's distracting to see both of us interpreting in stereo.

AN INTERPRETER'S PERSPECTIVE: This seems to be an issue of appropriate professional conduct on the job. Negotiating expectations with your team interpreter should take place outside of the interpreting arena, preferably before the assignment begins.

A DEAF CONSUMER'S PERSPECTIVE: You could gently sign, "Please hold," and then continue with your interpretation. At the break, discuss the situation with your partner.

- **Scenario 590**. I'm interpreting a college classroom when the professor announces that a reporter from the "Detroit News" will be coming to class to speak about their ongoing labor dispute. To my amazement, my team interpreter raises her hand and starts complaining to the professor. She says, "I can't believe you would let some scab reporter come into this classroom." I interpret as the professor defends his position, but that's beside the point. I think she should have stayed in role and kept her opinion to herself.

AN INTERPRETER'S PERSPECTIVE: This behavior is completely out of line! I would pull this interpreter aside and ask why she felt the need to step out of her role. I would also ask her to approach the instructor, explain her breach of ethics, and apologize. An encounter like this could give people the wrong impression about the role of an interpreter. The manner in which I would approach her would depend on our relationship. Regardless, I would also report this to our supervisor. If the other interpreter and I don't see eye-to-eye, I would request a different team. My trust in and respect for this person would be completely shattered at this point.

A DEAF CONSUMER'S PERSPECTIVE: You should report your team interpreter's inappropriate behavior to the supervisor. I, as a deaf student, would report it as well and request not to have the same team interpreter in future classes. I would expect the supervisor to discuss this situation with this team interpreter.

- **Scenario 591**. I team interpret an 8 a.m. college class. The student arrives at class 10 or 15 minutes late most days. Now, three weeks into class, my team interpreter starts showing up for class 15 minutes late every day. Sometimes she doesn't even beat the deaf student to class because she knows I'm always on time. I'm starting to get angry, but rocking the boat isn't my style.

AN INTERPRETER'S PERSPECTIVE: A discussion needs to occur. We have an obligation to provide accurate interpretation, and when a job requires two interpreters, they both need to be there for the full-time services that are needed. It's the deaf student's prerogative to show up whenever she wants. I would remind the interpreter of our obligation, as stated above, and that we won't be able to fully understand the rest of the class if one of us misses the first part. The first 15 minutes of "off" time should be considered part of the preparation for the class. It's important to work these things out right away. Otherwise, your feelings may come out in inappropriate ways, possibly skewing your interpretation or causing you to take it out on the deaf and hearing people with whom you're working. I would also let the other interpreter know that, if this situation continues, I will report it to the supervisor.

A DEAF CONSUMER'S PERSPECTIVE: The interpreter should report to the supervisor that her partner is not adhering to her time of the assignment. As a deaf student, as long as it doesn't affect the interpreting, then it's the team's problem, not mine. If the interpreter starts to show her "disgust" with her partner (through her signing or body language), then maybe I'll discuss it with the supervisor.

- **Scenario 592**. I'm interpreting a weekend college course, and I see the "off" interpreter pull out some earphones. The deaf student also notices and asks, "What's up?" My partner says she just wants to hear the score of the Michigan versus Ohio game. The next thing I know, they're both totally engrossed in the game, with my partner interpreting the game play by play.

AN INTERPRETER'S PERSPECTIVE: Some people! I was hired to interpret, and I will do my job if it's possible. If they're listening to the game during my turn to interpret, I would continue to interpret until it became too distracting. Then I would get the attention of the student and ask what she wants me to do. If she wants me to continue interpreting, I would ask my partner to please stop interpreting the game since it's too distracting for me. If the student says she doesn't care about the class and only cares about the game, I would ask the co-interpreter to switch with me and be the "on" interpreter. I will take over interpreting when the student is ready to attend to the class. However, don't expect me to fill in any missing information.

A DEAF CONSUMER'S PERSPECTIVE: Continue interpreting regardless of being ignored by the deaf client. If the team interpreter becomes a distraction, you can ask her to either stop or step out of the room. After the assignment, talk with the team interpreter and let her know that you didn't find her behavior appropriate or supportive. Request that it never happen again if she's to team with you. If it's a repeated behavior, report it to the agency or supervisor.

- **Scenario 593.** Last week, while team interpreting in a post-secondary setting, I couldn't believe my eyes when I noticed a shiny metal ball bouncing around on my partner's tongue. I found it very distracting and fascinating at the same time. Every time she opened her mouth, it was all I could see. I know our deaf client noticed it too. When she was called on in class, she admitted she was not concentrating and asked if the professor could please repeat the question. My question is: do I say something to my partner or wait for the deaf client to say something to her?

AN INTERPRETER'S PERSPECTIVE: Experienced interpreter teams often have pre- and post- feedback sessions, not only with each other but often with their consumers. If the deaf consumer does not address the issue, you should tell your partner that "you" found it distracting and minimally suggest she consider using a clear ball instead of a metal one.

A DEAF CONSUMER'S PERSPECTIVE: As deaf consumers have become more experienced and more empowered to speak up for ourselves in interpreting situations, we feel more comfortable addressing our needs directly with the interpreter. However, if for whatever reason the deaf student does not address this "visual noise" issue with your partner, you should.

- **Scenario 594.** I have noticed that an interpreter that I team with nearly every week (who has been an interpreter for over 20 years and never lets me forget it) tends to omit information. Either she doesn't think it's important or she just doesn't understand it herself. Forget suggesting giving her "feeds" from me; I've "only" been nationally certified for five years and am still a baby in her book. My problem is that she always asks me to do team interpreting assignments with her and nobody else. I know you're going to tell me to say something to her, but our community is so small I can't afford to anger her, financially or professionally. How can I handle this?

AN INTERPRETER'S PERSPECTIVE: Your situation might not have the negative conclusion you seem to fear. There is no reason at this point to think that saying something to her will anger her. Start by telling her that you have noticed that she omitted "xyz." Be specific. It is possible she has legitimate reasons for omitting certain information. Give her a chance to explain herself. For example, there are legitimate reasons why someone interpreting a "how to" computer software class will not sign everything a chatty trainer might say. You may get the opportunity to see something from a different perspective. If, however, it is as you infer and she is omitting valuable material, ask for her perspective in a positive way that does not put her on the defensive and indeed make her angry at you. Choose to say something like, "What leads you not to include that?" instead of asking her a confrontational question like, "Why are you leaving that material out?" Her answer will determine how you want to proceed with her.

A DEAF CONSUMER'S PERSPECTIVE: I had to fight and advocate for 10 weeks to have an interpreter replaced in a team setting during a 15-week graduate class. The supervisor of interpreters finally came and observed the interpreter's skills and agreed that, in spite of her certification and years of experience, her skills were indeed inadequate in that particular setting. Had her team interpreter reported her, I would not have had to go through 10 weeks of missing valuable classroom information and weeks spent advocating on my own. The supervisor was in fact reluctant to replace the interpreter because the team interpreter never said anything. I believe the team interpreter has a responsibility for communication the whole time she is on the job, not just during her own "on" time. Once an interpreter is out in the field, there is no other monitoring system other than peers in team situations. Interpreters shouldn't worry about angering the other interpreter, but instead focus on communication that the deaf person may not be getting that could result in failing a test, not getting a promotion, or any number of other negative consequences.

- **Scenario 595.** I am a teacher for the deaf in a mainstream high school. Our staff interpreter seems to be having a hard time getting used to the idea of working with a team interpreter. Occasionally we need to hire a second interpreter from a local interpreter referral agency. I have noticed our staff interpreter's facial expressions and attitude toward the outside interpreter when the outside interpreter asks me for information or feedback about content or the topic that day. I approached our staff interpreter about this and she freaked out, so I backed off. Now we stop sending in outside interpreters with her unless it is absolutely necessary, even though I know working with a certified interpreter would provide a valuable new perspective on her own skills.

AN INTERPRETER'S PERSPECTIVE: Feeling uncomfortable with team interpreting can occur for a variety of reasons, including one's own lack of training or experience and the fear of being compared and criticized. Additional issues may include: (1) The educational interpreter may not know that preparing for an assignment is part of an interpreter's job; (2) One or both of the interpreters may not have training or experience in the actual process of team interpreting. (Expectations of both interpreters and the deaf or hard of hearing consumer should be explicitly discussed — working out the details of team interpreting requires specialized knowledge and skill.); or (3) For community-based interpreters, educational interpreters, or certified interpreters, dynamics may interfere with the interpreter's comfort level.

I might approach the staff interpreter again and ask if she has specific concerns about working with outside interpreters. Maybe she is tiring from the additional responsibility of being the ongoing interpreter in an assignment where she has to update each new interpreter that appears on the scene. You could also encourage the interpreter to discuss the issue with someone else. If you or another person initiates a discussion, it is important to have a supportive, curious, problem-solving approach that acknowledges and validates her concerns. If the interpreter is simply resistant and uncooperative, it might require involving her supervisor. The supervisor could reiterate job expectations and responsibilities to the entire interpreting staff (therefore, not pinpointing this particular interpreter). The supervisor could emphasize the idea that staff interpreters are expected to work effectively with agency interpreters. "Working effectively" may need to be specifically defined in behavioral terms. The supervisor could also meet individually with the interpreter to help her identify problems and solutions. I would hesitate to "enable" the educational interpreter by altering your or the school district's use of outside interpreters. Instead, I would ask what ensures effective communication for the deaf or hard of hearing children in your district. This should be the basis for hiring decisions. A final note: This situation illustrates a stereotypical dynamic between educational and community-based interpreters. We need to remember that team interpreting challenges can occur between any two interpreters.

A DEAF CONSUMER'S PERSPECTIVE: The commitment for any and all interpreters is to aim for their best possible interpreter performance each and every time. The commitment for any and all consumers, deaf and hearing, is to aim to team as effectively as possible with interpreters. It is my feeling that you should not back off but continue to probe further to see what can be done to best address everyone's expectations. Extended interpreting time is harmful to the body, so there may be some wisdom in ignoring her protests, while simultaneously working toward a solution by arranging for a team interpreter. It is crucial that the staff interpreter is in the habit of practicing a healthy mindset and actions to avoid long-term negative consequences. Some tips may include identifying a core of interpreter responses and actions. There may be benefits to bringing in an independent expert or consultant for additional perspectives. Work toward a mutual understanding of what "team interpreting" means and when teaming is necessary. Consider professional development training that helps the staff interpreter to work comfortably with outside interpreters. Ask the staff interpreter to identify a pool of appropriately credentialed interpreters with whom she feels comfortable working (a "team preference list") and attempt to primarily contact the interpreters on both yours, the staff interpreter's, and the consumer's list.

- **Scenario 596.** What should an interpreter do when her team interpreter is wearing a totally inappropriate shirt, such as plaid or paisley? In my book, plain tops that contrast with the skin color are a basic rule, not a choice.

Should the team interpreter mention it? Keep quiet? In most situations I've been in, I have mentioned the appropriate clothing to the interpreter with varying but often negative results. Often I hear, "The deaf person doesn't mind it; why should you care?" I have seen this happen with a wide range of interpreters, from novice to experienced interpreters. Am I way off-base to mention this to my team interpreter and expect this adherence to the dress code?

AN INTERPRETER'S PERSPECTIVE: No, you are not off-base to expect adherence to a dress code that is perceived as an "industry standard." Expecting something to happen, even with training or length of time in the field, does not, however, ensure that it will happen — even something as simple as compliance to an accepted standard of dress in your profession. The question is what to do about it. I would hope that the deaf person receiving the interpreting services would approach the interpreter and request they wear appropriate attire the next time around, if the deaf person was bothered by it. Some deaf people are not bothered by clothing issues, but at the same time, many are. The point is you don't know which deaf people are bothered and which are not, so I prefer to always play it safe and dress in a manner that avoids controversy (i.e., plain tops that contrast with the skin color).

If the deaf person does not mention the clothing issue to the interpreter, I might be inclined to. At the end of the assignment, I might ask (not tell or preach to) my team interpreter if she has ever been approached and received any complaints about her clothing. If her answer was, "No, I've never been approached by a deaf person complaining about my attire," I would try to find a way to state my opinion. As tactfully as possible (and always using "I" statements), I would share my opinion that wearing plain tops that contrast with the skin color demonstrates respect and awareness of the physical requirements of a visual language and avoids controversy that could potentially lead to further complications. Interpreting is complicated enough; why add to it? I would further state my opinion about how lucky she has been to never have received a complaint. If the answer to my question was, "Why, yes, someone did complain to me once," I would have to ask them why they continued wearing controversial clothing while interpreting when she knew some deaf people were bothered by it.

A DEAF CONSUMER'S PERSPECTIVE: No, you're not off-base. Proper interpreter attire is part of professional conduct, and inappropriate clothing can be distracting for both the team interpreter and the client. To protect your own integrity, you should politely point out that the plaid or paisley shirt is ill-suited to interpreting and suggest that your team interpreter either replace it with a plain top or carry extra clothing in the car for such situations. Your team interpreter may thank you. However, if the team interpreter objects and says, "The deaf person doesn't mind,

why should you?" you have a choice: let the matter drop or let the interpreter know
that their inappropriate attire makes it difficult for you to concentrate and assist.
You're "off," yes, but you are affected. If it continues to be a problem, you can opt
not to work with this person anymore. Interpreters, as well as deaf people, have a
responsibility to uphold the standards of the interpreting profession. Sometimes
deaf people are reluctant to assert themselves with interpreters who exhibit cocky or
cavalier attitudes, or they may not be aware that plaid and paisley are no-no's. They
have a right to request that interpreters dress in solid tops, and the team interpreter
does have a duty to speak up. Self-policing in interpreting is a must, as long as it's
done diplomatically and with discretion. Please, interpreters, save deaf people's
eyes! Wear plain tops that contrast with your skin color!

- **Scenario 597.** During a lull in a staff meeting where I was interpreting, I
  used my electronic calendar to enter some appointments (and check my
  grocery list). Afterwards my team interpreter told me she thought doing
  that was rude and unprofessional. Do you agree?

AN INTERPRETER'S PERSPECTIVE: I think each situation is different, but
I am taking a "lull during a staff meeting" to mean that no interpreting needed to
occur. In that case, I think it would be OK to check your electronic calendar. Always
checking with your partner beforehand would be a good idea. During breaks I often
use that time to discuss how we think things are going and any ideas for the rest of
the meeting. We need to be prepared to interpret during breaks as well. This would
prevent resentments or misunderstandings like this from surfacing later.

A DEAF CONSUMER'S PERSPECTIVE: If by "lull" you mean checking your
electronic calendar while your partner is interpreting, then yes, it is rude — you
should be working. However, if by "lull" you mean "break" and that everyone is out
of the room or standing around and talking, then no, generally that's not a problem.
I understand when interpreters need to use the phone or check messages during
breaks. I do too. However, if I needed to speak to the "big boss" during the break
and I saw you checking your grocery list, it would make me feel uncomfortable
because this is still work time for me. In the future I suggest checking with your
client and partner before doing personal things on work time.

- **Scenario 598.** My team interpreter and I were recently interpreting for a
  deaf client who promptly fell sound asleep. Sounds like the same old story,
  I know, but this one has a slight twist. I chose to continue interpreting,
  but my partner wouldn't. This made the situation more noticeable, and we
  couldn't agree on how to proceed.

AN INTERPRETER'S PERSPECTIVE: The sleeping consumer is a classic
situation. The "twist," as you call it, seems to be the core issue. For me, an ideal

teaming situation is when two (or more) interpreters can work seamlessly to satisfy the goals of the assignment. This is why pre- and post-conferencing is essential. It's during these times when you and your team can play around with the "what ifs" such as: When do we switch? Who's going to start? Are you stronger at voicing or expressive interpreting? What kind of feeds do you want? If there's an environmental issue (e.g., lighting, sound), who's going to speak to the contact person? No matter what you decide, it is critical during the assignment that you show no disagreement or division. As you so rightly pointed out, disagreement just exacerbates the problem. A united front might also exemplify what deaf consumers mean when they say they want interpreters with good attitudes. After the assignment, or maybe during break, you can conference with your team to see if your plan is working. If not, that's the time to change your plan of action.

A DEAF CONSUMER'S PERSPECTIVE: When working with a team interpreter, especially with someone you do not know well or are not entirely comfortable with, you need to constantly remind yourself that the only person you can control is you. In any interpreting situation, you cannot control the client who may choose to sleep, your partner who may choose not to interpret, or even the presenter who may choose to use you as a prop. In this specific case, if you have decided that you want to continue interpreting, then for the time you are "on" proceed as usual. When it is your partner's turn, she can use her own discretion to decide what to do. If this is an interpreter with whom you have reasonably good rapport, then during the next break or after the assignment you could talk to the person about why she made that decision and perhaps come to a consensus of how to handle this situation in the future.

- **Scenario 599.** There are many interpreters out there who apparently still do not understand the concept of "team interpreting." I don't know if it's an inability or unwillingness on the part of these people to devote 100 percent of their energy or if they're just not taking interpreting jobs seriously. It has become all too common now for my interpreting partners to get up and walk out in the middle of a job in order to take or make a phone call. There are still interpreters who don't even watch me while I'm "on," much less offer me support. Don't you agree that it's high time we hold everyone accountable to the same rules of conduct?

AN INTERPRETER'S PERSPECTIVE: Unfortunately, we all know that the one interpreter "on" and one interpreter "off" philosophy exists. However, if I miss information, does that mean it's OK for my team to be busy text messaging an agency about another assignment? Or that teaming is only necessary if we are having an off day and need a bit more help? No, in fact, look at our "Standard Practice Paper on Team Interpreting." It contains statements such as, "All team members are constantly and actively involved," and "Support roles are necessary to enhance the team's performance." Now, have I ever checked my pager when I was the support interpreter? Absolutely. Would I consider it a best practice? Absolutely not. When we book an assignment, we often are asked to justify why we need a team. Having support and being actively involved in the process for the entire assignment benefits all consumers on that assignment. You have every right to expect that your team be with you 100 percent of the time. You should not feel that asking an interpreter to watch you when you are working equates to having a mentor. Use the "Standard Practice Paper" developed by our colleagues to support your belief that there is more to teaming than getting a break every 20 minutes.

A DEAF CONSUMER'S PERSPECTIVE: Notice the words "team interpreting;" what does one of those words mean? "Team" means two (or more) people working together on a common goal. As a deaf consumer, I have had numerous experiences with team interpreting, and one thing I have noticed is there is usually one dominant interpreter in the team. That dominant interpreter usually takes over everything and is the first one to leave early. Both interpreters are getting paid for the same number of hours worked, so both of them should stay to the end of the assignment unless one has a very good reason for leaving early (such as an emergency). The job of the "off" interpreter is to support the "on" interpreter doing the actual interpreting. It's not fair if you are left working alone while your team interpreter is either tired, doesn't understand what is going on, or misses what is being said. If someone can't work in a team (and that means supporting and providing feedback to each other until the very end), maybe she should stop taking jobs in which she'll be part of a team.

- **Scenario 600.** I interpreted with a partner who apparently has a bladder the size of a gerbil because every time we switched she left to go to the bathroom. She missed opportunities to feed me and see the signs the client and I had set up, and it just felt disjointed. The client was frustrated, but he never said anything to her. Neither did I; should I have?

AN INTERPRETER'S PERSPECTIVE: In my opinion, there certainly would be nothing wrong with pulling your partner aside during a break and expressing your concerns. There also certainly would be nothing wrong with the client expressing his concern. As professionals, we should all be able to give and accept constructive criticism. While you cannot control your partner, there is a reasonable expectation when working as part of a team. Usually these types of concerns can be worked out prior to the beginning of the assignment. If each team member states their expectations ahead of time, much trouble and misunderstanding can be avoided. Sometimes we are afraid to mention anything to our colleagues that might be perceived as negative. I have found that it is possible to address any situation in a calm, professional manner. Our common goal should be for the client to have as pleasant and seamless an experience as possible. That way, we are invited back and our reputation in the community is enhanced. Another course of action would be to say nothing and let it go. Chalk it up as a learning experience and make the decision not to partner with that particular interpreter in the future.

A DEAF CONSUMER'S PERSPECTIVE: It is very understandable that you had concerns about your interpreting partner's frequent leaves during the assignment. There are a number of legitimate reasons any person might make frequent trips to the bathroom, from the temporary (e.g., food poisoning, too much morning coffee, etc.) to the chronic (e.g., lactose intolerance, interstitial cystitis, truly tiny bladder). Your interpreting partner may have had a reason for not disclosing the need for these trips (e.g., too personal, too embarrassing, sincere belief and/or hope that the urgency will pass and she'll be able to get through the rest of the job without more interruptions). We don't know what the actual reasons were in this scenario, so we start with what we do know: frequent trips to the bathroom are not fun for anyone. If we do decide to say something to our team person, we start with sincere compassion: "Are you OK today?" followed by, "How can I be a good support today?" These questions can be on note paper since you are already in the midst of the job, and a note has the benefit of being private. Your partner, in turn, is still responsible for her own work she provides to the consumer and should be allowed to exercise her discretion in disclosing anything. With the possibility of a very personal circumstance causing the bathroom visits, the consumer (in this case, a male questioning a female) may have been uncomfortable mentioning it.

Other Scenarios

Identify the issue(s) involved and decide how you would respond. Discuss and compare your responses with your colleagues.

601. One hour before an assignment, your team interpreter calls to tell you she will be unable to make it but guarantees she will find a replacement. When you arrive at the assignment and see the substitute interpreter she has found, you're mortified. It's none other than your sworn mortal enemy. She's the same woman who steals your best clients, snubs you whenever you meet, and makes fun of your taste in clothes behind your back.

602. You are team interpreting a seminar. You're given a copy of the materials to be used today. The presenter is discussing some interesting personality tests included in the packet. You see that your partner has pulled out one of the tests and is filling in her answers. As if that weren't bad enough, when the audience starts discussing their answers, she raises her hand and participates.

603. You're team interpreting with an interpreter you have never worked with before. You talk about how to handle the switches and any necessary feeds. She seems very open to your ideas and says she has heard a lot about you and is looking forward to working with you. You start interpreting first and see that the deaf client and your partner are busy chatting. When it's time to switch, she's so engrossed in their conversation that she doesn't come up to switch. You can't get either her or the deaf client's attention.

604. You're team interpreting with another interpreter who you notice often uses unfamiliar sign choices. On break you ask her about them, and she tells you that she learned them in another state and is having a hard time switching to the signs used in your state. Normally you would buy it, but you know she has lived here 10 years now.

605. Your team interpreter has more certification than you, which she never lets you forget for a minute. When you watch her, though, you notice she tends to omit things that she either doesn't think are important or doesn't understand. You don't care much for her attitude or her interpreting, but you try to do the best job you can. One day she surprises you; she went to a mentoring workshop last weekend, and now she asks you for feedback. You feel certain she just wants affirmation of how wonderful she is.

606. While interpreting a lively, interactive group session, your team interpreter suddenly gets up and leaves the room. An hour later the group takes a break, and your partner has still not returned. Concerned, you go looking for him and find him in the lobby reading a newspaper. When you ask him what is wrong, he tells you the deaf client gets on his nerves and he just had to get out of there.

607. Your team interpreter at the college level is young, but very skilled. However, her appearance for classroom interpreting is a little too flashy in your book. She dresses like she's going to a nightclub afterwards. Granted, she always wears solid, contrasting colors; there's just a little too much cleavage and thigh showing for your taste. She's obviously attracted to the deaf student and he to her; they flirt constantly. If you say anything about her clothes, you'll only offend her.

608. You have been hired to interpret a conference, and so far most of the speakers have been very interesting. The particular speaker you're interpreting for right now is incredibly boring. Both the deaf and hearing attendees are either fidgeting or nodding off. You look over at your partner to switch, and he's sound asleep too.

609. During a break, your team interpreter is filling you in on all the details of her love life, and you have to admit, it's quite fascinating. When the break is over, she hasn't finished her saga, so while you're interpreting, she's still trying to tell you the rest of the story.

610. While interpreting a college class scheduled to go from 12 to 3 p.m., your team interpreter tells you she has booked another job at 3 o'clock, so she needs to leave a little early. She asks if you would mind setting it up so she would start and then you would do the last 30 minutes on your own.

611. While interpreting in a large college classroom, sometimes the acoustics are bad, and you miss information, at which point you always look over to your team interpreter for a feed. At one of those times, you look over to your partner for a feed, but she's engrossed in a crossword puzzle.

612. While team interpreting for a deaf client getting some training specifically to help him get a promotion, you see your partner leaving out a lot of important information. You feed her the information, but she ignores you. The client knows he's not getting everything and looks back and forth between the two of you for what she's signing and what you're feeding in an attempt to get all the information. When it's time to switch, she whispers, "Thanks a lot!" and you know you're going to hear about this later.

613. While team interpreting in a college classroom, your partner keeps feeding you signs that she wants you to use, but you feel pretty confident about the sign choices you're using. She's becoming more distracting to you now than helpful.

614. While team interpreting in a college classroom, your team interpreter starts clipping her nails. Then a little while later, you smell something and she's putting on nail polish. After class you quickly put on your coat and leave rather than stick around and chat like you normally do. You're afraid you'll say something you'll regret later. She follows you and tries to badger you into telling her what is wrong.

615. While your team interpreter is interpreting a meeting at the university where you both are on staff, the university's vice president leans over to you and tries to start a friendly side conversation with you.

616. You're interpreting a day-long church seminar. Your usual team interpreter is out of town so you're working with someone new. Two hours into the seminar, you're already fed up with him. He never pays attention when you're interpreting, much less feeds you when you need it. They break for lunch, and so you run out for a quick lunch alone and then head back to the church. The afternoon session begins. Within the first 10 minutes, your stomach starts churning and you're sure you're going to toss your veggie burrito right then and there. You can't get your team interpreter's attention in order to switch; in fact, it looks like he's sleeping.

617. You're seated close to your team interpreter, voicing for a well-known deaf presenter at a charity auction. You see your partner continually sipping something as you switch back and forth. You assume it's a Coke, but eventually you realize she's uncharacteristically slurring her words and giggling at her mistakes. You happen to know she's going through a rather nasty divorce and suspect her drink contains alcohol. The auction is scheduled to last at least another hour.

618. You're standing to the left of the speaker interpreting when, for some reason, your team interpreter jumps up and starts interpreting at the same time on the speaker's right.

619. You're team interpreting a meeting, and during a break several deaf people in the audience come up to you and say they understand you better than your partner. They ask you to do the rest of the meeting instead of your partner.

620. You're team interpreting a presentation by a deaf presenter when your partner leans over and whispers in your ear, "I think it's time for a break." Completely focused and trusting your partner's feed, you voice, "I think it's time for a break." The audience, also obviously ready for a break, gets up to leave. When the deaf presenter looks up from writing on the overhead, he's confused to see the room is now half empty. Meanwhile, your partner is apologizing to you profusely, explaining that those were his sentiments about being ready for a break, not the deaf presenter's.

621. You're team interpreting an all-day workshop. You and your partner agreed beforehand that you would switch every 20 minutes. You notice though that while you switch on time, her switches tend to leave you up there interpreting for 30 or 40 minutes at a stretch.

622. You're team interpreting with an interpreter who also happens to be a minister. You're both interpreting a large conference with a number of deaf people in the audience. At one point the presenter starts telling a dirty joke. You see your partner sign, "The speaker is telling a dirty joke," and then stand there with his arms by his side, not interpreting the joke. When the presenter resumes his lecture, your team interpreter starts interpreting again.

623. You're team interpreting with someone you have just met today. At one point in the presentation, there's a convenient break when the speakers switch. You signal to your partner to come up on stage now and switch. You don't know what to say, however, when your partner loudly hisses at you, "I've still got two more minutes before it's my turn!"

Challenges in Working Relationships with Other Interpreters

- **Scenario 624.** There's an interpreter in my area with whom I have a personality conflict. Even worse, it seems like every time I'm offered an assignment and I ask who my team interpreter is, it turns out to be her. I turn down the assignments because although she's a competent interpreter, I simply can't stand to be in the same room with her. I've turned down so many assignments, I'm afraid the agency will stop offering me jobs. The next call comes in, and it's for eight hours at the premium weekend rate. Guess who my team interpreter is?

AN INTERPRETER'S PERSPECTIVE: If you're normally easy to get along with, but you can't stand this person, chances are there are others who don't like her either. It may be time to mention this to the interpreting agency; you may be helping others as well. Explain there's a personality conflict and that working with this person would affect the quality of your work. You could also mention that other interpreters (no names!) have complained about this person, if that is the case. I would make it clear that I'd love to take these jobs, but I can't accept any jobs where I would be working with this person. From now on, if the agency wants me, they will need to find a different team interpreter.

A DEAF CONSUMER'S PERSPECTIVE: First of all, try to resolve the conflict with that interpreter in a neutral setting. If you can't do this, just do your best, leaving the personality conflict out of it. It's your attitude toward the other interpreter that's creating the problem, so change it to a positive attitude.

- **Scenario 625.** What do I say to my colleague when she tells me, "J says I'm the best interpreter he's ever had," knowing that I have interpreted for J as well? I'm not too bothered that J said this to her, but I am bothered that she tells me about it. I feel like this introduces an ugly, competitive flavor. What can I say to her without appearing jealous?

AN INTERPRETER'S PERSPECTIVE: The situation has the look and feel of a breach of the CPC, but you might not want to fight that battle by filing a grievance. A simpler approach might be to respond neutrally to the interpreter's comment (e.g., "It's nice to work with someone who likes your work") and let it go. Don't stoop to her level by competing with her on the issue. Continue to accept work with J as well as others and strive to make your interpreting solid. Work with interpreters on your team or in the community whom you trust and respect, and who offer you support and uphold your (as well as their own) professional integrity. Furthermore, continue to exhibit those qualities of trust, respect, and integrity to others in the field, especially newcomers. We can't afford to lose good (or potentially good) interpreters because of competitive, insensitive remarks made by a few.

A DEAF CONSUMER'S PERSPECTIVE: The deaf consumer most likely did not expect his comment that this particular interpreter is the "best interpreter he's ever had" to be shared with others. Assuming that this is a genuine comment, the interpreter should accept such a comment gracefully and keep it to herself for several reasons. First, such a comment may damage the relationship between this particular deaf consumer and other interpreters who perceive they have a strong relationship with this deaf consumer as well. Second, if this comment got back to the deaf consumer, it could lead to greater distrust about what these two interpreters disclose to each other about their deaf clients and the type of "gossip" they may share. Third, the comment reflects insecurity on the part of the speaker about her level of skill and relationship with deaf consumers, and reflects poorly on her (surely an unintended consequence of the comment). Finally, there is a possible risk, depending on the situation in which the comment was made, that the deaf person could perceive that there has been a breach of confidentiality in the sharing of his comment. The interpreter on the receiving end of such a comment might say something to the effect of, "I'm glad to hear you also have a nice working relationship with him; that's a very nice compliment he paid you." The interpreter could also add, "Can I suggest that you rephrase this comment in the future in order to make sure that the relationship the deaf consumer has with other interpreters is not damaged? I suggest that you just state that you have a good working relationship with the deaf consumer, instead of sharing his comment specifically. I'm sure the deaf consumer would prefer that other interpreters not know what he said specifically to you because that deaf person will still have to routinely work with other interpreters."

- **Scenario 626.** I am a male interpreter who has worked in an interpreter referral agency for about a year. I am professional in my demeanor, cordial but not overly friendly, and I do not tend to socialize with my colleagues outside the job. My female coworkers, however, continually engage in what I can only describe as intimate discussions during their downtime that, more often than not, get extremely graphic (mostly I suspect just to see my reactions). I'm not going to file a sexual harassment suit, but I believe this may be another reason why this field is predominately female and this profession is not taken seriously.

AN INTERPRETER'S PERSPECTIVE: You say, "This may be another reason why this field is predominately female and this profession is not taken seriously." I am not sure if you say this because of the intimacy among women, this group looking for your reactions, or something else. Rather than second guess the reasons for your statements, let me move to some reasons why our field has been traditionally dominated by women. Some of those reasons are because of low salary levels (the salary of a second family income), and we are a service profession. Gratefully, the field is changing and becoming advanced in some ways. The money is more lucrative so that some interpreters actually have decent incomes — incomes that can support a family and/or purchase a home and afford other luxuries. More men are becoming interested in the field, and education is raising the status of the profession.

I would like to make a few statements about your situation and how you state you are handling yourself. It sounds like you are conducting yourself in a professional manner. That is excellent and I encourage you to continue to be professional and cordial. You can be an example for others. I believe most women in this profession are not catty and sexist. I am saddened whenever I hear stories about my colleagues (men and women) who conduct themselves in this manner. Unfortunately, the colleagues of whom you speak would probably behave in the same manner regardless of their line of work. Interpreters represent deaf and hearing persons, as well as other interpreters. We need to always be mindful of this awesome responsibility in all aspects of our lives (work and play) — a responsibility that cannot/should not be taken lightly. My suggestion is to continue to talk the talk and walk the walk. We can only change ourselves and be examples for others to model.

A DEAF CONSUMER'S PERSPECTIVE: First of all, judging by your overall awareness of this situation, it sounds like you are on the right track with how you want to be seen and treated. If you feel this strongly, then you should continue to maintain boundaries between yourself and your coworkers by not encouraging any other relationship with them beyond what is required at work. Unfortunately, all relationships between colleagues can turn sour. These kinds of discussions could one day suddenly be turned around, and, who knows, you could be sued for sexual harassment by participating. I would recommend you first talk to your coworkers about your concerns, and hopefully, they will respect your wishes not to have these kinds of dialogues at work or, at least, not in your presence. You need to be up-front and clear with them about your desire to have strong professional relationships and not intimate ones with them. Should this situation not improve, you have no choice but to let your supervisor know what has been going on. I think it is important to protect yourself and your right to a safe working environment, regardless of your gender.

- **Scenario 627.** Another interpreter and I often team together and have become quite close. In between assignments, we began to share some of our personal lives with each other, which I didn't mind doing. Later my colleague started to tell me hair-raising stories about her sexual escapades and pressed me for details about my sex life. When I would tell her I didn't want to talk about it, she'd call me a prude! I don't mind sharing some things with her, just not everything! Now I'm reluctant to accept interpreting assignments with her. How do I continue to team with her without hurting her feelings?

AN INTERPRETER'S PERSPECTIVE: It seems as if you two have different ideas of where your boundaries are set. Some people's boundaries are more defined than others. While the other interpreter may feel comfortable disclosing more about her personal life than you would, her response to you about being a "prude" may just have been because she felt your boundaries were not as flexible as hers. You should not feel you cannot accept interpreting assignments if you are a good team. Sit down with the interpreter again and discuss your boundaries clearly. Remind the other interpreter, while you are on the job together, you need to maintain a degree of professionalism. If the other interpreter cannot accept your boundaries, you should not change yours in order to conform to hers. Remember, it is always a risk to bring up issues about your personal life at work because you are in fact enabling the interpreter to continue to cross your boundaries.

A DEAF CONSUMER'S PERSPECTIVE: The in-between assignment time can be difficult, whether it's with a deaf consumer or another interpreter. It can be very delicate, and we need to be aware of the kinds of conversations we get into during this time. If you are in a situation with a colleague with which you are uncomfortable, then you have a few choices. One solution would be to not work with that person anymore. I understand that this isn't the solution you'd prefer. You can talk with the person directly, and then you may be stuck with the first option. It does relate back to our CPC and "accepting assignments using discretion with regard to skill, setting, and the consumers involved." She may not respect your request, and then you have to decide how you can best perform your work.

- **Scenario 628.** I work as a staff interpreter at a large interpreter referral agency. I am openly gay, and most of my colleagues are comfortable around me. One particularly religious colleague, however, keeps leaving biblical tracts on my desk. I've told her I am not interested in her literature, but she insists on trying to save me. During team interpreting assignment breaks, she will talk about her beliefs and cite scriptures. I don't want to create waves within our agency, but this has turned into harassment.

AN INTERPRETER'S PERSPECTIVE: This colleague probably believes that sharing who she is and what she has is as important as being openly gay is to you. There are many 12-step programs that teach its members to practice principles before personalities. I am fortunate to be a member of one, and practicing principles helps me interact with those personalities with whom I disagree and have different beliefs and lifestyles. I would say to my colleague, "Thank you, I don't care for the literature, but I appreciate your offer. I have my own beliefs. They are different than yours, and although you want to share yours with me, please don't. I'm sure there are many other topics we would enjoy talking about. Thank you." This way, no waves are created, and you have made your honest and direct point. Now let it go, and remember you don't have to go home with that person.

A DEAF CONSUMER'S PERSPECTIVE: Whatever happened to common courtesy? I don't see that kind of behavior in this situation. You are right; this situation is definitely harassment. Before making an official grievance, however, I suggest you meet with her privately and explain you are not comfortable with her judgment of very personal aspects of your life. (According to your Constitutional rights, no one has the right to interfere.) If the problem is resolved and you can get along cordially and professionally, wonderful. If not, then the next step may be somewhat unpleasant, but necessary. State clearly to her what your next step will be if she doesn't stop, including a possible formal grievance. It is important that you communicate with your supervisor(s) and come prepared to those discussions with a journal or some kind of record of what has happened. Ideally though, I hope it doesn't have to come to that.

- **Scenario 629.** I chose the field of interpreting in college essentially on a whim because I took a class that I enjoyed, and I wanted to decide on a major quickly. I plugged along in the field mostly because it was the path of least resistance. I eventually earned my RID certification, but now I find myself growing weary of this field. Is it just me or does everyone else find this field to be full of backstabbers, critics, and gossipers?

AN INTERPRETER'S PERSPECTIVE: I think our field can be negative in that we can be critical of each other. However, I have also seen increasing attempts to move away from this and work together in a more positive and supportive manner, a trend I hope each and every one of us will continue to foster.

A DEAF CONSUMER'S PERSPECTIVE: Yes, it can be full of backstabbers, critics, and people who gossip. These people are never satisfied with their careers. My advice to you is to know who you are and determine if you really desire to be an interpreter for the deaf. If you know who you are, then you can distance yourself from the backstabbing behavior. Just keep in mind the quality interpreters you have met, and make it your goal to be counted among them.

- **Scenario 630.** Two interpreters recently came to me asking for advice about how they should deal with an interpreter who they believe is behaving unethically. Truthfully, I don't really want to get involved. I hate all the drama that always comes along with these things.

AN INTERPRETER'S PERSPECTIVE: Me too! I hate that we all judge each other so frequently and don't do enough to pump each other up. I would tell these two politely that I prefer not to get involved, unless I was there to witness the situation, as it is too easy to misunderstand as a third party. The most I would do is advise the two interpreters that confronting people on this sort of thing often leads to hurt feelings and could bring more harm than good to the interpreters themselves. I would then change the topic and move on.

A DEAF CONSUMER'S PERSPECTIVE: If I wasn't personally involved somehow with the actions of this purported unethical interpreter, I wouldn't get involved. Otherwise, your suggestions and advice may be repeated with your name attached to it.

Other Scenarios

Identify the issue(s) involved and decide how you would respond. Discuss and compare your responses with your colleagues.

631. You're a staff interpreter at an interpreter referral agency and become involved with another interpreter on staff. Unfortunately, after a few glorious months together, it ends badly. Now the two of you can't stand being in the same room together, much less team interpret together.

632. A fellow interpreter is telling you about an assignment that she has accepted that you believe is way beyond her abilities. Her voicing skills are still quite weak, and this assignment could mean some serious consequences for the client if she misses anything. You know she wouldn't take the suggestion to pass the job on to someone else as constructive criticism.

633. A fellow staff interpreter at the university where you work asks you to cover her night class. You have been interpreting all day and you're beat. When you hesitate, she reminds you of how many times she has covered for you.

634. You sit with your mentor at an educational interpreters' workshop. She has been your idol since you were an ITP student. She has always been there for you. Today, however, you think she's being petty and unkind as she gossips about the other interpreters in the room. You can't decide if she was always like this and you just never noticed or if she's just having a bad day.

635. You're at a Deaf social activity at a neighborhood church and are having a great time meeting new people. One interpreter you meet, though, is very vocal about her negative feelings about RID and how expensive their yearly dues are.

She's also complaining about the NAD test and their standards for testing. Basically, she's putting down everything and everyone. You can't seem to extricate yourself from her, but you don't want to look like you're associated with her either.

636. You're sick and tired of all the backbiting, backstabbing, and gossiping that seems to go on among the interpreters in your area. You're fine working alone, but the minute you work with another interpreter, either you find out later they've said terrible things about you behind your back or they say terrible things to you about other interpreters. When you get a newsletter announcing an upcoming, statewide workshop in your mailbox, you immediately pitch it. A room full of interpreters sounds more like a nightmare than a good time.

637. Your state's RID chapter is putting on a workshop this weekend, and you plan to attend with an interpreter with whom you work at an agency. You haven't been to a workshop in a couple of years. Your coworker seems to suspect this, because he keeps quizzing you — did you go to such-and-such workshop, and wasn't it great, and so on. You figure it's none of his business, and after all, you're trying to mend your ways.

638. Often I hear that hearing interpreters are competitive and not supportive of each other. I feel that CDIs are also competitive and not supportive of each other. Interestingly, my strongest support as a CDI has come from a core of hearing interpreters. These interpreters speak up to say that partnering with a CDI on an assignment ensures greater accuracy and comprehension. How can we all work together better?

Challenges in Handling Other Interpreters' Inappropriate Behavior

- **Scenario 639.** I've heard rumors from a large number of colleagues (both interpreters and deaf consumers) that another interpreter in the community has been bad mouthing me all over town. I even saw an e-mail a friend showed me with some very unflattering comments about me. Should I say anything? If so, what?

AN INTERPRETER'S PERSPECTIVE: In my experience, I don't see anything to be gained by confronting this person. Instead, I would work on teaching those around you who love you to either stand up for you or not tell you these hurtful rumors. Saying something critical about someone is fundamentally different from saying the same thing to the person directly. Even hearing criticism secondhand is like being shot by a gun with a silencer. You are shocked even more because you are struck by an attacker who is nowhere in sight, and you can't defend yourself. Repeating negative comments is unnecessarily hurtful even when the reporter has the best intentions. When you realize someone is about to tell you something that was said about you (even though a small part of you wants to know), stop the speaker in her tracks. You both know it's not true.

A DEAF CONSUMER'S PERSPECTIVE: Approach this person and say, "If you have a problem with something I've done, then I'd prefer you to tell me directly." Of course, you say it calmly and without anger; it is the perfect medicine. For one, it will catch her off guard. Usually, people who talk behind your back won't expect to be confronted. While she is still off balance, you can disarm her with kindness. Smile and (if possible) forgive. If you can do that, it will make it hard for her to continue to hate you.

- **Scenario 640.** I know for a fact that a colleague is cheating on her invoices. She always claims the full mileage from her home for every job even when, I know for a fact, she just came from another assignment close by.

AN INTERPRETER'S PERSPECTIVE: Unless you see her invoices or she tells you that she cheats, you can't always automatically assume this is truly happening. However, for the sake of argument, try opening a dialogue with this interpreter. You may say something like, "I don't like how my contract and invoicing work. How do you do billing?" Then in the context of the entire conversation, you can ask about specifics: "What do you charge for portal-to-portal? At what mileage do you start charging? Do you charge mileage from each place to home or just place to place?"

Then see how she responds. If she lies on top of cheating, then there is probably nothing you can do; some people just aren't honest. If she admits to charging from home to each place, you can come back with a simple, "I don't know if I agree with doing that, but I appreciate you sharing with me." That way, she knows how you feel without you attacking her, and maybe she will rethink how she does billing. You never know, maybe she thinks this is standard practice, and your dissent could inspire her to change her ways.

A DEAF CONSUMER'S PERSPECTIVE: Referral agencies handle mileage reimbursement in different ways. Some agencies consider each assignment as an independent entity for billing purposes. For example, you interpret a doctor's appointment from 9 to 10 a.m. and then a college class from 10:30 to 11:30 a.m. The two assignments are in close proximity to each other and require less miles than actually driving home and back. Some agencies consider these two assignments independent from each other and expect the interpreters to bill for the time and mileage as if each was the only assignment for the day. The agency then bills the requesting organization on that basis. Other agencies would divide the actual miles between the two assignments and bill accordingly. If the first case is true, then your colleague is not incorrectly billing for mileage. If the second case is true, then the agency should know that these two assignments are back to back and should notice a discrepancy in the mileage request. If it has gone unnoticed, this is when you could ask your colleague about her reporting methods or approach the coordinator of the agency.

I assume from your question that the assignments were given by the same agency. If the assignments were received through different venues and, therefore, would not be tracked by any one given agency, then this would be a matter of what is standard professional practice among the local interpreting community, as well as professional integrity. Interpreters may disagree on whether billing should be treated independently when assignments are obtained independently or linked in proximity and time. You could then have a discussion with your colleague on your feelings that it is inappropriate to charge full mileage from one's home when the assignments did not actually require that much mileage. You cannot monitor her billing practices, but can share your opinion and give the person something to think about. Just feel comfortable in your own decisions and that you are being forthright and trustworthy in your billing practices, and set a good example for other interpreters.

- **Scenario 641.** Another freelance interpreter and I are team interpreting one day. We both graduated from the same ITP and get most of our assignments from the same agency. After the assignment I'm surprised to see her giving out her own business card to the person in charge. We were both sent to the assignment by the agency, but she's telling the woman in charge to call her directly in the future, and she'll give them a better deal.

AN INTERPRETER'S PERSPECTIVE: I would approach them with an agency business card in hand, reinforcing that path of contact. Knowing this interpreter, I might approach her later and tactfully say that I was under the impression, since we were there via the agency, we were supposed to hand out the agency's business cards. I would also mention that it was uncomfortable for me to see her underbidding the agency. With someone I didn't know, I might say something like, "Hmmm, I've always thought I couldn't hand out my personal business card if I was on assignment through the agency." If the person disagreed, I might suggest calling the agency to clarify this. I might also say, "You know, I have a bunch of agency business cards in my car. Do you need a couple?"

A DEAF CONSUMER'S PERSPECTIVE: Ask the other interpreter directly if she felt that her actions were appropriate and see how she responds.

- **Scenario 642.** I've gone to several conferences over the years, and often there is a DJ scheduled for entertainment as part of the conference. I used to enjoy them, but not anymore! At the last two regional conferences, I witnessed people who had just earlier given presentations or sat at head tables suddenly becoming transformed. As the night went on, they became more suggestive and sexually explicit. I understand completely this is meant as a social event, but it is also part of the conference I paid to attend! Now all I can see when I look at these people in the light of day is their sloppy kisses or grinding their crotches into someone's face. How do we modify this trend of inappropriate behavior that reflects so poorly on them and the conference they worked so hard to put on?

AN INTERPRETER'S PERSPECTIVE: It seems this was a very uncomfortable situation for you. It probably was for others as well. Bravo to you for raising concern and asking the question. When someone in my profession behaves in a way that reflects poorly upon me and my other colleagues, I believe I have a responsibility to do something about it. There are several choices: (1) In the case you describe, I can ignore the situation which means, because I have said nothing, I accept it, even if I dislike or don't condone the behavior; (2) I can report to the "interpreting police" and expect them to take care of it for me. This means that I have found an easier solution than actually confronting it myself. I want someone else to take care of it for me; (3) I also can contact the persons showing the inappropriate behavior and share that it is and was uncomfortable for me, in this case, especially in front of an audience; or (4) I can write a positive evaluation regarding the conference content to the coordinators of the conference but also share what I observed and ask that my statement be included in the report to the next host conference committee. No matter what I choose, I must accept my decision and live with it. Our behavior, as interpreters, reflects upon our colleagues as well as our consumers, and I hope that my behavior is the kind that others want to emulate, regardless of whether I am on the job or not.

A DEAF CONSUMER'S PERSPECTIVE: Public displays like this make most onlookers uncomfortable and with good reason. This behavior is intimate and should only be done in a setting (e.g., a bar, party) where everyone in attendance knows this is the norm. I hope, on your conference evaluation, you brought this to the attention of the planning committee. In addition, I think a letter to your RID regional representative is appropriate. You won't get a refund, but unless you make your feelings known, this type of behavior will not stop. I don't want to see it at my regional or national conferences either!

Other Scenarios

Identify the issue(s) involved and decide how you would respond. Discuss and compare your responses with your colleagues.

643. You have decided to carpool with three other ITP students to a workshop scheduled for later that evening. You get there early, and the other two students want to stop in at a local pub for happy hour. You're thinking it's great to really get to know your fellow students, and you don't want to be seen as a stick-in-the-mud. However, one student ends up getting a little tipsy. Worse still, since "Ms. Happy Hour" didn't want to leave the bar, you all get there a little late, and everyone looks at you as you walk in.

644. You and a friend register for a workshop geared toward interpreting in a mental health setting. At the last minute, your friend can't go, and it's too late for you to get a refund. Afterward she asks you for a copy of your notes and handouts. She tells you she knew all the information covered anyway and plans to add this workshop to her resume since she already paid for it. She says she will have a receipt to prove it if anyone ever challenges it.

645. You hear through the grapevine that another interpreter has been criticizing your work and advising deaf clients not to hire you.

646. A fellow staff interpreter at the high school where you interpret has come to school dressed for Halloween as what she calls an "AIDS victim." The kids all think it's hysterical, but you personally think it's in extremely poor taste and are appalled.

647. You're a nationally certified interpreter attending a presentation about hearing ear dogs with a deaf friend. The organization is providing their own interpreter, someone on staff. The first thing the interpreter says is, "I'm sorry my skills are so bad, but it's been a long time since I last signed." You sigh and remind yourself you're just there to hear the presentation, not to interpret. Once the presentation begins, it's obvious the interpreter is lost, and you end up feeling sorry for her. Your deaf friend asks a question, and the interpreter freezes. You're sitting next to the interpreter at the table, and by instinct, quietly feed her the word she needs. She angrily turns to you and snaps, "Who's interpreting here, me or you?"

648. You're an ITP student doing your internship at a middle school. While you're up getting some hands-on time under the interpreter's supervision, she opens up your date book and starts reading your entries. You can't stop her unless you stop interpreting, but the book contains information about all your practicum sites.

649. You're at a workshop sitting with an interpreter you observe every week for your internship. You're dumbfounded as she introduces you to another interpreter and tells her all about the situation where you two work together.

Challenges Related to Inappropriate Comments and Questions When Not Interpreting

- **Scenario 650**. I was interpreting in court for a deaf man charged with sexually abusing a child. On break, a woman sitting in the audience approaches me and tells me she lives next door to him. She says she's worried because she has three small children. The woman asks if I have any kids and, if so, how I can stand to interpret for him.

AN INTERPRETER'S PERSPECTIVE: Giving your opinion on the matter would be a breach of the code of impartiality. However, you might inform this person about the role of an interpreter.

A DEAF CONSUMER'S PERSPECTIVE: Explain to the woman that you aren't personally involved, and that you're just doing your job. You might also explain that everyone has a right to equal access to information and communication, especially in the legal system.

- **Scenario 651**. A friend and I are at Dairy Queen one night when in walks a group of deaf people. Behind the counter, the teenage workers make rude remarks about the deaf group that are loud enough for everyone else to hear. Now my banana split has lost its flavor, and I want to throw it at these rude people. The deaf people are so engrossed in their own conversations they're not even paying attention to the smirking teenagers. And, after all, I'm just there to add a few inches to my hips.

AN INTERPRETER'S PERSPECTIVE: I may not be at the Dairy Queen to interpret, but I'm still a human being who has witnessed inexcusable mean-spiritedness against other human beings. The counter workers probably don't realize there's someone around who can tell them off in both spoken English and ASL. Once I positioned myself in clear view of the deaf people, I would do just that. I would say something like, "Did I just hear you say . . ." and then repeat the rude remark. What the deaf group decides to do about the situation at that point is completely up to them.

A DEAF CONSUMER'S PERSPECTIVE: I wouldn't say anything. You're not working; you're just there for ice cream. If the deaf people were aware of what was going on and it looked like a fight was brewing, then maybe I would get involved as a person who knows sign language and not as an interpreter.

- • **Scenario 652**. I interpret in a church with several other interpreters. Each of us takes turns interpreting the songs, sermon, prayers, or Sunday school service for the deaf kids. One day one of the deaf mothers comes up to me and starts complaining about the school her kids attend and where I also work as an interpreter. She doesn't feel the teachers give the kids enough attention. She wants my advice about how to approach the administration. One of the other church interpreters also works at the same school. She's standing there watching the conversation, but she isn't saying a word.

AN INTERPRETER'S PERSPECTIVE: Politely explain that you're not there as an expert on pedagogy or school-parent relations, and it would be inappropriate for you to advise her. I have found most deaf adults to be very understanding in cases like these. You could offer your services as an interpreter, however she decides to handle the situation. I would then find an excuse to politely cut the conversation short.

A DEAF CONSUMER'S PERSPECTIVE: Rather than give specific advice, encourage her to arrange a meeting with the school administrator, and offer to go with her as an interpreter.

Other Scenarios

Identify the issue(s) involved and decide how you would respond. Discuss and compare your responses with your colleagues.

653. You and your husband are at his company's Christmas party. One of his coworkers is fascinated with your job and asks you all kinds of questions about what it's like to be an interpreter. He asks you to please teach the table some "dirty" signs.

654. While out with a group of friends, they coax you into teaching them some sexual signs. You humor them since none of them know any deaf people. The following week a deaf friend comes up to you and says she's very offended because a student in her ASL 1 class showed her some signs you taught her. She says she and her colleagues are very disappointed in your lack of judgment regarding their language.

655. You have interpreted for a very wealthy, elderly deaf man in his attorney's office several times as he continually revised his will. As it turns out, the man decides to leave a lot of money to the ITP where you teach. After he dies and the will is read, the rumor on the grapevine is that you manipulated the old man for your personal gain.

656. You're at a bar one weekend and end up having a delightful conversation with a deaf man whom you've never met before. The next week you're at the local Deaf club when you see the same man with another group. A deaf friend comes over, points to him, and tells you he's telling everyone you slept with him.

657. A deaf friend of yours calls and asks you to go with him when he buys a motorcycle. He says he doesn't want you there as an interpreter, just as a friend. During the negotiations, the salesman doesn't realize you can hear and tells a coworker he doesn't want to sell a Harley to a "spic." You're both of Mexican-American decent.

658. The president of the university where you're a staff interpreter is pretty good about making sure there's an interpreter at all his public addresses. His secretary, however, never fails to gripe about what a drain to the budget these "access" jobs are because no deaf people ever show up. She acts like it's coming out of her own pocket.

659. After interpreting an all-day conference, as you pull out of the parking ramp, the deaf client is pulling out his car in front of you. He apparently doesn't look both ways before pulling out, and he's hit broadside by another car. You pull over to see if he's OK, and within minutes, the police arrive. The officer says he will need to talk to both drivers, and so you wait with the deaf man so he can give his statement. You can clearly hear the other driver talking to the police officer, and you hear the man say, "They shouldn't let deaf and dumb people drive." Then you hear the officer reply, "You got that right!"

660. You get a call to interpret a church service for a deaf woman whose son is being baptized this Sunday. The church secretary tells you, "If you don't come, there will be no one there to interpret for the poor deaf people. God will surely bless you."

Challenges Related to Making Mistakes

- **Scenario 661**. I'm interpreting in a chemistry class, and I'm trying hard to comprehend everything so I can interpret the meaning of the lecture accurately. The professor starts discussing the breaking apart of molecules and uses the term "cleavage" to describe the process. After about the fifth time the word is said, I see my team interpreter cracking up and trying to feed me a better sign choice. I must have been on auto-pilot because I suddenly realize I've been signing the word literally.

AN INTERPRETER'S PERSPECTIVE: I would accept the sign, thank my team member, smile to show I can laugh at myself, and just go on interpreting using the more appropriate sign. Mistakes happen; I'm human, and I can have a sense of humor.

A DEAF CONSUMER'S PERSPECTIVE: Just keep doing the job, and use the more correct sign for "cleavage." The student probably knew what the sign was supposed to be and didn't let it distract his attention.

- **Scenario 662**. I'm an interpreting student. I have arranged to get some observation hours at a site about an hour and a half from my home. I leave my house at 6:30 a.m. (which means I got up at 5:30), and on the drive I feel myself starting to fall asleep at the wheel. I decide to pull over and take a quick nap, rather than risk my life on the road any longer. By the time I get to the assignment, the class is half over. The interpreter shoots me a dirty look when I sit down, and I don't blame her. I'd be mad, too.

AN INTERPRETER'S PERSPECTIVE: Let the interpreter know what happened and apologize to the folks involved for being late. Unless showing up late is a pattern, then it really shouldn't be a problem. Also, let the ITP know what happened and why. Take responsibility for what you did, and everyone can move on. The time and location of a job or observation is always a factor to take into consideration. This might factor in more heavily in the future; it's probably a good lesson for you.

A DEAF CONSUMER'S PERSPECTIVE: The ITP student shouldn't get credit for observing. It's your responsibility to be ready for an observation the night before. If you show up late, no matter why, you have to start all over.

- **Scenario 663.** During some down time on an interpreting job, the client asked me how I was doing. Suddenly, I got all weepy and ended up blithering on more than I probably should have. Afterwards I could have kicked myself!

AN INTERPRETER'S PERSPECTIVE: It's OK; you are human. Apologize to the client, and explain that is not your normal behavior and that you won't ever unload like that again on the job. Chances are the client will be fine with your apology, and you'll have a chance to live up to your promise.

A DEAF CONSUMER'S PERSPECTIVE: First of all, recognize that you are a human being with thoughts, feelings, and emotions, and don't beat yourself up too much for expressing those. Learn from the experience. You realized your sharing those feelings was not the right thing to do at that time and place. When you think back on that event, consider what was going on that caused you to let down your guard more than was appropriate. What caused you to break down like that? Stress? Events in your personal life? What was the trigger? Use this as a learning experience and develop some strategies to deal with your own emotions when you are in a professional role. If you have the opportunity to talk with that deaf person again in the near future, just apologize for your behavior, and go from there.

- **Scenario 664.** I showed up at an assignment today underdressed. It wasn't intentional, but I felt like I stuck out like a sore thumb. I feel like I misrepresented the client by my casual attire.

AN INTERPRETER'S PERSPECTIVE: Since you didn't intend it, don't beat yourself up too much, but do use it as a learning experience. I would send a quick e-mail to apologize to the client and let her know that you will use this as a learning experience and did not intend to cause any distraction. You'll be sure to be better informed next time. Some interpreters carry a bag in their trunk for such emergencies.

A DEAF CONSUMER'S PERSPECTIVE: Why were you underdressed? Was it because other, more casual assignments were prior to this one? Did you misunderstand the type of assignment? Try to figure out why you dressed the way you did so that you might avoid a repeat performance. If it was because you dressed for other more casual assignments, you may need to carry a change of clothes with you for more formal assignments.

Other Scenarios

Identify the issue(s) involved and decide how you would respond. Discuss and compare your responses with your colleagues.

665. You have a full day of interpreting scheduled and just enough time to grab a quick lunch. You ordered extra onions on your sandwich and are totally embarrassed when one of the hearing clients at your next job asks you if you want a mint.

666. A deaf couple attending counseling sessions is requesting an additional session each week. The therapist asks you if you're available on the date the deaf couple is suggesting. You say it would be tight because you have got a job 40 minutes away from there interpreting for another couple. Whoops, it was enough information for the couple to say, "Oh, you must mean the Johnsons."

667. Money is tight right now, so you took an assignment interpreting for a deaf client for whom you wouldn't normally interpret. You figure it's your own fault now when he gets on your nerves, but it's affecting your interpreting. You're having trouble concentrating on the information because you're too busy kicking yourself for accepting the job.

668. You're a zealous ITP student signed up for a weekend retreat. You're thrilled to be paired up with a deaf roommate. The deaf woman is very patient with your signing skills and your many questions. In the room that night, you say goodnight and turn out the lights. As you're lying there, you hear a jet roar overhead. Wanting to share this information, you crawl over to the next bed and sign "jet" into her hand. The deaf woman feels your hand shape in the dark, suddenly sits up, turns on the light, and orders you to find a new roommate! She avoids you for the rest of the weekend, and it's not until a few weeks later that you realize what you signed. Meanwhile, word has gotten around about your "amorous advances."

669. During a lull in the elementary classroom where you interpret, you make a quick dash to the restroom. When you get back to the classroom, everyone is laughing at you. You stand there completely baffled, and finally the teacher suggests that the next time you go to the bathroom, you might want to remove your phonic microphone, or at least turn it off.

670. While interpreting in a college class on an exam day, you're looking out the window watching some construction going on while the deaf student is taking her test. You see a bulldozer coming closer and closer to the window, and it looks like it's going to come right through the wall. You scream and the whole class looks up, the test momentarily forgotten. The bulldozer, of course, doesn't come through the window. It has changed direction, and you now look like a fool.

671. One day while interpreting for a deaf woman, she tells her boss she recently had F.L.U. You're not familiar with the acronym, so you voice each individual letter out loud. Her boss's expression indicates that he also has no idea what she's saying, so you ask the deaf woman to repeat herself. This time she signs each letter two inches in front of your face in slow motion. Still confused, you go ahead and ask the client what it means. She has lost all patience by this time. She gives you an exasperated sign and says, "You know, cold, cough, headache. I recently had the flu!"

672. The high school history teacher is talking about a videotape they have just watched about the different groups of people persecuted by the Nazis during World War II. The title of the video is "Purple Triangles," and without thinking, you have repeatedly been making the sign for "vagina" instead of "triangle." It's too late to take back anything because the deaf students are now giggling and disrupting the class. The teacher stops and asks if you or the students would like to share what could possibly be so funny about such a serious topic.

673. The name of the sermon today in church is "Winners and Losers." The deaf congregation bursts out laughing when you accidentally sign the name of the sermon is "Winners and Intercourse."

674. While interpreting for a group of five deaf women attending a weight-loss program with 30 hearing women, you inadvertently make an obscene sign, and the deaf women start laughing hysterically. The leader of the group stops speaking and looks over with a puzzled look on her face. She's waiting for someone to explain to her what is so funny.

675. You're a returning missionary for your church and have been serving on a mission for deaf people in another country for two years. Now that you're home, the deaf members of your church are eagerly anticipating seeing you interpret the service and seeing how much your skills have improved. After the service, a deaf woman approaches you and asks you about an unfamiliar sign you used repeatedly today that just didn't seem to fit the sermon. The deaf woman shows you "the sign," and much to your chagrin it was only an itch you were scratching.

676. You're an experienced, nationally certified interpreter interpreting the opening ceremonies of a week-long festival. Before the governor speaks, there's an invocation. You start interpreting the invocation and every other word the minister says is "God." For the life of you, you can't remember the sign for the word "God."

677. You're interpreting at church, and the preacher is talking about how Mary was ashamed to tell Joseph she was pregnant. However, much to your chagrin, you realize too late that you have just signed Mary was a "whore."

678. You're interpreting for a deaf football player during a football game. With the noise from the crowd and the announcer over the PA system, it's hard to hear the coach's directions. At one point, the coach looks very angry, and he tells the deaf player he's going to have him arrested. The boy is confused and asks the coach, "Why? What have I done?" The coach ignores him and gestures for him to go sit on the bench. The boy is distraught trying to figure out what crime he could have been accused of. Finally at half time, the coach comes over and tells the deaf player why he wanted to "rest" him. You're sure that someday the deaf boy will look back on this and laugh. However, at the moment, he looks like he doesn't find your little mistake the least bit funny.

679. You're interpreting for a deaf student in a high school math class. The teacher is going around the room reviewing the answers to the homework problems. The teacher calls on the deaf student, and although you can see her answer on her paper, she gives a different answer, a wrong answer. You anticipated the right answer, and so you voiced the answer that was on her paper by mistake.

680. You're voicing for a deaf person making a presentation to a large audience. It's not possible to get the deaf speaker to stop in this situation, but you have just missed a sign. The first time the speaker uses the sign, you just work around it. However, then it comes up several more times, and even with the context nothing comes to mind that fits. You know you have done your client a disservice and that if you tell him he will lose confidence in you.

681. In a college algebra class, the deaf student wants to make an appointment with the professor to talk about some problems he is having with the class, and an appointment is made. In the following class, the professor angrily asks the student why he did not show up for his appointment, and the student is baffled. Turns out it was your mistake. The professor has a British accent; his pronunciation of "Tuesday" sounded just like "Thursday" to you, and so you interpreted the wrong day.

682. You had onions for lunch, so you grab a stick of gum to mask any offending odors. When you get back to the job, you forget you have the gum in your mouth. At one point the presenter turns to you and says the sound of your gum snapping is annoying him and asks you to remove it. You want to melt into the floor.

683. At a large conference, you're interpreting for a speaker who speaks in a monotone voice and pauses in the weirdest places. For example, he says, "And this next part is especially important today, I have begun," and then he pauses. You thought you heard him say, "Today, I have a gun." The deaf audience panics and starts to leave before you realize what has happened.

684. You're interpreting a graduate course where the professor is giving specific instructions about the upcoming exam. The professor is giving out a list of study questions, and then tells the students they will pick out 10 questions to answer on the final. On the day of the exam, the professor hands out the exam, and the deaf student looks at it and is so confused she raises her hand and says, "I thought you said we were going to be able to pick out the 10 questions we wanted to answer." The professor turns to the rest of the class and asks them if that is what they understood also, but they all say "no." Suddenly you realize that it was you who made the error because that is what you understood the professor to say. Now the deaf student is not prepared for her final exam.

Challenges in Handling the Unexpected

- **Scenario 685.** I am interpreting in church, and there's a guest minister today. He starts talking about handicapped people and sees me signing. He walks up to me and says, "Deaf woman, be healed," and smacks me on the forehead. I'm caught completely off guard and fall to the floor. He turns and walks over to a line of people now forming, waiting to be healed.

AN INTERPRETER'S PERSPECTIVE: "Oh, the places you'll go!" Dr. Seuss said. This is one of the many moments in your career when you'll need to try to regain your composure and continue the job. Control the urge to "heal" him back! After the sermon, you could talk with the deaf audience members about how to approach the guest minister and educate him. If the deaf attendees aren't comfortable addressing the minister, I would feel comfortable as the person who was smacked to explain what my role is and that being "spontaneously healed" doesn't allow me to perform my job.

A DEAF CONSUMER'S PERSPECTIVE: Too funny! My advice would be to regain your composure and continue interpreting. My guess is that some of the audience is laughing hysterically, and some may believe you were healed. Either way, stay in role.

- **Scenario 686.** I'm interpreting a summer school class when I notice a spider making its way down from the ceiling toward me. I'm phobic about spiders and ready to panic as the spider makes its way down in front of my face.

AN INTERPRETER'S PERSPECTIVE: My reaction might depend on many factors, such as the age of the students, the formality of the class, my location in the class, etc. In the final analysis, I would try to gracefully move to a new spot until the break, when I could recruit a bug relocation expert to get rid of the spider.

A DEAF CONSUMER'S PERSPECTIVE: If the interpreter is a true spiderphobe, she should ask her deaf client to please "pull the web and squash that beast!"

- **Scenario 687.** I'm interpreting an all-day conference where lunch is served, but the deaf client tells me and my partner this is a working lunch. We'll both need to interpret through lunch. I'm starving.

AN INTERPRETER'S PERSPECTIVE: My partner and I would need to quickly work out how we will take turns so that we each have a bit of time to eat. When I'm not "on," I would quickly eat and try to remain attentive enough to back up my partner, if needed.

A DEAF CONSUMER'S PERSPECTIVE: The interpreters should alternate: one interpreter is interpreting while the other is eating. Luckily, this assignment has two interpreters!

- **Scenario 688.** Recently I was hired to interpret for a doctor's appointment. The deaf client brought a friend along (whom I recognized, but don't know as another certified interpreter). During the appointment she and the deaf consumer were chatting (in ASL) while the doctor was trying to ask questions. She never introduced herself or used her voice so the doctor thought she was deaf too. The doctor used several medical terms the client clearly did not understand, and this other interpreter would take it upon herself to explain it further, rather than let me or the doctor do our jobs. It took me totally off guard, not to mention making me feel very uncomfortable. At one point the doctor looked at me when they were signing, and all I could say was that they were having a conversation. Later I misunderstood the client, and the friend herself finally voiced the correct response. This was not a life threatening situation. I believe that the incorrect response I gave would have caused the doctor to ask for clarification, at which point I would have realized my error and been able to correct it on my own. How should I have handled this situation better?

AN INTERPRETER'S PERSPECTIVE: This situation highlights a destructive dynamic within our profession that is difficult to understand. Interpreters who act in ways which make another feel inferior or incompetent in order to make themselves feel superior or competent undermine our profession in ways that no outside influence can. The actions of the interpreter/friend in this scenario not only affected you, but the deaf consumer and the doctor as well. The impressions that are made in these situations are formative and lasting and will have repercussions beyond that one day. As professionals, we need to interact in ways that positively impact both the attitudes and abilities of each other and those we serve. You did indeed allow the interpreter/friend to diminish your role, and that of the doctor as well.

It is important for you to continue to act as the interpreter of record, even with another interpreter in the room. You needed to assert your professional authority (and responsibility) by interpreting everything that was signed, regardless of who was signing. This would have given the doctor the opportunity to act within her professional authority to explain medical information that was confusing or misunderstood by the deaf consumer. By reducing your interpretation to "They are having a conversation" (About the weather? Baseball standings? The price of gas?), you eliminated the opportunity for the doctor to have meaningful interaction with the deaf consumer, while overly empowering the interpreter/friend with the responsibility of medical information, the content of which may or may not have been accurate. You did not mention if you had time for a moment to introduce (or re-introduce) yourself to the deaf consumer. It would have been an opportunity to acknowledge the interpreter friend and set professional boundaries: "Oh, hello. I know your name but I haven't had the chance to meet you. What a pleasure. What a great support for your friend that you can just be here for her, without worrying about interpreting." If we, as interpreters, can honor these boundaries and move beyond insecurity and self-doubt that needs to be bolstered by one-upmanship, we can truly and effectively serve consumers with professional confidence and assurance.

A DEAF CONSUMER'S PERSPECTIVE: This other interpreter's lack of professional cooperation was uncalled for. Friend of the deaf client or not, she is not deaf; and as an interpreter, she was very aware of the situation in which she was putting you. It was thoughtless and hurtful to play games. She can't have it both ways. If she's going as a (hearing) friend, then when introductions were made, she should have used her voice and identified herself. I understand if she chooses to sign with her deaf friend, but she can't have a side conversation without you needing to voice interpret her communication for the hearing doctor. Later if she decides to "assist" you with your interpreting (tongue in cheek here), you should stop and ask her if she wants to take over. No, she won't; she just wants to make points with the client or make herself feel bigger. Offering her the opportunity to "work" instead should shut her up and hopefully drive home your point that she is interfering.

- **Scenario 689.** I am hoping to find an answer or least get some feedback regarding a situation I encountered last week after an interpreting assignment. I arrived a few minutes before the consumer and when the assignment was over, I found out that the meeting was being "recorded." The only reason I found out was because I interpreted for the deaf consumer who stated at the very end of the meeting that she would get the transcript and write up the official minutes. The meeting was apparently being listened to by the Federal Relay Closed Caption (mentioned in their statement). This happened without our (the interpreters') knowledge. As interpreters, do we have a right to know that we are being recorded? I got the distinct impression that everyone else in the meeting knew because they acted so "matter of factly" about it. I wasn't sure what my rights were as an interpreter. Do we have the right to know when we are being recorded? There was no equipment (computer, monitor, video, etc.) indicating that we were being recorded.

AN INTERPRETER'S PERSPECTIVE: You experienced something that would frustrate me as well, and I'd be asking the same kind of questions. I am sure there are legal decisions that apply to this kind of situation. As you probably know, the quality of one's legal representative is often proportionate to the quality of the outcome for the represented. I doubt that you want to sue, but you certainly have to the right to let the consumers' organization know you did not appreciate being recorded without your knowledge. If this bothers you enough, contact a good legal resource. If you were on assignment as brokered through an interpreter referral agency, you may want to ask them the same questions. They should be an advocate for you in this matter.

A DEAF CONSUMER'S PERSPECTIVE: Actually, there are laws about audiotaping someone's private conversation without permission. However, as an interpreter, you are not actually involved in the conversation. Transcription distances this even more, since I assume someone was creating a written record of the conversation and not an actual recording. The transcription should reflect the words of the participants even when those come through an interpreter. My feeling is you should not be concerned about this.

Other Scenarios

Identify the issue(s) involved and decide how you would respond. Discuss and compare your responses with your colleagues.

690. You're called in to interpret in an emergency room for a young deaf driver brought in after a car accident. You're standing next to the boy's hospital bed when a man who identifies himself as the driver of the other car storms in and attacks the deaf boy. He says his wife was killed and now he's going to kill the deaf boy. The man reeks of alcohol, and no one else is in the room to help.

691. You're at an interpreting workshop, and at lunch some other interpreters ask if you know a certain deaf man. When you say no, they laugh and call you "fresh meat," and then drop the subject. You're a little unnerved when two weeks later you get a call to interpret for that same deaf man.

692. You're walking to your assignment at your local college. On the way, a man bumps into you and almost knocks you over. He doesn't apologize, and you give him a dirty look and exclaim angrily, "Well, excuse me!" You manage to get to your assignment and in walks the client. It's the same man that bumped into you. He introduces himself like nothing has happened.

693. A school administrator where you work will be presenting an award to a deaf student and asks you to teach her just enough signs to present the award herself. You gladly teach her the signs, and during the assembly, she demonstrates her sign skills, only to have the deaf students burst out laughing. Perplexed, she asks you in front of the whole student body what she did wrong. Instead of signing "trophy," she signed "vagina."

694. The interpreter referral agency that sent you to a church service either didn't know or neglected to tell you that the service is for a Spanish-speaking congregation. You don't know Spanish, and the deaf people in attendance don't know ASL.

695. You arrive at an appointment for marriage counseling, and the woman turns out to be someone you have dated recently. You have been intimate, and you even entertained the thought that this might be the woman of your dreams. Her husband is deaf but doesn't want an interpreter. He says he prefers to lipread. However, with the looks of guilt, embarrassment, and confusion written all over both your faces, the husband quickly becomes suspicious. He's demanding you tell him right now how you know his wife.

696. You're called in to interpret for a deaf patient in the emergency room who has suffered an injury to his genitals. The hospital tells you they tried to get a male interpreter without success, but the patient has agreed to a female interpreter. When you arrive, the deaf patient becomes very angry and says he agreed to no such thing. He wants you to leave immediately.

697. You're interpreting a home visit between a deaf mother and a social worker. The woman has four children who are all upstairs playing while the adults are meeting downstairs. All of a sudden you can hear the sound of shattering glass upstairs, and a child runs downstairs crying with blood gushing from his arm. The mother is so upset about the window being broken that she starts slapping the three remaining children. The social worker calls 911 and orders the mother outside. You're asked to ride to the hospital with the mother and her hurt son while the social worker stays with the remaining children.

698. You have worked hard preparing to interpret a theatrical performance. The day of the performance you have an allergic reaction to some medication, and you break out in hives. You feel terrible and you itch like crazy. There's no way you can interpret tonight, and you'll never find anybody crazy enough to substitute for this kind of job at the last minute.

699. You are an interpreter at a small church, and before the service you invite a few friends, including the deaf minister, to your home after the service for a spaghetti dinner. However, as soon as the minister gets up, he announces to the entire congregation (40 people) that "a spaghetti dinner will be provided by our very own, sweet and generous interpreter." The congregation enthusiastically applauds you.

700. You have been interpreting a college course this semester with only seven students, including the deaf student. The dynamics of the class are fantastic, and the group works well together. One day as you all are sitting in class waiting for the professor to show up, two university administrators walk in the room. They inform the class that the teacher committed suicide last night.

701. You are on an international flight to Japan with a deaf client you will be interpreting for on business. Right after take off, a man walks to the front of the plane and says that the plane is being hijacked. The hijacker tells everyone not to move. The deaf man is reading a magazine but looks up to see the man standing at the front of the plane with a gun, and he looks over to you to interpret what is being said. You are so terrified you can't move, but you know if you don't do something quick the deaf man could get hurt.

702. You are scheduled to interpret a job interview this afternoon. You and the deaf client go into the interview room. When you go to sit down, your chair falls over backwards, and you end up on your back looking up at the interviewers.

703. While interpreting at a doctor's office, the doctor describes in detail a procedure he will be performing on the deaf woman. The woman's husband starts feeling physically sick and is led out of the room by the doctor's nurse, and the doctor continues telling the woman about her surgery. You're torn in half because you can hear the nurse talking to the deaf husband and so you feel like you should be interpreting for him too.

704. You have interpreted for a young deaf couple through all of their natural childbirth classes, and it's the day of the big event. The mother-to-be is in labor, and the doctor takes one more look and says they still have a little more time to wait. He says he's going to grab a quick bite to eat and tells the deaf woman to use the call button if she wants the nurse to page him. The frightened deaf woman begs the doctor not to go. She's sure the baby is coming now, but he checks her again and assures her they have plenty of time. The nerve-racked father steps out to have a cigarette, and it's only the two of you left in the room. Suddenly the deaf woman starts screaming for help, and in the overhead mirror, you see the newborn's head emerging. You run around to the end of the table and see the baby starting to slide out.

705. You're interpreting for a deaf woman whose husband has suffered a massive heart attack. You're both waiting together in the husband's room for the doctor to come in with some test results. You both have been there all day, and you know the woman hasn't had anything to eat. She says she's going to go down to the cafeteria and grab something to eat, and she will be right back. She's not gone five minutes when an alarm goes off on her husband's heart monitor.

706. You have agreed to interpret a revival meeting in a large tent on Friday and Saturday night. The minister is responsible for finding a second interpreter but tells you he's not having much luck. He finally contacts someone who has interpreted for another congregation in the past, and she agrees to do it. She tells the minister she's internationally certified. The night of the revival, the woman gets up and dances on the stage. She finally has to be physically removed. You find out from the police that she has 27 documented personalities, one of whom she insists is an interpreter. Meanwhile you're left high and dry to interpret the rest of the revival.

707. On a warm summer day, you're interpreting on a platform in front of a large audience with a sleeveless blouse. You feel something on your arm, and when you look down, you see your bra strap has come undone and is now sticking out. There's no way to fix it, short of stopping and using two hands to reattach it.

708. You're a shadow interpreter for a play. During the performance, one of the actors accidentally turns the wrong way and bumps into you. To play it off naturally, he starts dancing with you and the audience loves it. You can't help but have a stunned look on your face, which just adds fuel to the audience's reaction.

709. You're hired to interpret a school event where several deaf students will be presenting. The deaf students' classroom teacher is present to supposedly provide moral support for the students. The teacher, however, keeps grunting and groaning over word choices you use during their presentation. Finally, she just takes over, and for a few seconds, you're both voicing. Not only is the audience confused by what is going on, so are you.

710. You're interpreting the opening ceremonies at a large festival in your community. There are approximately 50,000 people in the audience. You're interpreting the opening announcements when all of a sudden, in the process of making a sign, you knock off your glasses and they fly clear across stage.

711. While interpreting a confirmation ceremony at a church for two deaf children being confirmed, the pastor is trying valiantly to get the girls to understand different types of sins. You can see the point is to get them to recognize sins they themselves have possibly committed. The pastor asks the girls if they can think of an example of someone who has sinned. To everyone's surprise, both deaf girls simultaneously respond by nodding their heads, pointing at you, and saying, "She sins!"

712. You are an on-call interpreter for your local hospital, and late one night you get a call to interpret in the emergency room. The nurse tells you the deaf patient was in a serious car accident and is in critical condition. You rush to the hospital, and when you walk into the room, you see that it's a deaf neighbor. You know you can't function as both an interpreter and a friend right now.

713. You're scheduled to interpret for the President of the United States and are being searched by the Secret Service for illegal weapons. The metal detector keeps going off, and so they won't let you through. You assure them you have no metal pins or plates in your body. They inform you that you'll have to leave, when you suddenly realize what is causing the alarm to go off. You're now reluctant, however, to admit it to the group of Secret Service men surrounding you. Since you thought you might be on television, you recently went out and bought a new bra with underwires!

Challenges Related to Deaf Clients' Preferences for Interpreting

- **Scenario 714.** I am a certified interpreter interpreting a technology class for adults. The deaf consumer insists I interpret, not only what is lectured or announced, but also environmental noises like people walking in the hallway, side comments by fellow students, questions between one student and the instructor, and someone with a persistent cough. Is there any limit to how much is reasonable?

AN INTERPRETER'S PERSPECTIVE: Certainly there are limits to how much is reasonable. Interpreting requires many split second decisions. Sometimes we have to interpret one thing at the expense of another, but I think the choices can be successfully negotiated between interpreters and deaf people. When I have interpreted in postsecondary environments, some of the richest communication moments happened when I interpreted things other than the classroom lecture. For example, in working with graduate students in seminars, I have noticed that deaf students gain valuable information from the very examples you gave above. In many environments, such as business meetings, education, and medical appointments, the side comments or sounds can be powerful, peripheral information: which instructors are best for certain classes, who might make a good advisor, what kinds of grades others have received, research topics other students are considering, who is and isn't going to get tenure/a promotion, who's going to be responsible for an upcoming project, who the director thinks is funny, or when the nurse thinks the lab results will be ready. If the deaf person wants that kind of information, I'll work very hard to get that in and still monitor the other message. Of course, there will be times when we might lose information or have to summarize one message to concentrate on the other. Discussing preferences with the deaf person should help us with these decisions. I have found that sometimes they might not want to know about every airplane, sneeze, or cell phone. Once I asked a deaf professor if she wanted to know when hearing students' cell phones rang during class, and the answer was, "No, that doesn't really bother me; you don't have to interpret that." If we don't ask deaf people, we don't know. If we know someone's preferences include environmental information, I think we should look for a way to focus on those things.

A DEAF CONSUMER'S PERSPECTIVE: In most circumstances you will want to provide interpreting for the kinds of environmental noises you mention. There is always a limit to how much you provide. While I am not familiar with recent articles or sections of books addressing this issue (I suspect there are some good ones), it seems to me that the general principle is to interpret what you would normally notice if you were a hearing student in the class. That would mean an occasional, low cough is not usually noticed, but a persistent or loud cough or sneeze might be. The same holds true for any sounds that attract the "average hearing student's" attention. So a person walking the hall outside of class may not attract attention, while two people outside the classroom talking loudly and causing distraction for many within the class would be. However, sometimes classroom environmental sounds that normally would be distracting to students (e.g., in a math class) are so common that they cease to carry the same weight. At some point you could choose not to draw attention to those sounds by not interpreting them. Even the most obliging interpreter filters what she hears. No one could possibly listen for everything and interpret everything. There are many more sounds going on at any given time than any human can pay attention to.

- **Scenario 715.** I have just found out that the college student for whom I am interpreting this semester has requested another interpreter on staff next semester instead of me. I feel both hurt and embarrassed.

AN INTERPRETER'S PERSPECTIVE: While it may be upsetting at first, remember that you are providing a specialized service to a customer who is also an individual. The consumer should have the final say as to who provides the services they require. In the past when a shortage of qualified interpreters was the norm, many consumers had no choice. Consumers today are now in a position to greater exercise their right to choose. There could be several reasons why the student requested the change. However, be prepared; the answer you receive may not be one you want to hear. It is quite possible that the student is more comfortable with the style, personality, or level of professionalism that one of your other colleagues displays. You might even get the response that it is none of your business or that they want a change just because they can. Additionally, as providers of a specialized service as important as communication access, we have to be on top of our game. It is a competitive business, whether we like it or not. If a consumer wants to go with someone else, he most certainly has the right to do so. Don't take it so hard. It's just a fact that some consumers are more comfortable with certain interpreters. Just like there are thousands of qualified doctors out there; what makes us pick one over another? I say respect the student's wishes and move on.

A DEAF CONSUMER'S PERSPECTIVE: I understand how you feel. However, you have no idea what would make the client ask for another interpreter. It could be any number of reasons. Maybe it has nothing to do with you. If you really must know, and you think it may be related to something you can change about yourself, maybe it may help to ask the interpreter coordinator to facilitate getting some feedback for you. Nevertheless, it all works out in the end. Maybe this is just the opportunity you need to grow as an interpreter and gain new experiences. It may hurt for a short time, but I think you will be fine in the long term.

- **Scenario 716:** I swear I thought the RID ethics police were going to come and rip up my card. I was interpreting for a deaf professional at a conference who was the only deaf person in attendance. She said she had absolutely no interest in the conference, but she had to attend for her job. So instead of interpreting, the three of us (including my partner) spent the day chatting about everything under the sun. Afterwards I felt guilty, but ultimately it was the client's call, right?

AN INTERPRETER'S PERSPECTIVE: Go with the consumer. If the consumer decides to chat, so be it. You set aside the time; it's not like the time is your own to do whatever you want. You're getting paid.

A DEAF CONSUMER'S PERSPECTIVE: I've been guilty of this. I'm not saying it's right, but I ask one interpreter to continue interpreting. This way I can choose to participate.

- **Scenario 717.** I am curious in regard to the significance of an interpreter's sexual preference in this profession. I know this is an unusual question, but as an ITP student, I have been taught that we should be very concerned with how we represent ourselves professionally. If an interpreter is gay or lesbian, does it affect their reputation in the deaf community?

AN INTERPRETER'S PERSPECTIVE: This issue really goes across all professions (teachers, lawyers, etc.) and cultures. It seems, because there are a number of gays and lesbians in the Deaf and interpreting communities, there is more tolerance and perhaps acceptance. Frankly, I am not going to hide in the closet. I won't advertise or recruit, nor will I deny anything. When not working, my partner and I behave as any couple does in public. I realize there might be people who don't like or approve of my lifestyle in the Deaf and interpreting communities, but honestly I'd rather not work with or for someone who tries to oppress my freedom to love whom I choose. If you personally have a problem with it, you will need to choose your assignments very carefully, as well as whom you accept as clients and team interpreters.

A DEAF CONSUMER'S PERSPECTIVE: Sure, someone may not choose an interpreter because she or he is gay (same as in the straight community), just as they may not choose an interpreter because of race, gender, and even appearance. I don't think being gay/lesbian in and of itself is a deterrent to working as a professional interpreter. Deaf people make those kinds of subjective choices all the time. It seems to me often the bottom line for the deaf consumer is more about attitude. Skills can even be secondary. Attitude, plus skills, can cancel out potential concerns that may impact a professional interpreter's working life. If forced to choose, many deaf people prefer an interpreter with a good attitude and average skills over one with a bad attitude and good skills. This is the equivalent of bedside manners for doctors. A technically superb doctor might not know how to talk to patients and may have a hard time establishing trust with them, whereas a less talented doctor who has warm, friendly, comforting conversations with a patient and family is more likely to get business. It is interesting that interpreters worry a lot about boundaries, and yet we almost never seem to mention that as a concern. That is true of any people-oriented profession (e.g., social work, psychiatry, medicine, real estate). I think interpreters emphasize boundaries to protect their client's boundaries (and themselves). Until clients' boundaries have been crossed, it really isn't even an issue for them. I think it is critical for new interpreters-to-be to understand the concept that there may be a host of other reasons they were not called for a job. Do not jump to the conclusion that it is because "I'm Asian," "I'm gay," "I'm not a CODA," etc.

Other Scenarios

Identify the issue(s) involved and decide how you would respond. Discuss and compare your responses with your colleagues.

718. You have interpreted in the past for several deaf students at a small college in your area. You're well liked by both the deaf students and the administrators who hire you. A new deaf student at the college has requested a specific interpreter who works for a particular agency. The college administration calls you and says they would rather stick with you.

719. You have two clients; one is deaf, and one is hard of hearing. You ask them what method of communication they would prefer, and they both say, "ASL." During the course of the meeting, the hard of hearing client is asked a question, and he looks at you and says he doesn't understand. You repeat the question mouthing each word clearly in English order, and the client immediately answers the question. After the meeting, the hard of hearing client says he was confused while you were interpreting because you seemed always to be a sentence or so behind the speaker.

720. Your deaf friend is president of the local Deaf club. She has used your services several times in the past to interpret meetings with hearing guests. A fellow interpreter tells you about a big meeting coming up where a local member of congress will be speaking to the group. She tells you she has been asked to interpret. No matter how hard you try not to personalize it, you can't help but wonder why you weren't asked to interpret this time.

721. The deaf client has asked to speak to you alone for a moment and confides she's embarrassed by your team interpreter's appearance as she feels it reflects poorly on her. The client is a well-dressed professional, and your team interpreter is, well, overweight, loud, and inappropriately dressed. She's a very skilled interpreter, and while you empathize with the deaf client's feelings, this has nothing to do with you. However, the client says she plans to dismiss your partner, which would leave only you for the rest of the day.

Challenges in Dealing with Feedback from Clients

- **Scenario 722:** Interpreters who are not easy to lipread can be rough for me to understand. It makes it difficult for me to know the tone of the conversation. A lack of proper facial expressions just further compounds the problem. Is this something I should point out to even a nationally certified interpreter?

AN INTERPRETER'S PERSPECTIVE: Based on my experience, I think most interpreters — nationally certified, pre-certified, ITP students — appreciate feedback and are willing to attempt to put the feedback to use. Being nationally certified does not mean that an interpreter is not open to feedback (although, being easy to lipread is something that a person might not be able to change). I think it is fine to tell the interpreter you will be relying even more on facial expression during a meeting. I always appreciate that kind of heads-up because it gives me a better take on the deaf person's perspective, and I can attempt to adjust my work accordingly. Certified or not, let interpreters know what you're thinking.

A DEAF CONSUMER'S PERSPECTIVE: I feel that any time you are not happy about what the interpreter is doing, your concerns should be made known. This is especially crucial when the delivery of a message from the interpreter interferes with complete comprehension of the message. Your example of not being able to lipread is one issue, and not having any visible facial expressions which help clarify the message is another issue. Each issue should be addressed as they are both significant issues. It would be appropriate for you and the interpreter to look at each issue and see how improvements/modifications can be made. A nationally certified interpreter should definitely be told of these issues because they need to adjust their skills to meet different needs. You can feel better about telling nationally certified interpreters because they have invested a lot in the process of becoming nationally certified and usually have the deaf consumer's best interests at heart.

- **Scenario 723.** As a deaf consumer who utilizes interpreters frequently, I am astonished when interpreters apparently do not consider feedback from me to be a learning opportunity. Instead, interpreters seem to fear me, and I have this reputation in the interpreting community as an "outspoken" deaf person, like it is a bad thing. I assure you that I am never negative in my feedback to interpreters, and I go out of my way to be both professional and kind when giving it. However, apparently my behavior is not the norm. Should I just say "thank you" or a generic "good job" every time?

AN INTERPRETER'S PERSPECTIVE: Personally, I appreciate a deaf person who can give me good feedback. I think this is the best way to improve. If there are specific things that you need from an interpreter, you should just ask, regardless of the interpreter's reaction. You have the right to have your needs met. Like you, I have received negative reactions from interpreters when I have offered suggestions when they haven't asked for them. Often I have found, even when interpreters do ask for feedback, many can't take more than one or two pieces total. Therefore, I try to limit myself. In the hearing culture, we are taught to "sandwich" criticism between two compliments. An example might be: "You have very good facial expression, but your fingerspelling is a little too fast. You could also perhaps work on your use of classifiers. Overall, however, I think you did a pretty darn good job." I also appreciate it when a deaf client asks me before an assignment if I would like some feedback afterwards. That way, if I say yes, I am prepared. As an interpreter educator, I teach my students to always ask the consumer ahead of time to see if the deaf client is willing to give feedback, then to tell the deaf person something specific on which they would like to receive comments. I hope you continue to give feedback to your interpreters. That is the best way for us to improve. Perhaps in the future, interpreters will come around to being more open to what you have to say.

A DEAF CONSUMER'S PERSPECTIVE: The deaf consumer should re-examine her approach and selection of words in giving feedback. You may not realize that your words are too strong or culturally offensive. That said, interpreters need to learn to accept feedback in a professional manner from deaf consumers and not take it so personally.

- **Scenario 724.** I am currently wearing a brace on my wrist for Carpal Tunnel Syndrome. Today during a break, the deaf client came up to me and asked me to remove my brace because she found it distracting and it affected my clarity. She also said it made her feel guilty for having me work. What do you think I should have done?

AN INTERPRETER'S PERSPECTIVE: Our primary function as interpreters is to facilitate communication. If your client felt that your brace was truly affecting her access to equal communication, then you had several choices: (1) You could have removed the brace; (2) You could have not removed your brace and offered to reschedule for another day with another interpreter; (3) You could have offered to call the referral agency to try to find a replacement for yourself for the remainder of the assignment; or (4) You both could have made the best of the situation. You are the only person who knows your limits, and she's the only person who knows if she is satisfied. We as interpreters have to make sure that we are doing what is best, not only for our clients (and our profession), but also ourselves. It may mean admitting to yourself that you're not at 100 percent capability right now and taking some time off until you recover.

A DEAF CONSUMER'S PERSPECTIVE: Over the past 25 years, I have had several interpreters who wore braces due to Carpal Tunnel or other injuries in their arms or shoulders. My response was that I judged those interpreters on the accuracy of the information. If that was there, then I had no problem with it. However, if the interpreter's expressions or movements indicated that she was in pain or having difficulty keeping up, I would have said something. I would ask for a replacement until she is able to do the job fully again. I am acutely aware that interpreters are human beings and not easily replaced. I try to show understanding and compassion by trying to work with the interpreter. In the long run, this effort pays off because a good and healthy interpreter is worth it.

Other Scenarios

Identify the issue(s) involved and decide how you would respond. Discuss and compare your responses with your colleagues.

725. One of your regular deaf clients takes you aside and says your long fingernails and colored polish are distracting to her. You don't think they're that long, and the color is a subtle pink-beige. However, you thank her for sharing her opinion and decide to get a manicure and go back to clear polish. A week later she says she hates to mention it, but she finds all your jewelry distracting. You're only wearing your engagement ring and a pair of diamond stud earrings.

726. You're admittedly having a bad day and really struggling while interpreting. You didn't get much sleep last night, and the coffee you drank this morning to compensate is having an adverse effect on you. After the assignment, the deaf client is in your face, furious that the interpreter referral agency would send someone as incompetent as you. She says she will definitely be contacting them about her concerns and storms off.

727. A Deaf client who is a strong lipreader has asked you to place a call for him. You dial the number he gives you, which is supposed to be a direct line to his doctor, but it's not. It throws you, and it takes a few moments to figure out where you're calling. It's a line to a waiting room at the hospital. The elderly hospital volunteer is well-intentioned, but it takes a few minutes to get her off the phone. You hang up, and the deaf client is furious that you took over the conversation instead of letting him handle the confusion.

728. One night a week you interpret a college course for a deaf student reputed to be tough on interpreters. You two have had some clashes about sign choices, so you're careful to remember her sign preferences. Another interpreter you run into tells you she's interpreting for the same student for another class and that the deaf student has complained about your skills to her. The other interpreter says to take it with a grain of salt because everyone knows how mean the deaf student is, and nobody else wants to interpret for her anymore.

729. While interpreting a speech, a small group of people off to the side start laughing. You're focusing on what the speaker is saying, so you miss the side comment that made these folks laugh, but you smile too. The Deaf client asks you to tell him what they're laughing about, and you tell him you missed it. He accuses you of knowing because you laughed. This is absurd, but nothing you say can convince him. He has lost faith in you and is sure that you're keeping things from him.

730. You accept an interpreting job out of town, so you and your team interpreter decide to carpool. You get stuck in construction and then you get lost. By the time the two of you arrive at the workshop, you're about 30 minutes late. The deaf clients are rightfully upset with both of you. During the event, they spend the whole time complaining to each other about the two of you instead of paying attention. The workshop topic involves a lot of terminology, which you both have to laboriously fingerspell. On break, the deaf clients approach you and accuse you of not being good interpreters.

731. You're an experienced interpreter of many years. One day while interpreting for a mainstreamed deaf student, you use a sign you're familiar with for Santa Claus. The deaf girl proceeds to tell you you're wrong and shows you the sign she uses, which is fine, but you've never seen it before. You ask her where she learned that sign, and she tells you, "I didn't learn it from anywhere. I'm Deaf and I can use whatever sign I want!"

732. A local theater group putting on a play includes a large number of deaf people who have hired you to be their interpreter. While interpreting at a rehearsal, one of the deaf actresses comes over and proceeds to show you another way to sign the scene. You agree and incorporate it into your signing. Later, while rehearsing another scene, she again stops you and shows you exactly how she wants it signed. She creates a scene and embarrasses you in front of the rest of the cast and crew. You don't want to antagonize her, but now you're afraid to interpret anything for fear of setting her off. The play is only a week away now, and you're questioning your ability to perform.

Challenges Related to Legal Issues and Interpreting in Legal Situations

- **Scenario 733**. A deaf man invests a large amount of money in his company's stock. At the annual stockholders' meeting, the client has hired you to interpret. Right after the meeting, the client invests even more money in the company's stock. Within six months the stock drops through the floor, and when you hear about it, you know the client probably lost his shirt. Days later you get a call from an attorney informing you that you're being sued by his deaf client. The deaf man claims you didn't interpret all the information to him at that stockholders' meeting.

AN INTERPRETER'S PERSPECTIVE: To discuss the details of what was interpreted during the assignment would be a breach in confidentiality. Be prepared by consulting with an attorney about the situation, and explain that, unless you are taken to court and required to testify about what you interpreted during the assignment, you cannot discuss any of the details. It will be up to the deaf man to pursue legal action if he believes he has a case.

A DEAF CONSUMER'S PERSPECTIVE: As an ethical interpreter, do not discuss anything about the client or the annual stockholder's meeting during your conversation with the attorney. After hanging up, take a deep breath and be thankful that you renewed your RID membership.

- **Scenario 734**. I'm interpreting in a hospital emergency room for a man injured while drinking and driving. He's so drunk, he thinks he's going to die. Thinking this is his deathbed, he tells me that earlier in the evening he thinks he hit a pedestrian.

AN INTERPRETER'S PERSPECTIVE: An interpreter's worst nightmare — to be faced with not only interpreting under extreme circumstances, but also legally and morally having to report a potential crime. The law of the land supersedes our CPC, regardless of whether the information was divulged in confidence or in a drunken stupor. Try to maintain a professional attitude, and avoid letting the tragedy take over your emotions.

A DEAF CONSUMER'S PERSPECTIVE: You're there to interpret everything. If you voice everything the man says, the hospital staff will know what the deaf man thinks he did.

- **Scenario 735**. You go to a police station to interpret for a deaf person who has recently been arrested. Before the meeting, you ask the officer in charge to provide a video camera so that the interrogation can be videotaped for everyone's protection. The officer refuses your request and says, "That's not the way we do it. You've been watching too much television!"

AN INTERPRETER'S PERSPECTIVE: Explain that if there is a discrepancy or controversy about the information communicated during the interrogation, there would be no evidence available to clear up any misunderstandings, which could be grounds for dismissal. If the officer still refuses, stay in role and interpret the assignment.

A DEAF CONSUMER'S PERSPECTIVE: Assuming that you have the appropriate credentials to be in that situation, you shouldn't hesitate to take control. Remain calm and professional, and tell the officer that there must be a video camera recording of the interrogation. Take this opportunity to explain why it is a necessary procedure. If the officer still refuses to record the interrogation, then you should refuse to interpret.

- **Scenario 736**. While interpreting for an accused deaf man who is on the stand answering questions, you falter. The answer he gives to one question throws you because it's so out of context. The judge and attorneys are also confused and start to question your skills. They ask him the question again, and this time his answer is completely different and appropriate. This happens several times, and you can see everyone looking at you like you've lost your mind.

AN INTERPRETER'S PERSPECTIVE: Stay in role and interpret confidently the accused deaf man's responses.

A DEAF CONSUMER'S PERSPECTIVE: Even if everyone is staring you down, stay in role. Your job is to render the message faithfully and as accurately as possible.

- **Scenario 737**. You're interpreting in court, and the deaf client continually swears at everyone: the judge, his lawyers, and even you. The judge finally tells the deaf man that he will be held in contempt of court if he utters one more swear word. The judge asks the man if he understands him, and the deaf client sneers back a "y-e-s!" The judge promptly orders him to jail. The client is furious because he says "yes" is not a swear word. He tells you that when he gets out, he's going to kill you.

AN INTERPRETER'S PERSPECTIVE: Stay in role and interpret the information without personal response to the deaf client's threat. The client can see that you interpreted the response; now it is the judge's responsibility to explain the court's perception of the deaf client's response (if she so chooses). Court dialogue will be documented via the court reporter and available should the deaf client attempt to contact you.

A DEAF CONSUMER'S PERSPECTIVE: You maintain your impartiality, voice his "y-e-s" in a manner consistent with how he signed it, and continue voicing for him. You may want to consider making a police record of the incident for your protection in the future.

- **Scenario 738**. I'm a QA level interpreter, and my brother is a police officer. One night he calls me and begs me to come in and interpret for a deaf man they just picked up for allegedly raping a girl. My brother swears they tried all the interpreters on the list, and no one else is available.

AN INTERPRETER'S PERSPECTIVE: This scenario speaks to the need for discretion in accepting assignments. This is a legal situation and requires someone with skills in that field. Don't let others pressure you into taking the job by saying, "I'm sure you'll be fine," or "There's no one else." Your attempt to be accommodating could end up making things worse. Can you interpret the Miranda Warning accurately? What if the deaf man confesses while you're there? The confession could be thrown out in court if you can't prove you have the proper interpreting credentials. However, don't just turn the job down. Help your brother get an appropriately skilled interpreter there as soon as possible using the resources in your area. If an interpreter isn't available now, find out when an interpreter would be available and give your brother that information.

A DEAF CONSUMER'S PERSPECTIVE: No one tries all the interpreters on the list and gets no one. That's nonsense. However, you could offer to call a couple of interpreters to assist in the search. Under no circumstance should you interpret for the arrested man. This could lead to dismissal of all charges due to inadequate access. Most interpreting agencies have at least one interpreter on call 24 hours a day for emergencies such as this. As a deaf person myself, I would dismiss any Level I signer who chose to take this assignment, since it's in complete violation of the CPC in relation to knowing your own professional boundaries and limitations. Level I signers are nowhere near the level of being able to interpret in a situation like this.

- **Scenario 739**. I am interpreting for a trial in which an 18-year-old deaf man is charged with murder. The man was brought up in a cabin in the woods with no exposure to other deaf people, and his language skills are minimal. I quickly realized I couldn't handle this job alone and need a CDI to assist me. I stopped the proceedings to let the judge know, and he says, "If you can't handle this job alone, I'll find someone else who can!"

AN INTERPRETER'S PERSPECTIVE: If the judge refuses to understand why a relay interpreter is appropriate, take yourself off the case. My guess is that the judge will hear the same response from other professional interpreters.

A DEAF CONSUMER'S PERSPECTIVE: Respectfully explain that you won't be able to continue to interpret. You can try to explain that the current best practice in these situations is to use a team of interpreters (a certified ASL/English interpreter and a CDI). Although this is costly, all parties involved will be satisfied that this case was handled in the best way possible. If the judge still wants another interpreter, let him do that. You'll have a clear conscience.

- **Scenario 740**. While interpreting a police interrogation, the deaf client refuses to cooperate with the officers. The next thing I know, one of the officers dumps hot coffee on the client. The officer apologizes halfheartedly and actually sounds very sarcastic. I can't swear to it, but it looked intentional. Now the deaf person is screaming for an attorney and claiming police brutality. The officer mutters under his breath in my direction, "Remember, you didn't see a thing."

AN INTERPRETER'S PERSPECTIVE: I would continue to interpret everything that is being said/signed, and if asked what I saw, I would say that I saw the coffee spilled on the deaf person. I can't assume that the officer did it on purpose; I can only relay the events objectively.

A DEAF CONSUMER'S PERSPECTIVE: Interpret exactly what the deaf consumer is saying, such as, "I want an attorney." If you're asked for your eyewitness account, give it.

Other Scenarios

Identify the issue(s) involved and decide how you would respond. Discuss and compare your responses with your colleagues.

741. While waiting around for court to begin, you see the deaf client tell his wife it's her fault he got caught because, if she earned more money, he wouldn't have had to steal. At that point, you look away because you realize it's a private conversation. In fact, you decide to leave and go get a drink. Once in the courtroom, the deaf client vehemently tells the judge that he's not guilty.

742. You're interpreting for a deaf client at a bank where he's closing his account after a dispute with the customer service representative. One week later you receive a call from the deaf client's attorney accusing you of misinterpreting the information discussed at the bank. His client is alleging he lost thousands of dollars because he cashed in his bonds a day too early. He says he has lost six months of interest because of you, which you now owe him.

743. You and two other interpreters are hired for a trial. The judge has asked the three of you to meet with him in his chambers so he can review the case and give you your instructions. One of the interpreters hired is someone you have never seen before, but he tells the judge he worked at a deaf school for over 10 years. When asked about certification, he just nods his head "yes." The first time he gets up to interpret, it's obvious that he's barely a signer and certainly not an interpreter. However, the deaf client doesn't object at all.

744. While interpreting a court case, the deaf client is on the stand testifying about a telephone truck that hit her car. In response to one question, the deaf woman nods her head "yes" that she understands the question, but her answer to the question is "no." The judge sees this, immediately stops the proceedings, and asks if you're qualified to interpret this case.

745. Recently I was stopped for a routine traffic violation. The officer said I had to go to the police station because there was a warrant for my arrest. We went down to the police station. By the time we arrived, a CDI and a hearing interpreter were called in without my knowledge. I insisted that they leave as I felt perfectly capable of communicating on my own. After a long discussion, the officer finally agreed and sent them away. All charges against me were cleared. Now every time I see those two interpreters, I feel embarrassed even though I know I really don't have to explain anything to anyone. My question is: if I don't request an interpreter, does the officer have the right to try and force me to utilize one?

Challenges Related to Interpreting in Medical Settings

- **Scenario 746.** I've interpreted in a hospital emergency room a few times, and now I realize how much down time there is. What are some appropriate things I can do while waiting?

AN INTERPRETER'S PERSPECTIVE: Well, first I must say you should try above all else to stay outside the room or the curtain from the client when medical personnel are not in the room. The opening chat to develop your target language is fine, but if you stick around the entire time conversing with the client, I find it is much too difficult to close the door of involvement once it has been opened. I suggest a type of activity that will keep anyone from thinking you are just sitting around waiting to chat: anything to read to keep yourself from going crazy with boredom, something that you can drop so you can be ready to interpret at anytime.

A DEAF CONSUMER'S PERSPECTIVE: Keeping your activities unobtrusive and quiet is the first consideration, and also at a level of "intensity" that won't disrupt your concentration or understanding during your time at the hospital. Make yourself a bag filled with some of the following items: a book of crossword or Sudoku puzzles, a novel (new or beloved) that you can put down at a moment's notice, a memo pad so you can write your grocery list, and some stationery and envelopes with stamps already affixed (so you can send letters to family or friends with whom you haven't talked in a while). Buy an iPod and download books on tape. You can listen with one ear while waiting for the doctor or client to become available. If you're especially adept at handicrafts and know how to knit or crochet without using a pattern, you can make dishcloths, scarves, or small garments. As far as working on improving your interpreting skills during "downtime," bring along a thesaurus and memorize new English glosses for ASL terminology. Run through some fingerspelling exercises or stretch your muscles. Once in a while, if there's a lot of stress in your life, you can always meditate, pray, or do deep-breathing exercises to improve your concentration.

- **Scenario 747.** I'm interpreting for a series of chest x-rays. The technician gives the signal, I tell the deaf client to hold his breath, and then I go behind the protective shield with the technician. After the x-ray is taken, I run back and tell the deaf client to breathe again. I don't realize it at first, but I'm unconsciously holding and releasing my breath with the deaf client. Between all the running and holding my breath, I'm starting to feel light-headed.

AN INTERPRETER'S PERSPECTIVE: Let the deaf person and the technician know what is happening and ask for a quick break. Then take a moment to sit down and regain your breath. Consciously remember to breathe next time.

A DEAF CONSUMER'S PERSPECTIVE: Tell the x-ray technician to hold until you can get your breath, and then resume. It's important to do this job right.

Other Scenarios

Identify the issue(s) involved and decide how you would respond. Discuss and compare your responses with your colleagues.

748. You're called to interpret in an emergency room. The nurse on duty, however, won't let you into the deaf patient's room. You try to explain that you're needed to facilitate communication, but she says they don't need you yet. You ask her how she'll know when the deaf patient needs you. To prove her point, the nurse escorts you into the patient's room and yells a question at the deaf man to which he smiles and nods his head. The nurse is completely satisfied with his response and escorts you back out of his room. Five minutes later the deaf man starts having chest pains, and the same nurse is suddenly treating you like you're her best friend.

749. You arrive at the doctor's office and tell the receptionist you're the interpreter. She directs you to a deaf woman and her daughter. The child has red spots all over her body and you panic. You're an expectant mother and are afraid your unborn child could be exposed to something.

750. You have interpreted for a deaf client diagnosed with cancer through many months of tests, treatments, and nausea, during good days and bad. The woman and her doctors have always been optimistic about her recovery. That is why you're shocked when you find out about her unexpected and sudden death.

751. You're called to interpret in an emergency room for a deaf patient who has cut his finger at work while using an industrial saw. The cut requires a lot of stitches, and there's a lot of blood. You're normally OK in this kind of situation, but today you're suddenly feeling a little woozy.

752. You're interpreting a delivery, and every time the deaf mother has a contraction, she closes her eyes and communication becomes impossible. The umbilical cord has wrapped itself around the baby's neck, and the doctor is screaming, "Don't push." Another contraction comes along, but the woman's eyes are closed tight.

753. You're interpreting in an intensive care unit in a hospital. Things have been going along quietly for over an hour when suddenly the deaf patient begins to have difficulty breathing. The alarms go off on the machines he's hooked up to, and nurses and doctors come running into the room. Everyone is trying to figure out what the problem is before it becomes too late. The tension in the room is mounting, and then suddenly one of the nurses sarcastically says, "Well, if the interpreter would please not stand on his air hose, our patient will be just fine!"

754. You're sent to a medical exam for a deaf man being tested for venereal disease. The deaf client is a little embarrassed at first by having a woman interpreter. You work it out so that you leave the room during the actual exam. A few weeks later the doctor's office calls you again to interpret a follow-up visit.

755. You're called by an interpreter referral agency to interpret at a hospital for a vasectomy. When you walk into the patient's room, however, you realize there must have been a mix-up with the name of the patient, It's a deaf acquaintance of yours that is going under the knife.

756. You're interpreting for a deaf client who has recently received a kidney transplant. The hospital room is crammed with machines to which the client is hooked up. He has a tube down his throat and is on a lot of medication. Communication is nearly impossible, but the staff thinks you're just being difficult.

Challenges Related to Interpreting in Mental Health Settings

- **Scenario 757**. I get an emergency call to interpret for a deaf person who has just admitted himself to a crisis unit. I arrive at the hospital and interpret for the deaf man and the crisis worker. The crisis worker asks the man several questions, but the client refuses to answer her. Eventually, the woman excuses herself to go and get another colleague. As soon as the door closes behind her, the deaf client begins to "unload" on me.

AN INTERPRETER'S PERSPECTIVE: It's best to be pre-emptive in this case; that is, when the crisis worker leaves the room, I would also leave. Otherwise, I would tell the deaf consumer that it's better to wait until someone who is experienced at helping people in crisis returns. If the deaf consumer continues to unload and it's impossible or inappropriate for me to stop it, I would listen. However, I would keep reminding the person that the crisis worker is there to help, and that I would be happy to interpret between the two of them so he can get some relief.

A DEAF CONSUMER'S PERSPECTIVE: In this situation I would want the interpreter to say something like, "Great! That's exactly the kind of information that the social worker wanted. Hang on a second, and I'll call her back into the room."

- **Scenario 758**. You're interpreting for a deaf man who has been hospitalized for mental health problems. Whenever the man gets excited or agitated, his signs become larger and more pronounced. The staff perceives his thumps, thuds, grunts, and groans as being hostile, and they begin take-down procedures on him.

AN INTERPRETER'S PERSPECTIVE: It is sometimes our role as an interpreter to also be an educator. Oftentimes even medical staff is unaware of Deaf culture and their possible tendencies. In this scenario I would explain use of a larger sign space is only an indication that the deaf client is excited or agitated, not that he would necessarily cause any physical harm. In general, take-down procedures would make any person, hearing or deaf, more agitated. In addition, for a deaf client, this will make it impossible for him to communicate at all.

A DEAF CONSUMER'S PERSPECTIVE: Interject and try to stop the take-down by explaining to the staff that his exaggerated expressiveness is not intended to be threatening, but is his way of communicating his emotions. I understand, normally, staying in role is a must; however, in this situation it is clear that cultural clarity may be needed. As the qualified interpreter, you need to remain impartial, but you are there for the deaf client as well as the hearing client. In this case, providing cultural understanding is warranted.

- **Scenario 759.** While interpreting a counseling session for a deaf woman and her hearing husband, the therapist is interrupted by a phone call. The couple begins having an angry conversation and using profanity. When the therapist hangs up, he says, "So, what did I miss?" They look at you and say, "Nothing, nothing at all!"

AN INTERPRETER'S PERSPECTIVE: Remain neutral and interpret the deaf couple's response to the therapist's question. The therapist can see them having a discussion, so it is the therapist's responsibility to encourage open and honest dialogue. The interpreter is there to facilitate communication, not interject opinions or do counseling.

A DEAF CONSUMER'S PERSPECTIVE: You are the interpreter for the therapist, the deaf woman, and her hearing husband. It is your responsibility to continue interpreting whatever is said on either end during the phone conversation and the couples' conversation. However, the therapist chose to take a phone call during the counseling session. It is not your job to fill the therapist in on whatever information he chose to miss.

Other Scenarios

Identify the issue(s) involved and decide how you would respond. Discuss and compare your responses with your colleagues.

760. Prior to a counseling session, you and the deaf client are waiting to be called into the therapist's office. The client tells you some entertaining stories about his life to pass the time. Finally, the therapist comes out to get you both, and the client suddenly starts crying and leaves. The therapist asks you to tell her everything you two talked about in the waiting room.

761. You're called at 2 a.m. to interpret at an inpatient hospital for a schizophrenic deaf client who has become violent and is causing damage to the facility. The staff is explaining to the client the inappropriateness of his behavior. The client flies out of his chair and comes within an inch of your face and signs, "Hate you, stupid interpreter. Hate you."

762. You're interpreting a group therapy session when the deaf client becomes upset and exposes her large, unencumbered breasts to the other members of the therapy group. You look around and see several of the male members of the group start touching themselves in response to her actions.

763. You work as an interpreter at a mental health facility and have just had a long, long day. A therapist at the facility bawled you out for interpreting his disparaging side comments about a client during the therapy session. He says they were only meant for you. When you get home, your husband (also an interpreter) asks if you want to talk about what is obviously bothering you.

764. You're contacted by another interpreter to take over interpreting weekly counseling sessions for him. He says the job has become too personal for him, and he feels he can no longer be objective. You take the job, and a few weeks later you run into this interpreter at the mall. He asks you how the deaf client is doing in the counseling sessions.

765. You were once a victim of child abuse, and you still have nightmares about it. You get a call to interpret for a deaf child involved in a child abuse case who will be attending counseling sessions. Although you're aware that this probably isn't a good assignment for you since you never resolved your own abuse, you think you can resolve some of these issues by interpreting in this situation.

Challenges Related to Interpreting in Educational Settings

- **Scenario 766**. I am an interpreter for two deaf students in an elementary classroom. While the teacher is teaching and I'm interpreting, the students often have side conversations, such as: "Stop kicking me," "You stop touching me," "I didn't touch you," and "Yes, you did!"

AN INTERPRETER'S PERSPECTIVE: You should have already worked closely with the teacher to clarify your respective roles as interpreter and teacher. If the stage has been set in this way, then the teacher should make the decisions about how to handle it.

A DEAF CONSUMER'S PERSPECTIVE: I would suggest telling the students the first time around that you'll be voicing everything. If they continue to misbehave after the warning, I would voice everything said and let the teacher deal with it.

- **Scenario 767**. I interpret in a vocational training center, and one of the deaf clients has multiple handicaps and is in a wheelchair. While in class he drops his pencil. Usually when that happens, either I or a classmate pick it up for him. Today he decides to get it himself, and while he's leaning over to pick it up, he starts to fall out of his chair. I don't react quickly enough, and he lands on his face. I feel awful, and he has to go to the health center to have a gash on his forehead stitched up.

AN INTERPRETER'S PERSPECTIVE: I would go to the health center and interpret for him and the health care providers. I would feel badly, but I would also have to let it go at some point. The fact that he fell is no one's "fault"; it's just life.

A DEAF CONSUMER'S PERSPECTIVE: The vocational training center should decide what to do; it's not the interpreter's responsibility. Of course you would feel awful, but this could happen anywhere — at home, at a public facility, or at work. This fellow in a wheelchair needs help figuring out ways to prevent this from happening again.

- **Scenario 768**. One of the high school classes for which I interpret every day is Math. This wasn't my best subject when I was in school. However, so far I'm doing OK, until the deaf student fails a test and blames it on my interpreting. I have just enough insecurity in this content area to let it get to me, so I ask my supervisor to trade that class with another interpreter. At the end of the semester, I find out the student failed the course and has to repeat it during summer school. He has now requested me specifically.

AN INTERPRETER'S PERSPECTIVE: I wouldn't have asked my supervisor to replace me quite so readily after the student blamed his failure on me. I would have asked that someone qualified to assess the situation be brought in to observe and make recommendations to me, my supervisor, and the student on how to improve the situation. However, that not being the case here, I would request that an assessment be done at the beginning of the summer session. If the student's lack of success can be tied to problems with my interpretation, then steps should be taken either to improve the quality of my work or to find a different interpreter.

A DEAF CONSUMER'S PERSPECTIVE: You should inform your supervisor about the student blaming you for failing the class. Your request to trade is appropriate; however, you should go ahead and accept the assignment for the summer semester with the original student. I would talk to the student regarding the previous situation and try to work it out.

- **Scenario 769**. I'm an interpreter for a preschool class, and one of the little deaf girls is still struggling with toilet training. She has been promised a trip to Cedar Point if she doesn't wet her pants today. The class takes a field trip to the zoo. When everyone stops for a potty break, this girl doesn't go because she wants to see the monkeys first. Sure enough, she wets her pants, and she starts to cry when she realizes she won't be able to go to Cedar Point now. I could rinse out her clothes and hope they dry before the end of the day; then no one would need to know.

AN INTERPRETER'S PERSPECTIVE: Sorry, kid. I can't be a party to deceit. Although I wouldn't go out of my way to be a tattle-tale, I wouldn't encourage the deceit. I'm, after all, part of the educational team helping to teach her and shouldn't be working against my colleagues.

A DEAF CONSUMER'S PERSPECTIVE: If the position is interpreter/aide, it's appropriate to rinse out her clothes or have her change into dry clothes. However, the girl does need to accept the consequences of her actions, so I would tell the teacher. If the position is interpreter only, you'll need to let an aide or teacher know so they can clean her up.

- **Scenario 770**. I interpret for a deaf girl in a mainstream high school biology class. Instead of paying attention in class, the girl spends her time drooling over the handsome football player who sits next to her. She's failing the class.

AN INTERPRETER'S PERSPECTIVE: Girl gets an "F." Not my problem.

A DEAF CONSUMER'S PERSPECTIVE: Let her drool and fail. This is a lesson she needs to learn.

- **Scenario 771.** I have always enjoyed being an educational interpreter, but recently the student's teacher informed me that the deaf student is required to use her voice at all times, even if she doesn't want to. In the past, I was told to "encourage" her to use her voice, and she hated it. In a noneducational setting, I would never dream of telling a deaf person to voice. Please advise what, if anything, I can say.

AN INTERPRETER'S PERSPECTIVE: Often as interpreters, we know a lot more information than we need to. In educational settings, we become the child's confidante because we are the only one who can communicate with her. This puts us in an awkward position. When something is decided upon that is contradictory to the student's wishes, we feel there's something we should do. Since you mention that "she hated it," I am assuming she is clear about what she wants and does not want. So then, the main issue that needs to be addressed in your question is the Individual Education Plan (IEP). What does the IEP say? Has it been agreed upon by the team that the student will use her voice at all times? If this is the case, then your hands are somewhat tied (forgive the pun). If the IEP does not mention how the student will communicate, vis-à-vis her voice, then I would advise you to do nothing. If the student is truly uncomfortable using her voice, this is a great time to have her deal with the issue and hone her skills in negotiating for her right to choose her mode of communication. Best of luck.

A DEAF CONSUMER'S PERSPECTIVE: Your letter does not specify how old the deaf student is, so I'm going to suggest several options. Educational interpreters work in a different type of environment than community interpreters. Your employer is the school district that hired you, and you answer to them. However, you are still ethically bound to assist in determining the best communication mode and access for the deaf student, as you are considered a member of the child's educational team. If the student is in elementary or middle school, you might want to discuss the student's communication preferences with your immediate supervisor and see if this is an issue to review with the IEP team. If the child is in high school, then you can let the teacher know that you will interpret the teacher's request to the student to use her voice, which allows the student to comply or not. If I understand correctly, the Department of Education's (DOE) position is that the child is encouraged to actively participate in the formulation of her IEP goals. During this meeting, the deaf student could express her concerns/perspective to the IEP team and start the discussion from there.

- **Scenario 772.** Could someone please explain to me why most of the
  nationally certified interpreters out there tend to be freelance interpreters
  and the noncertified interpreters tend to be the K-12 interpreters? As a
  parent of a deaf child, I have to say that makes no sense to me when deaf
  children need the most skilled interpreters modeling language for them. No
  wonder the statistics say that deaf children's reading and comprehension
  levels are so far behind. Is it just about money?

AN INTERPRETER'S PERSPECTIVE: I can certainly understand your
frustration; you want the best for your deaf child. Furthermore, you are right to
say that your child needs the most skilled interpreters modeling language for her.
Unfortunately, you have also recognized that many certified interpreters have
invested a lot of time and money in developing the skills and knowledge needed
to become certified. They have every right to expect to recoup that investment
in a reasonable amount of time. Furthermore, they deserve pay commensurate
with their education and certification. Public schools often classify educational
interpreters as aides, which results in the interpreter getting neither the salary nor
the respect/status they deserve. The lack of respect is the second reason often cited
by certified interpreters for not wanting to work in the educational arena. Often
it is the interpreter who is the most knowledgeable about deafness, as well as
language, communication, and cultural issues. Yet, because they are not considered
part of the educational team, they are not allowed to give input. This can result in
the interpreter having to implement or abide by decisions that are not in the deaf
student's best interest. This frustrating work environment can quickly lead to health
problems and burnout. Let's move on and look at three other reasons interpreters
often give for not wanting to work in the public school setting.

Working is isolation- Often there is one educational interpreter in a school district.
This can mean that there is no one to bounce ideas off of, to help problem solve, or
to listen to your frustrations. It can also mean that there is no one knowledgeable
about interpreting or sign language, so the opportunities for personal growth and
meaningful feedback are minimal or nonexistent. The school district often does
not have the means or funds to send interpreters to conferences or even allow them
to have the time off to attend. Yet, all interpreters need to work in expanding their
knowledge and enhancing their skills.

Boredom- Some interpreters do not find it stimulating or challenging to work
with the same deaf consumer five days a week. In educational interpreting, some
interpreters end up working with the same deaf student for years!

Anti-culture- The Deaf community cherishes their language and culture. There is
a perception by some deaf people that the demise of their language and culture
is connected to what they see happening in the mainstream/inclusion settings in

the public schools. Because of their great respect for the Deaf community, some interpreters feel that they do not want to be contributing members of that demise, so they choose not to be interpreters in the public school setting.

I am sure that interpreters have other reasons, but these are the ones I hear most often. I would encourage you, as a parent, to work to bring about changes in your child's school system. Parents have more influence than interpreters in changing the pay and working conditions. Work with other parents and work behind the scenes during your child's Individualized Educational Planning Committee (IEPC) meeting to get what your child needs and deserves.

A DEAF CONSUMER'S PERSPECTIVE: No, I don't think it's about the money. Schools tend to include benefits in their salary, and it's a stable daily schedule. On the other hand, a freelance interpreter's income goes up and down, and they have to pay for health insurance, not to mention taxes. People also don't understand that educational interpreters are not tutors. If the teacher's lesson is bad, then the interpreter's message is bad too. Some states have laws for educational interpreters requiring licensure. Often the deaf students don't know their rights, and even if they don't understand their interpreter, they are very passive about it. Parents don't always realize the power they have to speak out at an IEP meeting about their child's education or the skill of the interpreter in the classroom. Bottom line: two-year programs aren't enough for someone to become a professional interpreter.

- **Scenario 773.** I interpret for a middle school student who has had a cochlear implant for a year now. He tells us every single day how much he hates it and that it doesn't help him. However, his parents and teacher insist that he wear it. I am not required to sign but to oral interpret for all of his classes. He tells me that he tells his parents how he feels (he's not shy), but his parents say he is too young to make that decision. I see how miserable he is and how much he wants me to sign again with him. Should I try to intervene? Or mind my own business?

AN INTERPRETER'S PERSPECTIVE: As interpreters, we certainly have the responsibility to inform the school's Deaf and Hard of Hearing services if we feel that our interpreting is not effective. As an oral interpreter myself (RID certified OTC), I am not sure how oral interpreting would support a student with a cochlear implant because the word sounds from the instructor would not match the oral interpreting mouth movements. With a middle school student, this issue could be referred to the IEP "team," which may include the interpreter as a resource rather than in the position of interpreter for the meeting. Since it is stated that this student is outspoken, we can assume he has already told his parents that he hates the cochlear implant. Is the student's school work suffering, and would a change to ASL help improve that? There would need to be some quantifiable reasons to indicate that ASL could help improve that. There would have to be some quantifiable reasons to convince the parents that oral interpreting is not benefiting this student and he is miserable because he is not getting the information in class. If the IEP support staff agrees that oral interpreting is not in the best interest of the student, that should be discussed as soon as possible with the parents and student involved.

A DEAF CONSUMER'S PERSPECTIVE: (1) Continue to encourage the student to speak to his parents. (2) Is there anyone within your school system who has the respect of the parents that could intervene on behalf of the student? Keep beating the bushes for an advocate; this student obviously needs one. I'm sure his parents consider him too young to make this kind of "life" decision. Thirteen is right on the fence for sure; he would be considered too much of a kid to really know his own mind yet. However, if he was 17 or 18, then they'd probably have to listen to him. It's a tough situation, and unfortunately, you've got a front row seat. I feel for you.

- **Scenario 774.** I am an educational interpreter who graduated from a program that taught us ASL. However, that is certainly not the language being taught or used by deaf children in mainstream programs. Why then are upcoming interpreters being taught ASL when the next generation of deaf consumers won't even use it?

AN INTERPRETER'S PERSPECTIVE: If you listen to college students who are learning English as a second language, you will notice they speak in what we might identify as a formal tone. They say "do not" instead of "don't," and have little or no incorporation of clichés, slang, idioms, or foul language. As they progress in the language, they begin to catch on to these terms and use more colloquial forms of English. The same is true for any language learner. You are first taught the purest form of the language from which to base future learning. Someone who has been trained in ASL may have some difficulty at first understanding Pidgin Signed English (PSE) or Signed Exact English (SEE); however, over time they are able to decode it. However, an individual who has been taught only a SEE or PSE system would not be able to correctly interpret using ASL. SEE's and PSE's grammars are much more closely based on English, therefore, making it easier to comprehend for hearing students. ASL's linguistic rules differ enough from English's that many beginning interpreting students cannot accurately voice ASL even after two or three years of study. All linguistic reasons aside, I don't feel it is appropriate for interpreters to decide what sign system the next generation of deaf children will use. At the same time that many mainstream children are using more English-based sign systems, there is a movement within residential schools toward bilingual-bicultural education which emphasizes the use of both ASL and English. At this point, it seems preemptive and oppressive for interpreters to decide that ASL is out and English is in.

A DEAF CONSUMER'S PERSPECTIVE: Your job is to ensure that the student understands the information presented through whatever means necessary. You are trained and qualified to be the best judge of that. During an IEP meeting, you should be looked at as the communication expert. I believe it is important for educational interpreters to advocate for the proper language choice to facilitate optimal learning. As part of your job, you can teach sign classes, not only to interested students but to willing staff members also. This will go a long way toward standardizing sign choices and lessening any confusion.

Other Scenarios

Identify the issue(s) involved and decide how you would respond. Discuss and compare your responses with your colleagues.

775. You interpret an 8 a.m. class at a community college. One morning you get up, and there has been a heavy snowfall. You check and the college is still open. To allow for road conditions, you leave a half-hour early. The professor is late, and the deaf student hasn't arrived. When the professor walks in, he tells you that the deaf student left a message at his office to say he wouldn't be in today.

776. While interpreting in a junior high school, the science teacher assigns the class some small-group projects. The teacher asks you to watch the class for a minute while she runs to the restroom. While she's gone, the deaf student is up at her desk in one of her drawers. When you ask him what he's doing, he says he's looking for his paper. You tell him to go back to his seat. At the end of the day, the science teacher tells you some money is missing from her desk drawer.

777. While interpreting for a deaf high school student, the student starts fiddling with his glasses. When he's done, he has taped a drawing of two eyeballs on his glasses and then leans back to take a nap. The teacher is oblivious to all this.

778. You don't believe half the things the deaf student for whom you interpret tells you. He tends to exaggerate all the time and comes up with elaborate stories. He's meeting with the high school guidance counselor about some absences and tells her a humdinger of a story. She apparently buys it, though, because she excuses his absences and clucks over him very protectively.

779. You have interpreted for the same deaf student all through high school, and you think the world of her. After graduation, she's excited about going to Gallaudet and meeting all kinds of deaf people. One day you see her and another girl outside at lunch smoking. When she comes in, it's not cigarette smoke you smell, but marijuana. You know the school has a tough policy on drugs, and she could be

expelled and jeopardize her graduation. As an adult employed by the school, you're expected to enforce the school's policies.

780. You're a staff interpreter at a high school and have been asked to chaperone (and interpret as needed) at the senior prom. You end up having a wonderful time, but then you notice that all the students seem to have developed a major thirst for the punch. You decide to sample the punch and realize it's definitely "spiked" with alcohol.

781. You're a staff interpreter at a high school. You're sitting in the teachers' lounge one morning before school when one of the teachers approaches you and asks you if you've noticed the deaf student's strong body odor. She asks if you would mind talking to her about it. The teacher's rationale is that the student seems to be most comfortable with you.

782. You're a staff interpreter at a university interpreting for an incoming deaf freshman during orientation. During the question and answer segment, one of the participants asks a question about the college's alcohol policy. The speaker responds that the college doesn't allow alcohol on campus. You know that the students at the university do bring alcohol on campus. The deaf student says to you that this college sounds way too strict.

783. A professor stops you in the hall and asks for your help. He says another interpreter in his class comes in late, and then she and the deaf student just giggle back and forth. He says he doesn't want to turn her in himself because he doesn't want her to get mad at him. He asks you to please talk to your supervisor about it for him.

784. After a bad snowstorm, many of the faculty and staff of the elementary school where you interpret don't report to work. You're scheduled to interpret an Individualized Educational Planning Committee (IEPC) meeting this morning and figure it will still go on since school was not canceled. You have just walked in when the principal hands you a shovel and tells you to help clear the sidewalks before the buses arrive. Normally you're as helpful as the next person and will go the extra mile for your job within reason, but today you have a dress and high heels on. You point this out to the principal, who angrily says, "That's just too damn bad. Start shoveling!"

785. While interpreting a particular high school class, you come to dread going to class. The teacher has no control over the students; and it's a free-for-all most of the time. Sometimes the students get so rowdy you actually fear for your own safety in class.

786. It's story time in the second grade where you interpret, and the little deaf boy is sitting in the front row, seemingly mesmerized by the story. Feeling rather proud of yourself to have captured the deaf student's full attention, you continue to pour your heart into interpreting the story. After the story is over, you can't resist talking to the little boy and asking him what was his favorite part of the story. The little boy grins, points to you, and signs, "You. You big breasts!"

787. You're an oral interpreter for a deaf girl in high school. She tells you she wants you to teach her sign language. You suggest that she take some classes at the local community college, but she says her parents would never allow it.

788. You're interpreting for a shy deaf student in her gym class. As you walk through the locker room on your way out, you overhear some of the other girls making fun of the Deaf student's body as she is changing her clothes.

789. While substitute interpreting, the deaf student asks you for the s-w-i-n-g-l-i-n-e. You have no idea what that is. The student finally gives an exasperated sigh and gets up to get the stapler on his own. Puzzled you look closely at the stapler and see it has "SWINGLINE" imprinted on the top.

790. You have been a staff interpreter at the same high school for the last 20 years. It's Friday morning, and you're interpreting a homecoming pep rally. You realize you just can't muster the enthusiasm to keep up with the kids anymore. The music and the screaming seems louder than ever before. You just can't wait to get back to the teacher's lounge for a second cup of coffee.

791. On the first day of school, you arrive in homeroom ahead of the eighth-grade deaf student. Before you can even introduce yourself to the teacher, he looks up from his desk and snaps, "I know who you are, and I just want you to know I don't do signs!" Then he goes right back to doing his paperwork.

792. You're an elementary school interpreter for a deaf student who has an identical twin sister in another class who is hearing. One day after recess, you start interpreting, and the little girl looks at you blankly and acts totally uninterested in what you're interpreting. As a test, you start signing the "Star Spangled Banner," and the girl doesn't bat an eye.

793. The deaf high school student for whom you interpret has ringworm and is currently being treated. He's a very physical boy and very touchy with his fellow students and you as well. The school nurse warns him he needs to take his medicines for six weeks or else he will have to be sent home because ringworm is highly contagious. Granted, ringworm isn't fatal, but it's certainly no fun. You cringe when he touches you. You're also sure he's not taking his medication regularly.

794. A deaf student at the college where you work consistently doesn't show up for class and doesn't call the office to inform them. The school policy is three no-shows, and the student loses her interpreter. The deaf student begs you not to tell the office when she doesn't make it to class. You consider it because you'll lose your hours if you report her.

795. During a writing class, the professor gave the class specific directions for their final paper. The deaf student gets an "F" on his paper, which means he fails the course. The student asks to see the professor after class and for you to stay and interpret. During the course of the meeting, the student proceeds to tell the professor that he didn't get a good grade because you didn't interpret the directions clearly.

796. In a high school class, the deaf student for whom you interpret continuously picks on a student he considers his inferior. The teacher sees the deaf student constantly shoving and picking on the kid but never says anything, obviously assuming that is your job. The poor kid is afraid to tell on the deaf student for fear it will only make things worse.

797. It's your first week as an educational interpreter in an elementary school. You're interpreting as the teacher walks around the room checking the students' work. You see that the deaf student keeps playing with his penis under his desk. You ask him if he needs to go to the bathroom. He says no and continues playing with himself. The teacher doesn't see what is going on.

798. The elementary classroom teacher has told all the students to throw out their gum. However, the deaf student doesn't want to throw hers out, so she's pretending that she doesn't have any in her mouth, even though you can still clearly see it.

799. You are interpreting in an elementary school. While the students are taking a test, the teacher says she needs to run to the restroom and asks if you would mind watching the class. As soon as the teacher walks out, one of the little boys in the class starts acting up and using profanity. All the kids in the class are looking at you now to see how you're going to react. The only one oblivious to what is going on is the deaf student, who is concentrating on her test.

800. You interpret for a deaf student in the sixth grade. You interpret five periods, plus homeroom. The only time you don't interpret for him is his lunch period. During his homeroom class, the deaf student buys a box of M&M's from another student. You're surprised when you hear the cost, but you don't say anything because the other boy said it was for a good cause. At lunch the principal calls you into his office, and the police are there. They ask you specifically about the boxes of M&M's because they think the kids are selling joints in them.

801. You interpret for a student who generally falls asleep the minute class begins. Eventually, you stop interpreting. When the deaf student wakes up, he asks why you didn't continue interpreting. He says that by stopping you let the professor know he was not paying attention. He accuses you of being lazy.

802. You show up to interpret for a deaf college student who, after 20 minutes, still hasn't come to class. The college policy for interpreters is to wait 20 minutes, then go back to the office for possible reassignment. As you get up to leave, the professor asks you to please stay and wait another 20 minutes in case the student shows up.

803. You're a staff interpreter at a university. A female deaf student for whom you're interpreting this semester has a crush on a male deaf student. She follows him around and knows his schedule almost down to the minute. She knows you interpret some of his classes and is always asking you about him during breaks. The boy has been complaining to you about her stalking him.

804. You're a staff interpreter in a high school mainstream program. One of the classes you interpret is Algebra, which is a subject in which you did poorly when you were in school. You're managing much better this time around, but now your supervisor is requesting that you also tutor the student twice a week during his resource room period. You think it would be pushing it to try and tutor him too.

805. You're an interpreter in a high school, and one day the deaf student tells you that she has a date with her boyfriend that night. You and she both know she has a big chemistry test the next day, but you figure it's her call. Before class the next day, the deaf student tells the teacher her mother was sick last night, that she was up all night taking care of her mother, so she couldn't study for the test. She asks to please be excused from today's test and allowed to make it up later when she has studied.

806. You're an interpreter in a mainstream junior high school setting. The deaf student thinks he's being cool by showing off a hunting knife he has brought to school. The school has strict rules about weapons. The classroom teacher hasn't arrived yet.

807. You're interpreting at an elementary school, and the kids are all working on individual projects at their seats. The teacher asks you if you would mind running to the office to run off a few copies because the classroom aide is gone all week. You agree, but ask her to please not do anything while you're gone. She gladly agrees. When you return, not only is she talking to the class, but the deaf student wants to know why you left her alone.

808. You're interpreting for a deaf elementary student taking a spelling test. The deaf student's best friend, who knows how to fingerspell, is helping her cheat on the test. Of course, they only do this when they think neither you nor the teacher is watching, and they're quite proud of themselves. They're good, but you weren't born yesterday.

809. You're interpreting for an elementary school gym class. The teacher is working with some of the kids while the rest of the class is running around the gym playing, including the deaf student. A couple of the little girls in the class come up and ask you to please hold the rope for jump rope.

810. You're interpreting in a high school special education classroom. One day the deaf student is amusing himself and all his classmates by signing his conversations using only his middle fingers. The special education teacher asks you to please talk to the student about his inappropriate behavior.

811. You're interpreting in a sixth-grade classroom, and you can see the student directly behind the deaf student making faces and mocking the teacher. The teacher, however, is writing math problems on the board, so she doesn't see the student's antics. The other students in the class are now all watching this student, except the deaf student, who is watching you. The class is starting to giggle at the boy's facial contortions.

812. You're the only interpreter in the school, and your day is quite full. One of the deaf students tells you she wants to join the yearbook committee. If you refuse to interpret for her, she won't be able to join.

813. You're called to substitute interpret at a high school. The secretary is on a personal call and makes you wait forever before she gets off so you can sign in. You introduce yourself, and she apologizes for making you wait. She says she thought you were a student. She tells you what room you need to go to, but on the way a hall monitor stops you and asks you for a pass. Not being able to produce one, the woman escorts you back to the main office to verify that you're really an interpreter, not a student.

814. A deaf student in a high school art class is having a difficult time holding the standard charcoal sticks provided to the students for drawing. The teacher suggests the student buy some special pencils, which she does. The student is supposed to bring them every day to class, but she often forgets. She asks you to keep them for her instead and bring them to class every day.

815. During some down time at your high school interpreting job, the deaf student comes up to you and asks if you think he should ask a very popular cheerleader out on a date. You know the girl has a different boyfriend every week, and you don't want to see him hurt. You also don't want to get involved in censoring his love life.

816. Every day, the teacher sends the deaf junior high school student home with a note outlining his disruptive behavior in class and asking to meet with his parents. The notes always come back signed. At the grocery store one evening, you run into the boy's mom, and she says she and her husband are very pleased with their son's progress in school. She says it has been at least six weeks since he's brought a note home from his teacher. They have doubled his allowance to encourage him to keep up the good work.

817. In the elementary school where you interpret, the students were watching a video called "Monsters: Truth or Myth?" After the video, the teacher tells the students to draw a picture of what they think a monster looks like. Whether the deaf student misunderstood or was in fact giving his opinion isn't clear, but when the deaf student shows the teacher his drawing, your name is written underneath it.

818. One day you and the teenage deaf girl for whom you're interpreting start talking about safe sex because several girls in school her age are pregnant. The next day you're called into the principal's office, and the deaf girl's parents are there. They're furious and demand that you be fired for trying to influence the way they're bringing up their daughter.

819. The junior high school deaf student for whom you interpret has missed many classes this quarter, and his grades have plummeted. You're aware that his parents are going through a divorce, and from what you understand, the custody battle is pretty nasty. The deaf student is stuck in the middle and not really accepting the divorce. He has told you that he feels responsible for the divorce. At the parent/teacher conference at the end of the quarter, his mom approaches you, and is very concerned about his grades.

820. The seventh-grade deaf boy for whom you interpret attends a Deaf Pride Day where deaf students from various schools around the state attend. The boy is so overwhelmed to meet other deaf students his own age that when it comes time to leave, he starts crying. He begs you to tell his parents he wants to go to school with all the other deaf kids.

821. You interpret for a deaf boy who attends a junior high school in a rough part of town. After lunch in the teacher's lounge, you walk through the cafeteria on your way back to class. You see the deaf student sitting by himself reading a book. Suddenly a group of boys surround him and begin mocking him and kicking his chair.

822. You're an elementary interpreter in a junior high school with four deaf girls. There are two other staff interpreters to cover all the classes. In one class, two of the girls are in the same class together. While you're interpreting, you see the girls try to have a private side conversation. You try not to watch them, but you're sure one girl just told the other one about how her daddy touched her when she was in bed.

823. You're interpreting an elementary school gym class, and the game today is called "dead bugs." When the gym teacher plays music, the students are supposed to run around acting like bugs. When the music stops, they're "dead bugs." There are three deaf students in the class, and two of them catch on to the game quickly. The third deaf student, no matter how many times it's explained, just doesn't get it. Finally, you grab the little boy's hand, run around the room with him until the music stops, and then flop down on the floor and act like a dead bug. The little deaf boy loves it and finally catches on, but the gym teacher looks at you contemptuously as you're flopping around on the floor.

824. A deaf high school student is being questioned about stealing money from you. This is the third time this has happened to you this year. Two other teachers in the building have also had money come up missing, and the deaf student is in both their classes. The student's mother is called in to be present while her daughter is searched. The exact amount of money is found in her possession, and the police are called in. You're asked to press charges.

825. You're a staff interpreter at a large university. Depending on the schedule that semester, the classes for which you interpret could be on opposite ends of the campus. On a given day, you may end up walking several miles to get from class to class. This is much more than you would like or think is reasonable for your job, but when you approach your supervisor, she's unsympathetic.

Challenges in Volunteer Interpreting Situations

- **Scenario 826**. I'm interpreting for a deaf woman attending a Mary Kay party. The Mary Kay representative helps everyone pick out makeup appropriate for their skin type and demonstrates application techniques. Afterwards she encourages the women to buy the products. I know this deaf woman has limited funds to work with; that's why I volunteered to interpret for this presentation for free. I'm more than a little surprised to see her order hundreds of dollars worth of products. I now wonder why I'm working for free.

AN INTERPRETER'S PERSPECTIVE: My advice is to be very careful about interpreting for free. If you do it, do it with an open heart, and don't feel taken advantage of later. Perhaps this experience will affect your decision the next time. Remember that how people spend their money is their business. It's well known that people will gladly spend money on themselves for direct benefits, but not on the service that got them that benefit. Ask any waitress.

A DEAF CONSUMER'S PERSPECTIVE: I would definitely be angry. I don't appreciate being taken advantage of. However, I wouldn't say anything to the deaf woman. I just wouldn't interpret for her for free again.

- **Scenario 827**. I am a CODA (child of deaf adults), and when I became a certified interpreter, my family and I agreed to establish some guidelines about when it would and wouldn't be ethical for me to interpret for them. However, I see interpreters interpreting for their spouses and family members all the time. Are there some guidelines you can suggest for when it is and is not appropriate?

AN INTERPRETER'S PERSPECTIVE: Open assignments (public record, open to everyone) would be fine. Don't interpret privileged communication (e.g., doctor/patient, lawyer/client, accountant/client, clergy/congregant). Avoid the appearance of impropriety and be a stickler for ethics. If your family members can't accept your ethical standards, don't do it. It's kind of like relatives borrowing money.

A DEAF CONSUMER'S PERSPECTIVE: Kudos to you for setting interpreting boundaries within your family. I grew up in a deaf family with one hearing sister. We were the classic CODA family where my sister had to interpret pizza orders, TV shows, meetings with professionals, and dialogues between our mother and hearing mothers. Now I see my young CODA nieces and nephews doing the same thing, and it bothers me because nothing has changed. I would hope interactions between hearing people and deaf family members would not have to be interpreted by a CODA anymore. I have noticed that my relationship with my neighbors and colleagues is enhanced when my hearing partner does not interpret even though she easily could. At first it aggravated me, but now I realize it is for the best because we both maintain a balance of power this way. The same thing is true with CODAs and their family members.

Other Scenarios

Identify the issue(s) involved and decide how you would respond. Discuss and compare your responses with your colleagues.

828. A close deaf friend of yours has cancer and is in the hospital. You go to the hospital every day to visit, and when you're there, the hospital staff takes advantage of your presence to interpret for one thing or another. You would like to be able to visit as a concerned friend only, but you know your deaf friend is also encouraging the staff to utilize you by telling them what time you plan to be there every day.

829. A deaf friend asks you to go Christmas shopping with her. On the way there, she stops off at the pharmacy to pick up a new prescription. The pharmacist needs to explain the new medications to her. Your friend asks if you would mind interpreting because the pharmacist has a beard, and she can't read his lips.

830. A deaf friend asks you to go with her to the hospital while she undergoes some tests. She has contacted the hospital directly and confirmed that they will provide an interpreter. She wants you there as a friend, not to work. Unfortunately, when you both walk in, the "interpreter" provided is a nurse's aide who has "The Joy of Signing" book tucked under her arm for reference. Your friend begs you to interpret for her.

831. While in Hawaii celebrating your recent RID certification with your husband, you're in line for a volcano helicopter tour. A deaf couple is at the front of the line. Everyone has to go through a metal detector, and the deaf man is detained. The man tries to turn and talk to his wife, but the security officers keep moving him forward. The deaf man becomes upset at what he believes is rough treatment. However, what actually happened is that they told him several times to move because a wheelchair was coming through, but he didn't hear them.

832. While standing in the check-out line at the grocery store, you see a deaf employee being reprimanded by the store manager for something. You can see the deaf woman doesn't understand her boss, and she begins crying out of frustration.

833. You have just arrived in scenic Michigan where you'll spend your much anticipated two-week vacation. As you step out of the cab and head to your hotel, you look up and see someone standing in a window 10 stories above the ground. A crowd is gathering around you. Suddenly someone yells, "Look, he's moving his hands. Is he deaf or something?" Sure enough, the man is signing and explaining to the crowd why he's going to jump.

834. You have worked for a year and a half without any breaks, and you really need to get away for a while. You're actually looking forward to the long plane trip to catch up on your reading. As the final passengers board the plane, you see a woman signing to the stewardess. They're both obviously upset and frustrated about something. The stewardess starts waving the deaf woman along, but she won't budge. You're close enough to assist them.

835. You live in a condo complex, and you get a call from your condo association president. She tells you that a deaf person has moved into the complex. She needs to meet with him, and she asks you to interpret. There have been complaints about him already because he keeps driving the wrong way on a one-way street in the complex. She assures you it will only take a few minutes. You and the president go over to the deaf resident's condo, and thirty minutes later the president says, "If you need me, just contact the interpreter. She lives in the condo complex. Here's her number."

836. You're an interpreter for a deaf student in high school who is experiencing her first homecoming. The homecoming activities that day include attending a pep rally, building a float, the football game, seeing the queen's court, and finally attending a dance. You're there when the girl's mother comes to pick her up after the dance, and you see the girl excitedly telling her mother about her day. Her mother, however, can barely sign, and the girl becomes so frustrated trying to fingerspell everything that she asks you to please come over and interpret.

837. You're an ITP student walking to your car after class when you see two policemen pull up, grab a man, and try to handcuff him. The man is struggling and yelling that he doesn't want to be handcuffed. You can tell from his speech that he's deaf, and you just learned in class tonight, as a matter of fact, that having his hands behind his back would naturally be upsetting to him. You're only 20 feet away and wonder if you should offer to help.

838. You're attending the drama club's most recent production at the high school where you work. A student ushers you to the front row of the auditorium to a deaf couple whose daughter is in the play. You have no intention of interpreting, but you don't think anyone is scheduled to interpret the play tonight.

839. You're on a plane headed home after an extended vacation. A few rows ahead, you see two deaf people signing back and forth. You don't bother to introduce yourself; instead, you spend the flight mentally readjusting to the real world. During the flight, however, the captain announces that the plane will be forced to make an unscheduled stop due to some electrical problems. You notice none of the flight attendants attempt to inform the deaf passengers of this significant piece of information.

840. You're on vacation when you board a sightseeing bus. A few minutes later a deaf couple also board the bus. The driver, however, keeps telling them that they're on the wrong bus. The deaf couple keeps pointing to the sign on the front of the bus, and then they go and sit down. The driver chases after them and tells them they have to get off the bus. The couple obviously doesn't want to leave and stays seated. The other passengers around you are becoming irritated at the delay.

841. You're shopping at your favorite department store when suddenly you see a commotion by the entrance. Security has apprehended someone for shoplifting. It's a deaf woman that you know, and she sees you too. You know she's afraid and probably doesn't understand a thing they're saying to her. She motions you to come over and help. Your husband is waiting for you at the food court, and you know he's in a hurry to go.

842. You're in the mall doing some last-minute Christmas shopping. You see a deaf woman in front of you, and a clerk is arguing about a problem with a refund. You'll feel like "a scrooge" if you don't at least offer to interpret. The mall will be closing soon, and you still have a few things left on your list. If you offer to interpret, maybe you'll be able to get served too.

843. You're an ITP student, and one day you're running errands with a deaf friend. She stops by her optometrist's office to pick up her new glasses, and the receptionist tells her the doctor would like to have a word with her about her insurance. Your friend asks you if you wouldn't mind interpreting for just a few minutes.

844. In exchange for your services interpreting his daughter's wedding, a deaf man offers to put you and your spouse up at the hotel that weekend, all expenses paid. You jump at it, but because the wedding party is in the same hotel, the family is always knocking at your door at inopportune moments to come interpret this or that minor crisis with the hotel staff. Your husband is frustrated, but you feel like you weren't clear about expectations beforehand. It doesn't seem right for you to impose limits now.

845. You're asked by a close deaf friend to interpret her wedding, and you're honored to have been asked. She asks you to come with her and her bridesmaids to pick out dresses, and you gladly agree. Once there, you realize you're expected to wear a matching dress. You don't want or need another bridesmaid's dress hanging in your closet collecting dust.

Challenges Related to Interpreter Business Issues

- **Scenario 846.** I have a situation that has bugged me for a while now. While I was team interpreting for a nonprofit organization, the "resting" interpreter was having a side conversation with the deaf consumer about the high cost of interpreters. A specific community function that is coming up was mentioned, and I saw this interpreter offer to interpret the upcoming event for free. What do you suggest I should have said afterwards, if anything?

AN INTERPRETER'S PERSPECTIVE: This is one of my personal favorites in terms of myth-busting. "Nonprofit" does not mean "has no budget." While many nonprofit agencies do depend on volunteer services to stretch their budget dollars, they have monies to pay for administration, rent, utilities, programs — and professional services rendered. They may negotiate with a plumber, an activities coordinator, or an interpreter for a reduced fee due to their nonprofit status, but each of those professionals is free to negotiate (or not) in return and accept or decline work based on the outcome of that exchange. The second myth in this scenario is that providing interpreting services is (exorbitantly, outrageously) expensive. Interpreters should expect to be paid for the professional services they render. Interpreters should expect to be paid a fair price in relation to their years of professional training, their continuing education, the professional development they have undertaken to receive certification, the patchwork assignment work interpreters piece together to make a living, and the costs interpreters incur to do their job (e.g., taxes, medical insurance, gas, car maintenance). Only when we start thinking of ourselves as professionals and balance the costs we bear to do our work, can we begin to educate consumers (deaf and hearing) of our value. If we apologize and concur that our services are an expensive burden, then we devalue ourselves and the profession. In specific response to this scenario, you should meet with the feed interpreter afterward. Explain to this interpreter, while you respect her decision to work *pro bono*, that that discussion, especially during a work setting when this interpreter was supposed to be the support/feed, really made you feel devalued.

A DEAF CONSUMER'S PERSPECTIVE: It is the "working" interpreter's responsibility to let the other interpreter know, after the interpreting assignment is done (and in a private place), it was unethical to do that in this situation. It is important it is addressed in a diplomatic way, as constructive criticism. A suggestion can be made that teamwork is needed by having the "resting" interpreter monitor the "working" interpreter to ensure quality of the translation. Also, have the "resting" interpreter sit where the "working" interpreter can see her for support and not beside the deaf consumer(s) so there is no opportunity for side conversations with the deaf consumer(s). Also, you can let that interpreter know it was a distraction (and as stated earlier, unprofessional as well) to watch them chatting/discussing while the meeting was happening.

- **Scenario 847.** I have been nationally certified for over 20 years, and lately I have discovered that recent ITP graduates with only state QA levels are charging as much as I do — sometimes more! So I asked around to see what others are charging, and I realize I'm not charging enough. However, it still feels to me like these less qualified interpreters are charging way too much for their limited skill level and minimal experience. Are they helping or hurting the rest of us? Do we experienced interpreters now look greedy by asking for more pay based on our advanced skills, or are all interpreters now benefiting from the recent graduates earning more money?

AN INTERPRETER'S PERSPECTIVE: Most importantly, I think RID as our national organization should educate Americans about what RID stands for, what a certified interpreter is, and what our role encompasses. Why not television commercials, magazine advertisements, etc., to introduce and promote us in the first place? I am a very strong advocate for using certified interpreters first. If more hearing and deaf clients knew about our certification and what those earned letters behind our names mean, then they would be educated enough to demand certified interpreters every time. Secondly, RID and its members should work together to define a national and/or regional pay scale — or at the very least, guidelines. I agree with you that recent graduates of ITPs usually do not graduate with the skills and experience that certified interpreters have; yet as you've stated, they can go out and charge the same, if not more than us. May I cite the example of individuals who go to school with the specific desire to become, say, a brain surgeon? No matter how badly they may want to be a brain surgeon, the reality is not every person actually possesses the skills to accomplish that goal. Consequently, they fail as a brain surgeon, but go on to discover another career at which they succeed. Yet, for some reason, we graduate just about every single student who goes to school to become an interpreter, seemingly regardless of their skill levels. So why are we graduating students from ITPs who cannot pass the CI and CT, i.e., cannot interpret? Certification should be a requirement for graduation. My analogy between brain surgeons and interpreters might at first seem like a stretch, but consider how serious our responsibility is to consistently interpret correctly, professionally, and ethically to ensure effective communication in such a wide variety of situations. Often outcomes of people's lives are, literally, in our own hands! To me, it is that serious. We should all be college graduates, certified, licensed, and be working on (or hold) a master's degree. Deaf Americans deserve no less than the very best interpreters, every time. This is the only way we will ever get our profession fully recognized and respected. In the meantime, raise your rates.

A DEAF CONSUMER'S PERSPECTIVE: I think it is up to us as deaf consumers to always request that we want only certified interpreters. I also think there should be a standardized pay scale starting with recent graduates up to certified interpreters. Then depending on how many certificates they have (if they have 2 or 3), interpreters should be compensated accordingly. To me, it is the same idea as when a person uses their time and resources to go to school and get their degree. By the same token, only those interpreters who have worked hard and put in the time are truly skilled enough to pass the national tests. Agencies for deaf consumers that send us interpreters "force" recent graduates and/or noncertified interpreters to achieve a certification level to demonstrate competency, before they can get paying jobs. After all, it seems only fair that interpreters who have put the time (and money) into acquiring the skills to become certified should be compensated accordingly.

Other Scenarios

Identify the issue(s) involved and decide how you would respond. Discuss and compare your responses with your colleagues.

848. A deaf client contacts you to interpret a social function he and his wife will be attending. It's a great party, and the deaf clients are very pleased with all the networking they're able to do for their business. The next day, though, the husband calls you and says while they were away from their home, their house was robbed. He's apologetic, but he says they won't be able to pay you for your services for at least six months or until they get their insurance check.

849. A deaf friend asks you to interpret a weekend retreat and tells you that lots of people you know will be there as an added enticement. It sounds like fun. You go and enjoy yourself immensely and are exhausted after a long weekend of working. You send your invoice, and a week later your friend calls you and says she assumed the free room and board was in exchange for your services.

850. A deaf person hires you directly to interpret for him at a counseling appointment, and payment is agreed upon in advance. When you get to the counselor's office, the deaf client is walking out with someone else. The deaf man introduces the woman he's with as a friend from out of town who is visiting. He says the counselor was able to get him in earlier, but he wasn't able to get in touch with you in time. His friend did the interpreting instead. No offer of compensation for the time you blocked off is made.

851. A deaf woman approaches you directly and asks if you would be willing to interpret a six-week Bible study class at her church. She explains that her church doesn't have the funds to pay you and neither does she, but she really wants to attend this class. She offers to clean your house once a week for six weeks in exchange for your interpreting services. You can't help but think you're actually getting the better end of the deal.

852. A doctor's office calls and asks if you're available to interpret for a deaf patient who has specifically asked for you. This particular doctor's office has been terrible about paying you in a timely manner in the past.

853. A friend asks you if you would interpret for her deaf brother at their father's retirement party. You tell her your rate, and there's dead silence on the other end of the line. She finally says that she assumed you would do it as a favor to her.

854. A woman you recently met socially through your husband calls you to interpret a lecture she's coordinating. She doesn't inquire about your hourly rate; instead, she offers you an exorbitant amount of money, which she has budgeted. She could get four interpreters for the money she's offering you.

855. After completing an assignment for a deaf client for whom you have interpreted for many years, you realize that you forgot to tell her that you recently raised your hourly rate. You're not sure if you should let it slide this time or just send her a bill reflecting your new rate.

856. An interpreter referral agency calls you to interpret for an employer interviewing a deaf person for a job opening. You arrive a little early and introduce yourself to the client. You're surprised when he becomes angry that the company has assumed he needed an interpreter. He says he's hard of hearing, not deaf. When the employer comes out to greet him, he says he resents their assumptions. The employer apologizes and says he thought he was doing the right thing. The employer tells you you're free to leave and thanks you for coming in. Later when your bill is never paid, you call to follow up, and the employer says he won't pay your fee because you never actually provided any services.

857. An organization you support both financially and with your time calls you to interpret a one-day program they're sponsoring. They indicate they don't have enough money in the budget to pay for interpreters, but you know that's not the case. The bottom line is that they just don't want to pay for an interpreter if they think they can get you for free.

858. The deaf client, who hired you directly to interpret for him, has discussed all the payment arrangements with you in advance. It has been two months, and you still have not seen a dime, even though you have called him several times already. You're ready to just call it a loss.

859. You charge $25 an hour with a two-hour minimum. A deaf client calls you at home and says he needs an interpreter and promises it will only take 30 minutes. He asks if you would please accept $25 instead of $50.

860. You have been interpreting a weekly story hour for deaf children. The kids love it and so do you. After story hour one week, the librarian approaches you and says they're not going to be able to continue because their budget doesn't allow for your weekly fees. She beats around the bush and finally asks you if you would consider reducing your fees or, better yet, volunteering your services.

861. You have interpreted several times for a state child protective services caseworker when she investigates deaf parents on her caseload. You work together well, but the problem is getting paid in a timely manner. You always get your money eventually, but it may be several months. She calls you today to ask you to interpret a home visit she's trying to set up.

862. You're a nationally certified interpreter asked to interpret for a deaf speaker coming in from out of town. When you tell the caller your rate, she says she's thrilled because they usually pay twice as much for a nationally certified interpreter.

863. You're called directly by a hospital for an emergency interpreting assignment. As soon as you hang up the phone, you realize you forgot to discuss payment. You know they expect to pay you, but you don't know what their hourly rates are.

864. Your attorney has just taken on a new deaf client, and he calls you to come in and interpret their meetings. The pay rate he suggests is much lower than what you usually charge, and you're somewhat offended considering how much he charges an hour. He obviously must not think much of interpreters. When you tell him your hourly rate, he's stunned.

865. A deaf friend comes to you and says she has just been to the parent/teacher conference at her daughter's high school. She says there was no interpreter present, and there seems to be some problems with her daughter's attendance. She asks if you would mind going back with her and interpreting. You agree, and afterwards the deaf woman tells you to send your bill to the school. They refuse to pay since your services were not authorized in advance.

866. You have been asked by a teacher to interpret her school's open house. She tells you the student's deaf parents can't afford to pay for an interpreter, and neither can the school district. She would just like you to volunteer.

867. You're interpreting a time management seminar that was scheduled to last an hour, but it's now going on almost two hours. You've got all the time in the world, but you hope they realize they've got to pay you for more than the agreed-upon time.

868. You're hired to interpret for an out-of-town, staff retreat that's supposed to last eight hours. The day of the meeting, you arrive early, and no one else is around. You wait for over an hour, but no one shows up. Once back home, you call the retreat organizer who contacted you in the first place, and she says she's sorry but the retreat was cancelled. She says the other interpreter was contacted and that she said she would call you and tell you. That's an eight-hour block you could have filled with other appointments had you only known the retreat was cancelled.

869. You're going to interpret at a formal dinner and presentation, so you splurge and buy an expensive powder-blue linen suit for the occasion. During the dinner, your deaf client spills a glass of red wine all over you.

870. You are interpreting for a deaf woman and her infant son in a pediatrician's office one afternoon when the 3-week-old boy urinates on your brand new, very expensive, dry-clean-only sweater!

Challenges Related to Interpreter Referral Agencies

- **Scenario 871.** I recently graduated from an ITP and have started working as a freelance interpreter. I was evaluated by an agency and have done some work for them. The coordinator, however, told me that she would prefer that I not work for any other agency. She even went so far as to say that if I turned down work with other agencies, the clients that normally called them would have to call her, and I would get the work anyway. The bottom line is that she assured me that she would get those job requests that I would turn down from other agencies in the area, and that there would be no need to accept work outside of her agency. If I turn down her offer to exclusively work with her agency, I fear she could make it harder for me to find work with other agencies. I'm confused. I understand that people have to make a living, but I am also sure that there is enough work for everyone. Why would an agency resort to trying to create a monopoly? How do experienced interpreters and deaf consumers view such aggressive business practices in our profession?

AN INTERPRETER'S PERSPECTIVE: The only time I would work exclusively for one agency is if I were given a staff position. With that, should come benefits and a guaranteed number of hours or a salary. Otherwise, this agency's practices are not appropriate. Even in the tiny world of sign language interpreting, competition is healthy. I would recommend that you explain your concerns to the coordinator, and if nothing changes, seek work elsewhere. Don't badmouth the agency to anyone, and be willing to go back to them if they change their ways. A big part of starting out as an interpreter is building a network of people you can trust. It sounds like these people don't fit the bill at this time.

A DEAF CONSUMER'S PERSPECTIVE: I would like to see interpreters and consumers unite to speak out against this type of ruthless exploitation. Agencies provide a valuable service to deaf and hearing consumers. Any spirit of competition between agencies, however, should be based on legitimate business practices — pay and benefits, interpreter education, and opportunities to earn CEUs, just to name a few examples.

- **Scenario 872.** I work for an interpreting agency. One of their contracts is with a local university. As a staff interpreter, I was sent to interpret one semester at the university for a deaf student enrolled there. Later I was contemplating switching to private practice interpreting, so I began to investigate work opportunities in my area by talking to other freelance interpreters. I learned that many freelancers work with several agencies, including this university and other organizations. I was unaware that this university had 15-20 deaf students and that they contract their classes with a variety of freelancers. Now as a new freelancer myself, one of the places I have contacted to work with is this university. However, when I gave my notice of resignation to my agency, my employer informed me that I could not work for any of their clients (specifically naming this university). My employer maintains, while his agency has no exclusivity clause for interpreters, there is a contract with the clients that they cannot hire his staff interpreters. This semester the university has scheduled me to interpret for one class with the same student for whom I interpreted when I worked for the agency. What do you think?

AN INTERPRETER'S PERSPECTIVE: At the time of hire with this agency, the agency should have presented you with a contract. Within the contract there should have been clauses regarding work restrictions specifically stating locations, time limits, your rate, guaranteed number of work hours per week, and their time frames with these restrictions in mind. In order for it to be effective and binding, there needs to be mutual assent and consideration by all parties involved either orally or written. One needs to make informed decisions which are shared prior to the date of hire as a staff interpreter for an agency so that one can participate in negotiations. Not only is it unlawful to inform an employee of work restrictions after the date of hire without consent, but it is also poor business practice on the agency's part to try to enforce a failure to perform a contractual duty of this nature. Since you have resigned, you are no longer an employee or staff interpreter of this particular agency; therefore, they are not your current employer. They are your former employer. This means you are now an independent contractor able to take on assignments according to your own ethical decisions and free will. You cannot be expected to agree to any work clauses if you were not fully informed and in agreement at the time of hire or during your employment; therefore, you are not being negligent in your duties at the time of terminating your contract. You could check with a lawyer just to be safe, but I would say that if you have no exclusivity agreement with the agency, there is no reason you can't take the job. If the university has such an agreement with the agency, the agency will have to take that up with the university.

A DEAF CONSUMER'S PERSPECTIVE: There are laws and unfavorable opinions regarding former employees "stealing" clients and business away from a previous employer — clients that the employee learned were on the employer's client list only through the virtue of being employed with that employer. On the other hand, clients are free to follow departed employees to their new workplace or employer in an increasingly global workforce and pursue efficient use of finite resources (e.g., personnel, talent, loyalty, money). It is public knowledge that the postsecondary setting is an employer of sign language interpreters. Interpreters work in a profession that is severely short in supply and great in demand; therefore, their mobility across employers and work opportunities make inevitable the predicament of being offered work with clients of a previous employer. It sounds to me that you are being honest, and that the information about the university's use of interpreters surfaced through networking with independent interpreters. It also sounds to me like there are no serious concerns among your colleagues and consumers in regard to your reputation. Furthermore, it is not reasonable to assume that an interpreter would know or remember *every* client of her previous employer, even if the interpreter chose to avoid accepting work with clients of the former agency. I think that the interpreting agency (if you choose to work with that agency again) should want to welcome you back, even if you joined the university's freelance interpreter list. Also, legally speaking, the agency has no ammunition to prevent your continued employment with the university other than to "make noise," as there is no exclusivity clause for interpreters. If there is any legal issue at all, it sounds to me that the interpreting agency can only fight the university and allege that there is a contract with the "client" (not a contract with its previous staff interpreters). Shouldn't ensuring the maximum availability and access of qualified interpreters for deaf and hearing consumers be the top priority here?

- **Scenario 873.** The agency for which I work went through a difficult time with several of their interpreters being unhappy with the working conditions at a job site. I didn't want to leave the agency during this rough time, so I stayed until things improved. Then the agency started a mentoring program, and I didn't want to leave then either because I was invested in the mentees. However, finally I decided there was never going to be a "good time" to leave and that I needed to just do it. My final decision came right after returning home from an RID conference. The agency paid for several of us to attend the conference (registration, half the hotel room, and a small amount for meals). My employer informed me that he was unhappy that I gave my notice after they'd just spent so much money on me for the RID conference. There was no agreement in place before the conference, and the only requirement for attending and having our expenses paid was to work at their booth, which I did. What really gets me about all of this is that there is another interpreter who also just left our agency. She gave her notice during the RID conference, but our employer has not asked for a penny back from her. I don't want to file a complaint against the agency. I'm just asking if I have crossed the line?

AN INTERPRETER'S PERSPECTIVE: It seems like one of the things that irks you most is that you would like to be acknowledged and given a pat on the back for your loyalty through the tough times. Now it feels like you're getting a double slap in the face from the agency's crankiness over the timing of your resignation. For some reason, our profession is not very good at separating our personal feelings and business. The reality is an agency is a business. However, too often, as contractors, we so want to be liked and acknowledged by the agencies that hire us, beyond the business element of filling job assignments. No employer is going to be happy it has spent continuing education money on a contractor, only to have that contractor quit soon after. That's just business. If you were hoping the agency would say, "We're so sorry to lose you because you've been so terrific during our ups and downs, and we'll consider the RID conference expenses a thank-you farewell gift," it's just not going to happen. You fulfilled your agreement by working the agency's booth. You don't owe the agency anything further, but neither does the agency owe you anything further.

A DEAF CONSUMER'S PERSPECTIVE: Your paid trip to the RID conference sounds well merited. You stayed through the difficult times at the agency, fulfilled a commitment to the mentees, and worked the booth as required. You demonstrated integrity and professional responsibility. Meanwhile, as you were proving yourself a valuable asset to the company, your employer was losing several employees. Perhaps he thought a guilt trip could convince you to stay with the agency. A lot of time went into arriving at your important decision, so regardless of the circumstances of the other interpreter's resignation, you can live comfortably with your thoughtful decision to leave the company when you knew the time was right for you. If this agency uses employment contracts or maintains an employee handbook, you could verify if you are an "at-will employee," and consult with an attorney as to any contractual obligations you might have in paying back your employer for the conference costs.

> • **Scenario 874.** In the past we have had discussions with certified interpreters who we contract about eating while on duty. We requested that they not eat our food while on duty. We requested hiring two interpreters back to back instead so they could quit after an hour and a half of interpreting. Recently at our fundraising event, when we were only expecting one interpreter, three interpreters arrived and took three seats and three dinners (at $35 each) that were reserved for our paid guests. We deducted those meals from their bill, but they continued to bill us for more interpreters than we requested and would not deduct the meals. I would appreciate your opinion on this occurrence.

AN INTERPRETER'S PERSPECTIVE: Did the coordinator of the event hire through an agency and receive written confirmation on the number and names of the interpreters who would be providing services? If not, this would be highly encouraged as to avoid the mishap of additional interpreters. If you were hiring through an agency and a confirmation of the assignment and its logistics was sent to you, including your request that meals weren't provided, you would be justified to request that the agency compensate or deduct the meals from the final invoice. I would hope the agency or private contractor would adhere to your requests and, if not, allow for flexibility in compensation when the errors occurred. It is also helpful if a contact person is arranged for the on-site event, thus alleviating some issues before they might arise. Typically, it is the norm in the profession to bill an initial two-hour fee or minimum. If this agency was following this policy, perhaps it may be the reason two interpreters arrived at the same time, thus maximizing the use of the interpreters for the two hours you would be billed for each of them, equaling four hours. If you contracted with individual contractors, it is highly recommended to have a written confirmation or contract for the event as well. Listing logistics, including the meal arrangements, helps avoid a potential problem at the event. Having this confirmation allows the coordinator to know if too many interpreters have been contracted, thus allowing you to cancel for those you do not need.

A DEAF CONSUMER'S PERSPECTIVE: Everyone loves a job that includes a good meal, but they should wait to be asked to partake, especially at a formal, sit-down dinner. On the other hand, interpreters should not be expected to work for long periods (particularly through a mealtime) without eating, especially if everyone else is eating. The requester needs to specify everything in the original request for an interpreter. If a meal will be served at the event, then they should state whether they will be providing a meal for the interpreter. If you include this information when you make the request, everyone will be on the same page, and there will be no surprises. You should not pay for two interpreters you didn't request, and if you didn't state that you would be providing a meal, you should not pay that as well.

Other Scenarios

Identify the issue(s) involved and decide how you would respond. Discuss and compare your responses with your colleagues.

875. An interpreter friend you know has decided to open her own interpreter referral agency. You don't have a problem with the idea of more than one interpreter referral agency. You think competition can be a healthy thing. One day on an interpreting assignment you accept through your friend, your team interpreter is hopelessly under-qualified for the job. Afterwards you voice your concern to your friend, and she says it saves her agency money to send noncertified interpreters.

876. An interpreter referral agency schedules you to interpret a staff meeting for a large corporation. You're told the meeting will last approximately two hours, but when you arrive, you look at the agenda and see that it's scheduled to last six hours.

877. An interpreter referral agency sends you out on an assignment. At the end of the job, the supervisor of the deaf client comes up to you and asks you for your business card. Without thinking, you give him one, and he tells you they're extremely pleased with your work and will be calling you directly in the future.

878. An interpreter referral agency sends you to interpret for a deaf client at the company where he works. On break, the client tells you his bosses are complaining about the rates the agency is charging for an interpreter. The deaf client says it would really make him look good if he could contract with you directly and save the overhead charges of the agency.

879. You were a staff interpreter at an interpreter referral agency, but quit because you wanted to be more independent. Now you're out on your own. You have let your clients know that if they want you, they can now call you directly. Your former supervisor calls you and says the agency is going to file a grievance with RID against you for stealing from their client list.

880. You were a staff interpreter at an interpreter referral agency, but because of a disagreement with your supervisor, you quit. Now you're freelancing and find out that your supervisor is bad-mouthing you to clients who call and specifically request you.

881. You're a nationally certified interpreter who works as an interpreter referral coordinator for a large agency. You work with several deaf people on staff, including your immediate supervisor. You're aware that he's currently applying for jobs elsewhere because you have taken a few of his messages. The director of the agency (your supervisor's boss) approaches you to verify the rumors that your boss is applying for jobs elsewhere during work time.

882. I have been interpreting in a weekly, mental health assignment as a freelance CDI. Last month I didn't get a call from the agency to interpret. Apparently, things didn't go well. Now the client and therapist want me back. However, the interpreter referral agency still isn't calling me. What can I do?

883. You're contacted by an interpreter referral agency to interpret a seminar. Upon arriving, you realize the client is deaf-blind. Of course, no one mentioned that to you when they set up the assignment. It's not that you can't do it, but there are a number of interpreters in your area who specialize in this field. It just would have been nice to know in advance.

Challenges Unique to Being an Interpreter/ Working with Deaf People

- **Scenario 884.** I am currently in an ITP, but I am starting to have doubts about the viability of my choice of careers. My concern is twofold. Recently it seems I've heard several experts say that interpreters will one day be replaced by technology! I also am aware that cochlear implants are a big deal right now for parents with young deaf children, so I'm wondering if maybe interpreters will become obsolete. What do you think?

AN INTERPRETER'S PERSPECTIVE: I too have concerns about all the technological advances we see continuing to creep into our lives. It seems like I'm always hearing or reading about new gizmos and inventions that sound pretty unbelievable, and the unknown can seem scary and daunting. In fact, I just read an article about children and adults who received cochlear implants, and interpreters are still very much in demand to augment what these individuals still cannot hear, especially when they are in group settings. Admittedly, technology usually intimidates me, but technology is only as good as those who are trained to use it. While these advances may invariably lighten our burdens, my sense is that deaf people are still going to want a real, live person rendering the message to them. The subtleties of facial expressions and non-manual markers, as well as the brain's ability to sift through the morass of our language to come up with the essence of what a speaker is saying, just can't be done by computer. I may sound naïve here because I know that technological improvements and discoveries are going to happen despite any protests or fear. I'd like to think, though, these new innovations will ultimately be positive in ameliorating difficult communication situations for deaf and hard of hearing people. We are human, after all, and communication replicated artificially is prone to misunderstandings. It cannot compare to the connection or human bond that is possible with a real, live person. Perhaps we need to reframe our apprehensions and instead look at technology as something that will hopefully make our jobs easier, better, and more efficient, as well as complement our craft.

A DEAF CONSUMER'S PERSPECTIVE: I understand how you might be concerned about the viability of your future career choice. However, speaking as a CDI, I feel more than ever that we (the Deaf community) will need ASL interpreters in schools, jobs, theaters, various performances, judicial settings, medical situations, etc. for many more years to come. As to your concerns about the prominence of technology eradicating the need for interpreters, you need to realize that not all deaf children will benefit from these advances. For example, children with profound or severe hearing losses will receive little to no advantage if they undergo cochlear implant surgery. Years ago I considered getting a cochlear implant, but my doctor advised against it because of the severe nerve damage in my ear. I strongly believe that ASL interpreters will be needed for many more deaf generations to come. I cannot and will not depend on technology to "cure" my deafness — that is impossible. Deafness is caused by a variety of factors, so finding a cure-all using technology is highly improbable. While it is true that the future is not "set in stone," I cannot imagine a world where ASL interpreters or the profession of interpreting will become obsolete.

- **Scenario 885.** I am an ITP student, and I think I already have three strikes against me before I even get into the field of interpreting. Strike one, I do not like to hug. Strike two, I have a young family and will rarely be able to attend Deaf interpreting events. Strike three, I prefer not to be called by my first name in the business world. Should I "walk?"

AN INTERPRETER'S PERSPECTIVE: As a professional interpreter, it is not necessary to hug your clients. You do not need to be warm and make a deaf client feel comfortable. When I meet someone for the first time, whether they are deaf or hearing, I always introduce myself by my full name, then indicate a name sign for myself to the deaf clients and an acceptable way to address me (i.e., Miss Smith). Not being able to attend Deaf events or interpreting events will limit your skill development and rapport with the Deaf community, but again, it is not a requirement for being an interpreter. I don't think you necessarily need to "walk," but you may want to try to develop some flexibility. As interpreters, we are language and cultural facilitators, so it is important to be comfortable with Deaf culture.

A DEAF CONSUMER'S PERSPECTIVE: My initial response is it seems as if you are lacking in areas of importance in interpreting. Why do you want to be an interpreter? However, since you are enrolled in an ITP, you obviously have the desire to interpret. Since you are hesitant to become overly familiar with your clients, you can select jobs that will not place you in that position. You could limit your jobs to interpreting for large groups and avoid one-on-one situations. As you become more comfortable with the interpreting and Deaf communities, you may find yourself relaxing your standards and appreciating the nuances of working with deaf people, such as hugging them and being on a first-name basis.

Other Scenarios

Identify the issue(s) involved and decide how you would respond. Discuss and compare your responses with your colleagues.

886. While driving to a musical performance you'll be interpreting, you're practicing to a cassette of the group's songs. The next thing you know a cop is pulling you over and accusing you of making obscene gestures to him when he passed you a few miles back. You explain to the officer what you were doing, but he doesn't believe you.

887. A deaf neighbor shows up on your doorstep one morning and asks you to proofread a letter she has written and make any necessary changes to her English. You agree, and by the time you're done, the letter she has written has your writing all over it. When you hand it back, she's visibly upset at how much you changed her letter.

888. The interpreter referral agency where you work also handles occasional relay calls for deaf clients. One day while you're covering the phones, a call comes in and you recognize the name of the person. You give your first name at the beginning of the call, but the deaf person doesn't acknowledge you. The call ends up being very personal, and you wonder if the caller really didn't recognize your name or he just didn't care and trusted that you would remain in role. The next time you interpret for him, you think he gives you a funny look, but neither of you says anything.

Challenges Related to Being an Interpreter Training Program (ITP) Student

- **Scenario 889**. You're out with some classmates from your ITP, and you all start discussing the vocabulary you learned in class that week. A deaf person comes over to your table and says he couldn't help but notice all of you signing and what you were discussing. He proceeds to correct some of the vocabulary and tells you, since your teacher is hearing and he is deaf, his signs are better.

AN ITP STUDENT'S PERSPECTIVE: Accept the signs that the deaf person gives and thank him for his helpful instruction. Explain to the man that we are instructed to use whatever signs our future deaf clients ask us to use. Therefore, our teacher is making sure we are well-educated as to all the possible sign choices because we will encounter them as future interpreters since not all deaf people use the same signs.

AN INTERPRETER'S PERSPECTIVE: You should thank the deaf person who came over to provide guidance for his input. You learn from each deaf person you meet. Recognizing that there are likely other deaf people out there using the same signs as him and knowing different modes of communication will likely help you with your receptive skills in the future. You should even take the suggestions given by this deaf man back to your classroom and share them with your teachers to get their feedback. As an outsider of Deaf culture, you should not under any circumstances correct the deaf person or say his choices of signs are wrong.

A DEAF CONSUMER'S PERSPECTIVE: You should graciously accept his signs without question. Everyone has their own style and different signs they prefer interpreters to use, and all you can do is try your best to accommodate each client. However, you surely shouldn't lose faith in your teacher. Her vast knowledge and experience most likely dictate the signs that are being taught in the classroom. Those signs are equally important to know.

- **Scenario 890**. You're an ITP student, but you also work in a hospital as a registered nurse. Your deaf friend is currently in the hospital for a colonoscopy. You stop by his room to visit him, and he tells you no interpreter has been provided so far. You tell him whom to contact, but the next day when you stop by again, he tells you he still hasn't had an interpreter for any of his tests or discussions with his doctor. He's very frightened, but you're afraid if you try to help, the hospital will try to make you interpret. They have tried it several times in the past.

AN ITP STUDENT'S PERSPECTIVE: Encourage the deaf friend to advocate for himself by having him explain to the doctor/nurses that he is unclear about the procedure and discussions with the doctor and, therefore, must refuse any treatment or signing of any documents until the hospital provides an interpreter as part of his legal right. As a friend, offer to be present during his meeting with the doctor/nurses (when you are off-duty), and let him know you'll keep an eye on him and monitor the situation.

AN INTERPRETER'S PERSPECTIVE: As a friend, you should attempt to advocate for your friend and his need for an interpreter. You should ask to speak with the hospital staff in charge of providing interpreting services. If the staff attempts to convince you to interpret, you should explain the numerous reasons why that would be inappropriate. You are only a student and not permitted or willing to interpret prior to receiving the appropriate credentials through state or national certification. I would also explain, because you are friends with the deaf person in need of an interpreter, it would be difficult for you to remain impartial, which is one of the key tenets of the interpreting profession. You should explain how you would be unable to maintain the role of being a supportive friend providing your own personal guidance and the role of interpreting professionally at the same time. You should direct them to an organization or agency in the community where professional interpreters can be located.

A DEAF CONSUMER'S PERSPECTIVE: It is important that you know your role as an ITP student/future interpreter. If you clearly know what your role is, then you can explain it to someone else who may not know or understand. In situations such as this, explain why you are not qualified to interpret and offer to help find someone who is. It always breaks my heart to see someone without equal access to communication; however, it is essential to remember that if you succumb to the pressure and agree to interpret, not only would you be going against the CPC, which you abide by as an ITP student, you would also be setting a precedent for accepting unqualified interpreters to do a job that only a qualified interpreter should do.

- **Scenario 891**. You're an ITP student working with an educational interpreter in a high school biology class. The educational interpreter asks if you would like to try interpreting while they do their lab project. You jump at the chance. Once the lab project is explained, however, the interpreter gets up and signs, "I will be right back," and leaves you to interpret the rest of the class.

AN ITP STUDENT'S PERSPECTIVE: This would be one of those times when wearing an "ITP Student" badge comes in handy and protects the ITP student. Explain to the client the interpreter had to leave suddenly and ask if it is acceptable to her for you to continue interpreting. If the client says "yes," then finish interpreting the class, and after completing the class, ask the student if she has any questions or needs any clarification about the information you interpreted. If the client says "no," inform the teacher that the interpreter left and that you, as an ITP student, cannot finish interpreting the class. Then try to contact the interpreter and make sure she is OK. Let the interpreter know that you depend heavily on her expertise and instruction, and without her, you are not comfortable that the client is getting all the information.

AN INTERPRETER'S PERSPECTIVE: Most interpreters work hard to make sure ITP students are learning what they need to know to become qualified interpreters. Therefore, if this happened, I would assume there was some kind of emergency that prevented the interpreter from coming back to the classroom. However, if you know for sure there wasn't an emergency and it was simply a poor judgment call on the part of the interpreter, then I would still refrain from speaking negatively about the interpreter or the situation to anyone. After all, you are a visitor at the school and should remain professional and respectful at all times. You should quietly pull the biology teacher aside and let her know that you are an ITP student and not qualified to be interpreting this class. Since the biology teacher is a member of the deaf student's academic team, she should be aware of the deaf student's needs and willing to help locate a qualified interpreter. After the class is over, you should seek out the interpreter and let her know how you handled the situation during her absence.

A DEAF CONSUMER'S PERSPECTIVE: The interpreter is there to interpret, not you. When the interpreter leaves, you leave.

- **Scenario 892**. You're an ITP student getting some observation hours for your internship. The two interpreters you're observing usually work well together, but today for some reason, there's no teamwork going on at all. When the interpreter who is currently interpreting misses information, she looks to you for a feed and, without thinking, you quickly supply it. The second interpreter suddenly snaps to attention and signs very clearly to you, "You're only a student; sit quietly and mind your own business." She makes you feel like a worm, but you're mad at her too.

AN ITP STUDENT'S PERSPECTIVE: Do as the interpreter instructs and sit quietly observing. After the assignment apologize to the interpreter, explaining that you were just trying to help and weren't sure if she had seen her partner's need for a feed. Add that no means did you mean to interrupt or imply that you are more skilled.

AN INTERPRETER'S PERSPECTIVE: After the meeting you should approach the second interpreter and ask to speak with her privately. Be honest about your uncontrollably supplying a feed, and apologize if she feels you overstepped your role while attempting to be of assistance. Exhibiting both professionalism and concern for interpreters and students will foster good relationships and encourage personal growth and development in the profession of interpreting.

A DEAF CONSUMER'S PERSPECTIVE: Everyone has bad days. That's true for the best of interpreters as well as ITP students. Wait until the next break or the end of the assignment, and approach both interpreters calmly and professionally. Sincerely apologize for overstepping your boundaries as an ITP student by giving a feed to a qualified interpreter. Make it clear that it was a mistake and not intended to be disrespectful in any way. As you thank them for allowing you to observe them, make a mental note never to let a situation like this happen again.

- **Scenario 893**. You're currently an ITP student and are contacted by the public school in your area to get on their interpreter substitute list. You assure them you're nowhere near ready to do substitute interpreting yet. However, they tell you getting on the list now will put you in a better position for any full-time jobs that come open next fall.

AN ITP STUDENT'S PERSPECTIVE: Decline, thank them for the wonderful opportunity, and tell them you must remain loyal to the CPC — that you're willing forego the offer to honor the code. Let them know that come fall, if an opportunity exists, you would be more than happy to come and meet with them.

AN INTERPRETER'S PERSPECTIVE: You should inform the school, while you appreciate their confidence in you and their concern for your potential future employment, you have to decline being included on their substitute interpreter list. You have no certification and are not be ready to interpret as a full-time employee or a substitute. Being uncertified disqualifies you from being a "reasonable accommodation," and utilizing you as an interpreter would not only be a hardship for the student, but might also possibly subject the school and yourself to the risk of legal action for working as an interpreter without appropriate credentials. Tell them you look forward to discussing full-time or substitute employment as an interpreter after completing your education and receiving certification.

A DEAF CONSUMER'S PERSPECTIVE: When you are a broke ITP student hoping to find a job after graduation, it may be very tempting to put your name on that list. However, the reality of the situation is your name wouldn't just be on a list. You would most likely to be called often to substitute interpret, and those sweet secretaries who are desperate to find a warm body to fill in can be unbelievably convincing! The right thing to do is explain to the school officials that you take great pride in the field of interpreting and won't work for them until you have the appropriate credentials. Also, let them know you will be sending them your resume in the fall and hope to be considered for an interview. Chances are, if they are having a hard time finding substitute interpreters, they will have just as much difficulty finding full-time interpreters in the fall. No matter what happens, you will be starting your interpreting career as an ethical interpreter!

- **Scenario 894**. I'm an interpreting student at a middle school doing my internship hours with a state QA level interpreter. In between classes, the deaf student keeps asking me if I would please interpret for him instead of his interpreter because he understands me better.

AN INTERPRETER'S PERSPECTIVE: Enjoy your one glorious minute of feeling wanted, then put that feeling aside, and keep your wits about you. Remind the student that you're an interpreter-in-training and not the school's employee. Encourage the student to discuss his needs directly with the school's interpreter coordinator. If you get overly involved, you may not only create hard feelings, but also ruin an opportunity for the student to advocate for his own needs.

A DEAF CONSUMER'S PERSPECTIVE: I would explain the set-up of the internship, and let him know that you're there to learn from the mentor interpreter. Encourage the student to talk with the mentor interpreter or a teacher to discuss the problems he's having with the mentor interpreter. The student needs to learn to be responsible for his own learning and communication access, and he should be encouraged to do so.

- **Scenario 895**. Another student and I from my program are hanging out after a Deaf club event, and a group of people are staying afterwards chatting. My friend and I are chatting away about our mutual teacher. A deaf person who is sitting nearby walks over and comments that he doesn't like our teacher.

AN INTERPRETER'S PERSPECTIVE: This is not a situation that involves the CPC. The CPC exists to guide our behavior as interpreters on the job. When we're being a part of the Deaf community or attending Deaf events, but not interpreting, our role is merely that of a signing member of the community. However, this situation gives us reason to review our behavior and realize how small the Deaf community is. Statements made in public about any person connected to the community are open for comment. It's best to try to stay neutral, professional, and discreet in this situation rather than getting involved in a critique of the instructor.

A DEAF CONSUMER'S PERSPECTIVE: I don't see a problem with sharing ITP teachers' names, as most deaf folks know who teaches in the ITP. As for the deaf person's remark, the student can say that she's sorry he doesn't like the teacher, but she herself has learned quite a lot from this teacher. Just leave no room for discussion. Deaf folks tend to be persistent, however, so if he keeps pushing, just nod, cut the conversation short, and then direct the conversation back to a neutral topic.

- **Scenario 896**. I'm an interpreting student and am always on the lookout for opportunities to get internship hours. A friend of mine suggests I come to their board meeting and "practice" just to get experience. She says there won't be any deaf people in attendance, so I agree. After the meeting, a board member comes over and offers to let me practice interpreting at his company's staff meetings. Jeez, this "practice" stuff is really starting to snowball.

AN INTERPRETER'S PERSPECTIVE: The practicum hours required in an ITP should be as close to real-life situations as possible. A setting where there are no consumers isn't full-fledged interpreting practice. In order to understand what it means to actively interpret — dealing with turn taking, questions, requests for clarification, backchanneling, and human interaction — there should be a consumer present who is aware of the practicum situation. I would look for informal situations where someone with my introductory skill level could gain "real world" experience.

A DEAF CONSUMER'S PERSPECTIVE: Without any feedback from deaf consumers or an experienced interpreter, I don't believe this is the best use of your time in an ITP. You should maximize your opportunities for learning while you're under the "umbrella of safety" of the student role.

- **Scenario 897**. I'm an interpreting student getting some of my internship hours observing an educational interpreter. Today I get there before the interpreter, and the deaf student and I are sitting and chatting. The deaf student asks, "So, do you think Mary Ann (the educational interpreter) is a good interpreter?"

AN INTERPRETER'S PERSPECTIVE: One little question can sometimes throw you into an instant ethical dilemma. I would say something like, "As a student, I wouldn't even begin to evaluate an interpreter's skills. I'm just happy to have the opportunity to observe and learn from an experienced, professional interpreter." Maybe that's not the answer the student was hoping for, but you maintain your professional decorum.

A DEAF CONSUMER'S PERSPECTIVE: The interpreter could respond to the student by saying, "She's here to do her job, and I'm here to learn from her. I think she's an excellent mentor." Leave it at that.

- **Scenario 898**. I am an interpreting student, and I do not appreciate the parental attitude everyone seems to have towards students. I am not a child; I am a college student. I do not appreciate being told what to wear and how to manicure my nails. My parents did a fine job of that, thank you very much. I would appreciate being treated as an adult who is responsible for making her own decisions. The point of this is, yes, I am still a student and here to learn from you, but I do not need you to lead me along. Believe it or not, I live every day on my own, and when I am not at school, I have survived just fine.

AN INTERPRETER'S PERSPECTIVE: Wow. Maybe you have heard this before from your parents: if you want to be treated like an adult, start acting like one. An adult understands and accepts that her chosen profession will have a code of professional conduct, which includes a particular way to dress and behave. An adult accepts critiques from her more experienced colleagues in order to learn and grow in the profession. An adult accepts that she must be open to, analyze, and accept constructive criticism. If the interpreters working with you are telling you that your dress (and nails) are inappropriate for the situation, I suggest you listen. First rule of becoming a professional in any field: check the attitude at the door. Honestly, the frustration I hear from you tells me that interpreting may not be a good fit for you. If you cannot abide by the professional requirements, then I would strongly recommend that you investigate another profession.

A DEAF CONSUMER'S PERSPECTIVE: Me, me, me! While it may not matter to some deaf people, it does matter to a whole lot of us what you wear and how you manicure your nails. Often we don't feel as though we can honestly tell interpreters what we prefer for fear of reactions such as yours. When you play, party, study, and sleep, you can go ahead and express your individuality however you want because that time is yours. However, as an interpreting student, you need to demonstrate to your professors, your colleagues, and the consumers involved that you know how to look like a professional. This means wearing plain, solid clothing that contrasts with your skin color so that we can clearly see the visual information presented. Other things like dangling earrings, visible tattoos and piercings, thumb rings, long nails, colored nail polish, etc. interfere with our visual comprehension as well. Dressing in a style that is compatible with that of the teachers, presenters, office workers, exercise instructors, and businesses with whom you work is not about you; it is about honoring all of us.

- **Scenario 899**. As an ITP student, you apply and are accepted to work as a staff member for a state chapter RID conference. You are responsible for monitoring workshops and providing services to the presenters, guests, and interpreters. Additional responsibilities include monitoring attendance of the participants and handing out the CEU credit at the conclusion of the workshop. It was explained to you that participants must not miss more than 15 minutes of the workshop in order to receive the CEUs. This includes arrival, restroom break, and departure times. If a participant misses more than 15 minutes during the workshop, they are not to receive CEU credit at the end. If you have any issues with that, you are told that you must notify the staff coordinator who will then address the situation. You are monitoring a specific workshop and in comes a national RID board member — 30 minutes late. At the conclusion of the workshop, the same board member approaches the student to receive CEU credits. How should you respond?

AN INTERPRETER'S PERSPECTIVE: First and foremost, your job as a staff member for an RID conference is an important job and one that should not be taken lightly. RID, as a national entity, prides itself on education, standards and excellence. As a representative of RID in the capacity of staff member at a state conference, it is your job to ensure RID's foundation of excellence is upheld. RID strives to maintain this foundation through leadership in membership. In your role in having been told nobody could miss more than 15 minutes of a workshop to earn CEUs, it would have been appropriate to inform the board member that you had been given guidelines by which to follow. They had missed more than 15 minutes of the workshop, meaning they were not eligible to receive the CEUs offered. In doing this, you have done your job as it was given to you, and you were fair to the other participants in the workshop. If the board member disagrees with your decision, they should take it up with the person in charge of conference staffing.

A DEAF CONSUMER'S PERSPECTIVE: Your response should have been, "I'm sorry, but participants can't miss more than 15 minutes of the workshop and still receive CEUs." This should have been your response whether this person was a board member or not.

Other Scenarios

Identify the issue(s) involved and decide how you would respond. Discuss and compare your responses with your colleagues.

900. You're an ITP student, and your deaf friend wants you to interpret a tryout she will be attending for the *American Gladiators* show. You're not ready to do any interpreting, but she assures you she wants you there only as a friend. Once there, your deaf friend is selected to compete, and one of the producers approaches you and offers you an incredible amount of money to appear on the show and interpret for your friend.

901. You're an ITP student and are at the top of your class. Your teachers have been quite complimentary about your skill development. One day you're approached by your local community education director to teach a beginning sign class. This is your idea of your dream job, but you know your ITP professor has repeatedly discouraged students from doing this kind of thing. She says it takes jobs away from qualified deaf professionals. You figure this is only a community education class in a rural community; it's not like deaf people are lining up for the job.

902. You're an ITP student asked to interpret a one-day computer class at school for one of your deaf instructors. She has excellent speech and lipreading skills, but prefers to utilize an interpreter. She knows you're still a student and not really ready but says she would like to give you the experience in a safe environment. You're extremely nervous, but can't imagine telling one of your teachers "no."

903. You don't believe in any God, but you're an ITP practicum student in need of practicum hours. You're told there's a "Passion Play" coming up. The play needs at least six interpreters, and they're willing to work with ITP students. It's going to be all volunteers, and they need a decision now. You sure could use the hours.

904. You and another ITP student are doing some internship hours at an interpreter referral agency in the office. One day a deaf client comes in the office and asks for assistance in placing a phone call to her doctor. She explains to both of you that she needs to follow up on a recent office visit to her doctor and ask for some more details about an upcoming surgical procedure he's recommending. You suggest the deaf woman wait a few minutes until a staff interpreter is free to assist her, but your fellow ITP student jumps right in and says she would be happy to interpret for the deaf woman's phone call.

905. You're an ITP student in search of practicum hours, and you find a church relatively close to home that provides an interpreter for their services. You contact the interpreter, and she welcomes you to attend an upcoming service to observe her. When you arrive, you go up to the interpreter and introduce yourself, and she directs you to sit off to one side of the room. When the service begins, you realize she has placed you on the opposite side of the room, and there's no way you'll be able to see her interpret from where she has you sitting. It seems to have been deliberate.

906. You're an ITP student observing a nationally certified interpreter. A couple of times, she misses some information and looks to you for a feed. Afterwards, though, she criticizes the sign choices you fed her.

907. You're an ITP student observing an interpreter who, in your opinion, dresses inappropriately. She tries too hard to dress like the kids, even down to the black nail polish. To prove her point, the interpreter asks the deaf student what she thinks of her nails, and the student says she loves them. It would drive you nuts if you had to watch those hands all day, but who are you to say? You're only a student.

908. You're an ITP student scheduled to observe two nationally certified interpreters who interpret in a college class. You're surprised when you see one of the interpreters pull out a romance novel and start reading it while her partner is interpreting. She only looks up to check the clock occasionally to see if it's time to switch.

909. You're an ITP student taking an ASL linguistics class in your program, and there's a deaf student in the class who sits next to you. During a test, the deaf student asks you the answer to a question. You think, "Gee, someday I may be the deaf student's interpreter, so I don't want to make him mad, do I?"

910. You're an ITP student who observes a nationally certified interpreter every week at a church. At the end of one of the services, the church deacon invites you to the front of the church for his blessing. You politely decline, but he doesn't give up. You now feel very uncomfortable.

Challenges Related to Certified Deaf Interpreter (CDI) Issues

- **Scenario 911.** I am deaf and have been utilizing interpreters for over 30 years. I was pulled over for a traffic violation, and when I told the state troopers that I was deaf, they were willing to write notes. After three pages of notes, they wanted me to come to the station. I then requested a sign language interpreter. They wanted to know why since our communication thus far was going so smoothly. I assured them, with an interpreter, we would be able to communicate more effectively. The interpreter referral agency they contacted sent two interpreters to the station, one hearing and one deaf. The CDI, however, was a distant cousin, a former classmate, and someone I see frequently at social events. I was shocked and speechless that she didn't excuse herself the moment she learned my name. I didn't have the courage to speak up and tell her to leave because I was afraid such a discussion would be voiced and possibly make matters worse. It was a conflict of interest for her to stay, and I believe it was motivated by greed and curiosity. The Deaf community is very small, and everyone knows everyone else. The CDIs are part of this community, and it is very awkward. Our interpreting needs can be very personal and private, and our peers have no business being present. This has now caused more situations where deaf individuals feel they have no choice but to write notes, read lips, or bring a family member to escape the embarrassment of an unwanted CDI showing up. I feel strongly that a hearing interpreter should be sent first and then call for back up if communication is determined not to be effective. Interpreter referral agencies are funded by work from the Deaf community.

AN INTERPRETER'S PERSPECTIVE: I think deaf consumers have a right to refuse the services of a specific interpreter if that's what the deaf person chooses to do. The best idea would be for you to contact the referral agency that is contracting with the interpreter with whom you are uncomfortable, and ask them not to send that interpreter for you again. I understand how awkward the situation was for you; however, the interpreter that you knew was certified and therefore carries with that certification the responsibility of maintaining confidentiality. I hope she abides by this essential tenet of the CPC, as all interpreters are required to do, thereby keeping your private information just that, private.

A DEAF CONSUMER'S PERSPECTIVE: As discomforting as this particular experience was for you, it reflects the ongoing evolution of the interpreting profession. Your concerns are not new. Most interpreters have had to face issues of being perceived as nosy or greedy, and most interpreters have encountered people for whom they've interpreted in social settings. CDIs are members of the Deaf community who have committed their time and funds to contribute professionally to both the Deaf community and the interpreting profession. As CDIs, they abide by, and are bound by, the same CPC all interpreters follow. They are invaluable in situations where the most accurate translation is critical, including legal and medical settings. Rather than creating an environment of suspicion, their participation in an interpreting team should provide consumers with even greater confidence that their messages are being accurately rendered. They represent a positive, innovative addition to the interpreting field.

- **Scenario 912**. I am a CDI who prefers to use ASL. Why would my hearing partner transliterate the message using ASL in English word order, including long fingerspelled words? They always tell me that is how it's supposed to work, but I disagree. I don't like when interpreters transliterate. I prefer that my partner interpret the information. I will then interpret it further to fit the client's needs.

AN INTERPRETER'S PERSPECTIVE: This could have been prevented if the interpreting team had met prior to the assignment and communicated their expectations. If you and this interpreter cannot agree on the communication mode, then don't team with her again.

A DEAF CONSUMER'S PERSPECTIVE: To me, a CDI must be bilingual (fluent in both ASL and English). The hearing interpreter is responsible for giving you all the information spoken in English so you can interpret it into ASL. Try to see it from the hearing interpreter's point of view. If the hearing interpreter already interprets the information into ASL, then why does she need you? Yes, I know you can further expand the information in ASL, but how is that interpreting? Interpreting means working between two languages, and right now you are only working in one language.

- **Scenario 913**. I'm a CDI and was teaming with a hearing interpreter with whom I had not previously worked. When the therapist spoke, my hearing partner transliterated the information to me, and then I interpreted the information to the client. What was unusual in this situation was that my hearing partner voiced my interpretation to the therapist. The therapist then kept interrupting me and saying, "No, that's not how I said it." The client also became frustrated because of all the interruptions. I don't think my partner should have been voicing when I was interpreting. Instead, she should have voiced only the client's responses. Right?

AN INTERPRETER'S PERSPECTIVE: I agree. I see no reason for the hearing interpreter to voice while you are interpreting. Yes, I understand this is consecutive interpreting. There will be a delay, but everyone will get used to it. I suggest both interpreters take some time before/after each session to debrief with the therapist to discuss any concerns about the communication process.

A DEAF CONSUMER'S PERSPECTIVE: I know that CDIs disagree on whether hearing interpreters should voice the dialogue between CDIs and deaf clients since it is consecutive interpreting. Personally, I find it helpful to let the hearing interpreter narrate (as opposed to interpret word for word) so that the hearing client can follow the deaf client's responses. I would find it intrusive to have my hearing partner voice. I feel it would be disruptive and take my focus away from the deaf client. This is a matter of trust.

Other Scenarios

Identify the issue(s) involved and decide how you would respond. Discuss and compare your responses with your colleagues.

914. A deaf client had been meeting with his employer regarding allegations of harassment for over a year with no resolution. Today's meeting was to discuss termination. The company hired me, a CDI. The client insisted that he was innocent of the charges of harassment. Right away I noticed the hearing interpreter continually spelled harassment and then followed up with examples (sexual harassment, physical harassment, verbal harassment, etc.). When it was my turn, I asked the employer to clarify the type of "harassment." The employer said he stopped by this female colleague's desk too often, he raised his voice when he was communicating with her, and he continually wrote her notes. The client readily admitted to all these things. He liked her, but did not physically or sexually harm her. There was clearly a misunderstanding. How can I explain this?

915. I am a CODA. I believe myself to be bilingual in ASL and English. I have always questioned the value and need for a CDI until today. A deaf client whom I have interpreted for many years confided to me that she too was reluctant to have "a deaf person" partner with me because she believed that CDIs were only for deaf persons with limited education. After an assignment with a CDI present, however, we both looked at each other and said we had gotten goose bumps. This CDI was truly able to see the information from both sides and interpret it more clearly than even the best interpreter I know ever could. I am now a believer, but how do we convince everyone else?

916. I was interpreting for a deaf resident of a group home. She was in the hospital being interviewed by the police. A staff member was suspected of raping her. Included in the meeting was a (non-signing) advocate for the deaf client who kept insisting the client be administered the rape test. The client, however, kept saying she didn't want the test because she liked him. The advocate insisted the client didn't understand the difference between consensual and forced intercourse. She kept pushing the hospital staff to administer the rape test. Now I am wondering if I should have stepped in because I believe the client was comprehending.

917. I was team interpreting (I'm a CDI) with an experienced interpreter in a jail while a deaf client was meeting with her attorney. The client told her attorney about how rough the police had treated her during her arrest. The attorney was asking her questions. The interpreter was role playing the officer's actions and physically pushed the client. The client became very angry, and all communication came to an abrupt halt. I stepped up and interpreted the rest of the interview. Now this interpreter refuses to work with me. I don't understand.

918. Recently I was teaming with a hearing interpreter who uses signs that are much more English-based. Afterwards she asked me about numerous ASL signs she saw me use with the client because she was unfamiliar with them. I feel like she was "stealing" my signs.

919. I am a CDI who has been interpreting a long-term assignment of weekly, group counseling sessions. A team of two hearing interpreters and two CDIs were assigned. After several months, a follow-up meeting was called by the caseworker. At the meeting, the deaf consumer mentioned being uncomfortable with having an "entourage" of interpreters. The caseworker asked the deaf consumer if she wanted the CDIs removed. The first hearing interpreter expressed her concern that she would be unable to perform the job to the best of her ability without a CDI. The second hearing interpreter said she would still be able to do the job without a CDI. The caseworker dismissed the first hearing interpreter and me. This doesn't seem fair to me.

920. Not all interpreters are created equal; that includes CDIs. Today I worked with another CDI who went through a mainstream program and often uses English-based signs when ASL would be more appropriate. Most of the time he just copied the hearing interpreter's signs, which was a waste of everyone's time. What can I do or say?

921. I was assigned to do an ongoing vocational rehabilitation case management meeting where the deaf consumer was expected to participate in developing his rehabilitation plan. It was determined that a psychiatric evaluation would be needed before the plan could be implemented. Unfortunately, the evaluation was scheduled for a time that conflicted with the case management meeting (which I was already scheduled to interpret). When the referral agency contacted me, I informed the agency that I was already scheduled at that time. The agency said they would reschedule the psychiatric evaluation and get back with me, but I never heard anything. I later learned that the agency went ahead and assigned a hearing interpreter to the psychiatric evaluation, instead of a CDI (as requested). This hearing interpreter knows that the deaf consumer has always had a CDI, but took the assignment anyway. Should I say something to her about it?

922. During a custody hearing, the deaf parents were told that they would get their child back in a few months. The parents kept asking the caseworker to tell them what day. The caseworker responded, "The last week in October." Still not satisfied, the parents insisted on knowing the exact date they would get their child back. The caseworker finally said, "October 29th." Well, October 29th went by, but they didn't get their child back. The parents filed a formal complaint. During the hearing, the caseworker denied ever having given an exact date. Suddenly everyone was looking at me and questioning me because I am a CDI. Obviously, I would never make up a date. What do I say?

923. As a CDI, I was asked to interpret a court case with a hearing interpreter. I interpreted numerous meetings with the Deaf person's lawyer. Often the lawyer would refer to other meetings that I had not attended. After asking for clarification, I learned that the consumer had several cases pending against him. I had only been hired to interpret for one of these cases, while the hearing interpreter had been hired to interpret all of the consumer's cases. This doesn't make sense to me.

924. Many interpreters believe that only low-functioning clients need CDIs. It's just not true. For example, I recently worked with a CDI for a senior citizen conference, and the audience loved it. Anytime I am assigned to work with a deaf client under 18, I insist on working with a CDI. There really is a difference, but I don't know how to convince my colleagues.

925. I attended two CDI training workshops. Both were superficial and inadequate. We need the same knowledge classes (e.g., Principles of Interpreting, Linguistics) hearing interpreters take to become interpreters. Otherwise, we have a hard time effectively integrating with our hearing counterparts who are formally trained.

926. When I do CDI interpreting, I add a lot of clarifying information. When I do this, I often see my hearing partner's eyebrows go up. Afterwards when I ask why, she tells me she thinks I went too far. I disagree. Deaf people are not like hearing people. We want/need examples.

927. As a CDI, I make a point to introduce myself to everyone at an interpreting assignment, instead of waiting for my hearing counterpart to take the lead. I think it's important for CDIs to be recognized as equal partners in business relationships. Do you agree?

928. Simply put, as a hearing interpreter, your native language is English. Your culture is hearing. There are going to be things that you don't even realize you missed because, in your mind, the information has been expressed and is understood. A CDI is part of the Deaf community. We live, work, and play in this community. We are invested in our community. We appreciate good hearing interpreters, but I don't think they always recognize what we add to the job, do you?

929. I recently realized that hearing interpreters and deaf interpreters are often paid different rates. When I ask the agency what my rate will be, they tell me a specific rate. However, when I ask my hearing partners what they are earning, they tell me a different rate. What can I do beforehand to make sure I'm being paid equitably?

930. I'm a CDI, and every time I work with a new hearing interpreter, it feels like a gamble. Many interpreters have never worked with a CDI. They do not know what to do. How can we bring hearing interpreters and deaf interpreters closer together?

931. I make my living as a CDI. Over the years I have worn many hats (e.g., social worker, teacher, friend). How do I separate my personal and professional involvement in the Deaf community?

932. I'm a CDI and have interpreted for the same deaf client for many years. Recently a new psychiatrist asked the client what medications he is on. He said, "You know, red medicine." The psychiatrist named several medications, but the client did not recognize any of the names. I knew exactly which medicine the client meant, but I wondered if I should just let the psychiatrist call his former doctors to be on the safe side.

933. A deaf client was assigned a public defender. The public defender was in a rush and barely reviewed the case with the client before it was time to appear before the judge. After the client was harshly sentenced, the client blamed me. He said CDIs don't know how to interrupt or force the attorney to listen.

934. Often court personnel do not know where to locate resources for deaf people. We as CDIs often have this information because of our personal and professional involvement in the Deaf community. I feel an obligation to share this information. Is that going too far?

935. Often deaf people will approach me when I'm not working (as a CDI) to ask me, because of my experience, to give them the name of a good lawyer for deaf people. I have opinions; can I share them?

936. As a CDI, I am required to get CEUs, but going to interpreter workshops is downright painful. I would like to see hearing people sit and watch an interpreter for six or eight hours straight! Whenever an interpreter workshop is conducted in ASL, I'm excited to attend. How can we help interpreter organizations be more CDI/Deaf friendly?

Challenges in Interpreting Addressed by Demand-Control Schema Analysis

Introduction by Robyn K. Dean, M.A., CI and CT, Rochester, NY

The scenarios in this chapter involve a *demand-control schema* (DC-S) analysis. The DC-S analyses were written by me, Robyn Dean, and my co-author, Robert Pollard, developers of the DC-S approach to interpreting work and interpreter education. We are grateful to Brenda Cartwright and the editors of *Encounters with Reality* for their invitation to include our perspective on several of the scenarios herein and for allowing us to write this introduction.

In our article, "From Best Practice to Best Practice Process: Shifting Ethical Thinking and Teaching" (Dean & Pollard, 2006), we provide a lengthier description of our approach to conceptualizing and thinking through ethical decisions. We refer to this approach as a "best practice *process*" to emphasize the dynamic nature of ethical decision-making in contrast to a static, rule-based decision-making approach. Two of the elements of our best practice process that will be particularly evident in our analyses of the scenarios included here are our emphasis on the specifics of the interpreting context or scenario provided and, secondly, our emphasis on the impact or consequences of the interpreter's decisions.

Ethical decision-making approaches that focus on the consequences of decisions are referred to as *teleological*. Teleological approaches often are contrasted with a different but equally valid ethical decision-making approach that focuses on principles or rules when reaching ethical decisions. This approach is referred to as *deontological*.

In a teleological approach, context plays a vital role. Teleologists are interested in consequences of an action, which can only be determined by considering the interaction of two factors: what is going on in a situation and how the people in the situation respond to what is going on. In our analyses here, we occasionally restructure what the interpreter described in her/his scenario in order to spotlight critical contextual factors and/or respondent actions. If such details were insufficient, we specifically note what hypothetical contextual factors in the scenario (what we call *job demands*) would need to be known or present before the fittingness of particular responses (what we call *control options*) could be determined. In cases where we do suggest specific responses, we offer a range of options based on our liberal-to-conservative *spectrum of ethical and effective decisions* (Dean & Pollard, 2005).

Our teleological emphasis on the consequences of interpreting decisions — including decisions to act in certain ways or refrain from acting — may be new to many interpreters. Shifting ethical thinking from a deontological, or rule-based approach, to a teleological, or outcomes-based approach, is not only a significant mental task, but a challenge to put into daily practice. Many interpreters were taught deontological decision-making approaches exclusively in their educational programs. Others have adopted this approach in light of the professional literature or consultation advice that emphasizes the use of rules (e.g., a tenet of the 1979 RID Code of Ethics) when making ethical decisions. A common rule or principle that influences many interpreters' decisions is to follow whatever course of action leads to the interpreter being the most transparent or invisible. To the degree that this principle, or other rules or principles have guided your ethical decision-making in the past, it may be disconcerting (or at least unfamiliar) to shift your focus to a teleological one that: (1) hinges on the details of the context of the interpreting scenario, (2) usually promotes more than one response option as ethical and effective, and (3) ultimately challenges the interpreter to make decisions primarily based on the consequences of one's actions.

Again, we are grateful for this opportunity to introduce the foundation underlying our DC-S analyses. Teleological views on ethics are relatively new to the interpreting profession. Noting this overtly helps minimize confusion which might otherwise counter the benefits that we believe could be gained — for interpreters and consumers alike — from this approach. We hope our additions to this book, as well as our publications referenced below, will help interpreters make this challenging but important shift toward ethical *process* reasoning.

Dean, R. K., & Pollard, R. Q. (2005). Consumers and service effectiveness in interpreting work: A practice profession perspective. In M. Marschark, R. Peterson, & E. Winston (Eds.), *Interpreting and interpreter education: Directions for research and practice* (pp. 259-282). New York: Oxford University Press.

Dean, R. K., & Pollard, R. Q. (2006). From best practice to best practice process: Shifting ethical thinking and teaching. In E. M. Maroney (Ed.), *A new chapter in interpreter education: Accreditation, research and technology* (pp. 119–131). Proceedings of the 16th national convention of the Conference of Interpreter Trainers (CIT). Monmouth, OR: CIT.

- **Scenario 937.** I recently interpreted for a conference with over 10,000 mostly hearing participants. The conference coordinators were an interpreter's dream. They gave us practically minute-by-minute schedules for both days, as well as song lyrics and scripts of the presentations. I wanted to divide the information in advance so I could prepare, but my team interpreter said she didn't want to do anything until the day of the conference. I didn't press the issue, but I was incredibly frustrated. What do you think we should have done?

A PERSPECTIVE USING DEMAND-CONTROL SCHEMA ANALYSIS:
What you are really talking about here is differences in control choices that you would have made versus your colleague. While I would agree that employing *pre-assignment controls* is always a good idea, it sounds like the team person didn't choose (for whatever reason) these same pre-assignment controls. Maybe your colleague brings sufficient pre-assignment controls to this constellation of demands and did not see the types of controls you suggested as necessary. Maybe she knows the topic inside and out. Maybe she knows the deaf consumers very well and feels she could sufficiently meet their needs without preparation. Maybe she perceives her skills to be sufficient for the job and that preparation for the job would not be worth it (in a cost/benefit way). What would be interesting to know is whether the resulting demand-control interaction turned out to be just fine, despite your concerns. (Often that is the case.) Sometimes I prepare for jobs and my colleagues do not, and they (because of their differing controls) do better work than me in the end. I am not suggesting this is the case in your particular situation, but I think it is interesting when we get to see the demand-control dynamics of individual interpreters play out in real life (versus how we imagine things will be).

It may be frustrating when our colleagues do not employ as many pre-assignment controls as we do, but at the same time, it does not keep you from employing those controls on your own. We are individually responsible for our work, even when we work as a team, and our colleagues hopefully will take on that same degree of responsibility. In the story you described, it occurs to me you could have just assigned your colleague parts of the conference for which she would be responsible and ones for which you would be responsible (since she did not want to participate in the divvying process).

Maybe you could have (or can in the future) started a very different conversation with your colleague. Instead of approaching it in terms of what nature (or timing) of controls you both will employ, maybe you could start the conversation by suggesting you consider what demands you both expect will be presented by this large conference assignment. Take the time together to list out the *environmental, interpersonal, paralinguistic*, and *intrapersonal* demands that likely will be present at this assignment. (If she won't, then do it alone and share your analysis with her.) Then begin brainstorming the pre-assignment controls you might employ to respond to the demands. It sounds like you were preparing for environmental demands mostly (e.g., topic areas, terminology, lyrics), but I wonder if you gave equal consideration to other types of demands in this situation (e.g., goal of the environment, interpersonal demands, paralinguistic demands of such a large venue).

After considering pre-assignment controls, you could begin considering *assignment controls* that might be used if a hypothesized demand actually does occur (e.g., a speaker is going too fast, the amplification system is faulty, visual information is referenced quickly on the screen but not long enough for the interpreter to read it, people walk in front of the interpreter on their way to and from the bathroom, the deaf client is intermittently checking and responding on their handheld e-mail device). The same thing can be done for *post-assignment controls*.

If, during your conversation, you and your colleague talk about the demand of songs and potentially "read" material (you mentioned that there were scripts, so it is quite possible that people will just read their presentation), then you could bring up the pre-assignment control of obtaining the material ahead of time. Then the conversation is more about "How will we respond to this job demand?" — either before or during the job — rather than "Why won't you prepare the way I would like to?" (Maybe your colleague would prefer to have the lyrics on a stand and read them as she goes along or preview them right before the song starts.) If your colleague does not think advance preparations are necessary, then ask her what controls she brings to the situation that she perceives will be equally effective in responding to these job demands. This is a very different type of conversation to have — one that empowers both colleagues to think about the job demands (beyond the issue of language translation per se) and allows for an appreciation of how colleagues may employ different types of controls (ones that can be equally effective as our own usual or preferred controls).

- **Scenario 938**. This week another ITP student and I were in the hallway talking, and she was venting about lack of feedback from one of her deaf instructors. We were talking in a normal tone, and we didn't see anyone around us so we weren't signing. However, a few minutes later a hearing faculty member came out of her office and informed us that the deaf instructor had asked her to interpret our conversation. I understand that the deaf person has the right to access environmental information, but if a situation appears to be private and not meant for others to hear, was it appropriate for this hearing faculty member to interpret our conversation without our knowledge? We feel the deaf faculty member should have just butted into our conversation and asked us what we were talking about.

A PERSPECTIVE USING DEMAND-CONTROL SCHEMA ANALYSIS: In this scenario, I am interested in the decision that the hearing faculty member made, to interpret the conversation — a conversation that was not intended for the deaf faculty member. One could argue in this case that it was not an interpreting demand at all (because the hearing individual was not in an interpreting role at the time), but instead, it was a demand related to being a faculty member that led her to "tell on" the students by translating their conversation. In other words, the first question to ask is: Was she responding in her role of faculty member and colleague or the role of an interpreter in that moment? I would assume the former.

Because I think she was responding in the role of a faculty member, I do not think it is appropriate for me to respond to this student's specific dilemma since I am not an ITP faculty member. It is not my intention to comment on what may or may not be ethical for other professions. However, I can analyze this type of event through the lens of DC-S because overhearing private conversations *is* a demand faced in interpreting.

It is true that this demand — being privy to conversations that are not intended *by the speaker(s)* to be translated — is a common interpreting demand. Of note, what these two students walk away with from this experience is a new control resource — greater awareness of what it feels like to have one's private conversation made known to an unintended audience. The demand of having access to a private conversation is something that all interpreters will face. Imagine that you are in a room with a deaf patient, and two hearing healthcare professionals are discussing another patient's case. Imagine being in a classroom and overhearing two kids talk to each other about cheating on a test or maybe "getting high" in the bathroom. Imagine that, prior to the beginning of a business staff meeting, the boss and a coworker are talking quietly, and the deaf employee asks you to eavesdrop and interpret what you can hear. Imagine that you are interpreting, and a deaf college student signs to another deaf college student that they think the teacher is boring.

See how that one demand could be couched in a variety of contexts (i.e., the *constellation of demands*)? Each of those contexts matters a great deal, and the likely response of a given interpreter will vary from situation to situation (see the liberal-to-conservative "ethical and effective" decision-making spectrum in Dean & Pollard, 2005). Further, since we view interpreting as a practice profession — where relationships matter — if interpreters behave in ways that are perceived by others as deceptive (eavesdropping on a conversation), as failing to appreciate the privacy of individuals, or are counter to the intention of an utterance or communication, then the interpreter should be prepared and willing to take responsibility for those actions.

The one thing I like about what the hearing faculty member did — which demonstrated responsibility for her actions — was to tell the students what she and the deaf faculty member had done. While I may disagree with her choice to interpret the private conversation (because it was initially deceptive), at the very least, she followed through and made her choice known to the people whom her decision impacted. I would suggest: if an interpreter chooses to make a private conversation known to an unintended audience (without first telling those individuals what is about to happen or asking them about it), then she/he needs to follow through in some way so that those who will be impacted by the decision can be notified and have the chance to respond to this decision.

I also noted above that the students gained a new control through this experience — knowing what it is like to be deceived in this way. This can be added to the control resources of these future interpreters, and hopefully, they will respond to this demand the next time it occurs with careful thought as they consider the very real consequences of that decision.

- **Scenario 939.** I recently interpreted an employee training workshop. During the break the deaf client left, and several of the employees were chatting. One employee started telling really offensive jokes. As a member of several minority groups (Jewish, Polish, Gay), what are my rights? I was not personally being harassed, but do we have rights in this situation?

A PERSPECTIVE USING DEMAND-CONTROL SCHEMA ANALYSIS: The better question to ask is, "Do I have options in the face of these demands?" Yes, you have options.

This is what we would call an *interpersonal demand*. Even though the deaf client had left, you and the employees are together, and in light of our practice profession approach, what happens in this scenario is still salient. The jokes being told outside of the context of the training workshop itself would be the interpersonal demand. However, because you were unable to respond to it (your control) sufficiently (e.g., by ignoring it, walking away, passing it off as ignorance), you then experienced an *intrapersonal demand*. I'll assume this intrapersonal demand was your negative feelings about the event (e.g., anger towards these individuals). So now you have two types of demands (interpersonal and intrapersonal) to deal with. Because many details are missing from this scenario, a full *constellation of demands* cannot be constructed, and accordingly a thorough demand-control schema analysis is not possible. Instead, I can outline a spectrum of conservative-to-liberal choices that an interpreter could make in this situation. A conservative response to the interpersonal demand (the jokes being told) would be to ignore them. A more liberal choice would be to walk away, where you can't hear them, until the break is over. A more liberal choice than that would be to communicate your disapproval through facial expressions or by saying something to the employees such as, "Jokes like that are offensive to me." These latter two choices are much more liberal in nature, and I would have to understand more specifically the *concurrent demands* (i.e., the other demands in the constellation, in addition to the main demand of the jokes themselves) to endorse them as effective in this case. For example, I could imagine a situation where the interpreter is a person of authority in an environment where there is an explicit policy that such comments will not be tolerated and, perhaps, must be reported.

As for the intrapersonal demand of feeling angry or upset by the comments, you will need to find ways to respond to these feelings that allow you to still do your work effectively. You could use *assignment controls* such as "self-talk" to acknowledge and manage the stress involved, including trying to find ways of empathizing with the individuals who made the jokes (e.g., "They must feel threatened by people who are different") or ways to gain helpful, distancing perspective (e.g., "I have more important issues to deal with in this job"). Depending on the nature of your relationship with the deaf person and the dynamics at the time, you might share what was talked about and how it impacted you with the deaf client to see what perspective she/he might have to offer. You could also use *post-assignment controls* by seeking comfort from your support system or employing other self-care approaches (e.g., meditation, exercise).

It is important to note that, as interpreters, we regularly contend with intrapersonal demands and need to be able to identify them as such (e.g., "I am feeling angry at these individuals for telling these jokes"). Recognizing *intra*personal demands as distinct from *inter*personal demands is also crucial. Responding to *intra*personal demands by involving other people in the assignment often has significant negative consequences and should be reconsidered. However, as I mentioned above, not always. If you had a close relationship with the deaf person or knew that the deaf person had a particular issue with these employees, then the control option of talking to the deaf person about the jokes and your response may be perfectly appropriate and effective. Again, in considering the value of possible responses along the liberal-to-conservative range of control options, it is the particular concurrent demands which complete the constellation of demands picture that typically will lead you to the best available choices.

- **Scenario 940.** I interpret weekly Alcoholics Anonymous (AA) meetings. Tonight my partner showed up looking especially haggard and under the weather, so I inquired about her health. She responded by saying that she "had a really massive hangover" and started laughing. I did not find this at all humorous, but maybe I'm overreacting.

A PERSPECTIVE USING DEMAND-CONTROL SCHEMA ANALYSIS:

I don't understand how not finding something humorous is an overreaction. A reaction must be a response of some kind (visible to others or noticeable to you). Did you get angry with her? Did you say to her, "I don't think that's funny"? Those would be reactions (or hypothetical overreactions), and we could discuss them in relation to their liberal versus conservative nature. More importantly, we could discuss where these responses might be coming from. However, just thinking that something is or isn't humorous is just a matter of opinion, not a reaction.

It sounds like the reaction to which you are referring was feeling upset or angry because of her comment, which is an intrapersonal demand. I will assume that the interpersonal demand of your interaction with your interpreter colleague was only between you two, and not an interpersonal demand between any other members of the AA group. If, in fact, her comment was heard or seen by either hearing or deaf AA members, then that is a completely different constellation of demands, and her choice to make her hung-over status known to those members would have significant negative consequences and *resulting demands* (e.g., distrust of her as an interpreter or even undermining someone's sobriety).

How an interpreter team member behaves on the job in response to interpreting demands will create resulting demands for us. We, as a team, represent the collective controls that we both bring to the interpreting assignment. Sometimes the *demand-control pairings* we then can offer are effective, and sometimes they are not. When resulting demands are created by controls that we or our team member bring to that situation, then we need to respond to them. A response can be as simple as acknowledgement that the demand is present, or it may require us to behave in more liberal ways (e.g., correcting a misinterpretation, attempting to repair a relationship).

It sounds like the question in this case is, "Where is this demand coming from —— an interpersonal place or an intrapersonal one?" Maybe it's both, but you have to figure out if, at its core, it is truly an interpersonal demand, which may be why you are characterizing it as an "overreaction." If it impacted only you, it is probably an intrapersonal demand. However, if it is impacting the working relationship between you and your colleague, then it is better framed as an interpersonal demand. One way to tease that out would be to ask yourself if this is something that upset you because of who you are (a clue that it is an intrapersonal demand) and, therefore, "your work to do." Maybe you are an AA member or related to an alcoholic, and this comment was an affront to your personal values or personality. Alternately, if this comment is impacting your current or future work with this colleague and, in that regard, needs a response for such work to be successful, then it is most likely an interpersonal demand. Again, it can be both, but it is best when intrapersonal demands are recognized as such and not "blamed" on being interpersonal demands.

I think that interpreters (and maybe people in general) take something that is intrapersonal and too easily make it the work of the interpersonal relationship, instead of dealing with it on their own. I can think of times as an interpreter where I have made comments to my colleague that I intended to be funny, and the other person did not take it as such. If my team member confronted me on the issue, I am not sure I would have thought that necessary. We all have done that in our careers. Understandably, if you think it is a pattern in your colleague's behavior and that it will affect her/his work with you or other interpreters, then addressing it appropriately is not an overreaction. You can make that decision on your own if you are careful to separate the intrapersonal from the interpersonal.

- **Scenario 941.** I am deaf and I work at a Center for Independent Living. I understand a deaf consumer's right to privacy, but our program often has interpreters go out on an assignment with our clients. And they see obvious needs for advocacy (e.g., a client living without heat). However, they don't tell us because they feel it would be violating confidentiality. Nonetheless, I feel interpreters need to share this information with the service provider. We need to work together for the best interest of the deaf consumers.

A PERSPECTIVE USING DEMAND-CONTROL SCHEMA ANALYSIS:
We have mentioned in our work that interpreters often have a skewed definition of "confidentiality." Confidentiality in other practice professions often means talking about your work with the appropriate people. (This is where the word confidential comes from — keeping something *in confidence* — which implies that you are sharing that information with another person.) In this regard, it is my opinion that providing such information to caseworkers at your center is not breaching confidentiality. Yet, at the same time, many interpreters feel nervous about doing anything that even remotely seems like a possible breach in confidentiality. On the one hand, this is good because interpreters often work within the very private sphere of other peoples' lives, and they should appreciate such a mantle of responsibility and take prudent measures to protect clients' privacy. On the other hand, as you point out, someone might actually be living without heat, and that is a significant consequence of an interpreter choosing not to say something to you or someone else at the center. We teach interpreters to consider the goal of the environment and respond to it accordingly in their work. I would suggest that working against the goal of the environment (in this case, the goal being maintaining safe and healthy conditions for clients) is an ethically problematic place for interpreters. Failing to mention that someone does not have heat would be working against this particular goal. Convincing interpreters to appreciate the goal of the environment as a crucial demand to which they always must respond would be your first step in helping them perceive their work in this practice professional manner.

Secondly, you could make disclosing problematic aspects of a client's health status a condition of employment. That is, make it an explicit expectation and, therefore, a demand of this job. If the interpreter is not willing to work as a member of the team in this way, then they should not take this assignment or job. Interpreters in educational and mental health settings commonly agree to such work conditions and responsibilities.

Last, maybe the deaf clients could be warned in advance that health risk observations made by the interpreter will be disclosed (if they did not disclose this information themselves which, of course, would be preferable). This too happens in mental health situations all the time. The therapist is understood to have a confidential relationship where they can (and sometimes must by law) share information with other colleagues, and the patient is aware of this and agrees to it. It is also understood by the patient and the therapist that those who are privy to this information will keep it in confidence. Could this type of design/policy be arranged at your center?

A good first step in getting interpreters to perceive their work differently would be to assign our 2005 book chapter and 2006 CIT proceedings article (references in the introduction to this chapter) and have a discussion about interpreting as a practice profession and the implications of this, given the independent living center's job descriptions.

Other Scenarios

Identify the issue(s) involved and decide how you would respond. Discuss and compare your responses with your colleagues.

942. You're interpreting in a veterinary class, and the students are going to be working on a cow cadaver today. The professor comes over and tells you that he feels it's very important for you to recognize each of the organs because the student's comprehension is dependent on your ability to understand the information. Both he and the deaf student insist that you literally get a feel for the material. They slap gloves, a gown, and a mask on you and point you toward the cow.

943. You're asked to interpret a televised debate between a couple of local politicians. When you arrive, you find out that they will project your image into an oval cameo in the corner of the screen. You have never interpreted in that kind of situation and are worried your sign space will exceed the parameters of the oval.

944. You're called to interpret at a business that will be having a meeting with their deaf employee. Upon arrival, you discover the meeting involves, not only the deaf employee, but also several agencies advocating for the deaf client. There are at least a dozen people in attendance, and you believe that the consumers' needs would be better met with two interpreters.

945. You're interpreting at a local dance studio. The deaf client is a very good dancer and only needs you to interpret from time to time, like when the teacher gives instructions to him or the rest of the class. You position yourself nearby so he can readily see you if the need arises. However, another dancer who is not so swift on his feet constantly barrels into you no matter where you stand and blocks your deaf client's view of you half the time.

946. You have agreed to interpret a large conference. Upon arriving, you learn that several of the sessions deal with highly technical information with which you're unfamiliar. It looks like it's going to be a long day and not an example of your best work. You wonder how you get yourself into these things.

947. A large grocery store has hired a deaf employee, and you're hired to interpret the employee training program. The trainer is reading straight from a manual at warp speed. You have stopped him several times to slow him down, without much luck. You stop him again to repeat information, and under his breath, you hear him mutter, "I knew hiring a retard was a bad idea."

948. While interpreting at church, the choir sings a song you have never heard before. Unfortunately, you can't understand a word. There's no one you can look to for a feed, and so you're standing there mortified with nothing to interpret.

949. The speaker at the conference you are interpreting is using Latin phrases to illustrate his point. Not knowing any Latin, you inform the deaf audience that he is speaking Latin. You try to fingerspell it and then realize you don't know how to spell most of it. Your team interpreter just shrugs. You can see some of the "off" interpreters smirking and shaking their heads at your predicament.

Challenges in Interpreting Addressed by Successful National Interpreter Certification (NIC) Candidates

- **Scenario 950.** I could kick myself. Yesterday I picked up the phone, and it was my deaf student's mother who was all chatty about how much her son liked me and school, etc. We talked for about a half-hour, and it didn't hit me until later that I never should have been talking to her about school matters at all. I know better. I should have referred her back to the classroom teacher. What do I do now?

AN NIC CANDIDATE'S PERSPECTIVE: This scenario falls under CPC Tenet 1.0, Confidentiality.

Problem/Conflict: For me to share information and have personal contact with a student's parents, I would be violating the confidentiality tenet.

Stakeholders' Perspectives:
1. *Deaf Consumer*: The student looks to the interpreter for communication access at school.
2. *Hearing Consumer*: Teacher – The teacher may view the interpreter as the student's helper (gopher, if you will). The teacher may not have cultural information on working with interpreters and probably has little to no previous experience working with the Deaf community.

Solution: I would avoid giving out personal information at all cost so this "boundary" is known when the assignment starts. This will prevent the teacher from having the assumption that the interpreter is on anyone's side.

Personal Experience: Of course, it would be a perfect world to be able to engage with the deaf student's parents on a personal level, but the real world hits home quite quickly when you realize you have to keep some distance and avoid becoming too friendly with the parents. The pressure is then on to get information from the interpreter which puts everyone in a sticky situation.

Implications:
1. *Short-term:* Contact with parents gives the parents some knowledge of the interpreter (e.g., who they are, skill level) but causes harm down the road with dependency on the interpreter for information that should be provided by the teacher.

2. *Long-term*: By keeping contact with the student's parents, the interpreter is hindering the success of the student due to the trust that has been built between the student and the interpreter.

- **Scenario 951:** One of the high school teachers never calls on the deaf student, ever! It's like the student is invisible and even if her hand is raised, he doesn't call on her. It is already midterms. What should I do?

AN NIC CANDIDATE'S PERSPECTIVE: This scenario falls under CPC Tenet 3.0, Conduct.

Problem/Conflict: The conflict in this situation is having personal concern for the role of the student in the classroom.

Stakeholders' Perspectives:
1. *Deaf Consumer*: The student who looks to the interpreter for communication access at school.
2. *Hearing Consumer*: Teacher – The teacher may view the interpreter as the student's helper (gopher if you will). He or she may or may not have cultural information on working with interpreters and probably has little to no previous experience working with the Deaf community.

Solution: The interpreter needs to be "unobtrusive" (Tenet 3.5) and "avoid performing dual or conflicting roles in interdisciplinary (e.g. educational or mental health teams) and other settings" (Tenet 3.3).

Personal Experience: We as interpreters want to save the day, right? We want our high school students to be successful with our help. This sets them up for failure! It is our job to show them our role in their educational experience and let them advocate for themselves or learn the hard way with a bad midterm grade.

Implications:
1. *Short-term:* The student will do well on their midterm exam as the interpreter inappropriately intervenes.
2. *Long-term:* The student will become an adult and have no confidence or self-esteem to figure things out on her own and will have no idea what the words "self advocacy" mean.

- **Scenario 952.** I interpret for a college student in a class where the students are required to make a formal group presentation. A week before the presentation another student in the group approaches the deaf student and tells him that the group has already met and they've got it all covered. The student seemed fine with it, but I'm not!

AN NIC CANDIDATE'S PERSPECTIVE: This scenario falls under the CPC Tenet 3.0, Conduct.

Problem/Conflict: The conflict in this situation is having personal concern for the role of the student in the classroom.

Stakeholders' Perspectives:
1. *Deaf Consumer:* The deaf student doesn't recognize there is a problem.
2. *Hearing Consumer:* Classmate – This classmate probably thinks she has done the deaf student a favor.

Solution: Tenet 3.0, 3.5, which states interpreters "avoid performing dual or conflicting roles in interdisciplinary (e.g., educational settings)," applies to this situation.

Personal Experience: Whether or not we agree with the hearing students not involving the deaf student in the planning of their group presentation, it is not our role to intercede.

Implications:
1. *Short term:* The deaf student may not get a good grade on this presentation because he doesn't know what caliber work the other students have done.
2. *Long term:* As long as I do not intervene, the student will gain an educational learning opportunity, as well as an opportunity to assert himself with his peers.

> • **Scenario 953.** Every day during the reading lesson the students all get a chance to read aloud, including the deaf student. She actually does a pretty good job, but invariably some of the boys snicker and make fun of her speech. I know the teacher is aware of it. She always gives the boys "the look," but it happens every time anyway. Fortunately, the deaf student isn't aware of this because it would surely devastate her if she knew. I've talked to the classroom teacher about this and she says she's open to suggestions, but what should I suggest?

AN NIC CANDIDATE'S PERSPECTIVE: This scenario falls under CPC Tenet 4.0, Respect for Consumers.

Problem/Conflict: The student is unaware of the comments and jokes being made about her speech.

Stakeholders' Perspectives:
1. *Deaf Consumer:* The student is assuming she is getting all of the communication that is happening around her
2. *Hearing Consumer:* The hearing students are making fun of the deaf student.

3. *Teacher*: The teacher assumes I am not telling the student what is going on.

Solution: The interpreter needs to facilitate communication and have equal independence of all consumers, Tenet 4.4.

Personal Experience: Nothing should be suggested to the teacher. Shame on the interpreter who decides what communication is to be given to the deaf client! As interpreters, our job is to interpret everything possible to provide equal access to communication. Who are we to make that decision?

Implications:
1. *Short-term*: The deaf student will assume everything is running smoothly and her classmates are accepting. The hearing students assume that it is OK to mock deaf people because they cannot hear anyway.
2. *Long-term*: The deaf student is (and will be) totally oblivious to what is happening around her and has no chance of educating her hearing peers about Deaf culture and the sensitivity that comes with that. The hearing students will miss out on a wonderful learning opportunity and treat deaf people as they used to decades ago, with little respect.

- **Scenario 954.** One of my students just got a videophone, and she is so excited about it that she calls everyone. She asked me if she could call me at home, and I said it would be fine. The first few phone calls were fine. However, I hoped the novelty of her new toy would wear off in time. Now I think I need to say something. I do not want to dampen her enthusiasm or strain our relationship, so what should I say?

AN NIC CANDIDATE'S PERSPECTIVE: This scenario falls under CPC Tenet 3.0, Conduct.

Problem/Conflict: The student is allowed to converse with the interpreter while not at school and is jeopardizing boundaries.

Stakeholders' Perspectives:
1. *Deaf Consumer*: The deaf student is viewing the interpreter as a friend figure instead of an interpreter.
2. *Hearing Consumer*: The hearing consumer can be the teacher in the long run and may assume the interpreter is a friend, as well as assume some "rule-bending" where the boundary is concerned.

Solution: The interpreter needs to be honest and explain that, while the student is great, there is a conflict of interest.

Personal Experience: If students want to give out their video phone number, it is our job to educate them on the role (do's and don'ts) of an interpreter. To give out our (interpreter's) phone number is enabling them to ignore (or be unaware) of our role and responsibilities.

Implications:
1. *Short term*: The deaf student assumes there is a friendship developing and may (depending on the student) take advantage of that.
2. *Long term*: The deaf student will not successfully have set boundaries as a deaf adult when it comes to interpreters for her doctor appointments, etc.

- **Scenario 955.** I think schools should be putting a premium on hiring male interpreters. There are so many male situations to which boys need exposure in school (e.g., physical education, locker rooms, health classes) that females can never give them.

AN NIC CANDIDATE'S PERSPECTIVE: This scenario falls under the CPC Tenet 4.0, Respect for Consumers.

Problem/Conflict: I would be assuming a male student needs more/different exposure than a female student. I would be "taking charge" of a situation.

Stakeholders' Perspectives:
1. *Deaf Consumer*: The deaf student may assume they must have male interpreters throughout every life experience and may lose respect for female interpreters. (This is all under the assumption the interpreter has encouraged this idea to the male student.)
2. *Hearing Consumer*: School – The school officials may assume male interpreters should be paid more than female interpreters, regardless of their certification credentials.

Solution: I would need to keep this thought to myself and keep to the business at hand-- interpreting the message faithfully and to the best of my knowledge.

Personal Experience: Interpreters are hired/contracted to do a thorough job of interpreting from one language to another without their own interjections. If the interpreter is doing her job well, there is no need for a male interpreter because the deaf student should be getting the whole message in the first place.

Implications:
1. *Short term*: The deaf student will assume a male interpreter is needed and will begin depending on the interpreter to make his decisions for him. The school would pay more for gender type versus certification level.

2. *Long term*: The deaf student would be less flexible with whom he has for an interpreter (preferring males only–of which there are not enough), while the ignorant hearing consumers would think to pay for gender, not credentials.

- **Scenario 956.** The high school student for whom I interpret is mainstreamed into regular classes most of the day, but he also works with a resource teacher two hours a day. The resource teacher signs, but not well, so the student constantly tells me it is a waste of his time. When he did not do well on his last report card, his parents asked for a meeting with the school. The parents now want me to interpret for the resource teacher, but that means I will not have a break all day. What can I say?

AN NIC CANDIDATE'S PERSPECTIVE: This scenario falls under the CPC Tenet 6.0, Business Practices.

Problem/Conflict: I am being asked to risk my health (overuse) and my mental ability because of the lack of signing skills from the resource teacher.

Stakeholders' Perspectives:
1. *Deaf Consumer*: The deaf consumer would have an interpreter who is there only because I have to be and may feel that I am taking my aggression out on him.
2. *Hearing Consumer*: Resource teacher – The resource teacher assumes I can go on forever without breaks.

Solution: I need to share my concern and perhaps offer another interpreter for that two-hour time.

Personal Experience: If we as interpreters do not advocate for ourselves, we will be forced to be on Social Security Disability Insurance at the age of 40! We need to stand our ground on these issues in a tactful, professional way, of course.

Implications:
1. *Short-term*: The deaf student will assume the interpreter can go on forever.
2. *Long-term*: The deaf student will not have an interpreter giving 100%, which will jeopardize the communication occurring (assuming I decide to do the extra work).

- **Scenario 957.** Two other interpreters and I were hired to interpret a medical conference. As you can imagine, the language of the conference was very technical. We each got a packet of reading material in advance, but it was still definitely a challenge to say the least. Two of us worked well together, but the third interpreter was useless. I don't think she should get paid for just being there when we did all the work.

AN NIC CANDIDATE'S PERSPECTIVE: This scenario falls under CPC Tenet 5.0, Respect for Colleagues, interns, and students of the profession.

Problem/Conflict: Two of the three interpreters are efficient, which gives less work to the inefficient interpreter.

Stakeholders' Perspectives:
1. *Deaf Consumer*: The deaf consumer is relying on accurate interpretation of the source message.
2. *Hearing Consumer*: The hearing consumer assumes all is well with the "trio," as well as clarity for the deaf participant.

Solution: The interpreter should be approached privately and offered any help with providing a fully accessible message.

Personal Experience: For myself and the other interpreter working, I say, "Suck it up!" We need to learn our lesson and move on. We need to try to be as sensitive as we can; we never know what is going on in the other interpreter's head. To the useless interpreter, I say, "Why did you take a job that you can't handle?" The information was given ahead of time, and there could have been a decision to decline at that time.

Implications:
1. *Short-term*: The efficient interpreters are doing all of the work.
2. *Long-term*: The useless interpreter's reputation will be on the line.

- **Scenario 958.** I am an educational interpreter who loves my job, except Bible class. Our students have a religious education class once a week for about 40 minutes. I interpret as professionally as I can, but I am a Jewish woman. This is more than I bargained for.

AN NIC CANDIDATE'S PERSPECTIVE: This scenario falls under CPC Tenet 6.0, Business Practices.

Problem/Conflict: I am in a dilemma with using discretion.

Stakeholders' Perspectives:
1. *Deaf Consumer*: The deaf consumer would not want an interpreter who is there because he or she has to be. The client will not get the worship connection like they would normally get.

2. *Hearing Consumer*: Pastor – The pastor is oblivious to the situation.

Solution: I need to share my concern and perhaps offer another interpreter for the Bible class.

Personal Experience: We have discretion in our CPC for a reason: to protect us! I utilized the CPC to find another interpreter for a similar situation. If we do not take care of ourselves, who will?

Implications:
1. *Short term*: The deaf student will not get the lesson (fully) that day, if the interpreter stays put. I would enjoy that assignment less and less everyday.
2. *Long term*: The deaf student will not have an interpreter giving 100 percent which will jeopardize the relationship with his or her God.

- **Scenario 959.** I am interpreting for a high school science class, and the teacher announced today that some of his equipment is missing. He knows it occurred during this period. He told the students if the equipment was returned by the next class there would be no questions asked. I don't have proof, but I suspect it was my deaf student. What should I do?

AN NIC CANDIDATE'S PERSPECTIVE: This scenario falls under CPC Tenet 2.0, Professionalism.

Problem/Conflict: Do I inform the appropriate person or do I keep quiet?

Stakeholders' Perspectives:
1. *Deaf Consumer*: The deaf consumer would think that I am breaching the CPC because I interjected my opinion regarding who I thought stole the equipment.
2. *Hearing Consumer*: The hearing consumer at first may appreciate my opinion.

Solution: I would keep quiet. I was hired to interpret for the student, not to "provide counsel, advice or personal opinions."

Implications:
1. *Short-term*: The deaf student would be upset with me if she found out that I told the teacher that I thought she stole the equipment. She would not want me to interpret anymore. The hearing consumer would appreciate it at first, but if I was wrong, he would be upset. Also, the hearing consumer would not respect me if he knew I was not following the CPC.
2. *Long-term*: The deaf student could file a complaint against me if I violated the CPC, and I could be fired. The hearing consumer may not want me to work for that school district in the future.

- **Scenario 960.** I am a successful private practice interpreter. My clients love my work so I get lots of referrals. However, even though the cost of living has gone up, I have yet to raise my hourly rate because I am worried if I do I will lose clients. So instead of charging more I take on more work to generate more income. However, I am working myself to the bone!

AN NIC CANDIDATE'S PERSPECTIVE: This scenario falls under CPC Tenet 6.0, Business Practices.

Problem/Conflict: The conflict in this situation is: do I raise my wages and continue to work myself to the bone, or do I increase my hourly rate?

I would follow Tenet 6.0 which states, "interpreters maintain ethical business practices." Tenet 6.0, 6.8 states that interpreters "charge fair and reasonable fees for the performance of interpreting services and arrange for payment in a professional and judicious manner." I would also refer to local agency/independent contractor pay scales, federal and local inflation rates, and cost of living data.

Stakeholders' Perspectives:
1. *Deaf Consumer:* The deaf consumers might be upset at first if I raise my prices. However, because at times they need to work with other interpreters, they would know that my rate is typical for services rendered.
2. *Hearing Consumer:* My colleagues would want me to raise my rates to an amount that would give them an opportunity to get assignments. They might think that I am undermining the profession by charging cheaper rates to get more interpreting jobs.
3. *Interpreter:* I would want to charge a rate with which I am comfortable, but I need to follow the CPC and think about the interpreting profession as a whole, not just my income.

Solution: I would determine my own pay scale. I would make sure to build in wage increases for education, years of experience, and some base percentage to cover inflation/cost of living. By being consistent with a yearly wage increase, the cost should be so incremental that few clients will really notice the difference. Just as with any doctor or other service professional, I will make sure to include a note about my fee increase before providing services and perhaps include a comment about cost of living, experience, etc. As long as consumers are aware of the cost ahead of time and the rate I settle on is reasonable and within the range charged in my area, there should be little resistance to the change.

Personal Experience: I interpreted a conference one year and was state qualified. The next year, the conference contacted me again to interpret, and when I told them my rate, they commented that was an increase from the previous year. I politely explained that I had earned my national certification since working for them previously and that with national certification there is a wage increase. They readily accepted this explanation, and I was re-hired for the conference.

Implications:
1. *Short-term – Deaf Consumer:* The deaf consumer may question my increase in rates initially, especially if the service providers have a problem with it.
2. *Hearing Consumer*: Some of the service providers may not want to utilize my services any longer and may look for an interpreter who still is not in line with agency and other interpreter rates.
3. *Interpreter:* I will have fewer assignments: Therefore, my income will be less. It may take a little time for the hearing consumer and deaf consumer to adjust to the increase, but if it is a gradual increase, that time should be limited.
4. *Long-term – Deaf Consumer:* Since the majority of my assignments are paid by the service provider, there would be very little short-term and long-term effects on the client.
5. *Hearing Consumer*: The hearing consumer may not like the increase, but anyone who has a business or does business service for a fee understands that reasonable increases are common practice. Most hearing consumers who hire me charge a fee for service and have increases to make ends meet. I think a negative effect on the hearing consumer for hiring me will be very minimal.
6. *Interpreter:* By charging a fair and reasonable rate, I not only adequately value myself and the services I provide, but also the profession as a whole. By bringing my rates in line with those of other local interpreters and agencies, the incentive to hire me is my skill and provision of services, not the bargain price. I would be able to work fewer hours and receive the same amount of pay, thus giving my body and mind the time they need to recuperate and, in turn, provide better quality interpreting services. Initially, this solution will require more leg work to inform clients of the rate change.

   • **Scenario 961.** I was interpreting an interactive workshop with another interpreter and while I was "off," the workshop leader initiated the first of many activities. To my horror the other interpreter started to participate in the activity; she actually requested an additional notebook so she could write her answers!

AN NIC CANDIDATE'S PERSPECTIVE: This scenario falls under CPC Tenets 3.0, Conduct, 4.0, Respect for Consumers and 5.0, Respect for Colleagues.

Problem/Conflict: As a participant, the interpreter partner is in an obvious role conflict. As the "off" interpreter, what is the best way to approach this situation? If the interpreter is participating, then she is probably not interpreting and thus not facilitating communication access.

I would follow the CPC Tenet 3.0, which states, "interpreters conduct themselves in a manner that is appropriate to the specific interpreting situation." Under Tenet 3.0, 3.3, interpreters "avoid performing dual or conflicting roles," and 3.5 states that interpreters should "conduct and present themselves in an unobtrusive manner." Tenet 4.0 indicates that interpreters must "demonstrate respect for consumers," and 4.4 requires interpreters to "facilitate communication access and equality." Finally, Tenet 5.0 states that interpreters "demonstrate respect for colleagues, interns and students of the profession," while 5.3 recommends "approaching colleagues privately to discuss and resolve breaches of ethical and professional conduct."

Stakeholders' Perspectives:

1. *Deaf Consumer:* The client may or may not have full communication access while the interpreter is participating in activities. As a member of the minority cultural group, the client may not feel empowered to approach the interpreter and advocate for his needs. However, with a history of role confusion in the field of interpreting, the deaf consumer may accept this as normal interpreter behavior and not find it to be a problem.

2. *Hearing Consumer:* With little to no experience working with interpreters, the hearing consumer may think this is standard fare and not question the interpreter's participation. On the other hand, if the person responsible for paying the interpreter is present, they may resent paying someone to participate in the workshop, instead of performing the job for which she was hired. The hearing consumer would feel that if they are paying the individual as a participant, then what right does the interpreter have to participate in the activities?

3. *Interpreter:* As a team interpreter, I would be embarrassed for my colleague. With any prior experience and knowledge of the CPC, my colleague should know that participating in such activities is a breach of professional and ethical behavior.

Solution: While my colleague is serving as a participant, I would take over interpreting, if necessary, to ensure communication access. During the next break, I would take my team interpreter aside to discuss the situation and voice my concerns about the role conflict. If my team interpreter wants to continue to act as a participant, I would interpret what I could to guarantee full communication access for the client, and later I would speak to the agency/supervisor responsible for hiring the team interpreter to discuss my concerns.

Personal Experience: Often there is confusion about my role as an interpreter, especially in a workshop setting where I may only work with these individuals for a finite amount of time. In a situation like this, not only do I find it helpful to clarify things with my team interpreter, but also the workshop presenter(s) in case they are unclear as to my role and may ask me to participate in an inappropriate manner. I find that giving the presenter clear cues as to my role (e.g., "I am happy to interpret that for you" or "I would be glad to interpret this activity") serves to clarify and remind while minimizing bruised egos.

Implications:

1. *Short-term – Deaf Consumer:* In not confronting this situation, communication access is compromised and role confusion persists. If the client is at all aware of his rights as a consumer and familiar with the CPC, he would be annoyed at my colleague's breach of professional conduct.
2. *Colleague:* My partner may be temporarily angered or upset with me, but hopefully this problem can be resolved in a private conversation.
3. *Interpreter:* I would need to put my frustrations aside until I had an opportunity to discuss this situation with my colleague. I would be very careful to make sure that the message being delivered to the deaf consumer is not compromised even further. The goal is to maintain the message and the deaf person's ability to participate in the workshop. To do nothing would be to compromise communication access and equality.
4. *Long-term – Deaf Consumer:* The deaf consumer may not want to utilize my colleague's services in the future. The client may not speak highly of my colleague in the Deaf community, and this would have a negative impact on her professional career.
5. *Hearing Consumer:* The hearing consumer may not want to hire my colleague in the future unless they are certain that my team member understands her role in an assignment. The hearing consumer would probably not have a negative attitude about the interpreting profession because I would be an example of an interpreter who honors the CPC.
6. *Colleague:* My colleague would receive more respect from the deaf consumer, the hearing consumer, and other interpreters, if she followed the guidelines set forth by the interpreting profession. Following the CPC, my team member would receive additional assignments in the future.
7. *Interpreter:* Working to clarify the interpreter's role (even just with the interpreter) serves to aid future interpreters working with members of that population to reduce struggle with role confusion, as well as establish reasonable expectations for an interpreter's work and level of involvement in a workshop setting.

- **Scenario 962.** My deaf friends often ask me to barter services for free interpreting. I agree to do it, but most of the time I really do not particularly want the services I will receive in trade. I usually agree because I am afraid of offending my friends. However, bartering does not pay my rent or my credit card bills!

AN NIC CANDIDATE'S PERSPECTIVE: This scenario falls under CPC Tenets
2.0, Professionalism, 4.0, Respect for Consumers, and 6.0, Business Practices.

Problem/Conflict: As a working interpreter, this is my livelihood and I am
dependent on it to pay my bills. At the same time, I do not want to offend my friends
by rejecting their offers of trade in exchange for interpreting.

I would follow the CPC Tenet 2.0 which states, "interpreters possess the
professional skills and knowledge required for a specific interpreting situation."
Tenet 2.0, 2.6 states that interpreters "judiciously provide information or referral
regarding available interpreting or community resources." Tenet 4.0, Respect for
Consumers, dictates, "interpreters demonstrate respect for consumers," and 4.2
recommends that interpreters "approach consumers with a professional demeanor
at all times." Tenet 6.0 dictates, "interpreters maintain ethical business practices."
Tenet 6.0, 6.7 states that interpreters "render pro bono services in a fair and
reasonable manner." Finally, I would refer to the Americans with Disabilities Act.

Stakeholders' Perspective:
1. *Deaf Consumer:* If I am not being honest with my friends and not telling them
    the "trade" is insufficient, they may be unaware a problem exists. Historically,
    those who served in the role of interpreter were friends and family members
    and did not charge for services. With the emergence of interpreting as a
    paid profession with credential carrying members, some consumers may be
    unaccustomed to paying for services and/or believe they are entitled to free
    interpreting. If they did not have to pay before, why should they start now?
2. *Hearing Consumer:* Hearing consumers may be unaware of any trade worked
    out between myself and the deaf consumer and thus assume that all interpreting
    is unpaid, volunteer work. The perspective could be that since it is unpaid, it is
    not really a profession and the interpreter probably does not hold credentials.
    If the hearing consumer knows I am friends with the deaf consumer, they may
    also assume it is okay to ask friends/family to interpret for deaf consumers and
    that there should not be an expectation that the interpreter be paid.
3. *Interpreter:* I would not be able to provide for my family if I continued to offer
    interpreting services for free. I feel I would be undermining the interpreting
    profession if I continued to work for trade.

Solution: First, I need to be honest with my friends. If they are truly my friends,
they will understand when I explain I need to pay my bills and that the trades are
not working. Perhaps I could set aside a certain amount of time to provide pro
bono services or maybe sit down with my friends and figure out if there is a trade
I am willing to accept for interpreting services. I included Tenet 2.6 because of
receiving these "trade" services in venues that would be ordinarily paid. If there
are issues with a hearing consumer not providing an interpreter in accordance with
the Americans with Disabilities Act, then I would help my friends get in touch with

local disability rights advocates (Tenet 2.0, 2.6) that can help them get the services to which they are entitled.

Personal Experience: Occasionally, I am willing to provide pro bono or trade services, but in a judicious manner. In some circumstances, an agency/professional may be unwilling to provide an interpreter even though they are legally mandated. In that situation, I may be willing to serve as a pro bono interpreter so the individual can access the needed services, with the understanding that the client has filed a complaint and is working to resolve the issue. On the other hand, for non-profit, grassroots-type organizations, if I support their cause, I may be willing to interpret as my "donation" on a continual or one-time basis.

Implications:
1. *Short Term – Deaf Consumer:* At first my friends and other deaf consumers may be angry and think I am being greedy for wanting payment for my services. If they do not view interpreting as a profession, they may not understand and may think badly of me.
2. *Hearing Consumer:* The hearing consumer may be shocked at first because they would not be used to me submitting an invoice for my time. The hearing consumer may also be annoyed, not want to pay me, and not understand they are obligated under ADA to provide interpreting services.
3. *Interpreter:* I may experience some difficult times at first with my friends and the deaf consumers. They may not want to talk with me or utilize my services at all.
4. *Long Term – Deaf Consumer:* I think my friends/deaf consumers will respect me because being a friend means being honest with them. I know I want my friends to be honest with me. Once they understand my situation, we will be able to work collaboratively to develop a solution instead of me drowning in financial woes.
5. *Hearing Consumer:* Once it is explained that interpreting is a "professional career," the hearing consumer will understand the importance of our role. This will set the stage for the hearing consumer utilizing interpreters in the future. The hearing consumer, now that they understand, can explain our role to other professionals with whom they associate.
6. *Interpreter:* By advocating for me to be paid, I serve to reinforce the professional work of interpreters. While it is important to give back to the community, it is also necessary to get paid for the work I do. Continuing to provide services on a trade basis denigrates my professional "worth" and can muddle an interpreter's status in the eyes of hearing and deaf consumers alike.

   • **Scenario 963.** I am a social worker for deaf clients with mental illnesses, but my goal is to become an interpreter. When I am no longer a social worker for these clients, would it ever be appropriate for me to interpret for them? I am trying to take into consideration the possible role confusion for all involved. Is it the client's responsibility to separate roles? Would waiting a certain amount of time between roles make it more acceptable?

AN NIC CANDIDATE'S PERSPECTIVE: This scenario falls under CPC Tenet 3.0, Professionalism.

Problem/Conflict: I wish to serve as an interpreter for these clients after previously working in the capacity of a social worker, which could cause role confusion and thus reduce the effectiveness of my interpretation.

I would follow the CPC Tenet 3.0, Professionalism, which states, "interpreters conduct themselves in a manner that is appropriate to the specific interpreting situation." Both 3.7 and 3.8 deal with "actual or perceived conflicts of interest." Additionally, there are federal and state guidelines regarding counselor/client interaction upon termination of the counseling relationship. Some localities have restrictions on the type of interaction allowable and may prohibit contact up to five years after termination of the relationship.

Stakeholders' Perspectives:
1. *Deaf Consumer:* As consumers with mental illness, what is their ability to separate the role of social worker and interpreter? They may not understand a shift in responsibility and could expect me to provide the same types of support as when I was a social worker. Depending on the type and severity of the illness, consumers may be able to distinguish my role. Historically, there has existed distrust of interpreters in the Deaf community as not being able to maintain confidentiality. As a social worker, I may be privy to a deeper level of sensitive information than in the role of an interpreter. Consumers may be uncomfortable with my ability to maintain their confidentiality once I have shifted my role from social worker to interpreter. As a social worker, clients may perceive me as "on their side," whereas in an interpreter role, I may be perceived as more neutral or siding with the hearing consumer.
2. *Hearing Consumer:* If an individual has interacted with me as a social worker and interpreter, there may be significant role confusion with an expectation that all interpreters also "help out" their clients. There also may be an expectation of me to divulge confidential background information about the client, and my refusal to do so in my role as interpreter could be perceived as uncooperative.
3. *Interpreter:* I would not perform both functions. Not only would I be violating CPC 3.0, I would not be adhering to Tenet 3.0, Conduct, 3.3 which states that interpreters "avoid performing dual or conflicting roles in interdisciplinary or other settings." Acting as their social worker and then as their interpreter would definitely be "conflicting roles in interdisciplinary."

Solution: When in doubt, do not do it. In a situation where I think it may be appropriate, it will be imperative to obtain deaf and hearing consumer consent and also make sure the deaf consumer fully understands the role shift. Again, as these are deaf consumers with mental illness, what is their mental capacity to make these distinctions?

Personal Experience: As an interpreter and program coordinator, I find those who frequently misunderstand my two roles are hearing consumers. They approach me to ask questions while I am busy interpreting and expect me to interpret when I am coordinating. In something as sensitive as mental health, this type of confusion could have serious negative consequences.

Implications:

1. *Short term – Deaf Consumer:* While there is the potential for role confusion, in situations where this can be minimized, I may be the best interpreter in the world for these deaf consumers since we tend to interpret best what we know. However, there still exists the potential for mental stress and strain associated with this role confusion, and thus in many instances avoiding the assignment is the best solution.
2. *Hearing Consumer:* Hearing consumers may not understand at first the "conflict of interest." For them it would be easier to use my services than find another interpreter. The hearing consumer may not want to go through the process of orienting a deaf consumer to a new interpreter.
3. *Long Term – Deaf Consumer:* The deaf consumer may have a hard time adjusting to a new interpreter. Because it is a mental health setting, the client may not understand why it would be a violation of the CPC for the social worker/interpreter to perform both duties or why it would be a conflict of interest.
4. *Hearing Consumer:* Since it is a professional setting, the other employees (after an explanation) will be able to understand the difficult situation in which an interpreter would be put if she had already provided social services for the client. The medical profession is very familiar with following a code of ethics.
5. *Interpreter:* I believe in this situation there will be positive and negative impacts for the short term and long term. I think this is a situation where there will be varying opinions among both hearing and deaf consumers. No matter the opinions of others with whom I work, I must follow the CPC. Being ethical can only help me be successful in my interpreting career.

- **Scenario 964.** A state qualified interpreter at only Level 1 is charging $25 per hour during the week and $45 per hour on the weekend. She is not very skilled! Should I tell her this is unethical or report her to someone?

AN NIC CANDIDATE'S PERSPECTIVE: This scenario falls under CPC Tenets 5.0, Respect for Colleagues and 6.0, Business Practices.

Problem/Conflict: Is this a fair/reasonable fee for this individual to be charging for her services? However, if the market can sustain this fee (meaning someone is willing to pay), what is the disincentive to continuing charging these high rates?

I would follow the CPC Tenet 5.0, Respect for Consumers, which states, "interpreters demonstrate respect for colleagues, interns and students of the profession." Tenet 5.0, 5.3 states that interpreters "approach colleagues privately to discuss and resolve breaches of ethical or professional conduct through standard conflict resolution methods." Additionally, I would adhere to Tenet 6.0, Business Practices, which states, "interpreters maintain ethical business practices" and Tenet 6.8 which states, "charge fair and reasonable fees for the performance of interpreting services."

Stakeholders' Perspectives:
1. *Deaf Consumer:* With the passage of the Americans with Disabilities Act, the burden of hiring and paying interpreters falls more toward the hearing consumer. The deaf consumers may be unaware of an interpreter's fees. If the consumers are satisfied with the interpreting services, then they have no reason to be concerned.
2. *Hearing Consumer:* The old adage "you get what you pay for" may lead the hearing consumer to believe this higher hourly rate guarantees them a higher quality interpreter. As the majority of hearing consumers do not understand the state qualification/national certification levels, they also may be unaware of the corresponding pay scales.
3. *Interpreter:* I feel interpreters earn their rate of pay as they develop their skills and experience. I do not think an interpreter who is just starting in the profession with a QA1 should get the same rate of pay as a seasoned interpreter. I feel $25 is too high for a QA1, let alone charging $45 on weekends. A QA1 charging those fees is "not fair and reasonable."

Solution: If I feel strongly that this interpreter is charging well above the market price for someone of her skill set, then it would be appropriate to approach her privately and discuss my concerns, making sure to include the potential short- and long-term implications. If this individual disregards my advice, then I am within my rights to file an ethical grievance.

Personal Experience: Working for an institution that employs multiple interpreters with differing education, certification, and experience levels, we do our best to set our pay rate to be competitive with the market. As someone working in the field, it is easy for me to identify someone charging far above or below what is appropriate for this locale. Unfortunately, others hiring interpreters may not be as savvy nor as aware of the profession, so it is within the scope of our responsibilities to ensure these individuals are not taken advantage of.

Implications:
1. *Short Term — Deaf Consumer:* Unless a deaf consumer personally hires an interpreter, he will not be involved in the interpreter's rate or pay. However, if any rumors spread about the unreasonable fees being charged by the inexperienced interpreter, the deaf consumer's respect for the interpreter would decrease.
2. *Hearing Consumer:* If the hearing consumer knew or was informed of the breach of ethical conduct by the QA1 interpreter, they would not hire that interpreter for other assignments.
3. *Interpreter:* The interpreter may be upset with me if I confront her about her rates. She may not want to team with me anymore. However, I would discuss it with her first, adhering to CPC 5.2. Maybe she was not aware that the level of qualification/certification and experience are factors in setting interpreter rates.
4. *Long Term — Deaf Consumer and Hearing Consumer:* Being cognizant of current rates in interpreter pay and addressing inequities advocates for those that may be less educated in the equitable pay of interpreters. If an individual/institution is paying these higher rates to this lesser qualified individual, they may eventually begin to question that interpreter once exposed to the pay rates of more qualified, but less costly, interpreters. This in turn brings embarrassment to the profession as a whole as the interpreter appears to be taking advantage of the deaf and hearing consumer's knowledge deficit.
5. *Interpreter:* This interpreter may or may not heed my warning, but I have done my part to uphold the CPC and high standards for the interpreting profession. It will then be up to me to decide about the next step if this interpreter chooses not to adhere to the standards of the CPC.

- **Scenario 965.** I interpret at a mental health facility for a young male client who has to be restrained at times. Today the person who was doing the restraint had his arm around the client's neck, and the client was screaming and crying. Later I was called into the supervisor's office to give my account of what happened. I knew if I told him that I thought the restraint was excessive, it would alienate me from the staff down the road.

AN NIC CANDIDATE'S PERSPECTIVE: This scenario falls under CPC Tenets 1.0, Confidentiality and 3.0, Conduct.

I would adhere to CPC Tenet 1.0, Confidentiality, which states, "interpreters adhere to standards of confidential communication." Tenet 1.0, 1.1 states that interpreters "share assignment-related information only on a confidential and 'as-needed' basis (e.g., supervisors, interpreter team members, members of the educational team, hiring entities)." Also under the CPC, 3.0 would apply which mandates that "interpreters conduct themselves in a manner appropriate to the specific interpreting situation." Tenet 3.0, 3.3 states that interpreters "avoid performing dual or conflicting roles in interdisciplinary or other settings," and 3.4 states that interpreters "comply with established workplace codes of conduct, notify appropriate personnel if there is a conflict with this Code of Professional Conduct, and actively seek resolution where warranted."

Problem/Conflict: On the one hand, I feel my loyalty is to my coworkers and do not wish to alienate myself from the staff. Additionally, I may be concerned about consumer confidentiality. On the other hand, if I were witness to something that brought harm to the deaf consumer, then what is my responsibility to pass along that information to prevent it from happening again?

Stakeholders' Perspectives:
1. *Deaf Consumer:* As a young man placed in a mental health facility, this individual probably has very little power and few rights. He may look to me to advocate on his behalf when in so many ways he has been silenced.
2. *Hearing Consumer:* Staff Member – If the restraint was truly excessive, this individual may be fearful of retaliation/punishment and might work to pressure me into keeping quiet. They may or may not be aware of client confidentiality guidelines and have little to no knowledge of the CPC.
3. *Supervisor:* The supervisor may or may not understand my role in the situation and probably has little to no knowledge of the CPC. In this situation, the supervisor may solely be looking to protect the facility from a lawsuit and/or is looking out for the well-being of the deaf consumer.
4. *Interpreter:* I was hired to interpret and nothing else. I am trained as an interpreter, not a mental health/restraint expert, and thus do not have the ability to pass judgment on how the situation was handled.

Solution: There are certain protected classes of individuals whom society has deemed in need of special protections. These classes include children, the elderly, those with severe cognitive impairments, and those placed in institutions. In this situation, I am able to provide a factual recount of what I saw but unable to pass judgment as to the appropriateness of the restraint. At that point, I would offer to interpret between the supervisor and my client if more clarification is necessary.

Personal Experience: I recently attended a legal workshop focused on interpreters' rights and responsibilities, and the information conveyed was that an interpreter cannot get in trouble if she stays within the area of expertise for which she was hired. If I am hired as an interpreter, I am able to make decisions about language and comprehension, but this is where the scope of my expertise ends. To venture beyond this knowledge base is to put myself in a situation that may result in litigation.

Implications:
1. *Short Term – Deaf Consumer and Hearing Consumer:* Both the supervisor and deaf consumer may be upset with me for not offering my perspective on the situation, and I may have to explain my ethical responsibility to the CPC.
2. *Interpreter:* I will feel pressure from both parties to give my opinion of what happened, but I must stand firm to ensure that my role as communication facilitator is better clarified for future situations. Both the hearing consumer and deaf consumer may not want me to continue interpreting.
3. *Long Term – Deaf Consumer:* Unless I can get the deaf consumer to understand my role/responsibility as an interpreter, he may not want me to interpret for him in the future.
4. *Hearing Consumer:* If I did not have a contract, the supervisor may decide to terminate my services and/or re-clarify my job description to include coverage of this type of situation.
5. *Interpreter:* I would hope that after discussing the situation, the deaf and hearing consumer would agree it is the mental health facility's responsibility to ensure consumer safety and the use of proper restraint techniques. If they understand I do not have experience regarding appropriate restraint, I can continue to work for the deaf consumer and hearing consumer. However, if both deaf and hearing consumers are dissatisfied with my response, I will not be interpreting at the facility any longer.

- **Scenario 966.** Another interpreter and I interpret weekly for a college student. Recently the two of us showed up for class in the usual location only to find the classroom dark and deserted. We happened to run into the professor who told us that the students were meeting in partner groups at a different location on campus. She knew where our client was meeting, so we proceeded to trek all the way across campus. However, when we got there, the client acted like we should have known where to find him. No apology, no excuse, nothing! In retrospect, I think we should have just not gone, and the client would have learned the hard way that he needs to communicate better.

AN NIC CANDIDATE'S PERSPECTIVE: This scenario falls under CPC Tenets 2.0, Professionalism and 4.0, Respect for Consumers.

Problem/Conflict: I am there to interpret but am unable to do my job if not informed of the location. I may be frustrated and angry and want to prove I am "right" and the client "wrong."

I would follow the CPC Tenet 2.0, Professionalism, which states, "interpreters possess the professional skills and knowledge required for the specific interpreting situation." Tenet 2.0, 2.1 states that interpreters "provide service delivery regardless of race, color, national origin, gender, religion, age, disability, sexual orientation, or any other factor." I would also follow 4.0, Respect for Consumers, which states, "interpreters demonstrate respect for consumers," and 4.2 which requires interpreters to "approach consumers in a professional demeanor at all times," and 4.4 which states that interpreters "facilitate communication access and equality and fully support the interaction and independence of consumers." Additional resources would be university/college policy on student "no-show" or student-interpreter communication.

Stakeholders' Perspectives
1. *Deaf Consumer:* Perhaps the deaf consumer just forgot and is hoping I can figure it out. Maybe he thought he told me; perhaps there was a breakdown in communication somewhere along the way–he could be thinking about what a lousy, disorganized interpreter I am. If this is a younger deaf consumer, then he may be used to high school where the coordinator/special education teacher was responsible for scheduling/informing interpreters of schedule changes. Perhaps it never crossed his mind that the interpreters would not know where to find the group.
2. *Hearing Consumer:* The fellow students might want to finish the project and be able to communicate with their deaf classmate. The hearing consumers may or may not understand why we are late and may see interpreters as untimely or perhaps uninformed.
3. *Professor:* The professor is aware of a lack of communication by the client and may or may not understand the interpreter role/responsibility.
4. *Interpreter:* I think there was an obligation for the instructor and/or student to let the interpreters know in advance that there had been a room change. If the decision was made that day, then a note should have been left on the classroom door indicating where the students were located.

Solution: Providing service delivery regardless of "any other factor" in this case could perhaps include rudeness or poor planning. In this scenario, the interpreter is the professional. Hearing and deaf consumers do not have their own CPC to follow, but we do. Oddly enough, nowhere in there does it mention teaching a client a lesson by not showing up. It does, however, mention professional demeanor and supporting the full interaction/independence of consumers. Luckily in this scenario, the interpreter was able to find the student. If that had failed to work, a "reasonable effort" should still be made to locate the student. Rather than assuming a vengeful, sadistic client, we could just give this person the benefit of the doubt and save ourselves a lot of angst. In terms of the client, perhaps after the assignment, it would be appropriate to remind him of the importance of communication when there is a change in class location, again keeping within the confines of a professional demeanor. Instead of it being about "me," the wronged interpreter, I would take the situation outside of myself and have it be about the message I am there to interpret; the message cannot be conveyed as efficiently without my presence.

Personal Experience: Sometimes I do not really like the clients I work with. If I met some of these individuals outside of a work environment, we would not be friends. That is the case with work–it is not about making friends. With older deaf clients who are used to family and friends serving as interpreters, this is a shift in the philosophy of the interpreter/client relationship.

Implications:
1. *Short term – Deaf Consumer:* Because the client is annoyed we did not arrive at our usual time, it may take the client a few minutes to settle down and focus on what is being interpreted.
2. *Hearing Consumer:* As long as there is not a lot of disruption by the interpreters coming in after all the students are paired, the hearing consumer should not be affected by the situation.
3. *Interpreter:* While there may be frustration on both parts for lateness and lack of information, these feelings can hopefully be set aside so that the work can continue.
4. *Long term – Deaf Consumer:* The student will be more aware of the importance of communication so that the interpreters can arrive to an assignment promptly. The deaf consumer is old enough to understand a problem with lack of communication between two parties. The deaf client may have a better understanding of his responsibility in the interpreting process.
5. *Hearing Consumer:* The hearing consumer may have seen a little tension between the interpreters and student but will be impressed to see the situation handled in a professional manner.
6. *Interpreter:* If handled well by the interpreters, we can help the consumer to shift the paradigm of interpreting from the interpreter's responsibility to a more holistic, team approach focused on effective communication.

- **Scenario 967.** Recently I observed platform interpreters who wore clunky necklaces and suits with different colored blouses underneath (e.g., black suits with red blouses). One interpreter had on a black suit coat, khakis, a big clunky blue necklace, and a big blue plastic watch! Many people were commenting about it. What's up with that?

AN NIC CANDIDATE'S PERSPECTIVE: This scenario falls under CPC Tenet 3.0, Conduct.

Problem/Conflict: If the attire/accessories are distracting enough that "many people" were commenting, then it is reasonable to assume the attire was obtrusive. This distraction may make it difficult to concentrate on the interpretation. On the other hand, perhaps these individuals did exercise care in the choice of their attire and are unaware it creates a problem for audience members.

I would follow the CPC Tenet 3.0, Conduct, and present myself in an unobtrusive manner and exercise care in choice of attire.

Stakeholders' Perspectives:
1. *Deaf Consumer:* The deaf consumers would think interpreters look professional in suits and dressed appropriately to fit the platform environment. On the other hand, the deaf consumers could be bothered by the colored blouses and chunky jewelry to the point where it is difficult for them to attend to the message. Even if the deaf consumers were bothered by the interpreter's attire, they may not feel comfortable approaching the interpreter, especially since in a platform setting, the interpreter may be perceived as being in line with the high-status, hearing presenter.
2. *Hearing Consumer:* With little to no experience with interpreters or their attire, the hearing consumers may believe the interpreters' attire fits the arena and is in line with other professionals on stage. The hearing consumers are probably unaware of the specialized needs in interpreter attire to avoid consumer eye strain.

Solution: As a participant and colleague, I would privately approach the interpreters after the event and inform them of audience member comments. For this to be successful, it is best to avoid value laden, judgmental statements such as, "I would never wear something like that," and instead stick to the facts–it was difficult to watch/understand the interpretation as the blouse/jewelry was distracting. Another approach is the compliment sandwich–one positive, one point for improvement, and another positive. For example, "Your placement on stage was great; I was really able to see you clearly, and I know fellow audience members were too. The only thing that made it a little tough was the colored blouses/jewelry. That chunky necklace is really cute but maybe not a great fit for interpreting. You sure did look sharp in that black suit!"

Personal Experience: Often if I am unsure of an outfit, I will ask my partner before starting and usually have a backup in the car. Sometimes it is a new color I am trying out or a particularly "loud" pair of pants. Regardless, team interpreters and even consumers can give you great feedback if you are ever unsure of your clothing choice.

Implications:
1. *Short term – Deaf Consumer:* Interpreters are informed that the choice of attire may not be the best fit for that arena.
2. *Long term – Interpreters:* Interpreters may or may not alter their choice of attire. A positive/professional relationship was maintained, and this modeling can be used to resolve conflicts with other professionals.

- **Scenario 968.** I am a full-time staff interpreter at a hospital and have an unpaid lunch hour. The other interpreter who was working with me today is a freelance interpreter who charges by the hour. At lunch the two of us and the deaf client were sitting together eating lunch and a drug rep came in to talk to the dietician. I interpreted the conversation. However, the other interpreter was the one being paid during lunch, but she did not offer to interpret. She just sat there, ate her lunch and listened. What should I have done?

AN NIC CANDIDATE'S PERSPECTIVE: This scenario falls under CPC Tenets 3.0, Conduct, 4.0, Respect for Consumers, 5.0, Respect for Colleagues, and 6.0, Business Practices.

Problem/Conflict: I recognize two apparent conflicts in this situation: the conflict between my need to eat and rest and my feelings of needing to interpret for the deaf consumer; as well as the conflict between me interpreting pro bono during my unpaid lunch versus my paid team interpreter.

Stakeholders' Perspectives:
1. *Deaf Consumer:* The deaf consumer may or may not be aware of the pay schedule for staff and freelance interpreters. If an interpreter is available and in the vicinity, the deaf consumer may forget it is a scheduled break and simply want the information being communicated by the drug rep.
2. *Hearing Consumer:* The hearing consumer wants the message communicated and is probably unaware of interpreters' need for breaks. The hearing consumer may assume that when the deaf consumer and interpreter are together, then the interpreter is "on" and available to interpret.
3. *Freelance Interpreter:* The freelance interpreter may be unaware of the pay schedule for a staff interpreter and does not realize that my lunch break is unpaid. The freelance interpreter may feel it is appropriate to defer to me as the staff member with "seniority" in this situation. Also, she may simply need a break and will not interpret during her "off" time.

Solution: If I really want to be "off" during lunch, then I need to not sit in the hospital cafeteria with the deaf consumer. If this is a recurring problem, then maybe going off-site for lunch is an option or taking my food to a more private area. If I decide to continue to eat in the cafeteria with the deaf consumer, then I know when other hearing consumers see me, they may assume I am ready and willing to interpret. I would first talk with the deaf consumer, explaining that while I enjoy eating lunch together, I need a break. Then we can work out a solution regarding how to address hearing consumers who want me to interpret during lunch. As far as my colleague is concerned, paid or unpaid, she needs a break too. Perhaps the previously mentioned conversation with the deaf consumer could include this interpreter as well, and the three of us can work out a system. If in the end, it seems I will interpret during lunch, then I can try talking with my supervisor to work out a system in which only half of my lunch is unpaid.

Personal Experience: As a staff interpreter in a similar situation, I sometimes am not able to take my fully scheduled, unpaid lunch due to the unpredictable nature of my work. I have talked with my supervisor, and he agrees it is reasonable for me to leave early or come in late on days when I know I will not be able to use my entire lunch hour. We have a similar system established for times when I work early, late, or on the weekends. As long as I communicate with him, he is amenable to flexing my schedule. If there are other staff interpreters, talk to them about how they handle the same situation. Your supervisor is also a good resource for how they believe this situation could be resolved.

Implications:
1. *Short Term:* The deaf consumer and team interpreter are made aware of my concerns and hopefully will work with me to ensure I get a break. My supervisor may or may not be understanding of the situation but will at a minimum be informed.
2. *Long Term:* There will be a better understanding of my need for a break and also my concerns about working through my unpaid lunch hour. I may need to make a different decision about where to eat if problems persist, which could in turn upset the deaf consumer and/or my interpreter colleague. However, by doing nothing and letting the situation continue, I perpetuate the misconception that whenever I am with the deaf consumer, I am working and ready to interpret. Advocating for my own needs helps deaf and hearing consumers better understand the need for break time in the interpreting process.

- **Scenario 969.** I am an ITP student, and I have been observing an elementary class for my internship hours. The interpreter has 20 years of experience. She makes up signs for vocabulary, so she does not have to fingerspell them over and over. Recently, I went to a workshop, and the presenter was emphatic that interpreters should fingerspell even to young children and that making up signs is oppressive! I do not know who to believe.

AN NIC CANDIDATE'S PERSPECTIVE: This scenario falls under CPC Tenets 2.0, Professionalism, and 7.0, Professional Development.
Tenet 2.0, 2.2 states interpreters should "assess consumer needs and the interpreting situation before and during the assignment and make adjustments as needed," and 7.1 states interpreters should "increase knowledge and strengthen skills."

Problem/Conflict: To fingerspell or not to fingerspell; that is the question; or, who do I believe?

Stakeholders' Perspective:
1. *Deaf Consumer:* The elementary school students see adults as high-status "experts" and thus will tend to model their behavior.
2. *Hearing Consumer:* The district may or may not be aware of the interpreter's language choices. As long as the information appears to be communicated, then no notice is taken. The hearing consumer may not understand the role of fingerspelling in American Sign Language and have little to no understanding of American Sign Language grammar and structure.
3. *Interpreter:* The interpreter may have little to no knowledge of a deaf child's language development. This individual may believe that deaf children are not capable of understanding fingerspelling, especially if she does not see children using fingerspelling in their own communication. The interpreter may believe that information is best communicated by using signs and omitting fingerspelling and relies on experience to guide her interpretation. The interpreter may have a mandate from the school district to use a form of Manually Coded English that discourages fingerspelling and advocates the use of initialized/made-up signs.
4. *Workshop Presenter:* The workshop presenter may have research to back her position on fingerspelling or could be relying on personal experience.

Solution: As an ITP student, you are to act as a sponge. However, after taking it all in, it is then your responsibility to fact check the information you have received. Consult with your instructors, other professionals, and academic resources. In any profession there exists conflicts in methodology, and it is the professional's responsibility to develop a well-researched position and philosophy for practice. The more conflicting views and opinions you encounter, the more well-rounded and informed you will be upon graduation.

Personal Experience: While it sounds like you are seeking an answer on the fingerspelling question, this is more about your development as an active learner in the profession and developing skills to find your own answers. Oftentimes you will be in situations where you are interpreting solo or with another interpreter that is equally stumped as to the appropriate way to handle a situation. The more you start considering these types of questions now, the better prepared you will be in the future.

Resources: CPC Tenet 2.2, current research on fingerspelling, interpreting texts, and interpreting program instructors.

Implications:
1. *Short Term:* After research, you are in a position to make your own decision regarding the incorporation of fingerspelling into your interpreting. In the short term, the solution dictates that you do nothing except learn.
2. *Long Term:* The hope is for you to emerge from your interpreter program as a well-rounded, researching, and informed professional. By continuing to research situations that seem to conflict with interpreting theory and methodology, you are able to develop your critical thinking skills and make informed decisions about pertinent issues.

- **Scenario 970.** I am a new and upcoming interpreter in the field, and recently I attended a presentation about job opportunities within a new company. I was impressed by their high standards and thought it sounded like a place I would want to work someday in the future. So you can imagine my shock and disappointment, when barely a month later, I found out that someone I knew had been offered a position. This individual has no QA, no RID, no NAD certifications. I was ticked. What's the point of their song and dance about high standards if they say one thing and do another?

AN NIC CANDIDATE'S PERSPECTIVE: This scenario falls under CPC Tenets 3.0, Conduct, 5.0, Respect for Consumers and 6.0, Business Practices.

Tenet: 3.2 Decline assignments and withdraw from interpreting profession when not competent due to physical, mental, or emotional factors; 5.3 approach colleagues privately to discuss and resolve breaches of ethical or professional conduct; and 6.1 accurately represent qualifications, such as certification, educational background, experience, and provide documentation when requested.

Problem/Conflict: While I support this company's *de jure* standards for interpreters, it seems the de facto are much lower than advertised. While this is disappointing, I next consider whether I want to work for this company in the future. If not, I must decide if I want to confront the "song and dancers" about their seemingly hypocritical actions.

Stakeholders' Perspectives:
1. *Deaf Consumer:* If this company continues to hire unqualified and potentially unskilled interpreters, deaf consumers will reject the use of their services. A poor reputation could drive the company out of business or force them to reconsider their hiring protocol.
2. *Hearing Consumer:* The hearing consumer may not understand the inner workings of interpreter certification but likes the reliability and "safety" of hiring a company versus an individual. If they do not receive negative feedback from the deaf consumer, the hearing consumer may assume that the

interpretation is satisfactory. As they are not typically immersed in the deaf community, they may not be aware of a company's reputation.

Solution: I would decide not to work for the company, and at the same time, I would not approach them about their hypocrisy. These kinds of business practices will catch up with the company (e.g., Enron, Arthur Andersen, Lehman Brothers), and eventually they will be forced to practice what they preach.

Personal Experience: There are good and bad interpreter agencies. There are reputable, ethical companies, and disreputable, unethical companies. In all cases, the competitive market and personal choice should weed out those without high standards. Unfortunately, due to the current interpreter shortage, some may continue to rely on unqualified/uncertified interpreters until supply and demand reaches equilibrium. The best we as interpreters can do is educate consumers, both hearing and deaf, about interpreter qualifications/certification and what is appropriate for certain settings and what is not. It is then up to them to make the best decision for their situation. In states where interpreter licensure is in place, the situation is resolved by filing a complaint with the governing authority regarding the unqualified/uncertified interpreter providing services.

Resources: CPC 3.2, 5.3, 6.1. Local/state laws related to interpreter qualification/certifications.

Implications:
1. *Short Term:* In the short term, nothing may come of my decision of inaction. When asked why I decided not to work for the company, I'll be diplomatic in my response and sure to include facts and not speculation in my answer. The community is small, and I do not want my words coming back to haunt me.
2. *Long Term:* If the company continues to hire and employ unqualified/unskilled interpreters, then the hope is the community will run them out of business by not utilizing their services. As previously mentioned, there is a severe interpreter shortage in some areas and thus demand exceeds supply. In this situation, the shortage of supply sometimes makes it necessary or "acceptable" to utilize these unqualified/unskilled interpreters. When supply and demand have reached equilibrium, competition should drive these individuals from the market or force them to improve their skill level. The big question though is when will the market reach equilibrium and how long are we willing to suffer the reign of these unqualified "interpreters" and the companies that employ them?

- **Scenario 971.** Is being employed by a video relay service (VRS) really an interpreter paradox? It appears that VRS organizations are dangling a decent hourly wage, benefits and flexible hours in front of our faces, while at the same time hiding behind the strength of the CPC to prevent interpreters from collaborating on equality in pay hours.

AN NIC CANDIDATE'S PERSPECTIVE: This scenario falls under the CPC Tenets 1.0, Confidentiality, and 3.0, Conduct.

Tenet: 1.1 Share assignment-related information only on a confidential and "as-needed" basis, and 3.4, comply with established workplace codes of conduct.

Problem/Conflict: VRS interpreters are asked to sign a confidentiality agreement regarding pay rate and are forbidden to discuss this rate with any other interpreter. Interpreters sign this agreement in exchange for the stability that VRS can offer, but at what cost? If interpreters breach this confidentiality, then they are at risk for termination and/or having an ethical complaint filed against them through RID.

Stakeholders' Perspectives:
Corporate America: The more information available about pay rates and benefits for individual employees, the less the company can afford to pay each new hire. This business practice has been in place for many years and is why many large corporations are resistant to unionizing, as unions make public record of pay rates, raises, and benefit packages and ensure that all unionized employees of equal education and experience enjoy the same benefits. By instilling the fear of a CPC breach into interpreters, VRS companies are able to minimize financial outlays and maximize profits.

Solution: I cannot have my cake and eat it too. If I want the stability and benefits of a corporate environment, then I must be willing to deal with the corporate culture, which is not necessarily a good fit for everyone. In this situation, I would say an interpreter could opt out if the emotional/financial cost of doing business is greater than the benefits received.

Personal Experience: With a background in economics and the corporate environment, it is easy to see why companies employ these tactics. If I do not have any idea that the person in the VRS booth next to me earns twice as much with half the experience, then I do not have any reason to complain. While this is probably not the case, by squelching interpreters' ability to organize, the company avoids the threat of collective bargaining and a uniform pay scale.

Implications:
1. *Short Term:* Upon deciding not to work for the company, I would be forced to deal with the instability of the freelance interpreter lifestyle and live without the benefits that VRS has to offer. However, in the freelance environment, I would be free to set my own pay scale and discuss rates with other interpreters

to ensure that I am close to the market price for someone of comparable certification, education, and experience.

2. *Long Term:* Ultimately interpreters need to decide whether the corporate environment is a good fit for them and their career goals. Historically, interpreters have been employed in mainly non-profit, social service, and educational settings. This shift to for-profit corporations has been swift, with unforeseen risks and benefits. Whether interpreters continue to settle for the "hush-hush" confidentiality standards or decide to organize and fight for collective bargaining remains to be seen.

- **Scenario 972:** I believe there should be truth in advertising, and an interpreter's business card is definitely a form of advertising. Therefore, I find it very misleading when I see business cards that do not clearly state the interpreter's level of certification. For example, in our state we have three levels of state interpreter certification, and there is a huge difference between the skills of a QA1 and a QA3. I have seen a number of interpreters' business cards simply say "state certified," so I ask them why they do not list their exact level. One responded, "This way I don't have to buy new business cards when I get a higher level." Another said, "Because if a potential client sees I have a QA1, they won't call me." And another said, "A knowledgeable employer always asks so it is their responsibility, not mine." What do you think?

AN NIC CANDIDATE'S PERSPECTIVE: This scenario falls under the CPC Tenet 6.1 which states, "Accurately represent qualifications, such as certification, educational background, and experience, and provide documentation when requested."

Problem/Conflict: A person is often hired based on their perceived level of skill. For someone outside of the deaf/interpreter community, "state certified" sounds legitimate. If there are different levels of state certification, then according to the CPC, these levels should be delineated. However, on the flip side, there is concern that if it is a low QA level, this person will not be able to find work and/or will need to purchase new business cards upon retesting. Is it the interpreter's responsibility to clearly express their qualifications, or is it the employer's responsibility to check?

Stakeholders' Perspectives:
1. *Deaf Consumer:* The deaf consumer is probably aware of the state QA levels and national certification and has a preference for which level fits their interpreting needs. The consumer may request a specific minimum level of state or national certification when requesting an interpreter.
2. *Hearing Consumer:* The hearing consumer probably has little to no awareness of the levels of state and national certification. They may have little to no

experience with the deaf community and hold a limited view of deaf people. They may be more comfortable interacting with a hearing individual and thus rely on the interpreter as the expert and disregard the request of the deaf consumer. They may also assume that like teachers, doctors, or lawyers, there is a singular certification or licensing standard, and as long as you are "certified," your skill level is equal to that of any other "certified" interpreter.

Solution: All excuses aside, interpreters need to accurately represent their qualification/certification level on their business cards and in any other forms of advertisement. It is explicitly stated in the CPC that interpreters must accurately represent themselves. Interpreters only open themselves up to litigation by doing otherwise. By accepting an assignment or being offered an assignment on the basis that we are "state certified," we are engaging in a nonverbal contract that says we are capable of interpreting that assignment. If we are later found to be under-qualified, we could be subject to legal ramifications. While it is the employer's responsibility to verify our credentials, it is first and foremost ours to accurately represent them.

Personal Experience: Recently two interpreters accepted an assignment that required nationally certified interpreters with a specialized skill set. When the hiring entity was confronted about their choice and use of these interpreters, they claimed that the two were certified. Once I was able to clarify for the hiring entity the difference between state and national certification, they were upset that the two interpreters had misrepresented their qualifications and ability to interpret in that venue.

Resources: CPC 6.1

Implications:
1. *Short Term:* By accurately representing our qualifications, especially if we are QA1, we may get fewer calls and have fewer clients. Hopefully though, the calls that we do receive will match our certification level and skill set and thus protect us from claims of under-qualification.
2. *Long Term:* If we want to put on our business cards that we are nationally certified interpreters or at the top level of state certification, we need to earn those levels. By accurately representing our qualifications, we give deaf and hearing consumers full access to information, and they are able to make their hiring decision accordingly. We may still receive calls for jobs that are above our skill sets, and out of respect for deaf consumers and their language needs, we need to politely decline. Again, this protects us from future litigation and embarrassment and builds our reputations as honest interpreters well aware of our strengths and limitations.

- **Scenario 973.** I volunteer at my church providing interpreting. Recently we had the rare occasion where, to our knowledge, no deaf or hard of hearing individuals attended the church service. After the service, a person, who attends our church and is a "registered interpreter for the deaf," approached the pastor who oversees the deaf ministry. This interpreter expressed her disgust with the fact that we provided interpreting when no one who required the services was present. This interpreter said she felt that "if a deaf person from the community knew about this, they would be seriously offended." Subsequently, we have been told that we must wait until a deaf or hard of hearing person is seated in the reserved section before interpreting. I feel this brings undue attention to the unsuspecting deaf or hard of hearing person who happens to arrive late, only to have the entire congregation notice someone now ascending to the platform to provide interpreting services. It also obliges people new to our church who might benefit from interpreting to sit in the reserved section. We also now run the risk of someone noticing the empty interpreting chair and leaving the service, assuming no interpreter is present. Are you aware of any protocol, guidelines or position statements I can provide our pastor which might help address this situation and resolve the issue?

AN NIC CANDIDATE'S PERSPECTIVE: I would follow the CPC Tenet 4.0, Respect for Consumers.

Tenet: 4.4 Facilitate communication access and equality and support the full interaction and independence of consumers.

Problem/Conflict: What are best practices in this situation? If a deaf consumer is not present, then should interpreting services still be provided? If a service or event is advertised as being interpreted, should it be interpreted regardless of anyone accessing the services?

Stakeholders' Perspectives:
1. *Deaf Consumer:* If an event is advertised as "interpreted," deaf consumers would assume interpreters will be providing interpreting regardless of whether the deaf consumer self-identifies or not. In a situation where services do not need to be requested ahead of time, deaf consumers are at their leisure to self-disclose their use of the interpreter or merely sit back and enjoy the communication access.
2. *Hearing Consumer:* The sight of an interpreter is a reminder of the need for accessibility of public events to deaf individuals and serves as a model for equal access.
3. *Interpreter – Congregation Member:* This interpreter may feel it is a waste of scarce interpreter resources to interpret when the need does not seem

to exist and that this type of "show" interpreting would offend the Deaf community. The interpreter may see the church as purporting themselves to be a deaf-friendly environment by setting up interpreters, but in reality, no deaf consumers are accessing the services.

Solution: If the service is advertised publicly as an interpreted service, then it needs to be interpreted. If there is a provision that persons requiring interpreting services self-identify and make a specific request for services, then interpreting should be provided if one of these specific individuals is in attendance.

Personal Experience: At one time I believed that I knew every deaf person that lived in my locale. I have come to realize that, in fact, I do not. Too many times I have been interpreting a platform public event where I thought no deaf people were in attendance, only to find out later they were. Deafness can be termed an "invisible" disability, meaning someone relying on an interpreter need not identify themselves ahead of time, and an interpreter or audience member may not be clear on who is or is not using the interpreter.

Resources: CPC 4.4

Implications:
1. *Short Term:* This fellow interpreter may be ticked at my decision to continue to provide services, but hopefully, after explaining the nature of church's advertisement, she will understand my choice.
2. *Long Term:* If interpreter services are consistently offered regardless of deaf consumer participation, the church will earn a reputation of consistency and equal access without necessitating deaf consumers prearranging services.

- **Scenario 974:** This week another ITP student and I were in the hallway talking and she was venting to me about one of her instructors. We were talking in a normal tone and did not see anyone around us, so we were not signing. However, a few minutes later, a hearing faculty member came out in the hall and told us that a deaf faculty member asked her to interpret our conversation. I understand that a deaf person has the right to equal access of communications, but this was a private conversation and not meant for others to hear. Do you think it was appropriate for this hearing faculty member to interpret our conversation without our knowledge? We feel that the deaf faculty member should have just come out in the hall herself and asked us what we were talking about.

AN NIC CANDIDATE'S PERSPECTIVE: I would follow the CPC Tenet 4.0, Respect for Consumers.

Tenet: 4.4 Facilitate communication access and equality.

Problem/Conflict: My desire to hold a private conversation versus the hearing faculty member's feelings of obligation to provide equal communication access for the deaf faculty member.

Stakeholders' Perspectives:
1. *Deaf Consumer:* Equal access means that if a hearing consumer could feasibly overhear enough to interpret, then that information should be provided to the deaf consumer as well. The deaf consumer may see this as a teachable moment and not want ITP students to think it is appropriate to hold private conversations in front of a deaf individual merely because that deaf person cannot hear. The deaf consumer feels it is appropriate for two individuals who want to have a private conversation to move to a private location where they cannot be overseen or overheard.
2. *Hearing Consumer:* If I was speaking loud enough for hearing faculty members to overhear, then they are within their rights to interpret what I am saying to ensure equal access to their fellow deaf faculty members. As faculty members and individuals working in the deaf community, they value communication access and also see this as a teachable moment.

Solution: If I want to have a private conversation, I probably should not stand near the office or classrooms of the faculty members I am talking about—hearing or deaf. This is a tough lesson to learn, and it sounds like a good opportunity for me to learn how to apologize to future colleagues.

Personal Experience: If I can hear it, I will be interpreting it. This seems a similar situation to the times when a hearing person asks me not to interpret something or "edit" my interpretation. By choosing what deaf people are and are not allowed to hear, we continue the pattern of paternalism and the idea that "hearing people know what is best" for deaf people.

Resources: CPC 4.4

Implications:
1. *Short Term:* Open mouth—insert foot. Hopefully if that situation occurred, my relationship/reputation in my interpreter program is merely tarnished and the two faculty members will be understanding regarding my mistake.
2. *Long Term:* Hopefully I will think twice before having a private or confidential conversation in a public location. As interpreters we deal with a lot of sensitive information, and not all settings are appropriate for divulging such information,

even with a team interpreter. Just as I never know who is listening—I also never know who is watching. I need to keep in mind that the door swings both ways, and I may be in an environment where I think I am the only person that knows sign language and be incorrect.

- **Scenario 975.** I am deaf and I work at an adult foster care home. I am aware of deaf consumers' rights to independence and their privacy. However, often our interpreters go out on assignments and observe blatant needs for advocacy (e.g., a home without proper heat), but the interpreter feels unsure about bringing this information to the attention of the home's management. Don't we need to work together for the best interest of the deaf consumer?

AN NIC CANDIDATE'S PERSPECTIVE: This scenario falls under the CPC Tenet 6.0, Business Practices.

Problem/Conflict: The conflict is: does the interpreter inform the appropriate parties about the lack of heat or not say anything about the situation? In the CPC, this conflict falls under Tenet 6.0, Business Practices, which states, "interpreters maintain ethical business practices." Additionally, Tenet 6.0, 6.3 states interpreters "promote conditions that are conducive to effective communication, inform the parties involved if such conditions do not exist, and seek appropriate remedies."

Stakeholders' Perspectives:
1. *Deaf Consumer:* In this situation the deaf consumer would not feel I am infringing on her rights because I am ensuring conditions are conducive to effective communication. The consumer would want the interpreter to be comfortable and able to sign efficiently. If the interpreter had cold hands and constantly felt chilled, it would be difficult to perform.
2. *Hearing Consumer:* If there was a hearing consumer present at the assignment, I'm sure he would want to be comfortable also. Most individuals have experienced a situation where having cold hands and being chilled has made it difficult to perform or concentrate to the best of their ability.
3. *Interpreter:* I would feel that I am taking the appropriate measures to make sure the client receives the information clearly and efficiently. I have interpreted assignments where my fingers/hands were cold and my ability to communicate suffers. The CPC states interpreters "promote conditions that are conductive to effective communication and inform the parties involved if such conditions do not exist." Therefore, it is my responsibility to address situations that would inhibit that communication.

Solution: I would inform the manager of the adult care home that the client does not have heat. However, before I did that, I would discuss the situation with the client. I could either inform management myself or go with the client.

Implications:
1. *Short term – Deaf Consumer*: The client would respect me for being concerned and taking appropriate steps to ensure communication of the message as accurately and clearly as possible.
2. *Hearing Consumer:* The manager may be upset at first but hopefully would understand through explanation how important "hands" are to effective communication.
3. *Interpreter:* I would feel good because the parties involved would be comfortable, and I would be doing my job to the best of my ability.
4. *Long term – Deaf Consumer*: The deaf consumer would appreciate an interpreter who follows the CPC and is vested in making sure the situation is conducive for effective communication. Also, the deaf consumer may want to utilize my services in the future and possibly share his experience with their friends in the deaf community.
5. *Interpreter:* I would feel I am known by the Deaf community as an interpreter who respects their rights to equal communication.

- **Scenario 976.** You show up at a court hearing for a deaf client, and you immediately recognize the police officer who will be testifying. Two days ago, he gave your son a ticket for reckless driving, and you gave him a piece of your mind! What would you do?

AN NIC CANDIDATE'S PERSPECTIVE: This scenario falls under the CPC Tenet 3.0, Conduct.

Problem/Conflict: The conflict in this situation is: does the interpreter continue the assignment or withdraw from the interpreting situation? Under the CPC, this conflict falls under Tenet 3.0, Conduct, which states, "interpreters conduct themselves in a manner that is appropriate to the specific interpreting situation." Additionally within Tenet 3.0, I would follow 3.7 and 3.8. 3.7 states interpreters "disclose any actual or perceived conflicts of interest," and 3.8 states interpreters "avoid any actual or perceived conflicts of interest that may harm or interfere with the effectiveness of interpreting services."

Stakeholders' Perspectives:
1. *Deaf Consumer:* The deaf consumer would not want anything to interfere with or influence the court hearing in a negative way. Initially, the consumer may not understand why I am withdrawing from the assignment, but once explained,

would appreciate the fact I did not continue, knowing there could be some bias that may harm the consumer's situation.

2. *Hearing Consumer:* The judge may be upset because I withdrew at the last moment but again, after explaining the conflict of interest, the judge would realize I acted in a responsible and reasonable manner.

3. *Interpreter:* I would not want to continue interpreting because of my reservations about my presence in the courtroom having a negative impact on the outcome. I would feel badly about the hearing being delayed, but I know I would be doing the right thing by following the CPC.

Solution: I would inform the parties that there is a conflict of interest due to my acquaintance with the officer and that in the best interest of the client I need to withdraw from the assignment. I would offer to assist in finding an alternate interpreter so that the hearing could take place as quickly as possible.

Implications:

1. *Short term – Deaf Consumer:* The client may be upset with me because he wants the hearing to take place. Initially, he might think I am irresponsible and may not want me to interpret for him at any other time.

2. *Hearing Consumers:* The judge and others involved in the process may be annoyed, thinking that their time was wasted, and not understand my decision.

3. *Long term – Deaf Consumer:* The deaf consumer would appreciate an interpreter who follows the CPC and takes her job seriously enough to create a possible uneasy situation for herself, but ultimately acts for the good of the deaf consumer. After understanding the reasoning behind my choice, the deaf consumer's respect for me would increase, and he would want me to interpret for him in the future.

4. *Interpreter:* I would hope the outcome of my decision would have a positive impact on how the client and deaf community feel about my ethics as an interpreter. I would hope the desire for my services would continue as the Deaf community experiences my dedication to follow the CPC.

- **Scenario 977.** In the middle of the minister's sermon, the deaf client falls asleep. You choose to continue interpreting anyway, but your partner will not. What do you do?

AN NIC CANDIDATE'S PERSPECTIVE: This scenario falls under the CPC Tenets 4.0, Respect for Consumers and 2.0, Professionalism.

Problem/Conflict: The conflict in this situation is: do I continue to interpret the message, especially since my colleague is not, or do I also stop interpreting until the client wakes up? Following the CPC, I would first address Tenet 4.0, Respect for Consumers, which states, "interpreters demonstrate respect for colleagues, interns, and students of the profession." Under 4.0 I would follow 4.4 which states interpreters "facilitate communication access and equality, and support the full interaction and independence of consumers."

Stakeholders' Perspectives:
1. *Deaf Consumer:* The deaf consumer feels she has a right to sleep if she wants to, but the interpreters are hired to "interpret," not pick and choose when they want to interpret. Plus, by not interpreting, I would draw more attention to the client sleeping.
2. *Colleague:* My colleague perhaps questions why he should continue interpreting the message if the client is sleeping, thus not receiving the message anyway.
3. *Hearing Consumer:* The hearing consumer may wonder why the interpreter has stopped signing since the minister is still speaking or why only one interpreter is signing. They may think the interpreters are rude.
4. *Interpreter:* I feel it is my responsibility to continue interpreting the message since that is what I was hired to do. Also, when the client does wake up, I will know what the speaker is talking about since I have been paying attention all along.

Solution: Tenet 2.0, Professionalism, states, "interpreters possess the professional skills and knowledge required for the specific interpreting situation." Under 2.0, 2.3 states interpreters "render the message faithfully by conveying the content and spirit of what is being communicated, using language that is readily understood by consumers, and correcting errors discreetly and expeditiously." Therefore, I would continue to render the message. The CPC does not give interpreters a choice in situations where the client is sleeping, not paying attention, etc.

Implications:
1. *Short term — Deaf Client:* The client may be upset when she wakes up and discovers no one is interpreting and the focus has been turned to her sleeping. If we continue interpreting, there will not be any ramifications to worry about.
2. *Hearing Consumer:* The hearing consumer may think the deaf consumer and interpreters were disrespectful if we did not continue signing the message. They may become irritated.
3. *Long term — Deaf Consumer:* The deaf consumer will appreciate an interpreter that follows the CPC by respecting deaf consumer rights. I think the deaf client will look favorably on the interpreter who continues no matter what the client is doing.
4. *Interpreter:* I think I would be viewed in a positive light in the future by the deaf consumer, speaker, and hearing audience. I would be thought of as a professional and someone consumers would like to work with at another time.

- **Scenario 978.** I just started working as an educational interpreter for the first time a few months ago, and I am very disappointed. My colleagues on staff are very comfortable in their paraprofessional role, but I was taught to consider myself a part of the professional educational team, so I work hard to maintain high professional standards for myself. I do not want to be considered a snob, but I worked hard to get a four-year degree in interpreting, and I want to be seen as the professional I was trained to be. What should I say or do?

AN NIC CANDIDATE'S PERSPECTIVE: This scenario falls under the CPC Tenet 5.0, Respect for Consumers.

Problem/Conflict: The conflict is: do I continue to follow my beliefs regarding interpreting as a "professional" career instead of "paraprofessional" and risk being thought of as a snob or succumb to the view of educational interpreting as a "paraprofessional" job?

The CPC 5.0 states, "interpreters demonstrate respect for colleagues, interns and students of the profession." Under Tenet 5.0, 5.1 states interpreters "maintain civility toward colleagues, interns and students."

Stakeholders' Perspectives:
1. *Deaf Consumer:* The deaf consumer would expect the interpreters to solve any problems among themselves and not have their personal feelings interfere with their interpreting assignment.
2. *Hearing Consumer:* The teachers involved would feel the same as the deaf consumer– that the interpreters should work things out between themselves and continue giving the client the information being conveyed.
3. *Interpreter:* I would be both civil and professional to my colleagues, but I would continue to consider myself the professional I worked so hard to become

Solution: I would continue to act in a manner that reflects I view interpreting as a professional career.

Implications:
1. *Short term – Deaf Consumer:* The deaf consumer would be appreciative that the interpreters are following the CPC.
2. *Hearing Consumers:* The teachers and other school professionals would expect the interpreters to behave in a professional manner and do the job for which they were hired.
3. *Interpreter:* I may have to deal with some adverse reactions from my colleagues if they are not willing to follow Tenet 5.0.
4. *Long term – Deaf Consumer:* The client would respect the interpreters who adhere to the CPC and be willing to work with these interpreters in the future.

5. *Hearing Consumers:* The hearing consumers as well would respect the interpreters who adhere to the CPC and be willing to work with them in the future.

6. *Interpreter:* I would hope more interpreters in the future would take on the professional outlook of being an interpreter. As more interpreters join the field, more will follow suit with the knowledge of the skills needed to interpret.

- **Scenario 979.** Sometimes during lectures, students do not watch the interpreter for an extended period of time. They may be reading something (unrelated to class), text messaging someone, or sleeping. When this happens, I tend to shrink my signing space to conserve energy, but I still keep up with the lecture. When the student looks up, I bring my signing back to normal. When I asked other interpreters how they handle this situation, I have gotten responses ranging from keep signing as usual to stop interpreting. Is there an accepted/expected action to this situation of which you are aware?

AN NIC CANDIDATE'S PERSPECTIVE: This scenario falls under the CPC Tenet 4.0, Respect for Consumers.

Problem/Conflict: The conflict in this situation is: do I continue to interpret the message when the students are distracted or stop signing until the students are again paying attention? Since the students are attending a lecture, I assume they are older, which places the responsibility of focusing on the lecture on the student. Therefore under the CPC, I would first address Tenet 4.0, Respect for Consumers, which states, "interpreters demonstrate respect for consumers." Under 4.0, I would follow 4.4 which states interpreters "facilitate communication access and equality, and support the full interaction and independence of consumers."

Stakeholders' Perspectives:
1. *Deaf Consumer:* As I mentioned before, these students are attending a lecture; they are not grade school students who need more direction. The deaf consumers would feel it is their responsibility to get whatever information from the lecture that they want. An older student would not want the interpreter to "scold" them by insisting they pay attention.

2. *Hearing Consumer:* The person giving the lecture may not even notice the students are sending text messages or otherwise not paying attention, and by my continued signing, focus would not be turned to the students. With older students, the lecturer would want to be the one to make any comments regarding their behavior instead of the interpreter.

3. *Interpreter:* At this point in their education, it is not my responsibility to interject regarding what the students are doing during a lecture. I was hired

to interpret, and as long as I am continuing to do so, I am fulfilling my commitment.

Solution: I would continue to sign the message until the lecture is completed.

Implications:
1. *Short term – Deaf Consumer:* The clients will respect me for not drawing attention to them when they send text messages, do not pay attention, or sleep.
2. *Hearing Consumers:* The hearing consumer may think the deaf consumer and interpreter were being disrespectful if I did not continue signing the message.
3. *Interpreter:* I know I am doing the job I was hired to do.
4. *Long term – Deaf Consumer:* The deaf consumers would have more respect for the interpreter because they know what their rights are and what role the interpreter plays in their education.
5. *Hearing Consumer:* The hearing consumer will appreciate the role the interpreter plays in the student's education at this point. Also, the hearing students will respect the occurrence of equal treatment for the deaf students and themselves.
6. *Interpreter:* The person giving the lecture and the students would see my role as a professional, not an enabler, and would look favorably on an interpreter in their class in the future.

- **Scenario 980:** I recently interpreted for a conference with over 10,000, mostly hearing participants. The conference coordinators were an interpreter's dream; they gave us practically minute by minute schedules for each day, as well as song lyrics and scripts of the presentations. I wanted to divide the information in advance so I could prepare, but my team interpreter said she did not want to do anything until the day of the conference. I did not press the issue, but I was incredibly frustrated. What do you think we should have done?

AN NIC CANDIDATE'S PERSPECTIVE: This scenario falls under the CPC Tenet 5.0, Respect for Colleagues.

Problem/Conflict: The conflict in this situation is: do I discuss with my team the importance of preparation or hope the other interpreter can handle the assignment without preparing beforehand? Under the CPC, this conflict is within 5.0, Respect for Colleagues, which states, "interpreters demonstrate respect for colleagues, interns and students of the profession." Additionally, Tenet 5.0, 5.2 states interpreters "work cooperatively with team members through consultation prior to the assignment, providing courteous and professional assistance when needed, monitoring the accuracy of the message while functioning in the role of the support interpreter."

Stakeholders' Perspectives:

1. *Deaf Consumer:* The deaf consumer would be upset if they knew an interpreter received materials prior to an assignment but did not take time to prepare. The deaf consumer would expect the message to be delivered as efficiently as possible.
2. *Hearing Consumer:* The hearing consumer wants the deaf consumer to receive the same message as the hearing audience.
3. *Interpreter:* I want my team interpreter to be at their best no matter what the interpreting assignment. I would hope an interpreter would have more respect for their profession.

Solution: I will continue to interpret the conference to the best of my ability until it is over. Then I would have a conversation with the interpreter that did not prepare. If the interpreter felt it was not necessary to prepare ahead of time, I would not agree to team with her again.

Implications:

1. *Short term – Deaf Consumer:* The client would be extremely upset knowing the other interpreter came to the assignment unprepared.
2. *Hearing Consumer:* The hearing consumer sent the documents in advance so the interpreters could prepare. Delivering the message accurately was obviously important enough that time was taken to make sure the interpreters had the information beforehand.
3. *Long term – Deaf Consumer:* For future assignments, the deaf consumer would want the interpreter who took the job seriously enough to prepare ahead of time. The deaf consumer would speak highly of the prepared interpreter in the deaf community.
4. *Hearing Consumer:* The hearing consumer would prefer to hire interpreters that prepare and therefore have a better possibility of conveying the spirit and content of the message.
5. *Interpreter:* I would refrain from interpreting with that colleague in the future unless the situation could be resolved and I was assured that nothing like that would happen again.

- **Scenario 981.** I recently interpreted an employee training workshop. During the break the deaf client left, and several of the employees were chatting. One employee started telling really offensive jokes. As a member of several minority groups (Jewish, Polish, Gay), what are my rights? I was not personally being harassed, but do we have rights in this situation?

AN NIC CANDIDATE'S PERSPECTIVE: This scenario falls under the CPC
Tenets 2.0, Professionalism, and 3.0, Conduct.

Problem/Conflict: The conflict in this situation is: if I continue interpreting, would
I be able to stay impartial, or would it be best to withdraw from the interpreting
situation? I would follow 2.0, Professionalism, which states interpreters "possess
the professional skills and knowledge required for a particular interpreting
situation." Tenet 2.0, 2.3 states interpreters should "render the message faithfully
conveying the spirit and content of the message being communicated in a language
that is readily understood by the consumer, correcting errors discreetly and
expeditiously." Also, I would follow Tenet 3.0, Conduct, which states, "interpreters
conduct themselves in a manner that is appropriate to a specific interpreting
situation." Under Tenet 3.0, 3.7 and 3.8 would apply because they both deal with an
"actual or perceived conflict of interest."

Stakeholders' Perspectives:
1. *Deaf Consumer:* The deaf consumer would expect me to continue to interpret
   the job for which I was hired and put my personal feelings aside.
2. *Hearing Consumer:* The hearing consumer would not be aware of any conflict
   at this point unless I confronted them regarding their comments. Therefore, they
   would expect to see me interpreting the rest of the training.
3. *Interpreter:* No matter how I feel about what was said by the other employees,
   it is my responsibility to finish the job for which I was hired. Under the CPC,
   my obligation is to render the message faithfully. At a later point, I could decide
   whether interpreting for that assignment would be a conflict.

Solution: I would continue to do the job for which I was hired but would avoid,
if possible, interpreting for this group in the future. I would keep my feelings to
myself, but it is something I would not easily forget.

Implications:
1. *Short term – Deaf Consumer:* If I let the comments interfere with my delivery
   of the message, it could affect the accuracy of what the client receives, which
   would be unethical.
2. *Hearing Consumer:* The hearing consumers would wonder what was wrong
   if I stopped interpreting. By not finishing the assignment, I would put a lot of
   unnecessary focus on the client.
3. *Interpreter:* I would continue to interpret the rest of the training and put my
   personal feelings aside.
4. *Long term - Deaf Consumer:* The deaf consumer would expect me to finish the
   job but would not want me to interpret in the future if I could not refrain from
   interjecting my own personal feelings.

5. *Hearing Consumer:* Depending on the employees and if they're aware of the situation, they may understand how I felt and be more careful in the future about making inappropriate jokes.
6. *Interpreter:* I would not interpret for this training in the future if I felt personally offended.

- **Scenario 982:** I interpret weekly AA meetings. Tonight my partner showed up looking especially haggard and under the weather, so I inquired about her health. She responded by saying she "had a really massive hangover" and started laughing. I did not find this at all humorous, but maybe I'm overreacting?

AN NIC CANDIDATE'S PERSPECTIVE: This scenario falls under the CPC Tenet 5.0, Respect for Colleagues.

Problem/Conflict: The conflict in this situation is: do I discuss the issue with my team member regarding coming to an assignment hungover or not?
Under the CPC, this conflict falls under 5.0, Respect for Colleagues, which states, "interpreters demonstrate respect for colleagues, interns and students of the profession." Additionally, Tenet 5.0, 5.3 states interpreters "approach team members to discuss and resolve breaches of ethical and professional conduct through the standard resolution conflict methods, file a grievance only when such attempts are unsuccessful or when breaches are harmful or habitual."

Stakeholders' Perspectives:
1. *Deaf Consumer:* I think it is obvious how unhappy a client would be to know an interpreter came to a scheduled assignment hungover, especially an AA meeting.
2. *Hearing Consumer:* The hearing consumers/participants would find the interpreter's condition inappropriate to say the least, especially under the circumstances.
3. *Interpreter:* I want my team interpreter to be at their best no matter what the interpreting assignment. I would hope an interpreter would have more respect for their profession.

Solution: I would continue interpreting the message with my partner, but I would have a conversation with her after the meeting. I think it is only fair to her and me that I let her know how I feel about having a team person performing at their best. I would express my concern regarding her lack of respect for the profession, and also for the type of meeting being interpreted.

Implications:

1. *Short term – Deaf Consumer:* The client would be extremely upset knowing the other interpreter came to the assignment hung over. The client may see AA meetings as a significant part of their sobriety and feel it is extremely rude of the interpreter to come to any assignment hungover, let alone an AA meeting.
2. *Hearing Consumers:* Many AA members take meetings seriously, would be offended by a hungover interpreter, and would probably question the interpreting profession.
3. *Long term – Deaf Consumer:* The deaf consumer would not want the interpreter to interpret in the future.
4. *Hearing Consumers:* The hearing consumer may lose respect for interpreters for future assignments or until they have had positive experiences with interpreters.
5. *Interpreter:* I would refrain from interpreting with that colleague in the future unless the situation could be resolved and I was assured nothing like that would happen in the future.

   - **Scenario 983.** Recently after interpreting a meeting between a deaf client and his supervisor, the deaf client asked me to write my own account of what transpired in the meeting. I said I could not do this because it would reflect my own personal opinion. The client then asked me if I would mind writing down what he signed to me but in English. I agreed because I felt that this was the same as interpreting the information. Later, however, I wondered if what I did could be considered "recorded interpretation," which places more responsibility for the information on the interpreter.

AN NIC CANDIDATE'S PERSPECTIVE: This scenario falls under the CPC Tenet 2.0, Professionalism.

Problem/Conflict: The conflict in this situation is: do I write down what transpired in the meeting or what the client signed to me, or do I indicate I cannot comply with their request?

From the beginning of this situation, I would follow the (CPC) Tenet 2.0, which indicates that interpreters "possess the professional skills and knowledge required for a specific interpreting situation." Tenet 2.0, 2.5 indicates that interpreters "refrain from providing advice, counsel or personal opinions."

Stakeholders' Perspectives:

1. *Deaf Consumer:* When the deaf consumer asks me, he may not realize it is hard to retain information while interpreting and be able to write it down later. Also, he may not be thinking how the CPC would apply in this situation.
2. *Hearing Consumer:* The hearing consumer would question the accuracy of the message written down after the provision of the assignment.

3. *Interpreter:* I would indicate to the client that I question my ability to remember accurately what he signed to me during the meeting. I feel writing down information after an assignment is completed would put my professional career in jeopardy. I would not want to be held accountable for any discrepancies.

Solution: I would explain to the client it is difficult to retain information that was interpreted. I would explain that because we are working with processing two different languages, retention is very limited and I would be concerned about the accuracy of what I would write.

Implications:
1. *Short term – Deaf Consumer:* Initially the client might feel upset with me. The client could look at me as being unreasonable and rude.
2. *Hearing Consumer:* The hearing supervisor would wonder how I could write down information for the client without interjecting my personal opinion. This situation could give the hearing consumer a negative impression of interpreters.
3. *Interpreter:* At first I might feel as if I was in the middle of the situation, even though I know I am ethically doing the right thing.
4. *Long term – Deaf Consumer:* The deaf consumer may not understand my reasoning nor want me to interpret in the future. The client may share with their family and friends that I was not very helpful, which could be bad for my reputation as an interpreter. On the other hand, they may appreciate and respect me for following the CPC.
5. *Hearing Consumer:* The hearing consumer will have a positive experience working with an interpreter and will feel comfortable using one in the future.
6. *Interpreter:* Part of an interpreter's responsibility is to educate the hearing consumer. If this is done in an effective way, the relationship between the deaf consumer, hearing consumer and interpreter will run smoothly. This positive working relationship between the parties can only benefit me and other interpreters coming into the profession.

- **Scenario 984.** During some downtime on a recent interpreting job, my client asked me how I was doing. Usually just "fine" works, but today her concern was so touching that I ended up getting weepy and telling her more than I should about my personal life. After the break, I was still trying to get a hold of my emotions and felt like such a fool, but the assignment would not be over for another three hours. What should I do?

AN NIC CANDIDATE'S PERSPECTIVE: This scenario falls under CPC Tenet 6.0, Business Practices.

Problem/Conflict: The conflict in this situation is: do I continue to interpret the assignment or not?

Under the CPC, I would follow 6.0, Business Practices, which states, "interpreters maintain ethical business practices." Tenet 6.0, 6.2 states interpreters "honor professional commitments and terminate assignments only when fair and justifiable grounds exist."

Stakeholders' Perspectives:
1. *Deaf Consumer:* The deaf consumer may not have had a problem with my becoming emotional, but the client would expect that I be able to put my emotions aside and continue interpreting until the assignment is completed. The deaf consumer would definitely not see any justifiable reason to terminate the assignment.
2. *Hearing Consumer:* The hearing consumer would also expect that I "get myself together" and continue the job as assigned.
3. *Interpreter:* I would adhere to 6.2 and continue the assignment because I was the one who became emotional during a job that had already started. If I had emotional problems before the assignment, I may be able to use Tenet 3.0, Conduct, 3.2 which states that an interpreter can "decline assignments or withdraw from the interpreting profession when not competent due to physical, mental or emotional factors." However, it is fully my responsibility to continue the assignment working efficiently and effectively.

Solution: I would continue to interpret until the assignment was finished.

Implications:
1. *Short term – Deaf Consumer:* The client would rightfully feel upset if I terminated the assignment at this point. On the other hand, she would see I have a human side but I am able to compose myself and continue to interpret in a professional manner.
2. *Hearing Consumer:* The hearing consumer would understand we are all human, and situations occur that we do not expect, but they would feel it is my obligation to complete the assignment.
3. *Interpreter:* I may be a little unsteady at first, but it would not take long for me to be interpreting as I did prior to my release of emotions.
4. *Long term – Deaf Consumer:* The deaf consumer would appreciate the fact I also have a caring/emotional side to me and respect me for putting those emotions aside and finishing the assignment as hired. The client would appreciate an interpreter who follows the CPC in respecting deaf consumer rights. I think the deaf client will look favorably on the interpreter who continues no matter what distraction has occurred.
5. *Hearing Consumer:* The hearing consumer would enjoy working with me in the future after observing how I take my assignments seriously by getting myself back together and returning to interpreting in a professional manner.

6. *Interpreter*: I think I would be looked on in a positive light in the future by the deaf consumer, speaker, and hearing audience. I would be viewed as professional and an interpreter who consumers would like to work with at another time.

- **Scenario 985.** I was working as a substitute for an educational interpreter who did not tell me there was a test scheduled for that day. When I arrived, the deaf student handed me a blank piece of paper and told me to write down the answers that he would sign to me. Obviously, this is what they have established for this situation, but what is your opinion of this practice?

AN NIC CANDIDATE'S PERSPECTIVE: This scenario falls under the CPC Tenet 3.0, Conduct.

Problem/Conflict: The conflict in this situation is: do I continue to write down the answers for the student as the other interpreter did, or follow my belief that writing down the answers for the student is not the responsibility of the interpreter?
I would adhere to the CPC Tenet 3.0 which states, "interpreters conduct themselves in a manner appropriate to the specific interpreting situation." Tenet 3.0, 3.3 states interpreters should "avoid performing dual or conflicting roles in interdisciplinary or other settings."

Stakeholders' Perspectives:
1. *Deaf Consumer:* The student may not understand why I would not want to write the answers since the other interpreter did. The student may feel I am being mean and uncooperative.
2. *Hearing Consumer:* The teacher may not have realized the other interpreter was doing the student's work. I do not think the teacher would approve of that since the other students in the class are writing themselves. The other students would feel the deaf student is getting special treatment.
3. *Interpreter:* I feel it is the student's responsibility to write his own answers. I am there to facilitate communication; not do his work for him.
4. *Solution:* I would not write down the answers for the student, and I would explain if the student asks me why I will not.

Implications:
1. *Short term – Deaf Consumer:* The client may be angry with me and not want me to interpret anymore. The client may act out and complain that the "other" interpreter would write his answers.
2. *Hearing Consumer:* The teacher would appreciate that I did not give the deaf student preferential treatment, and if the teacher saw the student get upset, it could be explained why it is important for the student to do his own work.

3. *Interpreter:* The situation may become awkward if the student gets upset with me, and a conversation may have to take place between the teacher, student, and myself.

4. *Long term – Deaf Consumer:* The student may not understand immediately, but hopefully as time passes he will better understand an interpreter's role and appreciate the benefit he gets from doing his own work. The student will also be thankful that a conflict was avoided from the hearing students thinking the deaf consumer was getting special help.

5. *Hearing Consumers:* The teacher will be grateful the interpreter did not cross interdisciplinary lines and interfere with the teaching process. The relationship between the deaf student and hearing students will be more positive with treatment being equal.

6. *Interpreter:* I would sit down with the other interpreter and explain my feelings about an interpreter's role and following the CPC. If the interpreter refused to follow the CPC, I would have a discussion with the teacher and/or principal. I know I would be taking the chance that I would not be called to substitute again, but I also would know I did what was in the best interest of the student and the interpreting profession.

- **Scenario 986.** I have a question I am hoping you can answer. Every Friday afternoon, I go to an interpreter referral agency for their social event. Oftentimes there are beginning sign students at the event who have a really hard time understanding anything the deaf people are saying. They often ask me what people are saying when they do not understand. I have no problem helping them, but I always wonder if it is appropriate. Sometimes I get the feeling the deaf person wants them to figure it out on their own, so I do not want to just give them the answers. However, then the students get frustrated and keep asking me. It is a very relaxed and comfortable setting, but I feel awkward during those times because I am not sure what to do.

AN NIC CANDIDATE'S PERSPECTIVE: This scenario falls under the CPC Tenet 2.0, Professionalism.

Problem/Conflict: The conflict in this situation is: do I continue to help the students or stay out of the situation unless asked?
I would follow the CPC 2.0, which states interpreters "possess the professional skills and knowledge required for a specific interpreting situation." Tenet 2.0, 2.6 indicates that interpreters "judiciously provide information or referral regarding available interpreting or community recourses without infringing upon consumer's rights."

Stakeholders' Perspectives:
1. *Deaf Consumer:* The deaf consumers may appreciate the assistance with the students but also feel they do not need to be "taken care of."
2. *Hearing Consumer:* The students may feel nervous and frustrated, but they would learn it is a safe environment. The students may not be familiar with the CPC and not understand at first why I would not be assisting in their communication with the deaf consumer.
3. *Interpreter:* I would look for cues from the deaf consumers indicating if they want assistance or not. If not, I would talk with the students and encourage them to think of the situation as a "teachable moment" and do the best they can.

Solution: I would wait for the deaf consumers to indicate if they wanted my assistance. I think it is only fair and respectful that I let the consumers make the decisions on what they need.

Implications:
1. *Short term – Deaf Consumer:* The deaf consumers would appreciate the students' willingness to attempt to communicate on their own and would respect me, the interpreter, for not infringing on their rights.
2. *Hearing Consumer:* The students will feel more comfortable interacting with deaf consumers the more experience they have interacting without outside assistance.
3. *Interpreter:* Tenet 2.0, 2.6 states to "provide information without infringing upon consumer's rights." I feel short term the deaf consumer would appreciate me following the CPC and also for setting clear boundaries.
4. *Long term – Deaf Consumer:* In the long term, the deaf consumers would see that as an interpreter I am acting as a facilitator of communication, not a "helper," and that I respect their privacy to carry on a conversation. The deaf consumers would look more favorably upon the interpreting profession.
5. *Hearing Consumer:* The students would gain more confidence and realize not all interpreting jobs will be easy. The students will observe different styles of signing which will be beneficial to their developing skills.
6. *Interpreter:* I will feel good about myself for following the CPC. I will be pleased the students had a safe learning experience and that the deaf consumers may want to utilize my services for appointments in the future.

- **Scenario 987.** One of the other interpreters at the hospital where I work wants me to interpret for her mother when she comes in next week as a patient. Is this unethical?

AN NIC CANDIDATE'S PERSPECTIVE: This scenario falls under the CPC Tenet 3.0, Professionalism.

Problem/Conflict: The conflict in this situation is: do I interpret for my friend's mother or tell her I do not think it would be ethical?

I would follow the CPC 3.0, which states, "interpreters conduct themselves in a manner appropriate to the specific interpreting situation." Tenet 3.0, 3.8 states that interpreters "avoid actual or perceived conflicts of interest that might cause harm or interfere with the effectiveness of interpreting services."

Stakeholders' Perspectives:
1. *Deaf Consumer:* The deaf consumer would want an interpreter who possesses the skills and knowledge needed for the assignment. My friend's mother may not have any strong feelings as to whether I was the interpreter or another equally qualified interpreter was hired.
2. *Hearing Consumer:* If I refuse the job, my friend may be upset with me initially. My friend knows my skills and the patient is "her mother," so of course she is concerned her mother gets the best qualified interpreter she knows.
3. *Interpreter:* I am honored my friend asked me and trusts me to interpret at a medical appointment for her mother. However, I cherish the relationship with my friend and would never want to do anything to jeopardize our friendship. I would not want to be in a position of knowing information that could come up in an appointment that my friend did not know. I would not want to be privy to confidential information not shared between my friend and her mother.

Solution: I would not interpret for my friend's mother as I would not want to jeopardize my friendship or my profession.

Implications:
1. *Short term – Deaf Consumer:* My friend's mother might be upset at first until a thorough explanation is given as to why my interpreting for her would be a violation of the CPC.
2. *Hearing Consumer:* My friend may feel I am being unreasonable. She may not want to talk to me for a while.
3. *Interpreter:* At first my friend might be mad at me, but I would explain to her the reason behind my decision. Also, I would help my friend find another interpreter she would feel comfortable having interpret for her mother.
4. *Long term – Deaf Consumer:* I think the deaf consumer would understand my position after I explained the ethical dilemma that could occur should a routine check-up ever turn into something serious. The deaf consumer would respect me for being able to keep my professional boundaries separate from my personal relationships.

5. *Hearing Consumer:* Since the friend who asked me to interpret for her mother is an interpreter also, she would understand the predicament in which I would be placed if I accepted an assignment to interpret for her mother. My friend would not want to put me in a potentially bad situation, nor would I to her.

6. *Interpreter:* I think not accepting the interpreting job for my friend's mother would reinforce to both of them how seriously I take my profession. My friend and her mother would respect me and share with their friends in the deaf community my ability to follow the CPC. I would potentially have an increase in assignments in the future.

- **Scenario 988.** The client has asked for a new interpreter because I have missed several appointments due to health reasons and am looking at surgery in the near future. She says that since I am unsure of my surgery date and future health status, it may cause me to be undependable. She also insists that I stand, but my doctor says I need to be off my feet as much as possible. Is this even legal? I am so frustrated.

AN NIC CANDIDATE'S PERSPECTIVE: This scenario falls under the CPC Tenet 3.0, Conduct.

Problem/Conflict: The conflict in this situation is: do I continue to sit when the client asked me to stand, and do I make an issue out of the fact that the client wants another interpreter?

I would follow the CPC 3.0, which states, "interpreters conduct themselves in a manner appropriate to the specific interpreting situation." Tenet 3.0, 3.2 states that interpreters "decline assignments or withdraw from the interpreting profession when not competent due to physical, mental, or emotional factors."

Stakeholders' Perspectives:

1. *Deaf Consumer:* The client feels she has the right to her preference as to whether the interpreter sits or stands and to ensure the interpreter facilitating her communication is dependable. The client needs to feel comfortable that all assignments will be covered.

2. *Hearing Consumer:* The hearing consumer would feel that if the interpreter is unable to fulfill the requirements of the assignment, the interpreter should withdraw from the assignment when no longer physically able to perform the duties.

3. *Interpreter:* I feel the deaf consumer does have the right to choose if the interpreter sits or stands. I also feel I would withdraw from the interpreting job because I can no longer fulfill my obligation in the manner required. I would consider myself no longer "competent due to physical factors."

Solution: I would go along with the wishes of the client and, if applicable, the agency that hired me.

Implications:
1. *Short term – Deaf Consumer:* The client would have more respect for me if I admitted I could no longer do the job as required. The client would be frustrated with me if I insisted on interpreting regardless of her feelings.
2. *Hearing Consumer:* The hearing consumer would respect an interpreter who focuses on what is best for the client. The hearing consumer would have a positive outlook on interpreters.
3. *Interpreter:* I would feel badly that I could not perform the job in the way my client desired. I would withdraw from the assignment even though I would feel disappointed in losing the job. I would assist in finding a replacement interpreter.
4. *Long term – Deaf Consumer:* My reaction to my client's wishes will impact how the client feels about utilizing my services in the future. If I react negatively, the deaf consumer would not want me to be hired after my surgery and would share my conduct with her friends. Therefore, it's possible other deaf consumers would not want me to interpret for them at any of their assignments.
5. *Hearing Consumer:* A positive interaction between the client and me will set the stage for how a hearing consumer feels about the interpreting profession in the future. If the experience for the hearing consumer is positive, they would look favorably on utilizing interpreters at future events.
6. *Interpreter:* How I handle this situation could affect how the client thinks about me and my reputation in the Deaf community. If I treat my client with respect, in the short term and long term, I will be treated with respect.

   •   **Scenario 989.** If I am in a meeting as a participant (not interpreting) and I hear the interpreter totally blowing the voicing, what do you think I should I do?

AN NIC CANDIDATE'S PERSPECTIVE: This scenario falls under the CPC Tenet 3.0, Conduct.

Problem/Conflict: The conflict in this situation is: do I inform the appropriate parties regarding the interpreter voicing incorrectly, or do I ignore the situation?
   I would follow the CPC Tenet 3.0, which states, "interpreters conduct themselves in a manner appropriate to the specific interpreting situation." Tenet 3.0, 3.4 states interpreters "comply with established workplace codes of conduct, notify appropriate personnel if there is a conflict with this CPC and actively seek resolution where warranted."

Stakeholders' Perspectives:

1. *Deaf Consumer:* The client has the right to have the message he is communicating conveyed accurately. The deaf consumer would be angry to find out after the meeting was over that what the interpreter voiced was nothing close to what he signed, especially if someone knew that the interpreter voicing was lacking the skills to perform the duty.

2. *Hearing Consumer:* The hearing consumer would be upset if the message voiced is inaccurate. Their response to the deaf consumer depends on how they receive the message being voiced by the interpreter.

3. *Interpreter:* I feel that even if I am only a participant, it is still my job as an interpreter to follow the CPC, Tenet 3.0, 3.4. I could not possibly live with a clear conscience if I did not convey to the appropriate parties, possibly the interpreter, that there was a problem with the accuracy of the message being voiced.

Solution: I would first talk with the interpreter either on a break or during lunch. Even though I am not a working interpreter at this function, I feel Tenet 5.0, 5.3, which states interpreters "approach colleagues privately," still applies. It is only fair I tell the interpreter, as professionally as I can, my observation regarding the accuracy of the message being voiced.

Implications:

1. *Short term – Deaf Consumer:* The client would either want another interpreter or would want a team to help.

2. *Hearing Consumer:* The hearing consumer would respect an interpreter who focuses on what is best for the client. The hearing consumer would have a positive outlook on interpreters.

3. *Interpreter:* The interpreter on duty may feel very embarrassed and hurt at first, but later would understand that being aware of the inaccuracies is very important. I know that I would want a fellow interpreter to confront me in a positive manner if the situation was reversed.

4. *Long term – Deaf Consumer:* If the interpreter on duty handled the situation professionally and worked on improving his skills, the deaf consumer may want to utilize his services at a later date.

5. *Hearing Consumer:* The hearing consumer would feel the same as the deaf consumer; how the interpreter reacts to the feedback will determine if their services will be requested in the future.

6. *Interpreter:* As the person giving the feedback, I would feel in good conscience I did the right thing. I kept in mind the rights of the deaf consumer and the hearing consumer. If appropriate, I could offer to work with the interpreter and help with his voicing skills.

- **Scenario 990.** What do I do if the university where I work wants me to tell them if the student does not show up? Would this be a breach of confidentiality? I also do not want to be asked to go interpret somewhere else instead, but neither do I want to risk losing pay. What do you think about this?

AN NIC CANDIDATE'S PERSPECTIVE: This scenario falls under the CPC Tenets 1.0, Confidentiality and 3.0, Conduct.

Problem/Conflict: The conflict in this situation is: do I keep quiet or do I let the university know when the student does not show up for class?

I would follow the CPC Tenet 1.0, 1.1, which states interpreters "share assignment-related information on confidential and 'as needed' basis" (e.g., supervisors, interpreter team members, members of the educational team, hiring entities). Also, I would adhere to Tenet 3.0, 3.4 which states interpreters "comply with established workplace codes of conduct, notify appropriate personnel if there is a conflict with this Code of Professional Conduct and actively seek resolution where warranted."

Stakeholders' Perspectives:
1. *Deaf Consumer:* The client may feel I am breaking confidentiality by informing the university when he does not show up. The client may also feel it is not the university's business if he goes to class or not--that he is paying for the class.
2. *Hearing Consumer:* The hearing consumer feels since they pay me it is their right to know if the student comes to class or not. The university would feel I am being insubordinate by not responding to their request.
3. *Interpreter:* I would not like that the student would feel I was being unethical, but I would have to follow the CPC. I would adhere to the CPC because I cannot pick and choose when I want to follow it depending on my personal feelings. The university hired me and Tenet 1.1 references "hiring entities" and 3.04 references "established workplace code of conduct."

Solution: As asked, I would let the university know when the student does not show up for class. I feel is my responsibility under the CPC and also because the university is my employer.

Implications:
1. *Short term – Deaf Consumer:* The client may feel I am breaking the CPC, become angry, and not want me to interpret for the rest of that class or any other time.
2. *Hearing Consumer:* If I did not let the university know about the student's attendance, I may be disciplined or even fired.
3. *Interpreter:* I could experience some difficulties with the student. I may have to talk with the instructor regarding the situation or have my supervisor schedule a meeting between all parties. I think initially the situation would be very tense.

4. *Long term – Deaf Consumer:* The student may not want me to interpret in the future. Hopefully, after explaining my obligation to the CPC and the university, the student will understand I did not have a choice and will continue to want to work with me.
5. *Hearing Consumer:* The university will respect me for honoring my professional responsibility, both to them and the CPC. The university would view me as honest and cooperative and would hire me for more interpreting assignments in the future. They will see me as part of the team and will think positively about working with interpreters.
6. *Interpreter:* If the student does not understand why I had to inform the university regarding their attendance, the student may not want to utilize my services in the future. I could also get a bad name in the Deaf community. However, if the student understands I am loyal to the interpreting profession, my client, and employer, he will respect me and request to have me interpret for future classes.

- **Scenario 991.** In our area, we provide 24-hour interpreting services for various nursing home patients who are in the hospital. One specific situation I encountered was interpreting for a deaf patient in ICU who had just had major surgery. Oftentimes, the patient was disoriented and confused. While the previous interpreter was on duty, the patient pulled out his IV tube in his sleep. When I come in to interpret for this patient, I see the patient is asleep and pulling on his IV tube. What should I do?

AN NIC CANDIDATE'S PERSPECTIVE: This scenario falls under the CPC Tenet 2.0, Professionalism.

Problem/Conflict: The conflict in this situation is: do I let appropriate personnel know what is taking place, or ignore it and wait for a nurse or doctor to come into the room and discover the situation?

I would follow CPC 2.0, which states interpreters "possess the professional skills and knowledge required for a specific interpreting situation." Tenet 2.0, 2.2 states interpreters "assess consumer needs and the interpreting situation before and during the assignment and make adjustments as needed."

Stakeholders' Perspectives:
1. *Deaf Consumer:* The deaf consumer at this point is unable to convey what is happening. The client would want me to intervene so there can be communication between him, a nurse or doctor, and myself. He would not want anything to happen such that he is harmed.
2. *Hearing Consumer:* The hospital personnel and family would be grateful I assessed the situation and attended to the client's needs.
3. *Interpreter:* Since it is my responsibility under CPC 2.2 to "assess consumer needs," I would be negligent if I did not let appropriate hospital personnel be

aware of the situation. I had a similar situation happen in a nursing home, and I had to seek a staff person to handle the safety of the patient while I facilitated the communication. All stakeholders were grateful for my action.

Solution: I would inform the appropriate personnel regarding the unsafe situation my client may be getting into.

Implications:

1. *Short term – Deaf Consumer:* The client may not understand at that moment what is happening but later would respect the fact that I followed the CPC and facilitated communication to assure his safety.
2. *Hearing Consumer:* The hospital personnel would be thankful for being made aware of the situation to prevent the client from unknowingly harming himself, especially since the client is in ICU. I think the hospital would have a better appreciation for the role an interpreter plays.
3. *Interpreter:* I would feel good I took the appropriate action by following Tenet 2.0, and I also would be relieved that the client was not hurt.
4. *Long term – Deaf Consumer:* Once the deaf consumer was aware of my actions, he would be pleased and feel extremely confident about my abilities as an interpreter. The client may share his trust of my actions with his friends in the Deaf community.
5. *Hearing Consumers:* The hospital personnel would enjoy working with me. They would have a good experience with an interpreter, which would set the stage for upcoming interpreters at the hospital. The family, either deaf or hearing, would respect me for making a prompt, accurate decision. The family's trust in me would increase immediately and for any assignment in the future.
6. *Interpreter:* I would be proud I established a higher level of trust with my client and also the Deaf community. I would suspect this increase in trust would open up more possibilities for me in my profession.

- **Scenario 992.** Another interpreter seems to have made it her mission to convert me. She treats every conversation as if it is a chance to make points about her religious beliefs. I cannot even congratulate her for getting shoes on sale without her saying something like, "The Lord favors his own!" If we are teaming together she'll say, "Oh, last night I was thinking about interpreting today, and the Lord told me we should." I have heard her on her cell phone during breaks with her church friends all pumped up about how "people are going to try to shut you up, but you've got to speak up for Jesus." I keep telling her I am not a believer, but my inclination to be respectful of others' views seems to put me at a disadvantage with someone who does not respect mine.

AN NIC CANDIDATE'S PERSPECTIVE: This scenario falls under the CPC
Tenets 5.0, Respect for Colleagues, and 3.0, Conduct.

Problem/Conflict: My partner is trying to force her religious beliefs on me, and I
am not comfortable with that. The work place is not an appropriate venue to be
discussing these things when we are both trying to work. Do I let it continue or
speak up and say something?

1. *What would you do?* CPC Tenet 5.0, Respect for Colleagues, states,
   "interpreters demonstrate respect for colleagues, interns and students of the
   profession." Tenet 5.0, 5.3 states in part that interpreters should "approach
   colleagues privately to discuss and resolve breaches of professional conduct
   through standard conflict resolution methods." I would chose to approach my
   partner at the end of the assignment. If I were to approach her during a break, I
   may upset her, and this would hinder the rest of the day working together and
   possibly affect our interpreting and hinder the message for our client(s). At the
   end of the assignment, I would approach my partner and explain that I would
   appreciate it if she could keep her religious beliefs to herself, as I do not feel
   that it is conducive to the interpreting environment. I would tell her that while
   I respect her views, I would like her to respect mine in return by keeping her
   beliefs to herself while working together. Following CPC Tenet 3.0, Conduct,
   under 3.8 in the future, I will "avoid any perceived conflicts of interest that
   may interfere with the effectiveness of interpreting services." After leaving
   the assignment and talking with my partner, I may decide not to work with that
   person again. It feels like a conflict of interest for me and could get in the way
   of the interpreted message.

2. *Why?* There will be short-term and long-term consequences of my actions. The
   stakeholders involved are the deaf client, the hearing consumers, my partner,
   the interpreting community, the Deaf community, and me. By confronting
   my partner, she may be upset with me and cause a scene. She may decide to
   badmouth me and potentially ruin my career or name with the Deaf community
   and other interpreters. The deaf client may notice the rift between us, and
   this may affect communication during the assignment. The deaf person may
   choose not to work with either of us again in the future. The hearing consumers
   may develop a misconception of interpreters and may not want to hire us
   or any interpreter in the future. Our actions could be setting a standard for
   future interpreters, and if we make a bad impression on the deaf client and the
   hearing consumers, that not only hurts us at the moment but our colleagues
   in the future. If my partner and I cannot resolve our conflict and put aside our
   differences to be able to work together, the Deaf community may notice and
   decide not to hire either of us in the future. Whether my partner chooses to
   accept my suggestion or not, I feel as though I did the right thing for me, and I

would hope that my colleagues, the Deaf community, and my potential hearing consumers respect me for my decision.

- **Scenario 993.** I'm writing about interpreter attire (yes, again!). The young interpreters coming into the field need to go to a class to learn what "conservative" really means. It is disgusting to see breasts and rear ends. Young women today wear skin tight clothes, low-cut blouses (and I mean low-cut), low-riding pants with their rear ends showing, and see-through dresses without the proper undergarments. One dress was so sheer I could see the moles on one interpreter's skin. She had on thong underwear, and the dress was the consistency of a nightgown.

AN NIC CANDIDATE'S PERSPECTIVE: This scenario falls under the CPC Tenets 3.0, Conduct, and 5.0, Respect for Colleagues.
Problem/Conflict: A fellow interpreter is dressed as though she were going out rather than going to work. Do I point this out or condone her appearance?

1. *What would you do?* Under the CPC Tenet 3.0, Conduct, "interpreters conduct themselves in a manner appropriate to the specific interpreting situation." I would approach her because Tenet 3.0, 3.5 says to "conduct and present yourself in an unobtrusive manner and exercise care in choice of attire." She is not following the CPC nor is representing our profession appropriately. I would not approach her in front of other people, but at the conclusion of the assignment, I would ask to talk with her privately. Under the CPC Tenet 5.0, Respect for Colleagues, "interpreters demonstrate respect for colleagues, interns and students of the profession." Tenet 5.0, 5.2 states "approach colleagues privately to discuss and resolve breaches of professional conduct through standard conflict resolution methods." I would point out that her clothes are not appropriate for interpreting. I would tell her that she is representing not only herself, but our profession as well; does she really want to be doing it that way? I would offer an example of what I was wearing and point out other appropriately dressed interpreters as examples as well. I would offer to help her go shopping and find interpreter-appropriate clothing. As this appears to be an on-going problem, I may offer to teach a class or have a workshop regarding interpreter professionalism. We could have a fashion show of do's and don'ts.

2. *Why?* There will be short-term and long-term consequences of my actions. The stakeholders involved are the interpreter I am confronting, other interpreters, the Deaf community, hearing consumers, and me. The interpreter with whom I ask to speak privately could choose to take my words and learn from them, or at that moment, she could become upset with me for calling her on her way of dressing. Short term, she may decide to do nothing about how she dresses and try to ruin my name by saying I meddle where I do not belong. She may choose

to take my advice and in the long run influence others to dress appropriately. If she does nothing, she is an example to future interpreters who come into the profession, and thus they may think it is OK to dress scandalously. If she changes the way she dresses, other interpreters may follow her example. The Deaf community may look down on her and not want to hire her because of the way she dresses, so she may not get jobs in the future. Hearing consumers may develop a misconception of how interpreters dress and may not want to hire interpreters who dress inappropriately for their events. I know I would be doing the right thing by speaking to her. We are raising the bar for our profession, and we all need to take part in supporting one another in the future.

- **Scenario 994.** I've just been bumped up to management at a video relay service (VRS) company, and I'm the same age as many of those I will be supervising. I was advised to "be friendly" with the interpreters, but not be their friend. Where do I draw the line?

AN NIC CANDIDATE'S PERSPECTIVE: This scenario falls under the CPC Tenet 2.0, Professionalism.

Problem/Conflict: I will be managing individuals that are close to my age. How do I be an effective manager and still "be friendly?"

1. *What would you do?* I was put in the management position to be a manager, not to be everyone's friend. This is a fine line to walk, because in the interpreting profession, we know a lot of our colleagues, not only on a professional basis but personally as well. It is probably safe to say that some of the people I am now managing are my close, personal friends. CPC Tenet 2.0, Professionalism, says that "interpreters possess the professional skills and knowledge required for the specific interpreting situation." Granted this situation is not an actual interpreting assignment, but it does have to do with interpreting. Tenet 2.0, 2.1 states "provide service regardless of age." I was put in management for a reason. My age has nothing to do with it, and my coworkers' ages will not prevent me from doing the job I was hired to do. After I am officially placed in the management position, I would call a staff meeting and lay out ground rules and my expectations.

2. *Why?* I teach sign language, and some of my students are older than me. However, I know I was hired to teach for a reason. If I approach a situation with confidence, people will respect me. Every time I go into the classroom, I never let them see me sweat. The same is true with this VRS management position. Do the job I was hired to do! There are stakeholders involved: my coworkers, the company, and myself. If I do not lay ground rules and establish my expectations, there is a chance my coworkers may walk all over me, and not just because of my age. I really do not think age is the issue. The issue is

can I do the job? If I come in and say, "These are my expectations, etc.," my coworkers will respect me. If I do not and try to be everyone's friend, I will lose their respect and trust and may not be able to regain those. If I do poorly at this management position, it will hurt the company, and they will remove me from my duties and replace me with someone who can handle the job. If I perform my job well, the company will notice and possibly give me more opportunities in the future. I am doing this job not only for my coworkers and the company, but for myself as well. How I handle this job will impact my future! I need to be friendly but not familiar.

- **Scenario 995.** I am an interpreter at a public middle school. The staff must practice good grooming and wear clothing that looks professional, but there is one young interpreter who, although her clothing looks professional, does not shave her armpits. This is something I really should not know, but I do because she sometimes wears sleeveless tops. Once when she, a teacher, and I were having a conversation about a deaf student, she raised her arms twice to gather her long hair into a ponytail, revealing her underarms. It felt almost as if she were flaunting them. My opinion is her personal hygiene is her own choice but that she should keep it her own business. I also think revealing her unshaven armpits is unprofessional. I would not want to see the hairy armpits of my male colleagues either! How should I handle this? Should I speak to our supervisor? Should I send her an anonymous but politely worded note? Or should I just deal?

AN NIC CANDIDATE'S PERSPECTIVE: This scenario falls under the CPC Tenets 3.0, Conduct, and 5.0, Respect for Colleagues.

Problem/Conflict: A fellow coworker has hairy armpits. She must think it is ok, but I find it distracting. Do I confront her or deal?

1. *What would you do?* Under CPC Tenet 3.0, Conduct, "interpreters should conduct themselves in a manner appropriate to the specific interpreting situation." Since I am working in a school setting and am part of the educational team, I would report this issue to my supervisor. Tenet 3.0, 3.4 says to "comply with established workplace codes of conduct and to notify appropriate personnel if there is a conflict with this Code of Professional Conduct." My coworker is not conducting or presenting herself in a manner that is unobtrusive and not exercising care in choice of attire. If she were, she would wear a shirt with sleeves. My coworker is not following the CPC 3.5. By approaching my supervisor, I am following CPC 5.0, Respect for Colleagues, which states "interpreters demonstrate respect for colleagues, interns and students of the profession." I am respecting my colleague by informing my supervisor of the problem.

2. *Why?* I once worked in an elementary school, and the interpreter I worked
    with had a tattoo on her forearm and a nose ring. I found this to be distracting
    for the students so I spoke with my boss, the principal, and within the week,
    the tattoo was covered and the nose ring was taken out. The stakeholders
    involved are my fellow interpreter, the middle school staff, the students, other
    interpreters, and me. I chose to report to my supervisor and allow her to handle
    the situation; however, the interpreter could assume it was me and confront
    me. I would play dumb and refer her to our supervisor if she has questions.
    In the short term, there could be some tension between us, which might carry
    over long term. Should a problem between the two of us continue, it could
    affect the middle school staff so we would need to meet with our supervisor
    to discuss it. Our conflict may affect the students, or her hairy armpits may
    serve as a conversational piece when she should be interpreting. I remember
    the interpreter I worked with would talk about her tattoo and nose ring with the
    students, which was another reason I spoke with my supervisor. The interpreter
    is setting an example for future interpreters, as am I by taking action. I would
    do what I felt was best for the students because I am part of a team.

    *   **Scenario 996.** Recently while interpreting, I saw a colleague's name on a
        layoff list at work. Should I tell her? She is a good friend. If she finds out I
        knew and did not tell her, I know she will be mad at me.

AN NIC CANDIDATE'S PERSPECTIVE: This scenario falls under the CPC
Tenet 1.0, Confidentiality.

Problem/Conflict: I was privy to information regarding a friend. If she knew I knew
and did not tell her, she would be upset. However, I am bound to follow the CPC.
1. *What would you do?* I would follow the CPC Tenet 1.0, Confidentiality, which
    states "interpreters adhere to standards of confidential communication." 1.1
    says interpreters "share assignment related information only on a confidential
    and "as-needed" basis." My friend does not fall into the group of "as-needed"
    people, who are supervisors, interpreter team members, members of the
    educational team and hiring entities. I would interpret the assignment, leave,
    and keep all information I learned, heard, and saw to myself.

2. *Why?* I have interpreted in a local school system where a family member
    works. I have heard information that has not been released to staff, but I do
    not run and tell them about it the minute the meeting is over. The stakeholders
    are my friend, the Deaf community and me. When my friend finds out she is
    being laid off, I will be a supportive friend. I would never tell her that I knew
    beforehand because I would be breaking confidentiality, and it would hurt her
    to know that I knew and did not tell her. If I did leave the assignment that day
    and tell her, she may be happy that I, her friend, told her. However, if it got

back to the Deaf community that I broke confidentiality, CPC Tenet 1.0, they may not want me to interpret for them in the future. Short term, I kept a friend; long term, my career is ruined. That would be a lose-lose situation and not a good decision to make. However, if I am truly confidential, my friend would not know that I had interpreted at that kind of a meeting where I would see information like that.

- **Scenario 997.** When a meeting is called for 10:00 am, I believe interpreters should arrive by at least 9:40 am. In short, interpreters need to show up at the location specified and the time indicated. However, some interpreters do not allow time to park, find the room, and meet the client. I understand things can happen, but if you believe it is OK to be late, you tend to be late. That says to me that you simply do not care.

AN NIC CANDIDATE'S PERSPECTIVE: This scenario falls under the CPC Tenet 6.0, Business Practices.

Problem/Conflict: Some individuals feel that if an assignment starts at 10:00 a.m., then arriving at 10:00 a.m., "on time," is acceptable. Others feel it is better to arrive early.

1. *What would you do?* If you are "on time," you are late. CPC Tenet 6.0 says "interpreters maintain ethical business practices." I find that 15 minutes is sufficient time to arrive, park, find where I am going, and meet my clients. One time I had an assignment on a college campus. When I arrived on campus, I realized how difficult it was to drive through. You never know when you will run into a difficult route or traffic. If you tend to be late and know that about yourself, plan accordingly. Tenet 6.0, 6.2 states that interpreters should "honor professional commitments."

2. *Why?* It is always better to be safe than sorry. There are consequences for my actions, both short term and long term. The stakeholders are interpreters, the deaf community, hearing consumers, and me. I am setting a standard for future interpreters. If I am always showing up late or just in time, it does not set a good example, and new interpreters will think it is OK to do the same. If I am always late, I will be known as "that interpreter who is never on time." For that day and assignment, it may start the day off bad if I am late, because maybe there was important information I needed to know beforehand. Maybe the deaf client wanted to talk with someone. In the future, that deaf person may not want to hire me and may spread the word to their friends. Hearing consumers may assume that interpreters show up when they want or at the last minute before the assignment starts. Yes, we may not be getting paid for being early, but do you really want to jump in to an assignment cold? If I arrive before the 10:00 a.m. start time, I have an opportunity to become comfortable with

my surroundings. If I make arriving early a good habit now, I will not have a problem in the future.

- **Scenario 998.** An interpreter I work with frequently comes to work smelling of alcohol. His performance is hit or miss on those days. If his work was consistently terrible, I feel like I could say, "Stop coming to work hung-over." So, in some ways, it is mostly the hygienic aspect that makes it difficult. It isn't easy to say, "You still reek of whatever you were drinking last night." Allowing such unprofessional behavior to continue makes me feel like a chump. What should I do?

AN NIC CANDIDATE'S PERSPECTIVE: This scenario falls under the CPC Tenets 5.0, Respect for Colleagues, 3.0, Conduct, and 6.0, Business Practices.

Problem/Conflict: A coworker smells of liquor, and sometimes his job performance seems "off." Should I say something or keep quiet?

1. *What would you do?* I would approach my colleague and bring to his attention the smell he is projecting and how it is affecting his work. Tenet 3.0, Conduct, of the CPC says "interpreters conduct themselves in a manner appropriate to the specific interpreting situation." He is definitely not. Tenet 3.0, 3.5 states "conduct yourself in an unobtrusive manner;" however, the smell is not unobtrusive. Tenet 3.0, 3.6 states "refrain from the use of mind-altering substances before or during the performance of duties," which he did not adhere to if I can smell alcohol and his performance is affected. He may not realize how he appears and comes across, so I would approach him after the assignment. Tenet 5.0 states "interpreters demonstrate respect for colleagues, interns and students of the profession." Tenet 5.0, 5.3 states "approach colleagues privately to discuss and resolve breaches of ethical conduct through standard conflict resolution methods." I would bring up these CPC examples to my partner, as well as tell him about 6.0, Business Practices, which says "interpreters maintain ethical business practices." We, as a team, need to "promote conditions that are conducive to effective communication," 6.3, and him smelling of alcohol is not a favorable interpreting situation. I may decide not to work with this person again, as we are seen as a team, and I am as much a reflection of him as he is of me.

2. *Why?* One person can make an impact on our profession. This one person happens to be making a negative impact. The stakeholders are my partner, other interpreters, the Deaf community, hearing consumers and myself. This man may cause other interpreters to think it is alright to arrive at an assignment smelly and possibly hungover. In the long term, this will affect how interpreters show up to jobs. He may also not get as many jobs because of his hygiene. Under the CPC Tenet 2.0, Professionalism, if his interpretation is hit or miss for

the assignment that day, the message might not be "rendered faithfully," 2.3. He may not get jobs in the future. Hearing consumers may have a misconception of interpreters and not want to hire us in the future. I want my partner to know I am concerned about him and that is why I am confronting him. He could become upset and maybe not want to partner with me in the future, but I would know that I followed the CPC and did the right thing.

- **Scenario 999.** A friend of mine just found out for the third time that he missed the cutoff for the lowest level on the state Quality Assurance screening test by five points. He wants to give up, but I keep telling him we need male interpreters in this field.

AN NIC CANDIDATE'S PERSPECTIVE: This scenario falls under the CPC Tenets 5.0, Respect for Colleagues, and 7.0, Professional Development. *Problem/Conflict*: A colleague wants to give up on interpreting; how do I support him?

1. *What would you do?* I would support that person and encourage him not to give up. Under the CPC Tenet 5.0, Respect for Colleagues, "interpreters demonstrate respect for colleagues, interns and students of the profession." Tenet 5.0, 5.4 states "assist and encourage colleagues by sharing information and serving as mentors when appropriate." I would offer to help him study, be his mentor, and give him feedback. I would tell him that everyone learns at a different pace, and he will succeed. I know that for some people it takes longer, and they have to work harder. I would also use a generic example of someone I know having to take the test three times, and now they are nationally certified! And he can be too! CPC Tenet 7.0, Professional Development, says "interpreters engage in professional development." I would recommend some classes for him to take and workshops to attend. I would also offer to observe him and give feedback.

2. *Why?* Interpreting is a relatively new profession, and while we are still growing, we do need more interpreters. The stakeholders are the male interpreter, other interpreters, the Deaf community, and me. This man may not want my help or appreciate me meddling in his business. He may not want to talk with me again and may feel that what I thought were helpful suggestions could push him to quit. He could decide to take me up on my offer, pass his test in the future, and have a career in interpreting. The Deaf community would see him as determined and possibly want him to interpret for them in the future now that he is qualified. The Deaf community appreciates seeing someone who works hard and is determined. Other interpreters will respect him for continuing to try and never giving up. If he does quit, he would be setting the example that it is OK to quit and give up if you do not easily get what you want. That is not the message we want to send to future interpreters. We want them to know that it can be done! I would feel good knowing that I helped someone achieve his

goal, but it is not about me. I help someone in the short term, which, in the long run, will help our profession; one more interpreter.

- **Scenario 1000.** My student has been out for a week already, and it looks like it might be a few more weeks before she comes back. The school has a policy that I have to be available for a different assignment until she comes back. It is awful. I have to drive to three different schools every day (elementary, junior high, and high school), and the other interpreters are too busy to help me catch up on the material. What do I do?

AN NIC CANDIDATE'S PERSPECTIVE: This scenario falls under the CPC Tenets 6.0, Business Practices, and 3.0, Conduct.

Problem/Conflict: The deaf student has been absent from school, and it looks like this may continue. Should I have to make myself available to interpret in other buildings or stay in my assigned building until the student returns?

1. *What would you do?* This sounds to me like the interpreter does not want to have to go to different buildings while waiting for the deaf student to return. I would relax until the student returns. Under CPC Tenet 6.0, Business Practices, "interpreters maintain ethical business practices." Tenet 6.0, 6.2 states interpreters "honor professional commitments." My commitment is to this school district, and I have to follow their procedures. Under CPC Tenet 3.0, Conduct, "interpreters conduct themselves in a manner appropriate to the specific interpreting situation." Tenet 3.0, 3.4 states, "interpreters will comply with established workplace codes of conduct." I worked at an elementary school for two years, and oftentimes the students would not come in or they would be late. The school had things for us to do; we were not allowed to go home or relax until the students returned. As an educational interpreter, I need to follow the procedures put in place by the school; I am part of the educational team. As for the interpreters in the other buildings not being able to help me catch up on the material, I could try phone conferencing, e-mailing, or meeting with the classroom teacher. If the driving from building to building is getting to me, I could ask the school to pay my mileage. I know interpreters at a local school who are paid mileage for their travel between buildings. If I have to go to three other buildings while the deaf student is absent, who interprets at those buildings when my deaf student is in school? That may be something to discuss with the school. I could assist them in various avenues of hiring another interpreter for those buildings or work something out with the other district interpreters.

2. *Why?* If I refuse to go to the three different schools, I could cause some hard feelings with the stakeholders: other district interpreters, administration of the school district, the deaf students, the families of the students, and myself.

If I stay in my building, relaxing, waiting for the student to return, the other interpreters may not appreciate my attitude. Short term, they may speak badly of me and spread it throughout the district. In the future, they may not depend on me or choose to work with me, in or out of the district. School administration may not look highly upon me if I refuse to do the job for which I was hired. I might get fired, acquire a bad name, and not get community jobs or another school district job in the future. The deaf students who need me in another building may have to go without an interpreter, and they may view me as undependable. They could also speak badly of me with the other students and refuse to use me as an interpreter in school and possibly out in the community when they graduate. Their families may not appreciate their children going without an interpreter, and if they find out I was available, they may request some sort of action by the school district. They could tell other families not to use me as an interpreter. The students should come before me; I was hired to do a job for the school, and I am part of a team.

- **Scenario 1001.** The deaf student for whom I interpret told me today she does not like it when I talk to the teachers. She is being paranoid. It is true we do talk, but we are not talking about her.

AN NIC CANDIDATE'S PERSPECTIVE: This scenario falls under the CPC Tenets 3.0, Conduct, and 4.0, Respect for Consumers.
Problem/Conflict: The deaf student requests I not to speak with her teachers; do I explain to her why I need to or allow a teacher or supervisor to do so?
1. *What would you do*? Tenet 4.0, Respect for Consumers, under the CPC states, "interpreters demonstrate respect for consumers." I would consider the student's request under 4.1, and I would turn over the responsibility of how to handle the situation to the classroom teacher(s) and/or my supervisor. I would request a meeting with the teacher(s), my supervisor, the student, myself, and an outside interpreter (to facilitate communication) so we could discuss the student's concern. Tenet 5.0, Respect for Colleagues, says, "interpreters demonstrate respect for colleagues, interns and students of the profession." By allowing the teacher(s) and my supervisor to handle the situation, I am following 5.2 of the CPC in which interpreters work cooperatively with team members, which is exactly what I am--part of the educational team. This also falls under the CPC Tenet 3.0, Conduct, which says, "interpreters conduct themselves in a manner appropriate to the specific interpreting situation." Tenet 3.0, 3.1 states "consult with appropriate persons regarding the interpreting situation." Tenet 3.0, 3.4 states "comply with established workplace codes of conduct and notify appropriate personnel if there is a conflict with this Code of Professional Conduct." I would like the team to be able to explain to the student we are all there for her best interest. We discuss the student on an "as-needed" basis, under CPC Tenet 1.1, Confidentiality. I would want to

emphasize that everyone on the educational team practices confidentiality. I would want the student to know it is good she felt she could bring her concerns to me (or anyone on the team) and that she could continue to do so should she have more questions or concerns. I worked in an elementary school, and if the student ever came to me with issues, I always turned it over to the teacher(s) and my supervisor to handle. Oftentimes the interpreter is the only contact deaf students have who share their language so they want to unload everything on us. It is important we do not take it upon ourselves to handle these situations but make everyone on the educational team aware so we can handle it as a group.

2. *Why?* It is important everyone on the educational team be on the same page. The stakeholders are the student, teacher(s), school administration or my supervisor, other deaf students, their families, and me. If the deaf student feels I am talking about her and not being confidential, there could be problems in the classroom. She could speak badly of me with other deaf students. If the student is uncooperative now, there could repercussions in her future. If the teacher(s) see me handle the situation, they might assume that is my role and let me handle everything that has to do with the deaf student. This is an incorrect assumption on their part, and they need to be educated on the role of the interpreter for the future. If not, they could have misconceptions of interpreters, and this would be problematic for interpreters to come. School administration may not appreciate it if I handle everything having to do with the deaf student. Depending on school policy, I may be removed from my job and not be able to work in another district. If I do not practice good ethics, word will get around to the Deaf community, other interpreters, and the interpreting community. The other deaf students may not want me to interpret for them within the district or out in the community once they graduate. Families may not appreciate it if their son or daughter comes home saying I talk about them with the teachers and may request action from the school district. If I say I am not talking about the student, I need to practice it. I will only talk about the student on an "as-needed" basis and make sure communication within the educational team is open. This may ensure my longevity as an interpreter, as well as a good school year with the student.

Appendix A

NAD-RID Code of Professional Conduct (CPC)

RID, along with the NAD, co-authored the ethical code of conduct for interpreters. Both organizations uphold high standards of professionalism and ethical conduct for interpreters. At the core of this code of conduct are the seven tenets, which are followed by guiding principles and illustrations.

The tenets are to be viewed holistically and as a guide to complete professional behavior. When in doubt, one should refer to the explicit language of the tenet.

TENETS

1. Interpreters adhere to standards of confidential communication.

2. Interpreters possess the professional skills and knowledge required for the specific interpreting situation.

3. Interpreters conduct themselves in a manner appropriate to the specific interpreting situation.

4. Interpreters demonstrate respect for consumers.

5. Interpreters demonstrate respect for colleagues, interns, and students of the profession.

6. Interpreters maintain ethical business practices.

7. Interpreters engage in professional development

NAD-RID CODE OF PROFESSIONAL CONDUCT
Reprint permission granted by the Registry of Interpreters for the Deaf

Scope
The National Association of the Deaf (NAD) and the Registry of Interpreters for the Deaf, Inc. (RID) uphold high standards of professionalism and ethical conduct for interpreters. Embodied in this Code of Professional Conduct (formerly known as the Code of Ethics) are seven tenets setting forth guiding principles, followed by illustrative behaviors.

The tenets of this Code of Professional Conduct are to be viewed holistically and as a guide to professional behavior. This document provides assistance in complying with the code. The guiding principles offer the basis upon which the tenets are articulated. The illustrative behaviors are not exhaustive, but are indicative of the conduct that may either conform to or violate a specific tenet or the code as a whole.

When in doubt, the reader should refer to the explicit language of the tenet. If further clarification is needed, questions may be directed to the national office of the Registry of Interpreters for the Deaf, Inc.

This Code of Professional Conduct is sufficient to encompass interpreter roles and responsibilities in every type of situation (e.g., educational, legal, medical). A separate code for each area of interpreting is neither necessary nor advisable.

Philosophy
The American Deaf community represents a cultural and linguistic group having the inalienable right to full and equal communication and to participation in all aspects of society. Members of the American Deaf community have the right to informed choice and the highest quality interpreting services. Recognition of the communication rights of America's women, men, and children who are deaf is the foundation of the tenets, principles, and behaviors set forth in this Code of Professional Conduct.

Voting Protocol
This Code of Professional Conduct was presented through mail referendum to certified interpreters who are members in good standing with the Registry of Interpreters for the Deaf, Inc. and the National Association of the Deaf. The vote was to adopt or to reject.

Adoption of this Code of Professional Conduct
Interpreters who are members in good standing with the Registry of Interpreters for the Deaf, Inc. and the National Association of the Deaf voted to adopt this Code of Professional Conduct, effective July 1, 2005. This Code of Professional Conduct is a working document that is expected to change over time. The aforementioned members may be called upon to vote, as may be needed from time to time, on the tenets of the code. The guiding principles and the illustrative behaviors may change periodically to meet the needs and requirements of the RID Ethical Practices System. These sections of the Code of Professional Conduct will not require a vote of the members. However, members are encouraged to recommend changes for future updates.

Function of the Guiding Principles
It is the obligation of every interpreter to exercise judgment, employ critical thinking, apply the benefits of practical experience, and reflect on past actions in the practice of their profession. The guiding principles in this document represent the concepts of confidentiality, linguistic and professional competence, impartiality, professional growth and development, ethical business practices, and the rights of participants in interpreted situations to informed choice. The driving force behind the guiding principles is the notion that the interpreter will do no harm.

When applying these principles to their conduct, interpreters remember that their choices are governed by a "reasonable interpreter" standard. This standard represents the hypothetical interpreter who is appropriately educated, informed, capable, aware of professional standards, and fair-minded.

Tenets
1. Interpreters adhere to standards of confidential communication.
2. Interpreters possess the professional skills and knowledge required for the specific interpreting situation.
3. Interpreters conduct themselves in a manner appropriate to the specific interpreting situation.
4. Interpreters demonstrate respect for consumers.
5. Interpreters demonstrate respect for colleagues, interns, and students of the profession.
6. Interpreters maintain ethical business practices.
7. Interpreters engage in professional development.

Applicability
A. This Code of Professional Conduct applies to certified and associate members of the Registry of Interpreters for the Deaf, Inc., Certified members of the National Association of the Deaf, interns, and students of the profession.

B. Federal, state or other statutes or regulations may supersede this Code of Professional Conduct. When there is a conflict between this code and local, state, or federal laws and regulations, the interpreter obeys the rule of law.

C. This Code of Professional Conduct applies to interpreted situations that are performed either face-to-face or remotely.

Definitions
For the purpose of this document, the following terms are used:
Colleagues: Other interpreters.
Conflict of Interest: A conflict between the private interests (personal, financial, or professional) and the official or professional responsibilities of an interpreter in a

position of trust, whether actual or perceived, deriving from a specific interpreting situation.

Consumers: Individuals and entities who are part of the interpreted situation. This includes individuals who are deaf, deaf-blind, hard of hearing, and hearing.

1.0 CONFIDENTIALITY

Tenet: Interpreters adhere to standards of confidential communication.

Guiding Principle: Interpreters hold a position of trust in their role as linguistic and cultural facilitators of communication. Confidentiality is highly valued by consumers and is essential to protecting all involved.

Each interpreting situation (e.g., elementary, secondary, and post-secondary education, legal, medical, mental health) has a standard of confidentiality. Under the reasonable interpreter standard, professional interpreters are expected to know the general requirements and applicability of various levels of confidentiality. Exceptions to confidentiality include, for example, federal and state laws requiring mandatory reporting of abuse or threats of suicide, or responding to subpoenas.

Illustrative Behavior - Interpreters:
1.1 Share assignment-related information only on a confidential and "as-needed" basis (e.g., supervisors, interpreter team members, members of the educational team, hiring entities).

1.2 Manage data, invoices, records, or other situational or consumer-specific information in a manner consistent with maintaining consumer confidentiality (e.g., shredding, locked files).

1.3 Inform consumers when federal or state mandates require disclosure of confidential information.

2.0 PROFESSIONALISM

Tenet: Interpreters possess the professional skills and knowledge required for the specific interpreting situation.

Guiding Principle: Interpreters are expected to stay abreast of evolving language use and trends in the profession of interpreting as well as in the American Deaf community.

Interpreters accept assignments using discretion with regard to skill, communication mode, setting, and consumer needs. Interpreters possess knowledge of American Deaf culture and deafness-related resources.

Illustrative Behavior - Interpreters:
2.1 Provide service delivery regardless of race, color, national origin, gender, religion, age, disability, sexual orientation, or any other factor.

2.2 Assess consumer needs and the interpreting situation before and during the assignment and make adjustments as needed.

2.3 Render the message faithfully by conveying the content and spirit of what is being communicated, using language most readily understood by consumers, and correcting errors discreetly and expeditiously.

2.4 Request support (e.g., certified deaf interpreters, team members, language facilitators) when needed to fully convey the message or to address exceptional communication challenges (e.g., cognitive disabilities, foreign sign language, emerging language ability, or lack of formal instruction or language).

2.5 Refrain from providing counsel, advice, or personal opinions.

2.6 Judiciously provide information or referral regarding available interpreting or community resources without infringing upon consumers' rights.

3.0 CONDUCT

Tenet: Interpreters conduct themselves in a manner appropriate to the specific interpreting situation.

Guiding Principle: Interpreters are expected to present themselves appropriately in demeanor and appearance. They avoid situations that result in conflicting roles or perceived or actual conflicts of interest.

Illustrative Behavior - Interpreters:
3.1 Consult with appropriate persons regarding the interpreting situation to determine issues such as placement and adaptations necessary to interpret effectively.

3.2 Decline assignments or withdraw from the interpreting profession when not competent due to physical, mental, or emotional factors.

3.3 Avoid performing dual or conflicting roles in interdisciplinary (e.g. educational or mental health teams) or other settings.

3.4 Comply with established workplace codes of conduct, notify appropriate personnel if there is a conflict with this Code of Professional Conduct, and actively seek resolution where warranted.

3.5 Conduct and present themselves in an unobtrusive manner and exercise care in choice of attire.

3.6 Refrain from the use of mind-altering substances before or during the performance of duties.

3.7 Disclose to parties involved any actual or perceived conflicts of interest.

3.8 Avoid actual or perceived conflicts of interest that might cause harm or interfere with the effectiveness of interpreting services.

3.9 Refrain from using confidential interpreted information for personal, monetary, or professional gain.

3.10 Refrain from using confidential interpreted information for the benefit of personal or professional affiliations or entities.

4.0 RESPECT FOR CONSUMERS

Tenet: Interpreters demonstrate respect for consumers.

Guiding Principle: Interpreters are expected to honor consumer preferences in selection of interpreters and interpreting dynamics, while recognizing the realities of qualifications, availability, and situation.

Illustrative Behavior - Interpreters:
4.1 Consider consumer requests or needs regarding language preferences, and render the message accordingly (interpreted or transliterated).

4.2 Approach consumers with a professional demeanor at all times.

4.3 Obtain the consent of consumers before bringing an intern to an assignment.

4.4 Facilitate communication access and equality, and support the full interaction and independence of consumers.

5.0 RESPECT FOR COLLEAGUES

Tenet: Interpreters demonstrate respect for colleagues, interns and students of the profession.

Guiding Principle: Interpreters are expected to collaborate with colleagues to foster the delivery of effective interpreting services. They also understand that the manner in which they relate to colleagues reflects upon the profession in general.

Illustrative Behavior - Interpreters:
5.1 Maintain civility toward colleagues, interns, and students.

5.2 Work cooperatively with team members through consultation before assignments regarding logistics, providing professional and courteous assistance when asked and monitoring the accuracy of the message while functioning in the role of the support interpreter.

5.3 Approach colleagues privately to discuss and resolve breaches of ethical or professional conduct through standard conflict resolution methods; file a formal grievance only after such attempts have been unsuccessful or the breaches are harmful or habitual.

5.4 Assist and encourage colleagues by sharing information and serving as mentors when appropriate.

5.5 Obtain the consent of colleagues before bringing an intern to an assignment.

6.0 BUSINESS PRACTICES

Tenet: Interpreters maintain ethical business practices.

Guiding Principle: Interpreters are expected to conduct their business in a professional manner whether in private practice or in the employ of an agency or other entity. Professional interpreters are entitled to a living wage based on their qualifications and expertise. Interpreters are also entitled to working conditions conducive to effective service delivery.

Illustrative Behavior - Interpreters:
6.1 Accurately represent qualifications, such as certification, educational background, and experience, and provide documentation when requested.

6.2 Honor professional commitments and terminate assignments only when fair and justifiable grounds exist.

6.3 Promote conditions that are conducive to effective communication, inform the parties involved if such conditions do not exist, and seek appropriate remedies.

6.4 Inform appropriate parties in a timely manner when delayed or unable to fulfill assignments.

6.5 Reserve the option to decline or discontinue assignments if working conditions are not safe, healthy, or conducive to interpreting.

6.6 Refrain from harassment or coercion before, during, or after the provision of interpreting services.

6.7 Render pro bono services in a fair and reasonable manner.

6.8 Charge fair and reasonable fees for the performance of interpreting services and arrange for payment in a professional and judicious manner.

7.0 PROFESSIONAL DEVELOPMENT

Tenet: Interpreters engage in professional development.

Guiding Principle: Interpreters are expected to foster and maintain interpreting competence and the stature of the profession through ongoing development of knowledge and skills.

Illustrative Behavior - Interpreters:
7.1 Increase knowledge and strengthen skills through activities such as:
- pursuing higher education;
- attending workshops and conferences;
- seeking mentoring and supervision opportunities;
- participating in community events; and
- engaging in independent studies.

7.2 Keep abreast of laws, policies, rules, and regulations that affect the profession.

Appendix B

Code of Professional Conduct

A Table of the Tenets and Illustrative Behaviors

1.0 Confidentiality Tenet: Interpreters adhere to standards of confidential communication.	2.0 Professionalism Tenet: Interpreters possess the professional skills and knowledge required for the specific interpreting situation.	3.0 Conduct Tenet: Interpreters conduct themselves in a manner appropriate to the specific interpreting situation.
1.1 Share assignment-related information only on a confidential and "as-needed" basis (e.g., supervisors, interpreter team members of the educational team, hiring entities).	2.1 Provide service delivery regardless of race, color, national origin, gender, religion, age, disability, sexual orientation, or any other factor.	3.1 Consult with appropriate persons regarding the interpreting situation to determine issues such as placement and adaptations necessary to interpret effectively.
1.2 Manage data, invoices, records, or other situational or consumer-specific information in a manner consistent with maintaining consumer confidentiality (e.g., shredding, locked files).	2.2 Assess consumer needs and the interpreting situation before and during the assignment and make adjustments as needed.	3.2 Decline assignments or withdraw from the interpreting profession when not competent due to physical, mental, or emotional factors.
1.3 Inform consumers when federal or state mandates require disclosure of confidential information.	2.3 Render the message faithfully by conveying the content and spirit of what is being communicated, using language most readily understood by consumers, and correcting errors discreetly and expeditiously.	3.3 Avoid performing dual or conflicting roles in interdisciplinary (e.g. educational or mental health teams) or other settings.
	2.4 Request support (e.g., certified deaf interpreters, team members, language facilitators) when needed to fully convey the message or to address exceptional communication challenges (e.g. cognitive disabilities, foreign sign language, emerging language ability, or lack of formal instruction or language).	3.4 Comply with established workplace codes of conduct, notify appropriate personnel if there is a conflict with this Code of Professional Conduct, and actively seek resolution where warranted.
	2.5 Refrain from providing counsel, advice, or personal opinions.	3.5 Conduct and present themselves in an unobtrusive manner and exercise care in choice of attire.
	2.6 Judiciously provide information or referral regarding available interpreting or community resources without infringing upon consumers' rights.	3.6 Refrain from the use of mind-altering substances before or during the performance of duties.
		3.7 Disclose to parties involved any actual or perceived conflicts of interest.
		3.8 Avoid actual or perceived conflicts of interest that might cause harm or interfere with the effectiveness of interpreting services.
		3.9 Refrain from using confidential interpreted information for personal, monetary, or professional gain.
		3.10 Refrain from using confidential interpreted information for the benefit of personal or professional affiliations or entities.

King, R. (2008). A Table of the Tenets from the Code of Professional Conduct for Interpreters. Unpublished manuscript.

4.0 Respect for Consumers Tenet: Interpreters demonstrate respect for consumers.	5.0 Respect for Colleagues Tenet: Interpreters demonstrate respect for colleagues, interns and students of the profession.	6.0 Business Practices Tenet: Interpreters maintain ethical business practices.	7.0 Professional Deve. Tenet: Interpreters engage in professional development.
4.1 Consider consumer requests or needs regarding language preferences, and render the message accordingly (interpreted or transliterated).	5.1 Maintain civility toward colleagues, interns, and students.	6.1 Accurately represent qualifications, such as certification, educational background, and experience, and provide documentation when requested.	7.1 Increase knowledge and strengthen skills through activities such as: • Pursuing higher education; • Attending workshops and conferences; • Seeking mentoring and supervision opportunities; • Participating in community events; and • Engaging in independent studies.
4.2 Approach consumers with a professional demeanor at all times.	5.2 Work cooperatively with team members through consultation before assignments regarding logistics, providing professional and courteous assistance when asked and monitoring the accuracy of the message while functioning in the role of the support interpreter.	6.2 Honor professional commitments and terminate assignments only when fair and justifiable grounds exist.	7.2 Keep abreast of laws, policies, rules, and regulations that affect the profession.
4.3 Obtain the consent of consumers before bringing an intern to an assignment.	5.3 Approach colleagues privately to discuss and resolve breaches of ethical or professional conduct through standard conflict resolution methods; file a formal grievance only after such attempts have been unsuccessful or the breaches are harmful or habitual.	6.3 Promote conditions that are conductive to effective communication, inform the parties involved if such conditions do not exist, and seek appropriate remedies.	
4.4 Facilitate communication access and equality, and support the full interaction and independence of consumers.	5.4 Assist and encourage colleagues by sharing information and serving as mentors when appropriate.	6.4 Inform appropriate parties in a timely manner when delayed or unable to fulfill assignments.	
	5.5 Obtain the consent of colleagues before bringing an intern to an assignment.	6.5 Reserve the option to decline or discontinue assignments if working conditions are not safe, healthy, or conductive to interpreting.	
		6.6 Refrain from harassment or coercion before, during, or after the provision of interpreting services.	
		6.7 Render pro bono services in a fair and reasonable manner.	
		6.8 Charge fair and reasonable fees for the performance of interpreting services and arrange for payment in a professional and judicious manner.	

King, R. (2008). A Table of the Tenets from the Code of Professional Conduct for Interpreters. Unpublished manuscript

Appendix C

Lessons From Geese:
An Interpreter Can Learn a Lot From a Goose!

"Lessons From Geese" was transcribed from a speech given by Angeles Arrien at the 1991 Organizational Development Network and was based on the work of Milton Olson. It was circulated by the Outward Bound Staff through the United States. I have adapted it to fit the interpreting field, as I think we can all learn from our feathered friends.

FACT 1:

As each goose flaps its wings, it creates an uplift for the birds that follow. By flying in a "V" formation, the whole flock adds 71% greater flying range than if each bird flew alone.

When interpreters act as reliable professionals (e.g., adhering to the CPC, following guidelines such as dressing appropriately, arriving at assignments on time, maintaining a positive attitude), they create a more standardized working environment in which interpreters and deaf clients benefit, and hearing onlookers are positively impacted.

FACT 2:

When a goose falls out of formation, it suddenly feels the drag and resistance of flying alone. It quickly moves back into formation to take advantage of the lifting power of the bird immediately in front of it.

When an interpreter experiences difficulty or failure despite her best efforts, other interpreters give their best encouragement and support. They remember that self-confidence improves performance, and no one is exempt from challenges that can be emotionally trying. They focus on their similarities rather than their differences and take their turn at offering and accepting the support of others.

FACT 3:

When the lead goose tires, it rotates back into the formation, and another goose flies to the point position.

Interpreters work together fostering one another's best efforts and sharing information freely (e.g., class, workshop, new signs). They are enabled to learn from one another by readily asking questions and freely requesting constructive criticism. They offer to mentor those who are newer to the profession or have an immediate need for bolstering and nurturing.

FACT 4:

The geese flying in formation honk to encourage those up front to keep up their speed.

When interpreters demonstrate their skills to one another at workshops or on the job, the observing interpreters realize the vulnerability of the individual presenting and participate by demonstrating encouragement through facial expression, deserved compliments, and useful suggestions. They are quicker to praise than criticize.

FACT 5:

When a goose gets sick, wounded, or shot down, two geese drop out of formation and follow it down to help and protect it. They stay with it until it dies or is able to fly again. Then they launch out with another formation or catch up with the flock.

Interpreters are loyal to one another. When one does not receive the certification level anticipated or makes a major error, other interpreters join to give reassurance, camaraderie, and specific assistance when appropriate. Interpreters offer support to one another and continue to network throughout their professional lives. They offer comfort through difficult times and celebrate success.

Interpreters who follow these guidelines ensure better working conditions for everyone: continued skill improvement, higher professional standards, greater job satisfaction, and a better served Deaf community. Everybody wins.

Appendix D

NO ONE EVER TOLD ME I'D HAVE DAYS LIKE THESE!

An interpreter was asked to interpret for the President. The day of the assignment, she was picked up from the school where she worked by the police. Next, she was searched by some rather intimidating Secret Service agents. After they'd finished, she was shown to her "position," a small square outlined to the President's right. They placed her in her spot and warned her not to move from her position. If she did, she might be mistaken as a threat to the President, and the Secret Service agents would be forced to "neutralize" her. Afraid to move, this 90 pound interpreter stayed in that square shivering violently as the cold wind whipped right through her.

ENCOUNTERS WITH REALITY

An interpreter was called to a police station and was met by an officer who told her she could leave because the deaf client was able to read lips. The interpreter looked at the officer and silently mouthed her reply. The police officer's face went blank. The interpreter then said aloud, "I asked you if I could borrow 15 cents." The officer turned red, then thought about it for a moment, and said, "I see your point, follow me please."

-Brenda Cartwright

ENCOUNTERS WITH REALITY

Near the end of school, the high school students had a party for their parents. One of the deaf students brought over her parents to proudly introduce them to the interpreter. The parents turned to the interpreter and said, "When will Jane stop acting like she is deaf and talk like a normal person?"

-Brenda Cartwright

ENCOUNTERS WITH REALITY

An interpreter was subbing one day in a print shop vocational training class. The room where she was to interpret was very small. There were huge machines everywhere and very little open space to stand. She turned to the shop teacher and asked him where he suggested she should stand. The man looked at her blankly and said, "Well, the other 'terminator' stood over there!"

-Brenda Cartwright

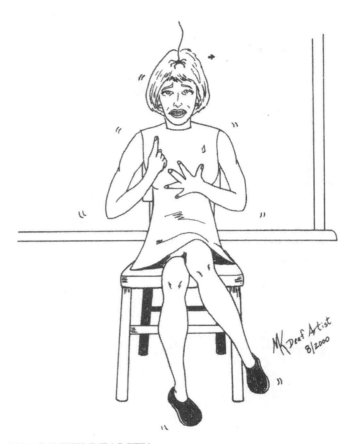

ENCOUNTERS WITH REALITY

You're interpreting a summer school class when you notice a spider making its way down from the ceiling toward you. You're phobic about spiders, and you're ready to panic as the spider makes its way down in front of your face.

ENCOUNTERS WITH REALITY

After a bad snowstorm, many of the faculty and staff of the elementary school
where you interpret don't report to work. You're scheduled to interpret an IEPC
meeting this morning and figure it will still go on since school was not canceled.
You have just walked in when the principal hands you a shovel and tells you to
help clear the sidewalks before the buses arrive. Normally you're as helpful as the
next person and would go the extra mile for your job within reason, but today you
have a dress and high heels on. You point this out to the principal, who angrily says,
"That's just too damn bad. Start shoveling!"

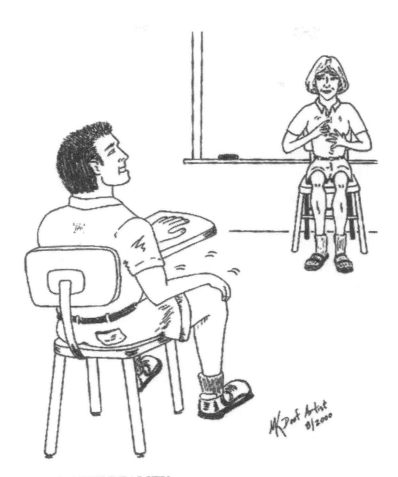

ENCOUNTERS WITH REALITY

One summer day in a college classroom, you're interpreting the professor's lecture and you notice that the deaf student, who is wearing shorts, keeps crossing and un- crossing his legs. You figure he's just trying to get comfortable. Suddenly out of the corner of your eye, it becomes obvious that the student is not wearing underwear. When you look up at the deaf student's face and see his smirk, you know he's doing it on purpose.

ENCOUNTERS WITH REALITY

While interpreting in a college class on an exam day, you're looking out the window watching some construction going on while the deaf student is taking her test. You see a bulldozer coming closer and closer to the window, and it looks like it's going to come right through the wall. You scream and the whole class looks up, and the test is momentarily forgotten. The bulldozer, of course, doesn't come through the window. It has changed direction, and you now look like a fool.

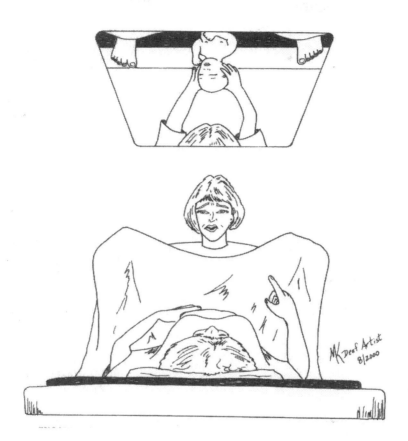

ENCOUNTERS WITH REALITY

You have interpreted for a young deaf couple through all of their natural childbirth classes and it's the day of the big event. The mother-to-be is in labor, and the doctor takes one more look and says they still have a little more time to wait. He says he's going to grab a quick bite to eat and tells the deaf woman to use the call button if she wants the nurse to page him. The frightened deaf woman begs the doctor not to go. She's sure the baby is coming now but he checks her again and assures her they have plenty of time. The nerve-racked father steps out to have a cigarette and it's only the two of you left in the room. Suddenly the deaf woman starts screaming for help and in the overhead mirror, you see the newborn's head emerging. You run around to the end of the table and see the baby starting to slide out.

ENCOUNTERS WITH REALITY

You have rehearsed for weeks for a theatrical performance you'll be interpreting tonight. You decide to take a quick nap to refresh yourself, and when you wake up you realize you have overslept and only have 20 minutes to get to the theater. You dress in record time, drive like a maniac, and walk on stage just as the curtain is going up. After the performance is over, you let out a sigh of relief as you walk out to your car eager to go home and relax. As you approach your car, you can see you reflection in your car window. You audibly groan as you realize you still have two pink curlers in your hair.

ENCOUNTERS WITH REALITY

An interpreter was interpreting a high school history class for a student who seldom paid attention. When asked a question to which he did not know the answer, the student responded with, "My interpreter isn't signing all the information to me that I need to answer your questions."

-Brenda Cartwright

Made in the USA
San Bernardino, CA
28 January 2019